Psychobiology of
Behavioral Development

Psychobiology of Behavioral Development

RONALD GANDELMAN

Rutgers University

New York   Oxford
Oxford University Press
1992

Oxford University Press

Oxford   New York   Toronto
Delhi   Bombay   Calcutta   Madras   Karachi
Kuala Lumpur   Singapore   Hong Kong   Tokyo
Nairobi   Dar es Salaam   Cape Town
Melbourne   Auckland

and associated companies in
Berlin   Ibadan

Copyright © 1992 by Oxford University Press, Inc.

Published by Oxford University Press, Inc.,
200 Madison Avenue, New York, New York 10016

Oxford is a registered trademark of Oxford University Press

Library of Congress Cataloging-in-Publication Data
Gandelman, Ronald.
The psychobiology of behavioral development / Ronald Gandelman.
p.   cm.   Includes bibliographical references and index.
ISBN 0-19-503941-6
1. Developmental psychology.
2. Developmental psychobiology.
I. Title.   [DNLM:
1. Child Behavior—physiology.
2. Child Development.
3. Psychophysiology.
WS 105 G195p]   BF713.G36
1992   155—dc20   DNLM/DLC
for Library of Congress
91-45760

9 8 7 6 5 4 3 2 1

Printed in the United States of America
on acid-free paper

To
D. and Z.

Preface

Research in behavioral development, specifically the contributions of physiological and experiential factors acting alone and in concert, has been carried out for many years. Given the breadth of the subject matter, it is no wonder that the questions posed about the forces that shape the development of behavior and the experimental methodologies established to answer them have been extraordinarily diverse. Despite such diversity, or perhaps because of it, a formal research specialty known as *developmental psychobiology* has emerged. I call it a formal specialty because it is represented by a research society, The International Society for Developmental Psychobiology, and the journal *Developmental Psychobiology*. Furthermore, departments of psychology on occasion advertise specifically for developmental psychobiologists.

The purpose of this endeavor is to provide developmental psychobiology with a textbook, one appropriate for both undergraduate and graduate students. Undergraduates will best profit from the book if they already have completed an introductory psychology course. It also would be helpful if they have taken a course with some emphasis on conditioning and learning. Graduate students with a background in psychology should have little difficulty with the material.

A colleague once remarked that psychology courses are defined by whatever the instructors wish to teach. In other words, the discipline is so broad that instructors have great latitude in selecting topics for coverage. Therefore they essentially define the subject matter of the specialty areas in question. The same is true for writers of textbooks, who also must select a rather small subset of topics. Regarding this book, I have tried to choose for consideration those topics regarding the psychobiology of development that have received enduring attention: embryonic behavior, early stimulation, and the influence of hormones, to name a few. The reader, however, might be struck by one notable omission— the relation of genes to behavioral development—a topic that obviously must not be excluded from the education of future developmental psychobiologists. I chose to omit the subject because it requires the mastery of so much background information about genetics it cannot be adequately considered in a chapter or two. The interested reader should consult one of the excellent specialty textbooks, such as Plomin, DeFries, and McClearn's *Behavioral Genetics: A Primer.*

As will become readily apparent, close attention has been paid to the older literature as well as to data of a recent vintage. I used this approach for two reasons. First, as historians tell us, the present is more clearly understood by examining the past, a point that is certainly true for science. The questions investigators ask and the way in which they attempt to answer them do not spring de novo from their fertile imaginations but are in large measure a product of what has come before. By considering the early literature the reader is able to place current research in perspective, thereby fostering a better understanding of it and allowing one to make informed predictions about future research directions.

There is another reason for paying such close attention to early research; much of it is outstanding and remains current. This point serves to demonstrate that research should not be dismissed merely because it was performed prior to the advent of high-powered technology; electron microscopy, radioimmunoassays, computer science, and so forth. Much of those data were collected by observation. A prime example is the 1885 study of Wilhelm Preyer, who meticulously monitored the reactions of chick embryos of differing ages to various forms of stimulation. Advances in our knowledge about the development of behavior have been and continue to be made by careful observation of behavior.

ACKNOWLEDGMENTS

There are many individuals to whom I am indebted for inspiring this book and providing valuable assistance in its preparation. I am indebted to the undergraduate and graduate students who have taken my course in developmental psychobiology over the past 20 years and asked those seemingly simple questions that, after periods of numbing silence, I realized I could not answer. I thank them also for informing me that, my lectures notwithstanding, they would have greatly benefited from a textbook. Thanks also are extended to some anonymous reviewers, to former graduate student Scott Graham, and especially to my colleague Richard Lore, all of whom helped with insightful comments on less developed versions of the manuscript.

September 1991   R. G.
New Brunswick, N.J.

Contents

**Psychobiology of
Behavioral Development**

1

Origin and Function of
Embryonic Behavior

The organism is inexplicable without environment. Every characteristic of it has some relation to environmental factors. And
particularly the organism as a whole, i.e., the unity and order,
the physiological differences, relations and harmonies between
its parts, are entirely meaningless except in relation to an external world.   C. M. Child, 1924

"I am born." So begins the chronicle of David Copperfield's development. Like Dickens, most psychologists, at least until recently, also began their study of behavioral development with the neonate, thereby discounting the potential import of activities and events that occur during the embryonic period. Even embryologists, whose attention by definition is focused on prenatal or prehatching processes, have been concerned principally with the development of structure. Because most viewed behavior as a by-product of structural development, they seldom considered the possibility that embryonic activity might influence the very structures they were examining.

During the 1980s, however, embryonic behavior became the focus of increasing attention. We now recognize that consideration of such behavior is central to an understanding of development—that activity of the embryo[1] is a critical element in ontogenesis. It has become clear that behavioral development does not only proceed in a structure → function direction but that behavior itself contributes to the structural development of the nervous system (function → structure). Moreover, we now understand that various aspects of postnatal/posthatching behavior have their origins in the interaction between the embryo and particular types of environmental stimulation. Hofer (1988) was indeed correct when he remarked that prenatal behavior is one of the sculptors of the organism.

A number of factors have contributed to the attention being paid to embryonic behavior. One is the development of noninvasive ultrasonic imaging techniques that permit monitoring of human fetal behavior repeatedly and over rel-

[1]The distinction between *embryo* and *fetus* is not well defined. For example, according to *Webster's Ninth Collegiate Dictionary,* an embryo becomes a fetus after "attaining the basic structural plan of its kind." Regardless of what that actually means, the timing of the transition from embryo to fetus is species-dependent. Therefore for the sake of simplicity and consistency, the term *embryo* is used throughout the text.

3

atively long periods of time. Before these techniques were available, data were gathered from aborted fetuses whose viability, because of the immediate onset of asphyxia, was questionable. Also, the emergence of new techniques in various subfields of neuroscience, e.g., neuroendocrinology, enables researchers to address questions central to important theoretical issues in behavioral development. Finally, concern with the consequences to the newborn of embryonic exposure to drugs and other substances has proved highly influential.

This chapter considers factors that influence the initiation and maintenance of embryonic behavior, the modifiability of embryonic behavior, and the relation of such activity to postnatal behavior. Early research, in addition to providing much of the basic information (which remains current) yielded a surprising amount of theory (as well as a surprising amount of vitriol among investigators with opposing theoretical viewpoints). Some of those theories are mentioned here for historical reasons and because they provide a useful framework within which to examine the data.

EMBRYONIC MOTILITY AND SPONTANEOUS NEURONAL DISCHARGE

Modern research on the study of embryonic behavior had its origins in 1885 with the publication of W. Preyer's *Specielle Physiologie des Embryo.* Among other findings, Preyer reported that the chick embryo begins to display movement several days prior to the time a reaction can be evoked by a tactile stimulus. A similar result was reported later for another species, the toadfish (Tracy, 1926). The first movement of the toadfish—bending the trunk in the anterior region—also occurred before movement could be evoked by tactile stimulation. Tracy referred to this behavior as "spontaneous" and suggested that it is caused by changes in blood chemistry, such as accumulation of carbon dioxide. Only later does the embryo begin to respond to sensory stimulation, the initial modality being tactile. Later still, the organism responds to light, vibration, and acid (pain).

In fact, through the work of several researchers it was found that differences exist among species with regard to whether a sensory system becomes functional during the embryonic period. Receptor complexes generally become morphologically mature in the embryos of species with long gestation periods. Also, the more mature the motor system at birth or hatching, the more likely it is that particular sensory systems, especially vision, will possess the capacity to function during the embryonic period (Gottlieb, 1971; Bradley & Mistretta, 1975).

Preyer's and Tracy's results indicated that the initiation of embryonic motility is not caused by the development of reflex mechanisms. Rather, it is generated endogenously by spontaneous discharges of motor neurons, i.e., by the automatic firing of nerves that arise in the spinal cord and innervate muscle tissue. In other words, early movement is a product of the neuromotor system and thus is solely a consequence of the development of that system. This early account of the genesis of embryonic motility probably did little to pique the interest of psychologists, as it discounted the role of stimulation. In the parlance of psychologists, that means that the environment is of little or no consequence. Because it generally was regarded that neuromotor development follows a preset course, early behavior was viewed as being *predetermined.*

The notion that embryonic motility is caused by the spontaneous discharge of motor neurons received additional support from early neuroanatomical experimentation. The neuronal circuitry that mediates reflex activity of the chick embryo is completed *subsequent* to about day 6 of the 21-day incubation period (Visitini & Levi-Montalcini, 1939; Windle & Orr, 1934), well after movement is first observed.

Research of a more recent vintage was presented by Hamburger and his associates who, in an elegant series of experiments, provide strong support for the notion that embryonic movement can be initiated and maintained by the spinal cord independent of stimulation. These researchers began by carefully monitoring the behavior of the chick embryo (Hamburger, 1963; Hamburger & Balaban, 1963). Their observations were summarized as follows:

> [W]e have characterized the motility of the chick embryo, up to 17 days, as random movements that are performed periodically, activity phases alternating with inactivity phases. All parts of the embryo which are capable of motility at a given stage participate during the activity phase; however, the movements of the different parts are not related to each other. For instance, the two wings do not move together in a coordinated manner as in flight, nor do the two legs move in an alternating pattern as in walking. Yet, both wings and legs may perform flexions and extensions simultaneously. Head movements, beak clapping and opening or closing of the beak and of the lower eyelid may all occur independently or as part of a total body movement. (Hamburger & Oppenheim, 1967, p. 171)

The duration of the activity phases increases with advancing age of the embryo (see Figure 1.1).

Hamburger and his associates (1965) then asked if motility could be elicited by the spinal cord itself. A section of the cervical portion of the cord was surgically removed in 2-day-old chick embryos, thereby severing the spinal cord from the brain. Any movement of the embryo thus would necessarily be produced by efferent or motor neurons that exit the cord and innervate muscle. As shown in Figure 1.2, although overall activity was reduced (by about 20%), the spinally transected embryos did exhibit motility in an age-related pattern similar to that of the intact preparations. These findings are in agreement with the electrophysiological work of Provine (1972), who recorded electrical activity directly from the spinal cord. Bursts of electrical activity, which are taken as indicative of complex bioelectrical events, were seen as early as day 5 of incubation. Moreover, the electrical bursts appeared coincident with body movement (Ripley & Provine, 1972) (see Figure 1.3). O'Donovan and Landmiesser (1987) reported a similar result by recording electrical activity in the ventral root of the isolated cord. Moreover, it appears that it is the initial portion of the electrical burst that actually triggers muscle activity (Landmiesser & O'Donovan, 1984). Lastly, Provine and Rogers (1977), whose findings are in close agreement with those of Ham-

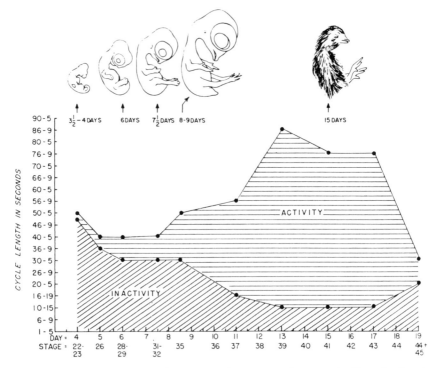

Figure 1.1   Mean duration of activity and inactivity phases and of length of cycle at different stages of development of the chick embryo. (From Hamburger et al., "Periodic motility of normal and spinal chick embryos between 8 and 17 days of incubation." *Journal of Experimental Zoology, 159,* 1–13. © 1965 by Wiley-Liss, a division of John Wiley and Sons. Reprinted by permission.)

burger, reported similar patterns of electrical activity from the spinal cords of intact embryos and those whose brains were severed from the cord.

The work of Hamburger and others, though demonstrating that embryonic motility can be generated by the discharge of spinal neurons, did not address the issue of stimulation. Perhaps motility is the result of spinal reflexes, i.e., sensory (afferent) input into the cord that triggers output to muscle fibers. Although it was not the purpose of the studies reviewed here to stimulate the embryo, it is possible that such stimulation either was given inadvertently or was produced by the embryo itself. Hamburger, Wenger, and Oppenheim (1966) asked specifically if stimulation is necessary for the display of embryonic motility. To that end, the thoracic portions of the spinal cords of 2-day-old embryos were removed so sensory input originating from the legs could be eliminated. Leg motility was then assessed in 8.5-, 11-, 13-, 15-, and 17-day-old embryos. Except for the 17-day-old embryos, the percent of leg motility during a 15-minute test period was the same for experimental and intact preparations (17-day-old experimental embryos showed a deficit). There is, then, direct support for the notion that sensory input is not required for embryonic motility.

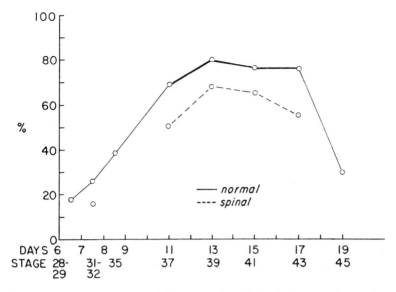

Figure 1.2   Mean percent of time spent in activity during 15-minute observation periods for normal and spinally transected chick embryos. (From Hamburger et al., "Periodic motility of normal and spinal chick embryos between 8 and 17 days of incubation." *Journal of Experimental Zoology, 159,* 1–13. © 1965 by Wiley-Liss, a division of John Wiley and Sons. Reprinted by permission.)

The early findings that embryonic movement occurs prior to the time embryos respond to the application of stimulation and the work of Hamburger, Provine, and others lend strong support to the notion that embryonic motility can be initiated by spontaneous discharge of the neuromotor system. Is it the case, however, that stimulation is really without influence? Whereas Hamburger et al. (1966) demonstrated that surgically prepared embryos can exhibit motility in the absence of afferent input, perhaps under *normal* conditions embryos do respond to exteroceptive stimulation. As we will see, other data show that embryos are indeed responsive to such stimulation. In other words, although embryos possess the *capacity* to respond spontaneously, they may not normally do so.

EMBRYONIC MOTILITY AND SENSORY STIMULATION

Stimulation and Assessment of Nervous System Development

Initially, researchers stimulated an embryo to assess nervous system development rather than to examine the relation between the embryo and its prenatal milieu. Stimulation was thought not to influence the course of development; behavioral development was viewed even by those interested in reactivity to

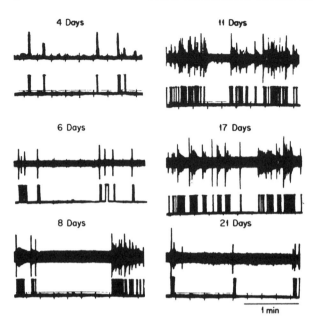

Figure 1.3 Comparison of cord burst discharges (upper traces) with visually observed body movements (lower traces) on days 4 to 21. The 4-day cord activity was integrated to emphasize the low-amplitude activity. Cord discharges were made from the lumbosacral region, except at 4 days, when the brachial cord was monitored. (From Ripley and Provine, "Neural correlates of embryonic motility in the chick." *Brain Research, 45,* 127–34. © 1972 by Elsevier Science Publishers. Reprinted by permission.)

stimulation as an inevitable and invariant outcome of nervous system maturation. Those examining embryonic responsiveness to stimulation also recognized that motility can occur in the absence of overt stimulation.

The neuroanatomist G. E. Coghill, whose work first appeared in 1902, was a pioneer in the study of embryonic development because of his carefully performed empirical research and his views concerning the development of embryonic motility (e.g., Hooker, 1936; Oppenheim, 1978). The salamander embryo served as the subject for most of his investigations. Correlations were drawn between the extent to which tactile stimulation (from a human hair) elicited movements and the level of nervous system development. Responsiveness to the stimulus initially appears near the snout because, according to Coghill, it is in the head region, that connections are first established between motor neurons and muscle tissue. The head typically is moved away from, and occasionally toward, the source of the stimulation (Coghill, 1929). Later, responses can be evoked from other areas, spreading in a rostrocaudal direction following the sequential development of neuronal innervation of muscle. Once again, behavioral development was seen as following a course determined by nervous system maturation.

Coghill also reported that the initial movements of individual structures, e.g., gills, hindlimbs, and forelimbs, are undifferentiated, resulting from the overall movement of the embryo's trunk. In other words, the motility of individual structures is part of a larger response involving motility of the trunk. It is only later that the embryo is capable of performing discrete, independent movements of individual structures. Coghill called the process of going from undifferentiated to differentiated activity *individuation.* In his words, "Behavior develops from the beginning through the progressive expansion of a perfectly integrated total pattern and the individuation within it of partial patterns which acquire various degrees of discreteness" (Coghill, 1929, p. 38). At the time, this approach was considered revolutionary because it had been widely held that overall patterns of behavior resulted from the summation of discrete, simple reflexes.

Coghill's use of the term *pattern* with reference to behavior was reminiscent of the then popular Gestalt movement, which emphasized overall patterns of central neural activity in its quest to understand perceptual processes. Lest anyone confuse Coghill's interpretation of behavioral development with that of Gestalt theorists and perhaps place the subject of embryonic behavior within the intellectual domain of psychology, Hooker (1936) stated the following:

> In a way, I think it possibly unfortunate that Coghill has used the term "pattern." The existence of patterns is denied by many and is rather generally associated with the principles of Gestalt psychology. It is true that the emergence of individual reflexes from a total response, as described by Coghill for Amblystome, has been gathered to the Gestalt bosom. However, I wish to emphasize that the total response, from which individual reflexes emerge, was forced upon Coghill by his functional-morphological findings, and was not evolved to give aid and comfort to the Gestalt point of view. (p. 581)

A number of subsequent experiments with mammalian embryos supported Coghill's findings with the salamander. Experimentation with the mammalian embryo (except for certain marsupials, e.g., the opposum and kangaroo), however, faces two major problems. One concerns observation. Unlike amphibian embryos, which can be observed directly through the semitransparent gelatinous substance that surrounds them, or avian embryos, which can be easily observed by removing a portion of the shell and coating the underlying membrane with petroleum jelly, mammalian embryos must be removed from the uterus while maintaining the integrity of the placental connection. Relatively mature embryos can be observed through the amniotic membranes, which become taut and transparent during the later stages of gestation. Less mature embryos must also be taken from the amnion. The very act of abruptly removing the embryo from its normal intrauterine environment may itself affect motility. A second problem concerns anesthetizing the mother, which is performed prior to exteriorizing the uterus. Anesthesia must result in blockage of pain and prevention of movement without affecting the embryo. Therefore the administration of an agent such as sodium pentobarbital is unacceptable, as the drug crosses the placenta and anesthetizes the embryo as well as the adult. A number of techniques have been developed to obviate this problem, including occlusion of the carotid

artery, transection of the spinal cord, and production of a functional spinal transection by injecting ethyl alcohol or lidocaine and epinephrine into the cord
(Smotherman, Richards, & Robinson, 1983; Smotherman, Robinson, & Miller,
1986).

Another early researcher, Angulo Y Gonzalez (1932), turned to the rat
embryo. After rendering the adult unconscious by ligating the internal carotid
arteries (ether was used only when required as a supplement), the uterus was
exposed and the embryos were "shelled out" of the amnionic sacs. The entire
preparation was suspended in a temperature-controlled bath of physiological
saline, with the adult's head being kept above the level of the solution. The
responses of 643 embryos aged 14 to 21 days (gestation period 22 days) to stimulation from a coarse hair were recorded. Observation sessions lasted up to an
hour.

The development of rat embryonic activity was strikingly similar to that
reported by Coghill for the salamander. The earliest movement, seen at 15.7
days after insemination, was head movement in response to stimulation applied
to the snout region. Between days 16.0 and 16.9, movement spread in a caudal
direction, involving first the forelimbs, then the rump, and lastly the hindlimbs.
During that period the forelimbs moved only in conjunction with trunk movements. Thus a total pattern of behavior, movement of the trunk with accompanying limb activity, was seen. Another total pattern, observed between 17.0
and 17.9 days, consisted of head movement with accompanying opening of the
mouth and tongue protrusion. As with the salamander, it was only later that discrete movements developed. Similar results were presented by Narayanan, Fox,
and Hamburger (1971). (The problem of anesthetization was dealt with by tran-
secting the pregnant animal's spinal cord at a level that eliminates movement
and blocks the receipt of sensory information from the abdominal region but
does not prevent respiration.) Responses evoked by tactile stimulation generally
begin as a total pattern of motility, and areas of the body that cause movement
when stimulated spread over time in a caudal direction (see Figure 1.4).

Human embryos also respond to tactile stimulation. Hooker (1936, 1952)
performed a series of experiments with therapeutically aborted embryos. Prior
to summarizing the findings, his caveat should be noted: Aborted embryos
immediately undergo asphyxiation even when oxygen is provided. "As a result,
all conclusions drawn from human fetal activity must be carefully weighed with
the effects of asphyxia in mind" (Hooker, 1936, p. 591).

Hooker's findings are summarized in Table 1.1. We see again that tactile stimulation initially elicits a total pattern response and, later, discrete responses.
Humphrey (1964), whose results are in general accord with those of Hooker,
extended the research by demonstrating a relation between behavior elicited by
tactile stimulation and neural development (see Table 1.2).

The data described here supported Coghill's idea that a total pattern of motility precedes discrete activities such as the movement of limbs. Unanimity was
not to be reached, however. Windle (1944; Windle & Becker, 1940) argued that
the procedures used to study the mammalian embryo produced an artifact that
led to spurious data, and that in reality individualized behaviors do predate gen-

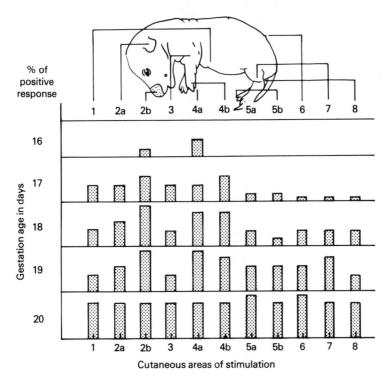

Figure 1.4 Semiquantitative representation of the appearance of motor responses evoked by stimulation of the cutaneous areas on the body surface of 16- to 20-day-old rat fetuses. Responses predominate in the rostral regions early, followed by gradual emergence of the response to cutaneous stimulations from caudal regions of the body. (From Narayanan et al., "Prenatal development of spontaneous and evoked activity in the rat." *Behaviour, 40,* 100–134. © 1971 by E. J. Brill. Reprinted by permission.)

eralized behavior. Based on information derived from the cat embryo, Windle concluded that impaired respiration, a condition that always arises when the embryo is removed from the uterus and amnionic sac, can abolish individual behaviors before they can be elicited by stimulation. Because asphyxia itself elicits rhythmic mass movement, the erroneous impression is gained that such mass activity is the precursor to individualized behaviors.

Whether individualized behaviors develop from mass activity or the opposite occurs is no longer a relevant controversy. The oft-cited monograph by Carmichael (1934) on the behavior of the guinea pig embryo argued for abandonment of the mass action and individuation concepts. His data supported both positions; although the first spontaneous and elicited responses of the guinea pig embryo were specific, each was itself part of a larger patterned response. Carmichael suggested that before generalization about behavioral ontogeny can be formulated we must collect more data from a wider variety of species.

Table 1.1 Periods of change in the character of fetal reflexes elicited by stimulating skin areas supplied by the trigeminal nerve

Menstrual Age	Nature of the Reflexes Observed
7.5–9.5 Weeks	"Total pattern" type of movements only.
9.5–12.0 Weeks	Movements stereotyped and repetition of a stimulus gives essentially an identical response.
	"Total pattern" type of movements disappearing and seen only with the onset of anoxia.
	Appearance of various local reflexes on stimulation of sensory trigeminal fibers.
12 Weeks and later	Newly appearing reflexes remain stereotyped for a time after first elicited, but repetition of a stimulus no longer always gives the same response.
	Combination of reflexes appear (e.g., ventral head flexion, mouth closure, swallowing) or local reflexes combine with such movements as lateral trunk flexion or ventral head flexion.
13–14 Weeks and later	Reflexes no longer at all stereotyped. Repeated stimulation may produce different reflexes or combinations of reflexes.
	Movements are graceful and flowing in nature.
	Local reflexes dominate the activity, either singly or in combinations.

Source: From Hooker. *The Prenatal Origin of Behavior.* © University of Kansas Press, 1952. Reprinted by permission.

Table 1.2 Development of peripheral sensory trigeminal receptors correlated with fetal reflexes elicited by their stimulation

Mentrual Age (Weeks)	Status of Nerve Endings	Activity on Trigeminal Stimulation
7.5	Nerve plexus in corium of lips and tongue	Contralateral flexion in neck region
8.0	Nerve fibers approaching epithelium of lips	Contralateral neck and upper trunk flexion. Rare ipsilateral neck and upper trunk flexion
8.5	Undifferentiated nerve tips mostly 40–50 μm from epithelial cells of lips; a few only 5 μm distant	Contralateral neck and upper trunk flexion now accompanied by extension at shoulders and rotation of pelvis to opposite side
		Comparable ipsilateral reflex rarely seen
9.5	A few nerve tips reach the basement membrane of the epithelium of the lips	First local reflex, lowering of mandible
		Contralateral trunk flexion extends farther caudalward
		Extension of trunk and neck
10–11	An increasing number of nerve fibers reach the basement membrane of the lips but do not appear to pierce it	Local reflex of swallowing appears
		Contralateral trunk flexion combined with rotation of face contralaterally

Table 1.2 (*Continued*)   Development of peripheral sensory trigeminal receptors correlated with fetal reflexes elicited by their stimulation

Mentrual Age (Weeks)	Status of Nerve Endings	Activity on Trigeminal Stimulation
	Rich nerve network just below epithelium of tongue	Trunk and neck extension combined with rotation of pelvis
	Nerve fibers approach epithelium between hair follicles of superciliary ridge	Orbicularis oculi contraction ("squint") and corrugator supercilii contraction ("scowl") on eyelid and eyebrow or eyelid stimulation alone
12–12.5	Some nerve fibers pierce the basement membrane of the lips and spread onto nearest epithelial cells to form crude discs resembling touch corpuscles of Merkel, expanding in a single large growth cone	Lip closure appears and may be accompanied by swallowing
		Ventral head flexion, with rotation of the face ipsilaterally and medial rotation of both arms
		Downward rotation of eyeballs on eyelid stimulation
	Nerve fibers now in sheaths of hair follicles on medial side of superciliary ridge and a few on upper lip	Consistent orbicularis oculi contraction ("squint") often accompanied by action of corrugator supercilii ("scowl")
13–14	Many nerve fibers have pierced the basement membrane of the lips and reach the epithelial cells	Mouth closure and swallowing with marked ventral head flexion
		Tongue movements
	Nerve fibers end on hair follicles of upper lip and cheek region, some with collateral branches; those of hair follicles of superciliary ridge and upper lip better developed than those of cheek and lower lip	Elevation of angle of mouth and ala of nose ("sneer" type of reflex) with rotation of face away from stimulus about alae and upper lip
		Orbicularis oculi contraction ("squint") combined with neck and trunk extension
20	Free nerve fibers in deeper layers of epidermis	Closure and protrusion of both lips (upper lip 17 weeks; lower lip 20 weeks)
	Tongue papillae richly innervated but no taste buds	
>20	Network of fibers among epithelial cells of lip on either side of midline	Pursing of lips (22 weeks)
		Spontaneous sucking (22–23 weeks)
	Intraepithelial fibers frequent at 24 weeks and better developed at margins of lips	Side-to-side head turning (22–23 weeks; 28 weeks)
		Sneezing on stimulating nostrils (24 weeks)
		Audible sucking (29 weeks, perhaps earlier)
Newborn	Abundance of differentiated end-organs present	Turning face toward stimulation on touching around the lips

Source: From Humphrey. Some correlations between the appearance of human fetal reflexes and the development of the nervous system. *Progress in Brain Research 4*, 93–135, 1964. Reprinted by permission.

As we have seen, embryos, although capable of movement in the absence of stimulation, are responsive to the application of exteroceptive stimulation. However, the data we have thus far examined were garnered from the artificial experimental situation involving surgically prepared specimens confronted with stimuli (e.g., hair, needles, acid) obviously not normally encountered in the uterine environment. Therefore a basic issue awaited resolution, namely, whether under *normal* conditions embryos respond to naturally occurring environmental stimuli.

Motility and the Interaction Between Embryo and Environment

With Pavlov's publication of the now classic studies on conditioned reflexes and the debut of J. Watson's two works, *Psychology from the Standpoint of a Behaviorist* (1919) and *Behaviorism* (1924), not only did our thinking about behavioral analysis in general become revolutionized but our views of embryonic behavior were shaken. E. B. Holt (1931), a radical behaviorist insofar as the embryo was concerned, stated that "it is a perilous insouciance with which many biologists and the majority of psychologists rattle on about about ancestral habits, original nature, innate tendencies, inherited instincts, innate ideas, engrams, mneme and so on" (p. 22). Brushing aside earlier debates, he argued that behavior of the embryo is for the most part acquired in the form of conditioned reflexes. By definition, then, embryonic behavioral development is not merely an invariant product resulting from nervous system maturation but, rather, the result of an interaction between the embryo and its environment. Embryonic behavior was thus placed squarely within the purview of psychological inquiry.

Holt relied on what then was both known and hypothesized about neuronal growth to argue that the development of the nervous system, and hence behavior, is not predetermined—that the undifferentiated embryonic nervous system can form particular sensorimotor connections as a function of the pairing of sensory stimulation with initially spontaneous motor activity. The work of Bok (1915) and Ariens Kappers (1936), which purportedly demonstrated that electrical current radiating from a developing nerve bundle attracts axons and dendrites from a less developed bundle, played a central role in Holt's theory. (Excellent treatments of this early neurophysiological research are found in Gottlieb [1970, 1973].) According to Holt, "Precisely because no connections between afferent, central, and motor neurones are 'preformed,' or established by 'heredity,' the earliest movements of organisms are utterly random movements. The movements become biologically useful, significant, or 'purposive' only very slowly" (p. 31). During ontogeny reflex arcs are established; more developed efferent (motor) neurons, which initially function spontaneously, attract afferent (sensory) neurons, forming a functional unit. Thus "the possibility is open for *any* sense-organ to acquire functional connection with *any* muscle" (p. 33). The ontogeny of the infantile grasping reflex is given as an example:

> Consider a random impulse reaching the flexor muscle of a finger. In the foetal position the fingers are often closed over the palm of the hand, and the least random

flexion of a finger will cause it to press on the palm. Then (what is not random) afferent impulses ("tactile") from the two surfaces in contact (palm and finger) will be sent back to the central nervous system, where by the principle already cited they will find an outlet in the motor paths that were just now excited, that is, those of the flexor muscle of the finger in question. When this has happened, a few times (as it is bound to happen) the reflex-circle will be established; and then a pressure stimulus on either palm or finger will cause the finger to flex and so close down on the object that caused the pressure. Such is the origin of the "grasping reflex," which is so useful through all the later life. With Pavlov's law . . . the reader can discover for himself the genesis of many of the earliest reflexes,—lip closure, jaw closure, "extensor-thrust" when the bottom of the foot is touched, knee-flexion when the posterior surface of either lower or upper leg is pressed . . . and many others. (Holt, 1931, p. 39)

For Holt, then, embryonic development exerts a significant influence on postnatal development; reflexes "acquired" by the embryo may be part of the behavioral repertoire of the neonate. Behavioral development of the embryo therefore is not an invariant product of neuromuscular maturation but is subject to the same vagaries that affect development of postembryonic behavior.

Z.-Y. Kuo, who focused much of his attention on behavior of the avian embryo during a career that spanned more than five decades, also believed that the environment or stimulation plays a critical role in the ontogeny of behavior. However, labeling Holt's view "environmentalistic," Kuo (1976) argued that behavior is the result of a *dynamic interaction* between the organism and its environment, both internal and external. In other words, rather than stimulation impinging on the embryo and resulting in the formation of a reflex, the environment and behavior are thought to act continually on each other (a "bidirectionalistic" view). In a sense, the environment and the organism can be thought of as a single, continually changing entity. Given the great diversity of stimulation that can impinge on embryos of the same species at any given moment in time, no two individuals can be expected to acquire the same behavioral repertoire. Kuo used the term "behavioral potentials" to refer to this wide range of possible outcomes of behavioral development. Behavioral potentials are, of course, constrained by such factors as morphology, and they diminish as the organism ages.

Kuo's theory of development and much of its supporting research are summarized in his book *The Dynamics of Behavior Development* published 3 years before his death in 1970 (and reprinted in 1976). One example of how the interaction between chick embryo and environment can affect behavioral ontogeny concerns the position of the embryo within the amnion. From the fifth through the tenth days of incubation, the position of embryos is variable. During that period motor activities are reduced by as much as 35% should the embryo lie on its ventral side. Movement is presumably curtailed because the ventrally positioned embryo is crowded by the yolk sac. This is akin to recent findings with the rat embryo demonstrating that both the uterus and the amnion restrain motility late in gestation (Smotherman & Robinson, 1986). The same is true for the human embryo, which, beginning at week 16, shows a dramatic decline in the rate at which it changes its position in utero (de Vries, Visser, and Prechtl, 1982). Effective stimulation is also thought to arise from the embryo's internal environment. Returning to the chick embryo, the heartbeat, for instance, has been credited with causing the head to move in a direction away from the source of stimulation.

Kuo rejected the concept of reflex and replaced it with the broader notion of "behavioral gradients." He argued that the *entire* embryo, all body parts and organs, is involved in every response. He defined *behavioral gradient* as the extent to which a particular structure participates in a behavior. With his repudiation of the reflex, Kuo was led to criticize what he considered to be the overly simplistic work of Hamburger and others, which, if you remember, involves local and what they believe to be spontaneous activities such as leg movement. Wrote Kuo:

> [I]n their desire to prove their point, they have inadvertently overlooked most of the complex behavioral events in the chick's development. . . . Thus, the motility of the embryo was reduced to such simplicity that the kymograph [a simple recording device] alone sufficed to record all the embryonic movements for several hours. With such experimental procedures it is hard for one who is quite familiar with the ontogeny of the bird embryo in all its usual complexity to assess Hamburger's findings and harder still to evaluate the theoretical interpretation of the findings. (Kuo, 1976, pp. 53–54)

Kuo studied the embryo in much the same manner as ethologists examine the postembryonic organism; behavior was examined as unobtrusively as possible within the organism's natural habitat. For Kuo, the habitat was the egg rather than the forest. Also, like the ethologist, Kuo imposed few if any experimental manipulations on the subject. In other words, the independent variables were naturally occurring events be they the position of a nest site relative to food sources or the position of the embryo relative to the yolk sac. To verify certain predictions, however, it often becomes necessary to manipulate the subject, to impose conditions that allow one to test hypotheses. A number of such experiments have provided important information concerning the role of environmental stimulation in embryonic development.

Peters, Vanderahe, and Powers (1958), using the chick embryo, recorded electrical activity from the optic lobes and eye in response to flashes of light at frequencies ranging from 5 to 60 Hz. Although the experiment was performed to assess the functional development of the visual system, the work has become noteworthy as a result of a serendipitous finding. Exposure to the light stimulus 2 to 3 days prior to hatching advanced the development of electrical responsivity of both the eye and the optic lobe. In other words, the stimulus appeared to hasten maturation of the visual system. A similar finding was reported with the duck embryo (Paulson, 1965). Embryos having had 24 hours of exposure to a flashing light exhibited shorter response latencies and more consistent waveform patterns in the optic lobe, retina, and telencephalon in response to light stimuli than controls. In both of these studies the embryos were *directly* exposed to light by removing a portion of the shell. It is not known, then, if the embryonic visual system is influenced by light passing through the shell—if ambient illumination is a factor that *normally* modulates visual system maturation. It would be an easy matter, of course, to compare the visual systems of embryos incubated in intact eggs under varying degrees of illumination.

Embryonic exposure to light also affects time of hatching. *Intact* chicken eggs exposed continuously to incandescent light from the first day of incubation hatched approximately 16 hours earlier than controls (Shutze, Lauber, Kato, & Wilson, 1962). (The authors stated that the light source, three 40-watt bulbs, did not produce an appreciable increase in air temperature surrounding the eggs.) An advancement of hatching can be produced even when exposure to light does not include the entire incubation period; light applied only during the first week of incubation is effective (see Figure 1.5) (Lauber & Shutze, 1964). Because the eyes are not functional at week 1, the authors speculated that some other organ must serve as the light detector. These data suggest that sunlight passing through the shell may be one factor that normally governs rate of development. This proposal is supported by the fact that incandescent light, which contains more wavelengths found in the sun's spectrum than does fluorescent light, is much more effective for advancing hatching.

The development of brain lateralization also is related to prehatching experience with light. As demonstrated by Rogers and Anson (1979), chickens normally exhibit asymmetry in forebrain function; the administration of the protein synthesis inhibitor cycloheximide into the left forebrain on posthatching day 2 led to retarded visual and auditory learning and elevated levels of attack and copulatory behavior. Treatment of the right forebrain did not affect those behaviors. Therefore visual and auditory learning as well as attack and copulation are con-

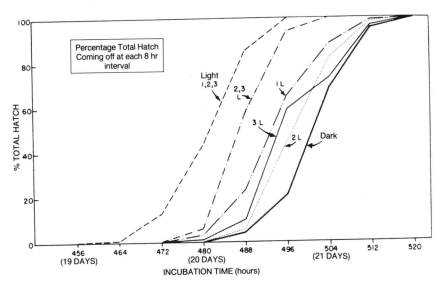

Figure 1.5 Hatching curves for chicken eggs under incandescent lights during week 1, 2, or 3 of incubation or combinations thereof. (From Lauber and Shutze, "Accelerated growth of embryo chicks under the influence of light." *Growth, 28,* 179–90. © 1964 by Growth Publishing Co. Reprinted with permission.)

trolled by the left hemisphere. However, left forebrain lateralization of attack and copulation is not reliably observed if the eggs are incubated throughout the incubation period in darkness (Zappia & Rogers, 1983). Furthermore, exposure to light for 4 hours, but not for 1 hour, on day 19 of incubation is sufficient to produce lateralization.

Light also affects mammalian fetuses. We know, for example, that certain biological (circadian) rhythms are found in embryos and that they often are in synchrony with those of the dam (Weaver & Reppert, 1987). The rhythms of the dam, in turn, are synchronized with the external lighting conditions. It has been proposed that this synchrony eventually functions to coordinate the pup with both the dam and the environment, thereby permitting the youngster to "assume its temporal niche" (Reppert & Weaver, 1988). One such rhythm is metabolic activity of the suprachiasmatic nucleus (SCN) of the embryonic rat brain, which is synchronized with that of the dam and the external lighting cycle (Reppert & Schwartz, 1983). If the maternal SCN is destroyed, the rhythm in the embryo brain no longer is synchronized with the external lighting condition (Reppert & Schwartz, 1986). Light therefore stimulates the maternal SCN, which, in turn, activates the embryonic SCN.

Maternal lighting condition also has been shown to influence the development of the coats of meadow voles. Coats were more developed in the offspring of dams that experienced 2 weeks of daily periods of short light cycles and least developed in those from dams that had 26 weeks of such treatment (Lee & Zucker, 1988).

Sound, as well as light, appears to play a significant role in the development of the avian embryo. It is important that hatching occurs at about the same time in the multiegg clutch to permit the hen to lead her entire brood away from the nest. Vince and her colleagues (1964, 1966; Vince, Reader, & Tolhurst, 1976) discovered that a particular sound regulates the timing of hatching, speeding up development in more slowly maturing embryos. Quail embryos emit a clicking sound coincident with the onset of regular breathing. That hatching is regulated by the clicking sound is supported by the following: (1) when the eggs are in physical contact, hatching is virtually synchronous; (2) when eggs are kept physically apart, the range of hatching times for a given clutch is markedly increased, presumably because the clicking sounds are not transmitted among the eggs; and (3) playing the appropriate clicking sounds to eggs not in physical contact leads to synchronized hatching. Observations of the embryos revealed that the clicks elicit activity. During a 15-minute test period during which clicks were presented, 20-day-old embryos displayed a significant increase in coordinated behaviors, e.g., wriggling of the entire body including the head, lifting the trunk, and movement of both wings—behaviors that bring the embryo into the hatching position. A determiner of the efficacy of the click stimulus is its rate of presentation. Presentation of clicks at rates different from those that normally occur may even retard hatching (Vince & Cheng, 1970). Vince's findings have since been replicated by White (1984) using the domestic chick.

Internal (interoceptive) as well as exteroceptive stimuli have been implicated in embryonic development, specifically hatching behavior. At the initiation of hatching, the chick embryo adopts a characteristic posture consisting in tightly flexed legs, beak angled upward toward the airspace in the blunt end of the egg, and head bent to the right and tucked underneath the right wing. Hatching behaviors can be reelicited in the posthatching chick by forcing them to assume the hatching posture. It has been accomplished by "folding" them into the hatching posture and placing them in artificial glass eggs (Bekoff & Kauer, 1984) or by simply bending the neck to the right or left (Bekoff & Kauer, 1982). It was hypothesized that sensory receptors located in the neck are activiated by the bending of the head, and it is this signal that initiates hatching (Bekoff & Sabichi, 1987). Bekoff and Sabichi used three groups of 0- and 1-day-old chicks to test this idea. Two of the groups were injected with the local anesthetic lidocaine, one group in the thigh and the other in the neck. A third group of chicks was injected with saline in the neck. The animals were then folded into the glass eggs and observed for hatching movements. The group of subjects that received the anesthetic in the neck exhibited hatching activity much later than did the other two groups, presumably after the effect of the anesthetic wore off. This finding supports the idea that interoceptive stimulation from the neck initiates hatching behavior.

The observational studies of Kuo and the experiments reviewed here provide ample support for the idea that the embryo not only is capable of responding to stimulation but does so as a matter of course. Stimulation may arise from sources internal to the embryo, external to the embryo but internal to the amnion, external to the amnion but internal to the membranes or uterus, or external to the shell or the adult female. The amnion and uterus themselves are also sources of stimulation. As stated by Smotherman and Robinson (1986), "Far from an incomplete organism passively reflecting random stimulation, the mammalian fetus should be viewed as an active, fitted organism capable of interacting with a complex and changing environment" (p. 1872). More is said about this subject in Chapter 2, in which the ability of environmental stimulation to establish behavioral potentials is discussed.

FUNCTIONS OF EMBRYONIC BEHAVIOR

Thus far we have considered factors that initiate and modulate the embryo's behavior. Now we turn to another issue, the function(s) of such behavior. Given that the embryo is the precursor of the adult, it is natural, even despite the pitfalls inherent in teleological argument, that we subject embryonic behavior to a functional analysis.

One way to ascertain the function of embryonic behavior is to assess the effects of its *absence*. This tactic requires experimental immobilization of the embryo. A number of early studies examined the influence of motor paralysis on amphibian embryos (Carmichael, 1926; Harrison, 1904; Mathews & Detwiler, 1926) by maintaining the embryos prior to the free-swimming stage in water containing an anesthetic. Whereas the results of these experiments all showed that the embryos eventually could swim, Fromme (1941) later found that their swimming was inferior to that of normal embryos.

Drachman and Coulombre (1962) infused the paralytic agent curare into 7- to 15-day-old chick embryos for periods of 24 and 48 hours. At hatching the chicks exhibited abnormal formation of toes and joints. The toes were hyperextended, clawed, and frequently crossed; and the ankle joints were rigid. This anomaly, referred to as "clubfoot," can be seen in Figure 1.6. Note the similarity between the immobilized chick embryo and amyoplasia, or "clubfoot" syndrome of the human infant, which is related to attenuated intrauterine movement (see Figure 1.7) (Hall, 1985). The problem resides in the formation of joint cavities, which, in the paralyzed preparation, fill with connective tissue, causing the limb to become rigid (Drachman & Sokoloff, 1966). Drachman and Coulombre stated that "joint differentiation proceeds to a considerable extent in the absence of movement, but articular cavity formation and fine sculpturing of the cartilaginous surfaces require the mechanical action normally provided by the embryo's own skeletal muscle" (p. 525). Extension movements of limbs in

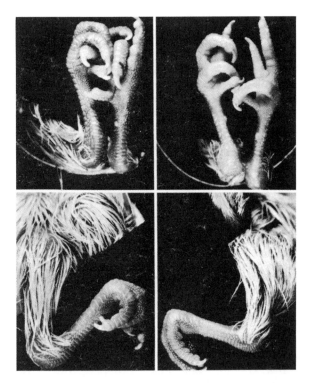

Figure 1.6 Feet of four chicks that had received 48-hour infusions of curare. (From Drachman and Coulombre, "Experimental clubfoot and anthrogryposis multiplex congenita." *Lancet, 14,* 401–20. © 1962 by Williams & Wilkins. Reprinted by permission.)

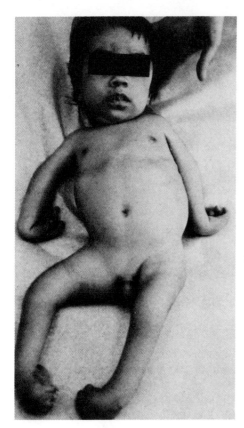

Figure 1.7 Infant with amyoplasia. (From Hall, "Genetic aspects of ary-throgryposis." *Clinical Orthopaedics and Related Research, 194,* 45–53. © 1985 by J.B. Lippincott. Reprinted by permission.)

the human embryo, which commence at about 10 weeks, may be similarly required to induce cavity formation (Swinyard & Bleck, 1985). Furthermore, it has been suggested that the spontaneous activity that Hamburger and others have shown to be of spinal origin may act as a safeguard to ensure necessary motor activity in the absence of sensory stimulation (Bekoff, Byers, & Bekoff, 1980; Oppenheim, 1982).

Embryonic immobilization leads to abnormalities in addition to those related to joint formation. Moessinger (1983) exposed rat embryos to curare from days 18 to 21 of gestation. The embryos, apart from multiple joint contractures, exhibited pulmonary hypoplasia, growth retardation, short umbilical cords, microgastria (abnormally small stomachs), and polyhydramnia (excessive accumulation of amniotic fluid). These symptoms are similar to those of the Pena-Shokeir syndrome, a genetic disorder afflicting humans. It has been suggested that the defects are caused by fetal immobilization (Hall, 1986).

It is clear that embryonic motility contributes to the normal development of structure and thus to the normal development of behavior. Chicks with leg malformations obviously cannot exhibit proper locomotor activity. Embryonic behavior also may contribute *directly* to behavioral development. That is, if postnatal/posthatching behavior is a continuation and elaboration of embryonic behavior as suggested by Kuo (1976) and others, behavior of the embryo might be a precursor for later, more complex behavior. Normal postembryonic development therefore may be contingent on normal embryonic development. Stated another way, embryonic behavior may be preparatory for postembryonic behavior.

As a precursor of infant behavior, one would expect embryonic activity to increase in complexity and become coordinated as the age of the embryo advances. A number of investigators have found this expectation to be true. Hamburger and Oppenheim (1967), for example, reported that by about day 17 of incubation the chick embryo for the first time exhibits coordinated movements involved in hatching. It is worth noting that these investigators suggested that the coordinated movements, unlike earlier spontaneous activity, may be guided by sensory information. Similar data from the rat embryo were presented by Robinson and Smotherman (1987), who reported a dramatic rise in synchronous activity (simultaneous movement of more than one body region) by day 17 of gestation. These authors defined this synchronous activity as "true" behavior, apparently in contrast to the asynchronous activities of the younger embryo. Complex and coordinated activities also appear during the latter stages of mouse embryo development (Kodama & Sekiguchi, 1982).

One also might suppose that, as a precursor of postembryonic behavior, embryonic behavior should resemble later behavior to some extent. Comparisons of pre- and postembryonic behavior are difficult. As discussed by Bekoff (1988), because of the marked structural changes in limb segmentation seen during embryonic development, behaviors that appear to differ between the embryo and the neonate may actually be similar. Also, the small size of embryos of species typically studied in the laboratory make observation of movements troublesome. For these reasons, two techniques in addition to the direct observation of the preparation are used to study embryonic–postembryonic behavioral continuity: electromyographic (EMG) recording and joint angle analysis. EMG recordings, obtained by inserting wire electrodes into muscle tissue and recording the electrical potentials, provide a direct assessment of the pattern of muscle contractions and an indirect assessment of the motor output pattern of the central nervous system. The analysis of joint angles and other parameters such as movement cycles is accomplished by videotaping the behavior and playing it back at slow speed. The data are then quantified and usually represented graphically.

Joint angle analyses and EMG recordings have yielded data showing that postembryonic behavior does not appear de novo—that continuity exists between the behavior of the embryo and that of the hatchling/neonate. Bekoff and Lau (1980) reported that the forelimb-forelimb and hindlimb-hindlimb coordinated movements of the 20-day-old rat fetus are similar to those observed in the postnatal rat while swimming. More recently, Bekoff (1988) reported that the neural circuitry that controls leg movements of the chick embryo during hatching is used again later to control leg movements of walking. Therefore, although these two behaviors clearly look different, leg movements of hatching may be a precursor to walking.

Continuity between embryonic and postembryonic behaviors also can be assessed by providing the embryo with stimulation it normally would encounter after hatching or birth. If such stimulation elicits a behavior similar to that of the neonate or hatchling, the view that embryonic behavior may be preparatory to later activity receives added support. Smotherman and Robinson (1987) infused milk or lemon juice directly into the mouths of 19- to 21-day-old rat embryos. By day 20 milk elicited a stretching response, and lemon produced face wiping (see Figure 1.8). Stretching is typically displayed by the postnatal rat in response

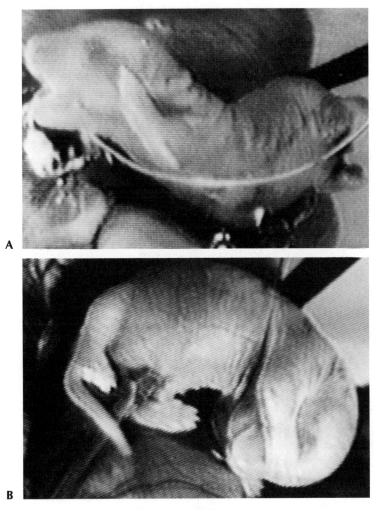

A

B

Figure 1.8 Photographs from videotape records of a 20-day rat fetus engaging in (A) stretching and face (B) wiping. (From Smotherman and Robinson, ''Prenatal expression of species-typical action patterns in rat fetus *(Rattus norvegicus).*'' *Journal of Comparative Psychology, 101,* 190–96. © 1987 by the American Psychological Association. Reprinted by permission.)

to the ejection of milk from the mammary gland while suckling. Face wiping, on the other hand, is exhibited by pups and adults when exposed to bitter tasting substances. Smotherman and Robinson (1990) went on to show that rat embryos are responsive to odorous gas as well as taste stimuli.

Embryos also react to tactile stimulation in a manner similar to that of the neonate. The newborn rat responds to maternal licking of its anogenital area by elevating its hindquarters and straightening its hindlegs. This reaction, referred to as the leg extension response, facilitates the mother's access to the perineum. Anogenital licking is important because it stimulates urination and defecation. Twenty-day-old fetuses also exhibit the leg extension response to stimulation of the anogenital region with a camel-hair brush (Smotherman & Robinson, 1988a).

Embryonic–postembryonic behavioral continuity dictates that the rate of embryonic behavioral development should be reflected during the postembryonic period. In other words, if we somehow increase the rate at which an embryo develops, the neonate also should be developmentally advanced. This prediction is supported by the results of an experiment by Gandelman and Graham (1986) in which singleton mouse fetuses were created by surgically removing all but one embryo from the uterus. Presumably because of enhanced nutrition (the singleton receives all of the nutrients it normally would share with the other embryos), 17-day-old embryos displayed more overall activity as evidenced by augmented frequencies and durations of forelimb and trunk-plus-forelimb movement than did controls. Other singletons that were permitted to develop to term and delivered by cesarean section exhibited walking (and eye-opening) earlier than did controls. Not only does this finding support the idea of embryonic-postembryonic behavioral continuity, but it also suggests that the number of embryos in a uterus normally may govern the rate of development.

Data have demonstrated rather convincingly (and not surprisingly) that embryonic behavior serves important developmental functions. It must also be kept in mind, however, that embryonic behavior may also serve to facilitate the survival of the embryo. The embryo, like organisms at every stage of postembryonic life, exists in an environment in which perturbations are the norm. Behavior often permits the postnatal organism to cope with those perturbations, thereby enhancing its chances of survival. Embryonic activities may serve the same function. For example, embryonic motility may function, in part, to maintain the embryo in an optimal position within the amnion so as to benefit maximally from the buffering property of the amniotic fluid. The hatching posture of the chick embryo also can be cast in similar terms. Assumption of the posture can be viewed as a precursor to escaping from a cramped and what is rapidly becoming an inhospitable environment rather than as a precursor to hatching— a subtle but not insignificant distinction.

If prenatal behavior functions in part to help ensure survival of the fetus, because of differences between the pre- and postnatal environment certain fetal behaviors should differ from those of the neonate. This issue has been addressed by Smotherman and Robinson (1988b), who studied the behavior of rat fetuses in response to hypoxia induced by clamping the umbilical cord. A characteristic three-phase sequence of behavior was observed: (1) suppression of activity; (2)

hyperactivity consisting principally of exaggerated flexions of the body; and (3) suppression of activity with rostrol extensions of the head. Because such reactivity is virtually opposite to that displayed by neonatal rats deprived of oxygen, it may be an adaptive response serving to alleviate accidental occlusion of the umbilical cord.

CONCLUDING COMMENTS

Very early embryonic behavior is likely caused by the spontaneous discharge of spinal motor neurons. Later, the embryo is responsive to stimulation, and behavior becomes more complex. Data show that prehatching and prenatal behavior fulfill two functions: permitting the development of structure and serving as a precursor for later behavioral development. One also can view the behavior as adjustments to a changing environment, adjustments that enhance the probability that the embryo will survive. In Chapter 2 we see that embryonic and postembryonic behavior can be modified by exposing the embryo to certain environmental events.

REFERENCES

Angulo Y, Gonzalez, A. W. (1932). The prenatal development of behavior in the albino rat. *Journal of Comparative Neurology, 55,* 395–442.

Ariens Kappers, C. V. (1936). *The comparative anatomy of the nervous system of vertebrates including man* (Vol. 1). New York: Macmillan.

Bekoff, A. (1988). Embryonic motor output and movement patterns: Relationship to postnatal behavior. In W. P. Smotherman and S. R. Robinson (Eds.), *Behavior of the fetus* (pp. 191–206). Caldwell, NJ: The Telford Press.

Bekoff, A., and Kauer, J. A. (1982). Neural control of hatching: role of neck position in turning on hatching leg movements in post-hatching chicks. *Journal of Comparative Physiology, 145,* 497–504.

Bekoff, A., and Kauer, J. A. (1984). Neural control of hatching: fate of the pattern generator for the leg movements of hatching in post-hatching chicks. *Journal of Neuroscience, 4,* 2659–666.

Bekoff, A., and Lau, B. (1980). Interlimb coordination in 20-day-old rat fetuses. *Journal of Experimental Zoology, 214,* 173–75.

Bekoff, A., and Sabichi, A. L. (1987). Sensory control of the initiation of hatching in chicks: Effect of a local anesthetic injected into the neck. *Developmental Psychobiology, 20,* 489–95.

Bekoff, M., Byers, J. A., and Bekoff, A. (1980). Prenatal motility and postnatal play: functional continuity. *Developmental Psychobiology, 13,* 225–28.

Bok, S. T. (1915). Stimulogenous fibrillations as the cause of the structures of the nervous system. *Psychiatry en Neurology Amsterdam, 119,* 393–408.

Bradley, R. M., and Mistretta, C. M. (1975). Fetal sensory receptors. *Physiological Reviews, 55,* 352–82.

Carmichael, L. (1926). The development of behavior in vertebrates experimentally removed from the influence of external stimulation. *Psychological Review, 33,* 51–58.

Carmichael, L. (1934). An experimental study in the prenatal guinea-pig of the origin and development of reflexes and patterns of behavior in relation to the stimulation of specific receptor areas during the period of active fetal life. *Genetic Psychology Monographs, 16,* 338–491.

Coghill, G. E. (1902). The cranial nerves of *Amblystoma tigrinum. Journal of Comparative Neurology, 12,* 205–91.

Coghill, G. E. (1929). *Anatomy and the problem of behaviour.* Cambridge: Cambridge University Press.

DeVries, J.I.P., Visser, G.H.A., and Prechtl, H.F.R. (1982). The emergence of fetal behavior: I. Qualitative aspects. *Early Human Development, 7,* 301–22.

Drachman, D. B., and Coulombre, A. J. (1962). Experimental clubfoot and arthrogryposis multiplex congenita. *The Lancet, 2,* 523–26.

Drachman, D. B., and Sokoloff, L. (1966). The role of movement in embryonic joint development. *Developmental Biology, 14,* 401–20.

Fromme, E. (1941). Embryonic immobilization and later swimming. *American Journal of Anatomy, 38,* 142–61.

Gandelman, R., and Graham, S. (1986). Development of the surgically produced singleton mouse fetus. *Developmental Psychobiology, 19,* 343–50.

Gottlieb, G. (1970). Conceptions of prenatal behavior. In L. R. Aronson, E. Tobach, D. S. Lehrman, and J. S. Rosenblatt (Eds.), *Development and evolution of behavior* (pp. 111–37). San Francisco: W. H. Freeman.

Gottlieb, G. (1971). Ontogenesis of sensory function in birds and mammals. In E. Tobach, L. R. Aronson, and E. Shaw (Eds.), *The biopsychology of development* (pp. 678–728). Orlando, FL: Academic Press.

Gottlieb, G. (1973). Introduction to behavioral embryology. In G. Gottlieb (Ed.), *Behavioral Embryology* (pp. 3–45). Orlando, FL: Academic Press.

Hall, J. G. (1985). Genetic aspects of arythrogryposis. *Clinical Orthopaedics and Related Research, 194,* 45–53.

Hall, J. G. (1986). Analysis of the Pena Shokeir phenotype. *American Journal of Medical Genetics, 25,* 99–117.

Hamburger, V. (1963). Some aspects of the embryology of behavior. *Quarterly Review of Biology, 38,* 342–65.

Hamburger, V., and Balaban, M. (1963). Observations and experiments on spontaneous rhythmical behavior in the chick embryo. *Developmental Biology, 7,* 533–45.

Hamburger, V., Balaban, M., Oppenheim, R., and Wenger, E. (1965). Periodic motility of normal and spinal chick embryos between 8 and 17 days of incubation. *Journal of Experimental Zoology, 159,* 1–13.

Hamburger, V., and Oppenheim, R. (1967). Prehatching motility and hatching behavior in the chick. *Journal of Experimental Zoology, 166,* 171–204.

Hamburger, V., Wenger, E., and Oppenheim, R. (1966). Motility in the chick embryo in the absence of sensory input. *Journal of Experimental Zoology, 162,* 133–60.

Harrison, R. G. (1904). An experimental study of the relation of the nervous system to the developing musculature of the frog. *American Journal of Anatomy, 3,* 171–204.

Hofer, M. A. (1988). On the nature and function of prenatal behavior. In W. P. Smotherman and S. R. Robinson (Eds.), *Behavior of the fetus* (pp. 3–18). Caldwell, NJ: The Telford Press.

Holt, E. B. (1931). *Animal drive and the learning process.* New York: Holt.

Hooker, D. (1936). Early activities in mammals. *Yale Journal of Biology and Medicine, 8,* 579–602.

Hooker, D. (1952). The prenatal origin of behavior. *18th Porter Lecture.* Lawrence, KS: Kansas University Press.

Humphrey, T. (1964). Some correlations between the appearance of human fetal reflexes and the development of the nervous system. *Progress in Brain Research, 4,* 93–135.

Kodama, N., and Sekiguchi, S. (1982). The development of spontaneous body movement in prenatal and perinatal mice. *Developmental Psychobiology, 17,* 139–50.

Kuo, Z. -Y. (1976). *The dynamics of behavior development.* New York: Plenum Press.

Landmiesser, L., and O'Donovan, M. J. (1984). Activation patterns of embryonic hindlimb muscle recorded in ovo in an isolated spinal cord preparation. *Journal of Physiology, 347,* 189–204.

Lauber, J. K., and Shutze, J. V. (1964). Accelerated growth of embryo chicks under the influence of light. *Growth, 28,* 179–90.

Lee, T. M., and Zucker, I. (1988). Vole infant development is influenced perinatally by maternal photoperiodic history. *American Journal of Physiology, 255,* R831–38.

Matthews, S. A., and Detwiler, S. R. (1926). The reactions of *Amblystoma* embryos following prolonged treated with chloretone. *Journal of Experimental Zoology, 45,* 279–92.

Moessinger, A. C. (1983). Fetal akinesia deformation sequence: An animal model. *Pediatrics, 72,* 857–63.

Narayanan, C. H., Fox, M. W., and Hamburger, V. (1971). Prenatal development of spontaneous and evoked activity in the rat. *Behaviour, 40,* 100–34.

O'Donovan, M. J., and Landmiesser, L. (1987). The development of hindlimb motor activity studied in the isolated spinal cord of the chick embryo. *Journal of Neuroscience, 7,* 3256–264.

Oppenheim, R. W. (1978). G. E. Coghill (1872–1941): Pioneer neuroembryologist and developmental psychobiologist. *Perspectives in Biology and Medicine, 22,* 44–64.

Oppenheim, R. W. (1982). The neuroembryological study of behavior: progress, problems, perspectives. *Current Topics in Developmental Biology, 17,* 257–309.

Paulson, G. W. (1965). Maturation of evoked responses in the duckling. *Experimental Neurology, 11,* 324–33.

Peters, J. J., Vanderahe, A. R., and Powers, T. H. (1958). Electrical studies of functional development of the eye and optic lobes in the chick embryo. *Journal of Experimental Zoology, 139,* 459–68.

Preyer, W. (1885). *Specielle physiologie des embryo.* Leipzig: Grieben.

Provine, R. R. (1972). Ontogeny of bioelectric activity in the spinal cord of the chick embryo and its behavioral implications. *Brain Research, 41,* 365–78.

Provine, R. R., and Rogers, L. (1977). Development of spinal cord bioelectric activity in spinal chick embryos and its behavioral implications. *Journal of Neurobiology, 8,* 217–28.

Reppert, S. M., and Schwartz, W. J. (1983). Maternal coordination of the fetal biological clock. *Science, 220,* 969–71.

Reppert, S. M., and Schwartz, W. J. (1986). The maternal suprachiasmatic nuclei are necessary for maternal coordination of the developing circadian system. *Journal of Neuroscience, 6,* 2724–729.

Reppert, S. M., and Weaver, D. R. (1988). Maternal transduction of light-dark information for the fetus. In W. P. Smotherman and S. R. Robinson (Eds.), *Behavior of the fetus* (pp. 119–39). Caldwell, NJ: The Telford Press.

Ripley, K. L., and Provine, R. R. (1972). Neural correlates of embryonic motility in the chick. *Brain Research, 45,* 127–34.

Robinson, S. R., and Smotherman, W. P. (1987). Environmental determinants of behavior in the rat fetus: II. The emergence of synchronous movement. *Animal Behaviour, 35,* 1652–662.

Rogers, L. J., and Anson, J. M. (1979). Lateralisation of function in the chicken forebrain. *Pharmacology, Biochemistry and Behavior, 10,* 679–86.

Shutze, J., Lauber, J. K., Kato, M., and Wilson, W. (1962). Influence of incandescent and colored light on chicken embryos during incubation. *Nature, 96,* 594–95.

Smotherman, W. P., Richards, L. A., and Robinson, S. R. (1983). Techniques for observing fetal behavior in utero: A comparison of chemomyelotomy and spinal transection. *Developmental Psychobiology, 17,* 661–74.

Smotherman, W. P., and Robinson, S. R. (1986). Environmental determinants of behaviour in the rat fetus. *Animal Behaviour, 34,* 1859–873.

Smotherman, W. P., and Robinson, S. R. (1987). Prenatal expression of species-typical action patterns in the rat fetus (*Rattus norvegicus*). *Journal of Comparative Psychology, 101,* 190–96.

Smotherman, W. P., and Robinson, S. R. (1988a). Fetal expression of the leg extension response to anogenital stimulation. *Physiology and Behavior, 43,* 243–44.

Smotherman, W. P., and Robinson, S. R. (1988b). Response of the fetus to acute umbilical cord occlusion: An ontogenetic adaptation? *Physiology and Behavior, 44,* 131–35.

Smotherman, W. P., and Robinson, S. R. (1990). Rat fetuses respond to chemical stimuli in gas phase. *Physiology and Behavior, 47,* 863–68.

Smotherman, W. P., Robinson, S. R., and Miller, B. J. (1986). A reversible preparation for observing the behavior of fetal rats in utero: Spinal anesthesia with lidocaine. *Physiology and Behavior, 37,* 57–60.

Swinyard, C. A., and Bleck, E. E. (1985). The etiology of arthrogryposis (multiple congenital contracture). *Clinical Orthopaedics, 194,* 15–29.

Tracy, H. C. (1926). The development of motility and behavior reactions in the toadfish (*Opsanus tau*). *Journal of Comparative Neurology, 40,* 253–369.

Vince, M. A. (1964). Social facilitation of hatching in the bobwhite quail. *Animal Behaviour, 12,* 531–34.

Vince, M. A. (1966). Artificial acceleration of hatching in quail embryos. *Animal Behaviour, 14,* 389–94.

Vince, M. A., and Cheng, R.C.H. (1970). The retardation of hatching in Japanese quail. *Animal Behaviour, 18,* 210–14.

Vince, M., Reader, M., and Talhurst, L. (1976). Effects of stimulation on embryonic activity in the chick. *Journal of Comparative and Physiological Psychology, 90,* 221–30.

Visitini, F., and Levi-Montalcini, R. (1939). Relazione tra differenziazone strutturale e funzionale di centri e delle vie nervose nell'embrione di pollo. *Swiss Archives of Neurology and Psychiatry, 43,* 1–45.

Watson, J. B. (1919). *Psychology from the standpoint of a behaviorist.* Philadelphia: Lippincott.

Watson, J. B. (1924). *Behaviorism,* New York: Norton.

Weaver, D. R., and Reppert, S. M. (1987). Maternal-fetal communication of circadian phase in a precocious rodent, the spiny mouse. *American Journal of Physiology, 253,* E401–9.

White, N. R. (1984). Effects of embryonic auditory stimulation on hatch time in the domestic chick. *Bird Behaviour, 5,* 122–26.

Windle, W. F. (1944). Genesis of somatic motor function in mammalian embryos: A synthesizing article. *Physiological Zoology, 17,* 247–60.

Windle, W. F., and Becker, R. F. (1940). Relation of anoxemia to early activity in the fetal nervous system. *Archives of Neurology and Psychiatry, 43,* 90–114.

Windle, W. F., and Orr, D. W. (1934). The development of behavior in chick embryos: spinal cord structure correlated with early somatic motility. *Journal of Comparative Neurology, 60,* 287–307.

Zappia, J. V., and Rogers, L. J. (1983). Light experience during development affects asymmetry of forebrain function in chickens. *Developmental Brain Research, 11,* 93–106.

2

Early Modification of
Behavioral Development

When studying the interaction of genetic and environmental
factors in the acquisition of taste preference and aversion, it is
not valid to conclude that the presence of a preference at birth
demonstrates a genetic basis.

C. M. Mistretta and R. M. Bradley, 1977

A major postulate of Z.-Y. Kuo's theory of development is the concept of *behavioral potentials:* "By behavioral potentials we mean the enormous possibilities or potentialities of behavior patterns that each neonate possesses within the limits or range of the normal morphological structure of its species" (Kuo, 1976, p. 125). Whether one concurs with Kuo's overall view of behavioral development, it is probably true that most agree with the concept of behavioral potentials. Except for specific motor activities, e.g., bipedal locomotion, which are dictated by morphology, the elaboration of behavior can proceed in several directions.

A principal task of developmental researchers is identification of the factors that shape the course of development. Because of the historical precedent of commencing the search for those factors with the neonate, much more is known about the effects of events that occur during the postembryonic period (e.g., mother–young interaction, environmental stimulation and complexity, and nutrition) than about factors that impinge on the embryo. (An exception is the study of the adverse effects of certain agents on developing organisms, a topic considered separately in Chapter 4.) Nonetheless, the relatively limited data do show that the embryo can be affected by simple exposure to particular types of stimuli and by more complicated classical and instrumental conditioning procedures. Embryonic stimulus exposure often channels postembryonic preference behavior so that, when given a choice, the organism is likely to select the stimulus to which it had been exposed prior to birth or hatching. Conditioning, on the other hand, leads to the display of conditioned responses not only during the postembryonic period but also by the embryo itself. Both of these manipulations are considered in this chapter, beginning with conditioning. For the sake of simplicity, the data derived from insects, amphibians, and mammals are treated separately.

CONDITIONING

Insects

Given the small size of insect embryos and the fact that they generally exhibit little if any motility, conditioning experiments have been performed using larvae, an ontogenetically later form of the organism. Following the embryonic period, the insect enters the larval stage during which it passes through a number of molts and is transformed into a pupa or chrysalis. It is from the latter that the adult form emerges. Investigators have asked if larva that have been conditioned exhibit the acquired behavior following metamorphosis. This question is particularly interesting because the central nervous system undergoes major modification during metamorphosis.

Borsellino, Pierantoni, and Schieti-Cavazza (1970), using an instrumental conditioning procedure, trained mealworm beetle larvae to move either left or right in a circular maze by punishing an incorrect response with bright light and rewarding a correct response with darkness. A control group received no punishment. Larvae underwent one trial a day. (The authors failed to mention when during the 17-day larval stage conditioning began.)[1] When the adult forms were tested in the maze without punishment, they exhibited significantly more responses to the side of the apparatus to which they were reinforced as larvae. Similar findings are presented by Somberg, Happ, and Schnerden (1970), who demonstrated retention by adult mealworms of a passive avoidance response acquired during the larval stage. The discriminative stimuli were floor textures. Somberg et al. suggested that such conditioning causes adults to remain in the area that was favorable to their larval growth.

Amphibia

Larval salamanders can be conditioned to swim to the left or right in a Y maze when incorrect responses are punished by the onset of a bright light (Frankhauser, Vernon, Frank, & Slack, 1955). Schneider (1968) reported that salamander larvae also can be taught to swim out of a spot of light to avoid electric shock. Similar findings have been presented for larval frogs (Hoyer, Shafer, Mouldin, & Corbett, 1971). Tadpoles learned to avoid electric current by swimming to an adjoining compartment in the testing chamber in response to the onset of light. I am aware of no attempt to examine the transfer of conditioning from the larval to the adult form.

---

[1] This omission is important because the level of learning exhibited by mealworm larvae varies according to the period of the larval stage during which conditioning trials are given; it is poorest in the middle of an intermolting period and greatest just before and immediately following a molt (Sheimann, Khutzian, & Ignatovitch, 1980).

Birds

A number of experiments have demonstrated both classical (e.g., Gos, 1935; Hunt, 1949) and instrumental (e.g., Heaton, 1978; Impekoven, 1973) conditioning of avian embryos. Fried and Glick (1966) attached electrodes to an exposed leg of 14-day-old chick embryos. The electrodes were used to moniter the electrical resistance of the skin (galvanic skin response [GSR]) and administer electric shock, which served as an unconditioned stimulus (UCS). The UCS evoked an unconditioned response (UCR), a decrease in the magnitude of the GSR. The conditioned stimulus (CS) was a tone. Conditioning, as evidenced by a decrease in the GSR in response to CS presentations, was observed.

The most complete account of classical conditioning was given by Hunt (1949). The UCS consisted of electric current that was passed directly through the shell; the UCR was leg movement; and the CS was the sounding of a bell. Control groups received the CS alone, the UCS alone, or neither stimulus. The results showed that conditioning could not be established prior to the 15th day of incubation. Thirty-eight percent of embryos 15 days of age and older attained the conditioning criterion by exhibiting five consecutive CRs. This experiment is noteworthy in that some subjects were tested after hatching. Of 15 embryos that attained the conditioning criterion and were permitted to hatch, 9 exhibited conditioning. (Only 2 of 68 control embryos and hatchlings exhibited CRs.) It is interesting that the conditioning exhibited by the hatchlings was short-lived, as the CR could no longer be elicited after the chick had been exposed to light and other stimuli such as food and water for about an hour. So long as the chick was kept in the dark under conditions similar to those of the incubator, CRs continued to be elicited.

Avian embryos also have been conditioned using instrumental procedures. The first demonstration was presented by Impekoven (1973), who capitalized on the fact that Peking ducks, a domesticated form of mallard, are selectively responsive to maternal calls. (More is said about this point later in the chapter.) The presentation of reinforcement, a 3.6-second burst of mallard call was made contingent on an embryo's foot movement. Each experimental subject was compared to a control embryo that received the identical amounts and spacings of the mallard call except that the administration of the call bore no systematic relation to foot movement. (This technique has been referred to as a *yoked-control.*) Testing occurred a few hours prior to hatching on day 28 of incubation. The results showed that the frequency of foot movements was reliably higher in the experimental subjects than in the controls. (If chicken rather than mallard calls were used, no such difference was obtained.) Impekoven suggested that because embryonic vocalizations, which are known to accompany embryonic movement, stimulate the adult to emit vocalizations, a contingency might normally exist between the adult call and embryonic movement. Such a contingency might result in a hastening of hatching.

Duck embryos also have been trained to perform escape responses (Heaton, 1978). Termination of electric shock applied to the wing was made contingent on leg flexion in one group of embryos. A second group received inescapable shock. As illustrated in Figure 2.1, conditioning, as evidenced by decreased latencies of the flexion response, was exhibted by day 24 of the 28-day incubation period.

There has been no attempt, to my knowledge, to determine if instrumentally conditioned responses acquired by the embryo persist into the postembryonic period. Such a determination would be difficult using the method of either Impokoven or Heaton because the hatchling could simply and quickly *relearn* the instrumental response (foot movement contingent on the presentation of the maternal call or termination of electric shock) rather than exhibit a transfer of an already acquired response. The problem of relearning can be obviated by the use of a discriminative stimulus. For example, one could condition an avoidance response in the embryo by having a tone precede the onset of shock. A foot movement that occurs after the onset of the warning signal but prior to the onset

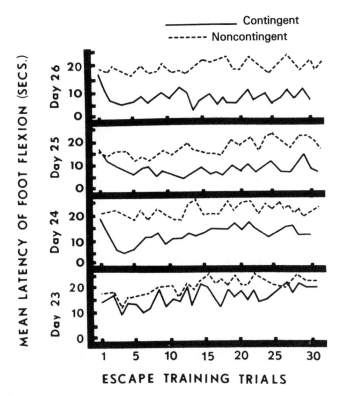

Figure 2.1 Latency of foot-flexion responses of 23- to 26-day Peking duck embryos during operant escape training trials. Note the process of acquisition in embryos in which reinforcement contingency was established (days 24, 25, and 26). (From Heaton, "Development of operant escape learning in the Peking duck embryo." *Journal of Comparative and Physiological Psychology, 92,* 397–405. © 1978 by The American Psychological Association. Reprinted by permission.)

of the shock would prevent the shock from being administered. Should embryos be able to acquire the response (an interesting question in itself), assessing transfer of the learned behavior from the embryo to the hatchling would be simple, requiring only the presentation of the discriminative stimulus (warning signal). Would the discriminative stimulus elicit foot movements?

Mammals

Smotherman and colleagues (Smotherman, 1982a,b; Smotherman & Robinson, 1985; Stickrod, Kimble, & Smotherman, 1982a,b) performed an interesting series of experiments showing that mammalian (rat) embryos are capable of acquiring a response that can be exhibited well after parturition. Stickrod et al. (1982a) injected either apple juice or saline into the amniotic fluid of 20-day-old embryos. Five minutes later the embryos were given intraperitoneal injections of either lithium chloride or saline. Four groups were thus formed: apple juice/ LiCl, saline/LiCl, apple juice/saline, saline/saline. It is well known that adult animals administered a toxic substance such as LiCl that produces gastric upset following the ingestion of a novel foodstuff subsequently avoid that food. This phenomenon is known as a *learned aversion.* The question asked by Stickrod et al. (1982a,b) was whether neonates exhibit a learned aversion acquired as embryos. On postnatal day 16 the pups were separated from the dam. Eight hours later the dam, now anesthetized, was placed at the choice point of a T maze with its ventrum exposed. The pups were permitted to traverse the stem of the maze and, if they made contact with the dam, to suckle. Each subject underwent 10 trials. The nipples to which it attached for a minimum of 15 seconds were recorded. Pups exhibited a preference for two or three nipples. The preferred nipples then were coated with apple juice and the others with saline, and additional trials in the runway were undertaken. Pups that had been exposed to apple juice and then to LiCl in utero showed the least preference for the apple juice-coated nipples relative to the other three groups. In other words, the previously preferred nipples were no longer favored, having assumed an aversive quality because they were coated with a taste stimulus the pups had associated with illness prior to birth.

Smotherman (1982a), in follow-up experiments, demonstrated that the olfactory component of the apple juice is sufficient to mediate the learned aversion; presentation of only the odor of the juice led to either slower traversing of the maze by the neonates or failure to make contact with the dam. Neonates also avoided wood shavings that had been scented with the aversive odor (Stickrod et al., 1982b). These findings suggest that the olfactory system functions prior to birth. Additional evidence for embryonic olfactory function is provided by Pederson, Stewart, and Shepard (1983), who reported that the embryonic rat brain shows uptake of radioactively labeled 2-deoxy-D-glucose (2DG) throughout the accessory olfactory bulb after 2DG administration to the pregnant animal. The uptake of 2DG is indicative of neuronal activity.

The experiments described here show that embryos are capable of forming associations and that those associations can be exhibited after parturition.

Smotherman and Robinson (1985) went a step further and asked if conditioning can be exhibited in utero. This was accomplished by pairing a mint extract CS with an injection of LiCl on day 17 of gestation. Two days later some embryos were again exposed to the mint CS. Would they respond to the CS in a manner similar to the way other 19-day-old embryos respond to LiCl? In other words, would the experimental embryos exhibit CRs? The answer was *yes*. Both the CS and the administration of LiCl suppressed overall activity while augmenting curls (flexion or torsion of the trunk) and twitches (a spasm along the side of the trunk). Based on these findings, the authors speculated that taste and odor aversions may be adventitiously established in human embryos as a consequence of the maternal ingestion of chemical substances such as alcohol that, like LiCl, also produce suppression of behavior.

The only account of conditioning of the human embryo was given many years ago by Spelt (1948). A classical conditioning procedure was used with a loud noise serving as the UCS and a vibrotactile stimulus placed on the abdomen as the CS. Fetal movement, the UCR and CR, was assessed by placing tambours on the abdomen. Abdominal movement caused displacement of the tambours which, in turn, activated a recording device. All subjects were past the seventh month of gestation. The conditioning procedure consisted in presenting the CS for 5 seconds followed by presentation of the noise for an unspecified period of time. A control group was included to assess the effects of the CS alone. Of the five women in the conditioning group, two were eliminated because of the onset of labor. Data gathered from the remaining women were interpreted as conditioning. Conditioned responses—embryonic movement after onset of the CS—were observed after 15 to 20 CS—UCS pairings. Extinction resulting from CS presentation alone and spontaneous recovery were reported as well.

Spelt concluded unequivocally that human embryos can be conditioned. His experiment, however, suffers from a serious flaw. It is possible that the mothers, not the embryos, were conditioned. The vibrotactile stimulus, as a consequence of being paired with the loud noise, might have come to elicit a response on the part of the women that, unbeknown to the investigator (and even the women), causes embryonic activity. Another potential problem concerns the vibrotactile stimulus itself. Whereas Spelt reported that it does not elicit movement prior to conditioning trials, a later study found that it does produce embryonic activity (Leader, Baille, Martin, & Vermeulen, 1982). This disparity may have to do with the activity assessment procedure. Leader et al. used ultrasonic monitoring, a much more sensitive procedure than the mechanical tambour arrangement used by Spelt.

The results of studies from various species have established that the behavior of embryos can be modified by conditioning procedures. Moreover, data have shown that the effects of conditioning may be observed during the postembryonic period. Although the single experiment on human embryonic conditioning is problematic owing to questionable methodology, it would be surprising if the human embryo, unlike embryos of other species, is not susceptible to the imposition of reinforcement contingencies.

EARLY SENSORY EXPOSURE

We turn now to the other method of influencing postembryonic behavior—providing the embryo with sensory stimulation. As mentioned previously, it is generally the case that such early exposure establishes a bias: The postembryonic organism tends to select the stimulus to which it was exposed. The influence of sound, light, and chemical stimulation is considered.

Sound Stimulation

An abundance of evidence is available demonstrating that the auditory system functions during the embryonic period of many species. A plethora of anecdotal reports exist, such as the case of a pregnant woman who reported that during musical concerts a great deal of embryonic movement occurred whenever the audience applauded (Forbes & Forbes, 1927). Such accounts are supported by the results of formal experimentation. The chicken embryo, for example, exhibits its initial response to sound by day 12 of incubation (Grier, Counter, & Shearer, 1967), and consistent movement occurs from day 14 onward (Jacken & Rubal, 1978). The auditory system of the guinea pig becomes functional about 13 days prior to birth (Rawdon-Smith, Carmichael, & Wellman, 1938). Moreover, the electroencephalographic response to an auditory stimulus is strikingly similar in late embryonic and newborn guinea pigs (Scibetta & Rosen, 1969). With regard to the human embryo, Birnholz and Benacerraf (1983) applied sound stimulation to the abdomen directly above the embryonic ear and, using ultrasonic imaging, recorded eye-blinks that were assumed to be startle responses. The embryo first exhibits eye-blink responses to auditory stimulation between the 24th and 25th weeks. Gelman et al. (1982) reported sound-elicited movement in response to the application of a 2000 cps (110 db) tone. As shown in Figure 2.2, the movement persisted well beyond the cessation of the stimulus.
Given that the embryonic auditory system is functional, one must ascertain the degree to which sound stimulation is normally available to the embryo. A number of studies have been performed in which sounds were monitored from microphones placed in the uteri of pregnant women (Henshall, 1972; Walker, Grimwade, & Wood, 1971) or placed against the cervix (Bench, 1968). The results of these experiments indicate that the predominant sounds accessible to the embryo are from the maternal cardiovascular and digestive systems. These sounds are relatively loud (68 to 95 dB) and of low frequency (20 to 700 Hz). Sounds arising from outside the adult are attenuated from 19 to 90 dB.

Because the embryo is surrounded by fluid and amniotic membranes, accurate data regarding the early sound environment obviously can be derived only by recording sounds from within the amnionic sac. Vince and her colleagues (Armitage, Baldwin, & Vince, 1980; Vince, Billing, Baldwin, & Toner, 1985) did just that by inserting a transmitting radiohydrophone into the amniotic sac of a pregnant ewe. The device was attached close to the embryo's ear. Sounds generated from within the ewe—drinking, eating, swallowing, breathing, and so

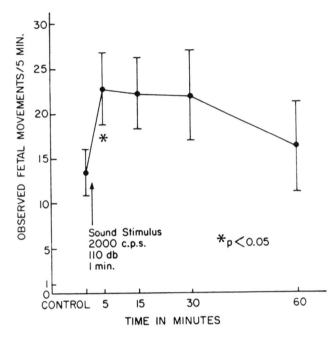

Figure 2.2 Direct ultrasound measurements of human fetal movement (mean ± SEM) before and after the abdominal sound stimulus of 2000 cps (110 db) for 1 minute. (From Gelman et al., "Fetal movements in response to sound stimulation." *American Journal of Obstetrics and Gynecology, 143,* 484–85. © 1982 by Mosby-Year Book. Reprinted by permission.)

forth—were recognizable. Sounds produced by external sources were attenuated by 16 to 37 dB. Moreover, the sound of the ewe's voice is a prominent part of the uterine sound environment, being well above background noise. The voice tends to be enhanced at low frequencies and less attenuated than external sounds at higher frequencies. This finding agrees with the results of intravaginal recordings made from humans indicating that the mother's voice is audible in utero (Querleu & Renard, 1981; Querleu, Renard, & Crepin, 1981).

Now that we have seen that the embryonic milieu is composed, in part, of various types of auditory stimulation derived from sources internal and external to the dam, we must consider the issue most germane to this discussion, namely, the significance of early auditory exposure to postembryonic behavior. We begin with a discussion of mammals, from which limited but intriguing information has been derived, and then turn to avian species, about which much more is known.

The only infrahuman mammals examined thus far with regard to the influence of prenatal auditory exposure, to my knowledge, have been guinea pigs and sheep. Vince (1979) asked if prenatal exposure to a particular auditory stimulus affects postnatal responsivity to that stimulus. At 2 to 3 weeks prior to parturition pregnant guinea pigs were exposed each day to the feeding call of the bantam hen. In addition to its obvious novelty, the call was chosen because it appears to be somewhat aversive to the adult guinea pig and because it includes a wide range of frequencies. Eleven presentations, each 5.5 seconds in duration and separated by 60 seconds, were given daily. Commencing on the day of birth and continuing for the next 4 days, animals were presented with the bantam call and control sounds produced by the adult guinea pig. The latter therefore also were present prior to birth. Control subjects were treated exactly as the experimental subjects but without the embryonic exposure to the bantam call. Dependent measures were heart rate and vocalizations.

Animals that had been exposed as embryos to bantam calls tended to exhibit a smaller change in heart rate upon the initial postnatal presentations of that stimulus than did the like-aged controls. No appreciable differences were observed in the incidence of vocalizations. In addition, there were no group differences in response to the postnatal presentation of the guinea pig-generated sounds.

Vince, Armitage, Walser, and Reader (1982) performed essentially the same experiment with sheep and reported a similar result. Lambs exposed as embryos to a novel sound pattern (200-, 400-, and 300-Hz tones, each separated by a brief interval) exhibited less heart rate acceleration in response to the postnatal presentation of that sound than did controls. No differences were noted between groups in overt behavior.

Vince (1979) interpreted her findings as demonstrating that repetitive embryonic exposure to auditory stimulation leads to habituation to those stimuli, that "animals become adapted to their sound environment before birth. Continuity of these conditions (a stable background of sound in the perinatal period) might well be beneficial: offspring relatively unaffected by normally occurring background sounds are likely to respond more readily to specific cues involved in the establishment of postnatal mother-infant bonds" (p. 917). In other words, embryos become adapted to auditory stimulation arising from within the mother (those sounds tend to be naturally repetitive) and to stimuli from the external environment that happen to be repetitive. Such adaptation facilitates the animal's ability to "focus" on novel postnatal cues by eliminating responsivity to familiar stimuli. Vince's interpretation, of course, assumes that heart rate is a significant index in that it reflects a behavioral disposition.

We now make a large leap—from the guinea pig and sheep to the human *and* from a nonbehavioral (heart rate) to a behavioral measure. Does prenatal auditory experience influence infant behavior? This question has been addressed by DeCasper and his associates, commencing with the report of two experiments demonstrating that during the first 3 days of life infants can discriminate the voice of the mother from that of a stranger and prefer the sound of the former (DeCasper & Fifer, 1980). Infants were provided with a nipple that allowed sucking but did not yield milk, a procedure aptly known as nonnutritive sucking. Infants normally exhibit nonnutritive sucking in bursts of individual sucks followed by brief interburst intervals (IBIs) of no sucking. A sucking burst was defined as a group of sucks separated from one another by less than 2 seconds.

The idea was to determine if the mother's voice could be used to reinforce the production of particular IBIs, that is, periods of nonsucking. For half of the infants, sucking bursts that terminated IBIs equal to or greater than their median baseline production of IBIs (i.e., nonsucking periods of either the same duration or longer than the median of those displayed just prior to the conditioning trials) yielded the sound of their mothers reading a passage from a children's storybook (the passage had been previously recorded, just after delivery). The production of IBIs of a duration shorter than the median baseline IBI generated the sound of another adult female reading the same passage. For a second group of neonates, the treatment conditions were reversed; short IBIs produced the mothers' voices and long IBIs those of strangers. A pressure transducer attached to the nipple automatically recorded the pattern of sucking during the 20-minute test. Sounds were presented to the infants through earphones.

Most of the infants (8 of 10) increased the proportion of IBIs that produced the maternal voice, thereby demonstrating the ability to discriminate between the voice of the mother and that of a stranger, as well as a preference for the former. These findings were verified and extended in a second experiment in which discriminative stimuli, 4 seconds of a 400-Hz tone and 4 seconds of silence, were used. Each IBI contained alternating periods of tone and no-tone. For half the infants, a burst of sucking that was begun during a tone period produced the recorded story read by the mother and turned off the tone, whereas a burst initiated during a no-tone period produced the nonmaternal voice. The conditions were reversed for the remaining subjects, a burst of sucking during a no-tone period produced the story recorded by the mother. In this experiment, then, gaining access to the mother's voice had nothing to do with manipulating the IBI but, rather, was governed by whether sucking occurred in the presence of a stimulus that signaled the availability of the mother's voice. The results verified the findings of the first experiment. By the latter third of the 20-minute test session, the probability of sucking during the tone and no-tone periods was greater when the stimuli signaled the availability of the maternal voice.

These findings demonstrate that either prenatal or very early postnatal experience with the maternal voice (the infants did have some, albeit limited, exposure to their mothers' voice) causes it to be differentially reinforcing. If experience is gained prenatally, one would predict that its elimination will prevent the maternal voice from acquiring reinforcing properties. Obviously, one cannot experimentally eliminate an embryo's exposure to the voice of its mother. It is possible, however, that, like the maternal voice, a passage of speech to which an embryo is repeatedly exposed also will exhibit reinforcing properties. No such prediction could be made if experience is gained postnatally because, except during the testing period, the newborn would not be exposed to the passage. These possibilities were addressed by DeCasper and Spence (1986), who asked pregnant woman to recite a passage aloud twice each day during the final 6 weeks of pregnancy. As before, the passages were excerpted from childrens' stories. Later, the infants, by controlling the IBIs, could produce a recording of either that passage or a novel passage. Unlike the first experiment, however, the recordings were made by strangers. The data revealed that the passage read by the mothers during pregnancy exhibited differentially reinforcing properties postnatally; these passages were preferred by the infant even though they were recorded by strangers. Therefore the embryo apparently learns something about repetitive auditory stimuli that persists into the postnatal period. The data also suggest that the previously demonstrated preference for the maternal voice is likely acquired by embryonic exposure to it (see also Spence & DeCasper [1987]).

That embryos have neither as much exposure to male voices nor the same type of exposure as is derived from a sound generated from within the pregnant woman may explain the lack of infants' preference for the father's voice (DeCasper & Prescott, 1984). Moreover, extensive prenatal experience with nonvoice sounds originating from the mother also may account for infants' predilection for intrauterine heartbeat stimuli. According to DeCasper and Sigafoos (1983), intrauterine heartbeat sounds can differentially reinforce short and long IBIs.

What is the functional significance of this ability to recognize the maternal voice? There is some indication that identification of the mother's voice might increase feeding efficiency (Noirot & Algeria, 1983), facilitate the mother's ability to reduce her child's distress (Thoman, Korner, & Beason-Williams, 1977), and facilitate new learning (Parry, 1972).

Regardless of the adaptive benefits, the data from mammals do show that embryonic auditory exposure plays a role in behavioral development, subserving recognition by the neonate of those sounds to which it was exposed prenatally. The rather limited data from mammals is buttressed by a great deal of information gathered from birds. The ease with which one can provide avian embryos with stimulation relative to embryos developing within a uterus probably contributed to the popularity of birds in this type of research. We now review the findings.

Hens of many species of precocial birds emit a species-typical call that attracts its young. Gottlieb (1971) tested newly hatched chickens, mallards, wood ducks, and Peking ducks in an apparatus that simultaneously presented two calls, one a maternal call of its own species and the other the call of another species. The subjects were allowed to approach the source of the sounds. In most cases the chicks and ducklings exhibited differential attraction to the maternal call of its own species. Not only can this type of between-species discrimination be made, but chicks have been reported to exhibit differential responding to the sound of a familiar hen relative to that of an unfamiliar hen (Falt, 1981).

Of relevance here is the possible role of prehatching auditory stimulation in establishing such preferences. That is, does embryonic exposure to species-typical maternal calls contribute to postembryonic attraction or preference for that call? If early exposure does mediate attraction, one would predict that attractions can be manipulated by varying the auditory stimuli to which the embryo is exposed. This prediction has been tested by providing embryos with nonavian sounds, sounds emitted by a member of another species, and vocalizations of specific species members.

Grier et al. (1967) continuously exposed incubator-reared chicken eggs to a series of 1-second 200-Hz beeps separated by 1 second of quiet from days 12 to

18 of incubation. After hatching, the chicks were placed in an apparatus that allowed them to approach one of two speakers. One speaker emitted the sound to which they were exposed as embryos, and the other emitted a novel sound (2000-Hz beeps). The stimuli were presented alternately, and the distance the chicks moved toward each speaker was recorded. As summarized in Table 2.1, the chicks were differentially attracted by the sound to which they were exposed prior to hatching. A second experiment showed that the chicks followed a model chicken that emitted the familiar sound more than it did a model that emitted the novel sound or no sound at all.

The influence of embryonic exposure to the call of a nonspecies member was assessed by Bailey and Ralph (1975), who exposed chick embryos during the final week of incubation to the attraction or alarm call of the male pheasant. After hatching, the chicks were tested in a two-choice apparatus and permitted to approach a speaker emitting the pheasant call or one emitting the sound of a human voice imitating the pheasant call. Chicks were tested in groups to simulate a brood. Preference for either the pheasant alarm or attraction call was displayed. Although no particular day of exposure was more effective than any other, a cumulative effect was noted; the greater the number of days of embryonic exposure, the greater was the attraction. What is not known here is whether the chicks would have preferred pheasant calls to novel hen maternal calls.

It is important that Guillemot young be able to identify their parents, as they live on cliff ledges without nests in colonies of high population density. Tschanz (1968) has shown that individual recognition derives from embryonic exposure to parental calls. Guillemot feeding calls consist of strings of pulses. Their duration, the duration of intervals between them, and their pitch are characteristic of an individual. Tschanz exposed embryos for about 2.5 days from the time they began to vocalize to the call of a particular individual. It was found that the embryos vocalized more often to the familiar than to a novel call. Also, when tested after hatching in a simultaneous choice apparatus, they preferred the call to which they had been exposed as embryos.

The most programmatical research on the issue of embryonic stimulation has been performed by Gottlieb. Among his many contributions are data relating embryonic auditory *self-stimulation* to posthatching auditory preference. The

Table 2.1 Average distance chicks moved toward a stationary sound source

Group	No. Tested	Distance Moved Toward Stimulus (cm)	
		200 Hz	2000 Hz
Experimental	15	25.22	11.84
Control	20	13.72	13.46

Source: From Grier et al. Prenatal auditory imprinting in chickens. *Science, 155,* 1692–1693. © 1967 by The American Association for the Advancement of Science. Reprinted by permission.

idea that the embryo is responsive to its own vocalizations derived from monitoring the behavior of embryos in response to the maternal call (Gottlieb, 1971). Normally, mallard duck embryos exhibit a decrease in oral activity (bill-clapping) in response to the maternal call presented on day 23 and an increase in bill-clapping in response to the call presented on day 24. If incubator-reared embryos are exposed experimentally to the vocalizations of siblings on days 21 and 22, they display the increased bill-clapping behavior a day earlier than usual. Because siblings can affect responsiveness to the maternal call, Gottlieb asked if exposure to a duck embryo's *own* vocalizations is involved in posthatching responsiveness to the maternal call.

Gottlieb's strategy was straightforward: The role of embryonic vocalizations was assessed by eliminating them. That condition was accomplished by placing the liquid surgical dressing collodion on the tympaniform membranes of embryonic mallard ducklings. The membranes become rigid, preventing them from vibrating and thus vocalizing. The embryos were incubated in isolation, and devocalization was performed on day 24. After hatching, the devocalized ducklings, although capable of discriminating the mallard call from that of the pintail duck, the wood duck, and mallard duckling calls, showed no reliable discrimination between the maternal mallard and chicken calls. According to Gottlieb, the latter discrimination is the most difficult because chicken calls are similar to the mallard call with respect to frequency and rate. Thus although the ability of mallard ducklings to discriminate between their own maternal call and that of a number of other species is present in the absence of embryonic auditory self-stimulation, self-stimulation is necessary for the *complete* development of discriminative abilities.

Subsequent research has refined the initial data. Even though selective responsiveness of the embryo to the maternal call at its normal 3.7 notes/second develops prior to being exposed to its own vocalizations, such responsiveness is not maintained after hatching unless the embryo is exposed to its own 4 notes/second vocalizations (Gottlieb, 1980). Moreover, it was subsequently shown (Gottlieb 1981, 1982) that embryonic exposure *only* to 4 notes/second vocalization, although maintaining posthatching discrimination, does so in an odd manner; discrimination is seen beginning 48 hours after hatching. Obviously, normal ducklings exhibit the preference immediately at hatching. Such an immediate preference requires that the embryos be exposed to calls consisting of normally occurring variation, e.g., 2.1, 4.0, and 5.8 notes/second rather than the abnormally invariant call of 4 notes/second.

Gottlieb (1975a,b) also showed that devocalized and isolated embryos are deficient in their perception of maternal call *frequency,* being relatively insensitive to the higher frequency components of the call. This deficiency presumably is due to the fact that because embryonic vocalizations themselves are in the high frequency range (> 1500 Hz), devocalized embryos lack specific high frequency experience. The deficiency was prevented by providing devocalized embryos with recorded high frequency embryonic calls.

The inability of devocalized duck embryos to later discriminate the call of the mallard from that of the chicken presumably results from the lack of embryonic exposure to auditory stimuli of particular frequency and range of rates. Moreover, although the embryos show selective responsivity to maternal calls of 3.7 notes/second *prior to* hearing its own vocalizations, such responsiveness is not maintained unless the embryos are exposed to their own vocalization. "Thus . . . the maintenance of seemingly innate postnatal behavioral development is dependent upon a highly specific, normally occurring prior experience; it will not be maintained if only rather general (nonspecific) life-sustaining conditions prevail during ontogeny, as has been assumed in the past" (Gottlieb, 1980, p. 584).

Light Stimulation

Although light reaches the embryo, it does so in a more restricted manner than does sound. To determine the fraction of light that penetrates the uterus, Jacques, Weaver, and Reppert (1987) surgically implanted optical fibers in uteri of 20-day pregnant rats and 51-day pregnant guinea pigs. A sensor was connected to the fibers to measure the amount of white fluorescent light reaching the uterus. As shown in Figure 2.3, the amount of light transmitted through all of the maternal tissue (hair, skin, abdominal wall, uterus) in both the guinea pig and rat is low (about 2% for wavelengths less than 600 nm). However, about 10% of a 650-nm stimulus penetrates the uterus. In a similar experiment with quail (Heaton, 1973), a bit of shell was removed, and a silicon photoelectric cell was placed as close to the embryo's eye as possible. The piece of shell then was replaced, and the eggs were placed in sunlight. A measurable amount of light was recorded from within the egg at intensities sufficient to elicit the embryonic pupillary reflex.

Assuming that light does stimulate the embryo and fetus, let us turn to behavior. Relative to the amount of literature on embryonic auditory stimulation, a paucity of information exists with regard to the influence of visual stimulation. Wiens (1970) studied larval frogs to determine if the preference for particular visual patterns can be established and, if so, if the preferences are maintained. Two weeks after hatching, tadpoles were assigned to one of the following four treatment groups: (1) tadpoles reared in featureless white pans through metamorphosis; (2) those reared through metamorphosis in an experimental chamber in which black stripes were affixed to the floor and wall *or* one in which black squares were affixed in a linear arrangement; (3) those reared in one or the other experimental chamber until the middle of larval development and then transferred to a featureless environment; and (4) tadpoles kept in a featureless chamber until "late tadpole age" and then placed in one of the two experimental chambers. Animals were housed in groups of six. Each subject was tested three times for visual preference: once when they were 15 to 20 mm in length, again when they displayed hindlimb development, and again when metamorphosis was virtually complete.

The results revealed that preference for the rearing environment was shown by the animals that were reared in the striped environment. The preference was maintained throughout the three tests. Moreover, there did not appear to be a

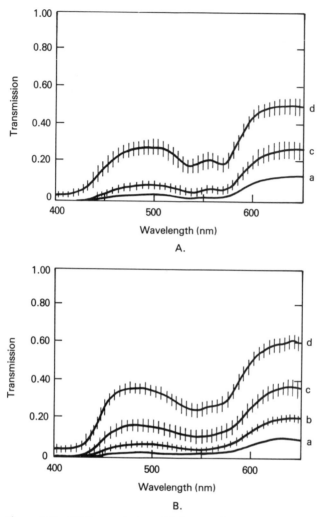

Figure 2.3 (A) Transmission of light into the uterus of the rat. Mean transmission levels by wavelength for five rats are indicated; vertical lines represent the SEM. Spectral scans for the following conditions are shown: (a) through full thickness; (c) after retraction of the skin; and (d) after retraction of the abdominal wall. (B) Transmission of light into the uterus of the guinea pig. Mean transmission for six placements (two positions in each of three animals) with the SEMs are indicated for each wavelength. Spectral scans for the following conditions are shown: (a) through full thickness; (b) with the hair shaved; (c) after retraction of the skin; and (d) after retraction of the abdominal wall. (Adapted from Jacques et al., "Penetration of light into the uterus of pregnant mammals." *Photochemistry and Photobiology, 45,* 637–41. © 1987 by Pergamon Press. By permission.)

critical period for establishing the preference; tadpoles placed in the experimental environments relatively late in their development (group 4) also displayed the preference. Wiens speculated that because the normal environment of the species of frog he used was characterized by the presence of vertical-stemmed plants on which young tadpoles cluster and around which adults tend to remain, it is not surprising that preference was established only for the striped environment. In other words, the organism is prepared to establish particular preferences and "incapable of forming a response to stimuli characteristic of unsuitable habitats" (p. 548).

Chicken embryos also appear capable of forming a visual preference. Metcalfe (1976) exposed embryos to one of two visual stimuli throughout the incubation period, a 200-W light flashing at a rate of 3/second or a 25-W light flashing at the same rate. At about 16 hours after hatching the chicks were given a simultaneous preference test in which they were allowed to approach one of two globes; one globe emitted the high intensity illumination and the other the low intensity stimulus. The results were clear; hatchlings exhibited a preference for the visual stimulus similar to that to which they were exposed as embryos.

In addition to the assessment of embryonic (or larval) exposure to light stimulation on subsequent preference, two studies have examined the effect of early light exposure on imprinting, the predisposition of hatchlings to follow the first moving object to which they are exposed. Chicken embryos exposed to light on day 19 of incubation required less time to approach the imprinting object and exhibited lower intensity of distress vocalization than did animals that had been exposed to light prior to day 19 (Adam & Dimond, 1971). Dimond and Adam (1972) subsequently reported that embryonic exposure to a light flashing at a rate of 20 minute has a greater effect on approach behavior than a light flashing at 6.6/minute.

Chemical Stimulation

Mammalian embryos have been reported to ingest amniotic fluid (see review by Bradley & Mistretta, 1975). Data from a study performed many years ago with human embryos appears to show that they not only ingest it but are responsive to its taste (De Snoo, 1927). In that study, saccharin was injected into the amnion of women suffering from excess levels of amniotic fluid. The idea was that the sweetener would induce the embryo to ingest elevated amounts of the fluid, which would eventually be excreted in the mother's urine, thereby alleviating the problem. To make the determination, a dye that shows in the urine also was injected into the amnion. Owing to the fact that embryos normally ingest small amounts of amniotic fluid, some dye appeared in the urine even without the saccharin injections. However, much more dye was seen in the urine after saccharin was administered. The procedure was only marginally successful with regard to its clinical application because the embryos eventually reduced their ingestion of the fluid, owing, according to De Snoo, to habituation to the sweet taste.

More recent evidence reveals that embryonic exposure to olfactory- and taste-related chemical stimuli can establish preferences for those stimuli. Smotherman (1982a,b) injected apple juice or saline into the amniotic fluid of 20-day-old rat embryos. When adults, the animals were given two-bottle preference tests. On one test the animals were allowed access to apple juice and water. The other test consisted in a choice between a maple solution and water. Water-deprived animals that had been exposed prenatally to apple juice ingested more of it during the 30-minute test than animals exposed as embryos to saline. Preference was not exhibited for the maple-flavored solution.

In addition to a long-term (prenatal to postnatal) consequence of exposure to a taste stimulus, Smotherman and Robinson (1988) reported a short-term (prenatal to prenatal) effect. Half of a group of 17-day-old rat fetuses were exposed to intra-amniotic injection of mint and the remaining subjects to saline. Two days later all fetuses were exposed to mint, and their behavior was monitored. Mint infusion increased fetal activity. Nineteen-day-old fetuses exposed to mint for the first time, however, displayed an immediate and brief suppression of activity prior to the increase in activity. In contrast, fetuses pretreated with mint on day 17 exhibited no such reduction. Based on this differential suppression of activity as a function of prior experience, one can conclude that fetuses discriminate between novel and familiar taste stimuli.

Hepper (1988) used a less direct technique to expose embryos to chemical stimulation. Instead of introducing the chemical directly into the amnion, he simply permitted the gravid female to ingest it. It has been shown that olfactory neurons respond electrophysiologically to olfactory/taste-related chemicals injected into the bloodstream (Maruniak, Silver, & Moulton, 1983). It was suggested that the chemical stimulates olfactory receptors after diffusing from the blood in the nasal capillary bed. Perhaps such chemicals ingested by pregnant animals reach the embryos through the blood and then stimulate their olfactory receptors.

Hepper fed some pregnant rats one clove of garlic a day from gestation day 15 through day 21. When the offspring were 12 days old, they were placed in a test apparatus and allowed to approach a dish containing garlic or one containing onion. Offspring of mothers that had been fed garlic during pregnancy exhibited a preference for the garlic, spending more time near the dish of garlic than near the dish of onion. (The preference was for the *odor* of garlic, as the animals ingested neither the garlic nor the onion.)

Was the preference for garlic actually established prenatally? Changes in the quality of milk have been associated with the ingestion of particular foods by the lactating animal (Ling, Kon, & Porter, 1961). Therefore the preference for garlic might have been established postnatally as a consequence of the ingestion of "garlic-tainted" milk. Hepper performed a second experiment in an attempt to show unequivocally the prenatal origin of the preference. It was identical to the first experiment except that the young were fostered to a nongarlic-fed mother within an hour after birth. Those offspring also exhibited the preference for garlic. However, the finding is still only suggestive (although *very* suggestive) of a prenatally established preference. It would have been best had the embryos been delivered surgically and then immediately fostered, a procedure that would obviate the possibility of even a brief bout of nursing.

Preference is exhibited not only for particular olfactory- and taste-related chemical stimuli to which embryos have been exposed as a result of an experimental manipulation, it also is displayed for stimuli to which embryos have been exposed naturally. Hepper (1987) has reported that rat pups prefer the odor of their mother's amniotic fluid when it is paired with fluid from another animal. He suggested that preference for one's own fluid (and thus the fluid of one's brothers and sisters) may be involved in the development of kin recognition. Allowing young to recognize their littermates soon after delivery may in some manner facilitate the later ability to recognize kin.

CONCLUDING COMMENTS

Embryos obey the laws of both classical and instrumental conditioning; they are capable of forming and maintaining associations between stimuli and responding predictably to the imposition of reinforcement contingencies. With a bit of imagination, one can suggest possible functions of embryonic conditioning. It is a different and difficult matter, however, to argue convincingly that conditioning *normally* plays a part in development. Two points must be established to prove the case. First, it must be shown that the factors that underlie conditioning (conditioned and unconditioned stimuli, reinforcing agents, and so forth) are normally present during the embryonic period. Second, the function of conditioning must be demonstrated. Thus far neither requirement has been met. All that can be concluded from the available evidence is that the embryonic nervous system attains a level of sophistication that *permits* conditioning to occur in response to the experimental imposition of appropriate contingencies. This "precocial" neural maturation does ensure, however, that the modification of behavior in response to certain environmental exigencies can occur *immediately* after birth and hatching.

We have seen, in addition to demonstrations of embryonic conditioning, that exposure of the embryo to particular types of stimulation can lead to postembryonic modifications of behavior. Does such exposure normally figure in development? An answer in the affirmative requires that the same two points be satisfied: that the conditions underlying embryonic stimulus exposure occur and that a behavior is dependent on such exposure. First, the conditions underlying embryonic stimulus exposure do indeed occur. The embryo is exposed to maternal vocalizations, chemicals from the adult, and the peculiarities of its own amniotic fluid. Moreover, research has demonstrated that embryonic stimulus exposure is an important, normally occurring event in the process of development, leading to the later recognition and preference for certain stimuli. Young animals, then, like adults (Zajonc, 1971), are differentially attracted to familiar stimuli. Such attraction may be advantageous if one assumes that familiar stimuli tend to be safer than novel stimuli. Therefore it is to the infant's benefit to form an attachment to the appropriate adult and, later, to ingest food items that were part of the mother's diet. Moreover, under certain circumstances it may be to the organism's advantage to remain in the environment in which it developed as an embryo or larva.

That embryonic stimulus exposure can apparently influence postnatal behavior is ironic. For many years pregnant women were encouraged to engage in certain activities, usually of an intellectual or artistic nature, that would later prove beneficial to their children. Accordingly, women went to concerts, art galleries, museums, and so forth in the hope of affecting their children's tastes. Such a prescription, assumed by many to be utterly nonsensical, may have some basis in fact—thus the irony.

REFERENCES

Adam, J., and Dimond, S. J. (1971). The effect of visual stimulation at different stages of embryonic development in approach behaviour. *Animal Behaviour, 19,* 51–54.

Armitage, S. E., Baldwin, B. A., and Vince, M. A. (1980). The fetal sound environment of sheep. *Science, 208,* 1173–174.

Bailey, E. D., and Ralph, K. M. (1975). The effects of embryonic exposure to pheasant vocalizations in later call identification by chicks. *Canadian Journal of Zoology, 53,* 1028–34.

Bench, J. (1968). Sound transmission in the human foetus through the maternal abdominal wall. *Journal of Genetic Psychology, 113,* 85–87.

Birnholz, J. C., and Benacerraf, B. B. (1983). The development of human fetal hearing. *Science, 222,* 516–518.

Borsellino, A., Pierantoni, R., and Schieti-Cavazza, B. (1970). Survival in adult mealworm beatles *(Tenebrio molitor)* of learning acquired at the larval stage. *Nature, 225,* 963–964.

Bradley, R. M., and Mistretta, C. M. (1975). Fetal sensory receptors. *Physiological Reviews, 55,* 352–382.

DeCasper, A. J., and Fifer, W. P. (1980). Of human bonding: Newborns prefer their mothers' voices. *Science, 208,* 1174–175.

DeCasper, A. J., and Prescott, P. A. (1984). Human newborns' perception of male voices: Preference, discriminations, and reinforcing value. *Developmental Psychobiology, 17,* 481–91.

DeCasper, A. J., and Sigafoos, A. D. (1983). The intrauterine heartbeat: A potent reinforcer for newborns. *Infant Behavior and Development, 6,* 19–25.

DeCasper, A. J., and Spence, M. J. (1986). Prenatal maternal speech influences newborns' perception of speech sounds. *Infant Behavior and Development, 9,* 133–50.

De Snoo, K. (1927). Das trinkende Kind im uterus. *Monatschrift fur Geburtshilfe und Gynakologie, 105,* 88–97.

Dimond, S. J., and Adam, J. H. (1972). Approach behaviour and embryonic visual experience in chicks: Studies of the effect of rate of visual flicker. *Animal Behaviour, 20,* 413–20.

Falt, B. (1981). Development of responsiveness to the individual maternal "clucking" by domestic chicks *(Gallus gallus domesticus). Behavioural Processes, 6,* 303–17.

Forbes, H., and Forbes, H. B. (1927). Fetal sense reactions: Hearing. *Journal of Comparative Psychology, 7,* 353–64.

Frankhauser, G., Vernon, J. A., Frank, W. H., and Slack, W. V. (1955). Effect of size and number of brain cells on learning in larvae of the salamander, *Triturus viridescens. Science, 122,* 692–93.

Fried, R., and Glick, S. (1966). Conditioned galvanic skin responses in the chick embryo. *Psychonomic Science, 6,* 319–20.

Gelman, S. R., Wood, S., Spellacy, W. N., and Abrams, R. M. (1982). Fetal movements in response to sound stimulation. *American Journal of Obstetrics and Gynecology, 143,* 484–85.

Gos, M. (1935). Les reflexes conditionnels chez l'enbryon d'oiseau. *Bulletin de la Societé Royale des Sciences de Liege, 4,* 194–200.

Gottlieb, G. (1971). *Development of species identification in birds.* Chicago: University of Chicago Press.

Gottlieb, G. (1975a). Development of species identification in ducklings: I. Nature of perceptual deficit caused by embryonic auditory deprivation. *Journal of Comparative and Physiological Psychology, 89,* 387–99.

Gottlieb, G. (1975b). Development of species identification in ducklings: II. Experiential prevention of perceptual deficit caused by embryonic auditory deprivation. *Journal of Comparative and Physiological Psychology, 89,* 675–84.

Gottlieb, G. (1980). Development of species identification in ducklings: VI. Specific embryonic experience required to maintain species-typical perception in Peking ducks. *Journal of Comparative and Physiological Psychology, 94,* 579–87.

Gottlieb, G. (1981). Development of species identification in ducklings: VIII. Embryonic vs. postnatal critical periods for the maintenance of species-typical perception. *Journal of Comparative and Physiological Psychology, 95,* 540–47.

Gottlieb, G. (1982). Development of species identification in ducklings: IX. The necessity of experiencing normal variations in embryonic auditory stimulation. *Developmental Psychobiology, 15,* 507–17.

Grier, J. B., Counter, S. A., and Shearer, W. M. (1967). Prenatal auditory imprinting in chickens. *Science, 155,* 1692–693.

Heaton, M. B. (1973). Early visual function in Bobwhite and Japanese quail embryos as reflected by pupillary reflex. *Journal of Comparative and Physiological Psychology, 84,* 134–39.

Heaton, M. B. (1978). Development of operant escape learning in the Peking duck embryo. *Journal of Comparative and Physiological Psychology, 92,* 397–405.

Henshall, W. R. (1972). Intrauterine sound levels. *American Journal of Obstetrics and Gynecology, 112,* 577–79.

Hepper, P. G. (1987). The amniotic fluid: an important priming role in kin recognition. *Animal Behaviour, 35,* 1343–346.

Hepper, P. G. (1988). Adaptive fetal learning: Prenatal exposure to garlic affects postnatal preferences. *Animal Behaviour, 36,* 935–36.

Hoyer, W. J., Shafer, J. N., Mauldin, J. E., and Corbett, H. T. (1971). Discriminated avoidance and escape conditioning with the tadpole *(Rana pipiens). Psychonomic Science, 24,* 247–48.

Hunt, E. L. (1949). Establishment of conditioned responses in chick embryos. *Journal of Comparative and Physiological Psychology, 42,* 107–17.

Impekoven, M. (1973). Response-contingent prenatal experience of maternal calls in the Peking duck *(Anas platyrhynchos). Animal Behaviour, 21,* 164–68.

Jacken, H., and Rubel, E. W. (1978). Ontogeny of behavioral responsiveness to sound in the chick embryo as indicated by electrical recordings of motility. *Journal of Comparative and Physiological Psychology, 92,* 682–96.

Jacques, S. L., Weaver, D. R., and Reppert, S. M. (1987). Penetration of light into the uterus of pregnant mammals. *Photochemistry and Photobiology, 45,* 637–41.

Kuo, Z. -Y. (1976). *The dynamics of behavior development.* New York: Plenum Press.

Ling, E. R., Kon, S. K., and Porter, J. W. (1961). The composition of milk and the nutritive value of its components. In S. K. Kon and A. T. Cowie (Eds.), *The mammary gland and its secretion.* Orlando, FL: Academic Press.

Leader, L. R., Baille, P., Martin, B., and Vermeulen, E. (1982). *Early Human Development, 7,* 211–19.

Maruniak, J. A., Silver, W. L., and Moulton, D. G. (1983). Olfactory receptors respond to blood-borne oderants. *Brain Research, 265,* 312–16.

Metcalfe, J. (1976). The influence of incubatory photic stimuli on chicks' visual intensity preference for approach behavior. *Developmental Psychobiology, 9,* 49–55.

Noirot, E., and Algeria, J. (1983). Neonate orientation towards human voice differs with type of feeding. *Behavioral Processes, 8,* 65–71.

Parry, M. H. (1972). Infants' responses to novelty in familiar and unfamiliar settings. *Child Development, 43,* 233–37.

Pederson, P. A., Stewart, W. B., and Shepard, G. M. (1983). Evidence for olfactory function in utero. *Science, 221,* 478–80.

Querleu, D., and Renard, K. (1981). Les perceptions auditives du foetus humain. *Medicine and Hygiene, 39,* 2102–110.

Querleu, D., Renard, K., and Crepin, G. (1981). Perception auditive et reactivite foetale aux stimulations sonores. *Journal de Gynecologie Obstetrique et Biologie de la Reproduction, 10,* 307–14.

Rawdon-Smith, A. F., Carmichael, L., and Wellman, G. (1938). Electrical responses from the cochlea of the fetal guinea pig. *Journal of Experimental Psychology, 23,* 531–35.

Schneider, C. W. (1968). Avoidance learning and the response tendencies of the larval salamander *Ambystoma punctatum* to photic stimulation. *Animal Behaviour, 16,* 492–95.

Scibetta, J. J., and Rosen, M. (1969). Response evoked by sound in the fetal guinea pig. *Obstetrics and Gynecology, 33,* 830–36.

Sheimann, I. M., Khutzian, S. S., and Ignatovitch, G. S. (1980). Periodicity in the behavior of grain bettle larvae. *Developmental Psychobiology, 13,* 585–90.

Smotherman, W. P. (1982a). Odor aversion learning by the rat fetus. *Physiology and Behavior, 29,* 769–71.

Smotherman, W. P. (1982b). In utero chemosensory experience alters taste preferences and corticosterone responsiveness. *Behavioral and Neural Biology, 36,* 61–68.

Smotherman, W. P., and Robinson, S. R. (1985). The rat fetus in its environment: Behavioral adjustments to novel, familiar, aversive and conditioned stimuli presented in utero. *Behavioral Neuroscience, 99,* 521–30.

Smotherman, W. P., and Robinson, S. R. (1988). Behavior of rat fetuses following chemical or tactile stimulation. *Behavioral Neuroscience, 102,* 24–34.

Somberg, J. C., Happ, G. M., and Schnerden, A. M. (1970). Retention of a conditioned avoidance response after metamorphosis in mealworms. *Nature, 228,* 87–88.

Spelt, D. K. (1948). The conditioning of the human fetus in utero. *Journal of Experimental Psychology, 38,* 338–46.

Spence, M. J., and DeCasper, A. J. (1987). Prenatal experience with low-frequency maternal-voice sounds influence neonatal perception of maternal voice samples. *Infant Behavior and Development, 10,* 133–42.

Stickrod, G., Kimble, D. P., and Smotherman, W. P. (1982a). In utero taste/odor aversion conditioning in the rat. *Physiology and Behavior, 28,* 5–7.

Stickrod, G., Kimble, D. P., and Smotherman, W. P. (1982b). Met-enkephalin effects on associations formed in utero. *Peptides, 3,* 881 = 83.

Thoman, E. G., Korner, A. F., and Beason-Williams, L. (1977). Modification of responsiveness to maternal vocalization in the neonate. *Child Development, 48,* 563–69.

Tschanz, B. T. (1968). Die Entstehung der persoenlichen Beziehungzwischen Jungvogel und Eltern. *Zeitschrift fur Teirpsychologie,* suppl. 4, 1–103.

Vince, M. A. (1979). Postnatal effects of prenatal sound stimulation in the guinea pig. *Animal Behaviour, 27,* 908–18.

Vince, M. A., Armitage, S. E., Walser, E. S., and Reader, M. (1982). Postnatal consequences of prenatal sound stimulation in the sheep. *Behaviour, 81,* 128–39.

Vince, M. A., Billing, A. E., Baldwin, B. A., Toner, J. N., and Weller, C. (1985). Maternal vocalisations and other sounds in the fetal lamb's sound environment. *Early Human Development, 11,* 179–90.

Walker, D., Grimwade, J., and Wood, C. (1971). Intrauterine noise: A component of the fetal environment. *American Journal of Obstetrics and Gynecology, 109,* 91–95.

Wiens, J. A. (1970). Effects of early experience on substrate pattern selections in *Rana aurora* tadpoles. *Copeia, 3,* 543–48.

Zajonc, R. B. (1971). Attraction, affiliation and attachment. In J. F. Eisenberg, W. S. Dillon, and S. D. Ripley (Eds.), *Man and beast* (pp. 141–79). Washington, DC: Smithsonian Institution Press.

3
Hormones

Becoming a male is a prolonged, uneasy, and risky venture; it is
a kind of a struggle against inherent trends toward femaleness.
                                                    A. Jost, 1969

Blood-borne substances secreted by specific tissues have long been implicated in the development and maintenance of both structure and behavior. As Aristotle wrote in *Historia Animalium,* "Some animals change their form and character, not only at certain ages and at certain seasons, but in consequence of being castrated. . . . The case is the same with men; if you mutilate them in boyhood, the later-growing hair never comes, and the voice never changes but remains high-pitched." By the eighth century BC accounts began to appear of the use of castration to deliberately eliminate libido in man. In what has been credited as "the first proof of endocrine function as we know it" (Forbes, 1949), Berthold (1849) castrated a group of young male fowl and returned a testis to each animal by placing it in the body cavity. Because the fowl continued to look and behave normally, Berthold was startled when, at autopsy, he found that a nerve supply to the grafted testis had *not* been reestablished. This finding led him to conclude the following: "So far as voice, sexual urge, belligerence, and growth of comb and wattles are concerned, such birds remained as cockerels. Since, however, transplanted testes are no longer connected with their original innervation, and since no specific secretory nerves are present, it follows that the results in question are determined by the productive functions of the testes, that is, by their action on the bloodstream" (translation from Forbes, 1949).

Historical precedent as well as factors that need not concern us here (Gandelman, 1984) have led to the widespread use of reproductive and reproduction-related activities as dependent measures in research on hormones and behavior. For that reason, the discussion opens with a consideration of hormones and the development of reproductive capacities, beginning with reproductive physiology and then turning to reproductive behavior. Afterward the influence of early hormone exposure on nonreproductive behaviors, including human personality, is considered.

HORMONES AND REPRODUCTION

Reproductive System

The view that the endocrine system regulates the development of reproduction-related morphology and behavior—in other words, that hormones are involved in *sexual differentiation*—was given impetus from various quarters. We consider only some of the major early developments beginning with study of the freemartin.

The freemartin, studied initially by Lillie (1916, 1917), is the female member of a pair of dizygotic bovine twins, the other member being a male. Although the male is normal, the female exhibits a number of anomalies, including sterility (about 90% are sterile), atrophic gonads that resemble both ovaries and testes, and variable development of the female genital tract, which in some instances may be absent (Burns, 1961). The freemartin is found only in cases in which there is a fusion (anastomosis) of some of the placental blood vessels, as depicted in Figure 3.1 (Lillie, 1917). Because of the fused vessels and because the male member of the dyad is normal, it was proposed that androgenic hormones, manufactured and secreted by the fetal testis, enter the blood and produce the effects seen in the female (Keller & Tandler, 1916; Lillie, 1917).

The hormone theory, proposed to explain the etiology of the anomalous female, had an explosive impact on research in the field of sexual differentiation. It led to the development of a variety of techniques for manipulating the endocrine milieu of the fetus as well as to new methods of assessing hormone levels

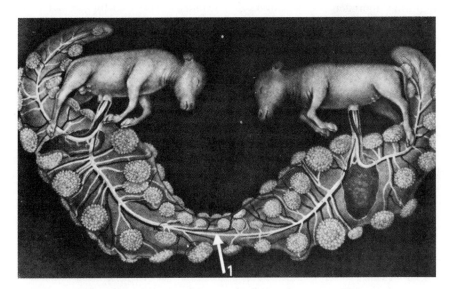

Figure 3.1 Lillie's (1917) famous illustration of confluent, anastomosing blood vessels connecting the two placental circulations in twin calf fetuses.

(see Price [1972] for a detailed historical account). Ironically, however, the hormone theory, as it applies to the freemartin, appears to be untenable. The single most damaging datum is that attempts to produce the freemartin syndrome by administering androgens to pregnant cows have failed (Jost, Chodkiewicz, & Mauleon, 1963). The differences between the freemartin and female fetuses exposed to exogenous androgen have been reviewed by Feder (1981) and are summarized in Table 3.1. It has since been proposed that freemartinism is caused by an exchange of germ cells from the male to the female (Herschler & Fechheimer, 1967) or by the presence of a nonandrogenic substance that supports testicular development (Short, 1970).

A vast amount has since been learned about the role of hormones in sexual differentiation. It is known, for example, that regardless of genetic sex, each embryo contains the anlagen, or basic material, from which *both* male and female genital ducts develop. The wolffian ducts are anlagen of epididymis, seminal vesicles, and vas deferens; and the müllerian ducts are the precursors of the uterus, oviduct, and portions of the vagina. During the embryonic period the endocrine system and, in particular, the fetal testicular secretion testosterone cause the wolffian ducts to develop (Jost, 1953; Price, 1970; Wilson & Gloyna, 1970); another hormone produced by the fetal testis, müllerian-inhibiting substance, causes the müllerian ducts to regress (Donahoe et al., 1982; Josso, Picard, & Tran, 1977). Therefore, whether male or female anlagen develops depends on the presence of functional fetal testes; a male duct system develops when they are present and a female system in their absence. These data led to the principle of *preferential female differentiation:* The embryo, being bipotential, develops in the female direction *except* when testicular secretions are present. In other words, female differentiation is passive, whereas male differentiation is active, requiring androgenic stimulation. This axiom is supported by the fact that, unlike the embryonic testis, which synthesizes and secretes high levels of testosterone, the embryonic ovary is relatively quiescent (e.g., Bloch, 1979).

Preferential female differentiation also can be seen in the elaboration of the urogenital sinus and genital tubercle. In the female the clitoris arises from the genital tubercle, whereas in the male the tubercle develops into the penis. The

Table 3.1 Differences between freemartins and female mammalian fetuses exposed to exogenous androgens

Subject	Type of Gonad	Type of Internal Genitalia	Type of External Genitalia
Freemartin	Atrophic (but may resemble testis more than ovary)	Male	Female
Androgenized female	Female	Female	Male (if dosage of androgen is sufficiently high)

Source: From Feder. Hormonal actions on the sexual differentiation of the genitalia and the gonadotrophin-regulating systems. In N. T. Adler (Ed.), *Neuroendocrinology of Reproduction.* © 1981 by Plenum Press. Reprinted by permission.

prostate gland and urethra arise from the urogenital sinus of the male. The urogenital sinus of the female elaborates into the urethra and a portion of the vagina. The direction of development depends solely on whether testicular secretions are present (Nathanielsz, 1976). The same is true for the mammary glands; they develop only in the absence of androgen (Goldman, Shapiro, & Neumann, 1976).

The outcome of a number of genetic disorders support the notion that differentiation proceeds in a female-like direction in lieu of androgenic intervention. One such disorder, *Turner's syndrome,* is the result of an XO chromosomal pattern; that is, it occurs when the embryo lacks a second sex chromosome. One characteristic of this genetic anomaly is that the embryonic gonads do not develop. Therefore differentiation should, and does, assume a female pattern, as shown in Figure 3.2.

The presence of functional embryonic testes is of no consequence, however, should the embryo lack tissue sensitive to androgen. The absence of androgen-sensitive tissue is inherited as an X-linked recessive trait, producing what is

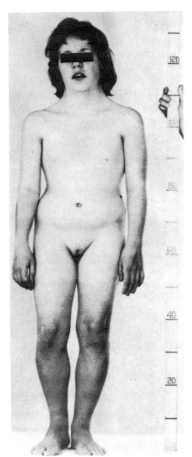

Figure 3.2 Turner's syndrome in a child 14 years 10 months old. Female secondary sex characteristics were induced with estrogen therapy. (From Grumbach and Van Wyk, "Disorders of sex differentiation." In R. H. Williams (Ed.), *Textbook of Endocrinology* (pp. 423–501). © 1974 by W. B. Saunders. Reprinted by permission.)

known as the *testicular feminizing syndrome*. It is tantamount to a genetic male developing in utero without testes, as androgen is useless in the absence of appropriate target tissue. Genetic males suffering from the testicular feminizing syndrome are often identified as female at birth. It is not until later, when puberty does not occur, that the disorder is identified; undescended testes are discovered, and the vaginal canal is seen as merely a blind pouch (see Figure 3.3). Because these boys are raised as girls prior to the diagnosis, they develop a female gender identity[1] that, after the age of about 2 years, is believed to be immutable. The only recourse, then, is to continue to raise them as female. Hormone treatment is given to bring about full feminine somatic development. The testicular feminizing syndrome also is found in animals, as shown in Figure 3.4.

We have seen that somatic development is profoundly affected by the endocrine system and that, in the absence of androgenic stimulation, development proceeds in a female direction. Pfeiffer (1936), in a classic study, demonstrated that the principle of preferential female differentiation applies as well to reproductive function. Hormones released cyclically by the pituitary (luteinizing and

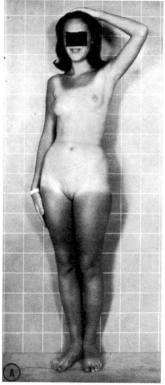

Figure 3.3 Syndrome of testicular feminization (male pseudohermaphroditism) in a 17-year-old (From Grumbach and Van Wyk, "Disorders of sex differentiation." In R. H. Williams (Ed.), *Textbook of Endocrinology* (pp. 423–501). © 1974 by W. B. Saunders. Reprinted with permission.)

[1]*Gender identity* refers to "a person's knowledge that he or she is male or female and to his or her satisfaction with that knowledge and adherence to the role it implies" (Hines, 1982, p. 61).

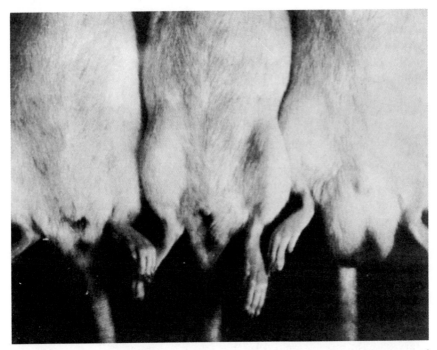

Figure 3.4 External genitalia of a rat with testicular feminization. The external genitalia are similar to those of a normal female rat (left) and different from those of a normal male rat (right). (From Bardin et al., "Testosterone metabolism in the androgen-insensitive rat: A model for testicular feminization." In D. Bergsma (Ed.), *The Endocrine System* (p. 185–192). © 1971 by Williams & Wilkins for the National Foundation-March of Dimes (BD:OAS VII[6]: *190*). Reprinted with permission of the National Foundation–March of Dimes.)

follicle-stimulating hormone, known collectively as gonadotropins) act on the ovary to induce ovulation.

Pfeiffer asked if the development of a cyclic pattern of gonadotropin release as characteristic of the female is dependent on the availability of hormones during early life. Neonatal rats of both sexes were gonadectomized, and some were given a testicular transplant to provide them with androgen. When they became adult, each was provided with an ovarian transplant and assessed for ovulation. Pfeiffer found that, regardless of genetic sex, ovulation does not occur if testicular secretions are present during early life. In other words, androgen leads to a tonic rather than a cyclic release of gonadotropins. Moreover, both females and males exhibit ovulation in the absence of androgen. Here again we have evidence for preferential female differentiation. These findings have since been repeated many times using the much simpler procedure of injecting pregnant animals with testosterone, thereby eliminating the need for testis transplants.

Given that gonadotropins are secreted by the pituitary, Pfeiffer logically interpreted his data to mean that the site of action of androgen is the pituitary. A "male" pituitary, one secreting gonadotropins tonically, results from early androgenic stimulation, and a "female" pituitary that secretes gonadotropins cyclically develops in the absence of androgen. Later research, however, proved him incorrect.

The existence of a masculine pituitary gland implies that a normal female would cease to ovulate if her pituitary were exchanged for that of a male. This prediction was not confirmed (Harris & Jacobsohn, 1952; Martinez & Bittner, 1956). Other research has demonstrated that the site of action of androgen involves the brain, most notably the arcuate and preoptic nuclei. Based on the effects of electrically stimulating those structures in females made anovulatory by the perinatal administration of testosterone, Gorski and Barraclough (1963) suggested that the preoptic nucleus causes the arcuate nucleus to change its firing pattern from tonic to cyclic. The arcuate nucleus, in turn, synthesizes and releases a hormone (gonadotropin-releasing hormone) that acts on the pituitary. When this releasing hormone is secreted cyclically, it causes the pituitary to release gonadotropins in a cyclic fashion and thus promotes ovulation. Related experiments have demonstrated that the placement of minute amounts of testosterone directly into the arcuate and preoptic nuclei cause ovulation to cease (Hayashi & Gorski, 1974; Nadler, 1972, 1973). Moreover, early androgen exposure affects the neuroanatomical development of both nuclei (Matsumoto & Arai, 1980; Raisman & Field, 1973).

Now that we have seen that early androgen exposure masculinizes both the soma and endocrine function, we consider the role of the endocrine system in the development of reproduction-related behaviors. Females of many mammalian species are sexually receptive only at particular times during the ovulatory cycle. Rats and mice, for example, have 4-day cycles and mate only during a period of a few hours. Because *both* ovulation and sexual receptivity are cyclic, it is reasonable to assume that early exposure to androgen eliminates not only the capacity to ovulate but also sexual receptivity. Moreover, perhaps early androgen stimulation promotes the later display of male-like reproductive behaviors.

Reproductive Behavior

Dantchakoff (1938a,b), whose primary interest was the influence of androgen on genital morphology, made reference to the fact that female guinea pigs that had been exposed to androgen prior to birth displayed enhanced levels of male sexual activity. It was not until the report of Phoenix, Goy, Gerall, & Young (1959), however, that the issue of hormones and the development of sexual behavior took center stage. Pregnant guinea pigs were injected daily with the widely used synthetic androgen testosterone propionate throughout most of the gestation period. When the prenatally hormone-exposed young were between 90 and 160 days of age they were gonadectomized and tested. Would prenatal exposure to androgen reduce the capacity of females to exhibit female sexual behavior? Female sex behavior of animals with discrete periods of receptivity is triggered by the cyclic release of relatively high levels of the ovarian hormones estrogen and progesterone. Sexual receptivity therefore can be induced in ovariectomized females by providing them with estrogen and progesterone replacement therapy, specifically, one injection of estrogen followed some time later by an injection of progesterone. Phoenix et al. discovered that prenatal exposure to testosterone permanently suppresses the females' capacity to respond to estrogen and progesterone by becoming sexually receptive. In addition, the exposed female guinea pigs exhibited elevated levels of *male* copulatory activities in response to testosterone propionate stimulation given in adult life. The sexual behavior of adult males exposed as embryos to androgen was unaffected.

Phoenix and co-workers interpreted their data as showing that, when present in sufficient quantity during very early development, androgen *organizes* particular portions of the brain. Such organization consists in reducing sensitivity to ovarian hormones and enhancing sensitivity to androgen. In other words, androgen prevents estrogen and progesterone from activating female sexual behavior while heightening the ability of androgen to elicit male sexual behavior. Here, then, we have partial support at a behavioral level for the concept of preferential female differentiation; regardless of genetic sex, the presence of androgen causes development to proceed in a male-like direction. The next step was to determine the applicability to behavior of the other facet of the concept: that in the absence of androgen, and regardless of genotype, development proceeds in a female-like direction. Will males castrated early in life exhibit augmented levels of female and reduced levels of male sex behavior?

Grady, Phoenix, and Young (1965) castrated male rats on either day 1, 5, 20, 30, 50, or 90 of life. Later, the animals were administered estrogen and progesterone and then tested for the display of female sexual behavior. The results were clear. Males castrated on days 1 and 5 displayed much more female sex behavior in response to estrogen plus progesterone treatment than did males castrated after day 5. They also exhibited less male sexual behavior in response to testosterone treatment than did animals castrated after day 5. These data support the notion that in the absence of androgen and regardless of genetic sex, differentiation of reproductive behavior proceeds in a female direction.

The data of Grady et al. demonstrated that, for the rat, androgen must be present beyond the fifth day of postnatal development to establish a permanent masculinizing (organizing) action on reproductive behavior. In general, animals with relatively long gestation periods (e.g., guinea pig, sheep, rhesus monkey) are maximally sensitive to the organizing property of androgen during the embryonic period (e.g., Goy, 1970; Goy, Bridson, & Young, 1964; Short, 1974). Short-gestation animals (e.g., mouse, rat, hamster) are maximally sensitive during the neonatal period (e.g., Carter, Clemens, & Hoekema, 1972; Edwards & Burge, 1971; Gerall, Hendricks, Johnson, & Bounds, 1967). As Feder (1981) pointed out, the critical factor determining the timing of the period of maximal sensitivity is the level of neural development at the time of androgen exposure rather than the pre- or postnatal status. An understanding of the factors that bring the period of maximal sensitivity to a close may help us understand how hormones and the central nervous system interact.

It should be noted that the outcome of several studies suggest that *postnatal* ovarian secretions may play an active role in the process of feminization (Dunlap, Gerall, & Carlton, 1978; Hendricks & Duffy, 1974). Gerall, Dunlap, and Hendricks (1972) castrated newborn male rats and gave them ovarian transplants. The ovaries were removed on day 60, and tests for female sexual behavior in response to estrogen plus progesterone treatment were conducted on days 90 to 160. Males given ovaries displayed more female behaviors than those not provided with ovarian transplants.

As discussed above, the organizational influence of early androgen exposure consists, in part, of rendering neural tissue sensitive to androgen so that later in life androgen can activate male sexual behaviors. However, perinatal androgen exposure *alone* has been reported to lead to elevated levels of male sexual activities. Manning and McGill (1974) found that 65% of females of the BDF$_1$ mouse strain given testosterone propionate on the day of birth mounted sexually receptive females. Similar findings have been reported for the rat (Sodersten, 1973), hamster (Lisk, 1980), rhesus monkey (Goy & Phoenix, 1971), and marmoset monkey (Abbott & Hearn, 1979). Therefore early androgen stimulation, along with its ability to render neural tissue sensitive to the male sex behavior-activating property of androgen, can produce permanent facilitatory effects on reproductive behavior. Curiously, this permanent influence of perinatal androgen exposure has not been studied in much detail. One obvious consideration is the degree to which masculine sex behavior produced by perinatal androgen exposure alone approximates that activated in the adult by additional androgenic stimulation.

A good deal of attention has been paid to determining the mechanism of action by which androgen exerts its organizing influence. Evidence indicates that testosterone per se may not be the agent responsible for masculinization. Normally, a fraction of testosterone is converted metabolically (aromatized) to estrogen in both peripheral tissue and the brain. It has been suggested (Reddy, Naftolin, & Ryan, 1974) that the aromatized androgen (i.e., estrogen) is the active masculinizing agent, at least for nonprimate species (Pomerantz, Goy, & Roy, 1986). When given to infant female rats and to embryonic guinea pigs, estrogen acts like testosterone by suppressing the later display of female sexual behavior and enhancing male sexual behavior (Hines & Goy, 1985; Whalen & Etgen, 1978; Whalen & Nadler, 1963). Moreover, embryonic exposure to antiestrogenic compounds can reduce the later display of male sexual behavior (McEwen, Lieberburg, Chaptol, & Krey, 1977; Tobet & Baum, 1987). It has been hypothesized (Dohler et al., 1984) that high levels of estrogen cause sexual differentiation to proceed in a male-typical direction, whereas moderate levels of estrogen lead to female differentiation.

HORMONES AND NONREPRODUCTIVE BEHAVIOR

Aggression

As is the case for reproduction, it was known long before the field of endocrinology came into existence that testicular secretions are involved in the display of aggressive behavior. Those engaged in animal husbandry realized that males, typically more aggressive than females, can be made tractable by castration. Laboratory study of the effects of the endocrine system on aggression began much later than work on hormones and reproduction. In initial studies, Clark and Birch (1945) and Beeman (1947) reported that aggression, reduced in the male following castration, can be reinstated by testosterone replacement therapy in both chimpanzee and rat. More than 20 years later Edwards (1968), studying mice, described results suggesting that aggression, like sexual behavior, follows the principle of preferential female differentiation: In the absence of androgen exposure and regardless of genetic sex, a relatively nonaggressive organism develops.

Edwards injected testosterone propionate into some newborn female mice and gave others only the oil vehicle (steroid hormones are routinely dissolved in sesame or peanut oil). Later, when adult, the animals were ovariectomized and administered daily injections of testosterone propionate in dosages that were initially low but increased weekly. Once each week the females were paired with a male, and the presence or absence of fighting was noted. The results of this experiment are depicted in Figure 3.5. It is apparent that neonatal androgen exposure promotes later responsiveness to androgen; females attacked the males only if testosterone propionate was administered soon after birth. Edwards assumed that "the usually observed difference between normal male and female mice, with respect to fighting, is due to the fact that males are stimulated by testicular androgens early in life. One may presume that the stimulation by endogenous testosterone in the male (and exogenous testosterone in the female) can 'organize' or cause the differentiation of a neural substrate for fighting" (p. 108). Edwards (1969) later showed that removal of neonatal males' endogenous source of androgen by castration reduces the percentage of animals that later fight in response to testosterone treatment.

Although Edwards contended that early androgen exposure is a necessary condition for the later induction of aggression, subsequent research proved otherwise. Fighting *can* be activated in animals that have not been exposed to androgen during the period of perinatal development, i.e., in animals whose

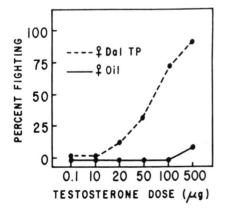

Figure 3.5 Percentage of female mice administered testosterone propionate (Da 1 TP) or oil on the day of birth that fought in response to testosterone exposure during adult life. The dosage of testosterone increased weekly. (Adapted from Edwards, "Fighting by neonatally androgenized females." *Science, 161,* 1027–28. © 1968 by The American Association for the Advancement of Science. By permission.)

brains have not been organized. However, such activation proceeds at a much slower pace than does the triggering of aggression in perinatally androgen-exposed subjects. Instead of requiring three or four injections of testosterone to activate fighting, as is the case for females administered testosterone during infancy and for males castrated when adult, nonperinatally androgenized animals require upward of a month of daily injections (Svare, Davis, & Gandelman, 1974; vom Saal, Svare, & Gandelman, 1976). Therefore androgen stimulation during early development does not institute behavioral responsiveness to testosterone. Rather, it functions to *enhance* responsiveness by markedly augmenting sensitivity to androgen's aggression-activating property.

Beyond the principle of preferential female differentiation, additional parallels exist between the hormonal involvement in reproduction and aggression. One concerns the period of maximum sensitivity to the organizational effects of androgen. As stated above, the major difference between perinatally androgenized and nonandrogenized animals is that as adults the former require a much shorter period of exposure to androgen to produce fighting. The period of maximum sensitivity, then, is that point in development at which exposure to androgen produces the greatest reduction in the time required to fight following the commencement of hormone treatment later in life. Two findings are relevant in this regard. First, in the mouse, early *postnatal* androgen exposure is more effective than embryonic exposure (Gandelman, 1980). Second, as found by administering testosterone at different times postnatally to gonadectomized animals, the period of maximum sensitivity comes to a close between the 6th and 12th postnatal days (vom Saal et al., 1976) (see Table 3.2). This time frame is similar to that of androgen on sexual behavior of rodents.

Another parallel between the endocrine involvement in aggression and reproduction concerns estrogen. As we saw with regard to reproductive behavior, perinatal estrogen as well as androgen can channel development in a male direction. The same is true for fighting behavior (Edwards & Herndon, 1970; Simon &

Table 3.2 Response of testosterone-treated adult mice that had been exposed to testerone as neonates

	Males		Females	
Days of Treatment	No. Fighting	No. Days Treatment Needed[a]	No. Fighting	No. Days Treatment Needed[a]
0	24/24	4.6	24/24	4.7
3	24/24	4.0	23/23	4.5
6	22/22	3.8	24/24	4.9
12	24/24	5.5	22/22	7.2

[a]Mean number of days of adult testosterone exposure required to establish fighting.

Source: Adapted from vom Saal et al. Time of neonatal androgen exposure influences length of testosterone treatment required to induce aggression in adult male and female mice. *Behavioral Biology, 17,* 391–97. © 1976 by Academic Press. By permission.

Gandelman, 1978), which suggests that estrogen aromatized from testosterone may be involved in organizing or masculinizing the central nervous system. Simon and Whalen (1987) have proposed that masculinization of the neural substrate mediating aggression may be a dual process involving *both* androgen and estrogen.

A final similarity is that fighting, like male copulatory activity, is enhanced in some cases by perinatal androgen exposure in the absence of androgen treatment later in life. Payne (1976) reported that female hamsters exposed to testosterone only on the day of birth had a median aggression score against males almost five times that of control females. Likewise, the administration of testosterone propionate to 3-day-old female mice of the Balb/c strain produced augmented levels of fighting during adult life (Vale, Ray, & Vale, 1972).

Thus far we have considered the influence of early androgen exposure on adults' propensity to fight. However, the endocrine system also affects the behavior of juveniles in the form of "play fighting." Although consisting of most of the components of aggression, play fighting does not result in physical injury. It is thought that such behavior may constitute practice for the authentic aggression of the adult.

The effect of androgen on play fighting is found in both the primate and the rodent. As shown in Figure 3.6, female rhesus monkeys exposed prior to birth to testosterone propionate by way of maternal injection exhibited elevated levels of play fighting and threat gestures (Goy & Phoenix, 1971). Play fighting of female marmoset monkeys also is augmented when testosterone treatment is begun at birth (Abbott & Hearn, 1979), and female rats given only a single injection of testosterone propionate exhibit enhanced play fighting as well (Olioff & Stewart, 1978). Much more is said about play fighting in Chapter 7.

Activity

Female rats generally exhibit higher levels of activity (assessed by ambulation in an open field) than do males (Broadhurst, 1958; Denenberg & Morton, 1962; Sines, 1961). This open field activity presumably is related to exploration and investigation. The sex difference can be modulated by the imposition of hormonal manipulations. Many investigators have reported that the administration of testosterone to females sometime between postnatal days 1 and 10 reduces their later display of spontaneous activity to a level approximately that of the male (e.g., Blizzard, Lippman, & Chen, 1975; Denti & Negroni, 1975; Stevens & Goldstein, 1981; Stewart, Skvarenina, & Pottier, 1975). Scouten, Grotelueschen, and Beatty (1975) reported that the open field activity of males can be made indistinguishable from that of females by eliminating early androgenic stimulation. Here the male embryo is exposed, by way of maternal injection, to an antiandrogenic chemical and then is castrated soon after birth (Scouten et al., 1975).

Running-wheel activity, which apparently is a regulatory behavior used to adjust energy expenditure to food intake, also differs quantitatively between

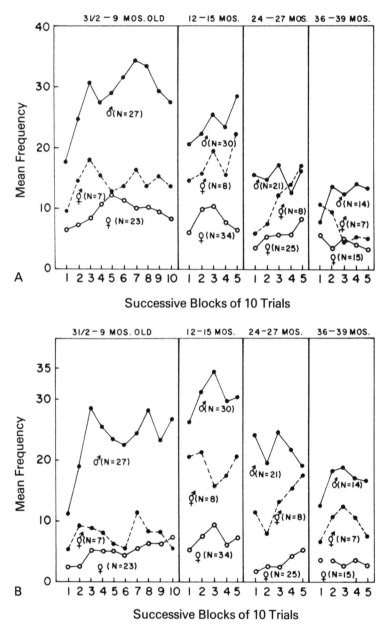

Figure 3.6 (A) Mean frequency of performance of rough-and-tumble play per block of 10 consecutive daily trials by normal intact male (♂), female (♀), and pseudohermaphroditic female (⚥) rhesus monkeys; (B) mean frequency of performance of threat gestures per block of 10 consecutive daily trials. (From Goy and Phoenix, "The effects of testosterone propionate administered before birth on the development of behavior in genetic female rhesus monkeys." In C. H. Sawyer and R. A. Gorski (Eds.), *Steroid Hormones and Brain Function.* © 1971 by The Regents of the University of California, The University of California Press. Reprinted by permission.)

male and female rats, with the latter exhibiting higher levels of running (Gentry & Wade, 1976; Hitchcock, 1925; Tokuyama, Saito, & Okudo, 1982). Neonatal injections of gonadal hormones have been shown to influence behavior significantly; testosterone markedly reduces activity of the female, whereas estrogen produces increased running among females and, to a lesser extent, males (Dawson, Cheung, & Lau, 1975; Gerall, 1967).

Another means of assessing activity is to place a series of photocell beams across the cage floor. As the subject moves about, it breaks the beams. The number of such interruptions constitutes a measure of activity. Broida and Svare (1984), using such a procedure with mice, presented perhaps the most thorough account to date of the influence of early hormone exposure on activity. Their findings can be summarized as follows: (1) adult females are more active than males; (2) gonadectomy of adult males and females, though reducing activity, does not eliminate the sex difference; (3) males gonadectomized on the day of birth are more active than males gonadectomized on day 5, 10, or 25; and (4) females injected with testosterone propionate on the day of birth are less active than females exposed to the hormone on day 10, whereas the latter do not differ from controls. Thus we see that neonatal androgen stimulation exerts a permanent attenuation of activity, and that the period of maximum sensitivity occurs within the first week of life.

The sex difference in activity and the activity-suppressing influence of neonatal androgen stimulation may account for findings pertaining to other types of behavior. Beatty and Beatty (1970), using rats, were the first to report a sex difference in terms of the acquisition of an active avoidance response: Females are superior to males. Furthermore, injections of testosterone during infancy and again during adult life masculinized (reduced) the females' avoidance performance. Denti and Negroni (1975) later reported that neonatal androgen exposure alone was sufficient to produce a decrement in the female rat's active avoidance behavior. The performance of the male can be augmented by eliminating early androgenic stimulation (Scouten et al., 1975).

In contrast to the females' advantage in the active avoidance task, males are superior in terms of learning the relatively complicated Lashley III maze; they make fewer errors and retracings than do females (Stewart et al., 1975). As you could now predict, exposing neonatal females to testosterone improves their performance. The data are reviewed in Table 3.3.

Table 3.3 Mean scores of rats run in the Lashley III maze

Group	Trials to Criterion	Errors	Retracings	Combined Errors and Retracings
Normal females ($n = 8$)	19.6	62.6	92.6	155.3
Androgen-treated females ($n = 8$)	13.0	30.4	47.6	78.0
Normal males ($n = 8$)	13.6	21.0	26.1	47.1

Source: Stewart et al. Effects of neonatal androgens on open-field behavior and maze learning in the prepubescent and adult rat. *Physiology and Behavior, 14,* 291–95. © 1975 by Pergamon Press. Reprinted by permission.

The sex differences in active avoidance behavior and maze learning probably are secondary to the activity differences described above. Being less active would retard active avoidance behavior and thus explain the superiority of the female. Conversely, being generally less active could be advantageous in complex learning situations that require deliberate responding—hence the superior performance of the male.

Taste Preference

A sex difference in the preference for salt and its modification by early hormone exposure has been demonstrated by Krecek (1973; Krecek, Novakova, & Stilbral, 1972). By day 60 of life, female rats begin to consume more of a 3% saline solution than do males. The appearance of this difference can be prevented by injecting 2-day-old females with testosterone. Injections on day 12 are without effect. A sex difference again favoring the female rat is seen for sweet tastes (Valenstein, Kakoluwski, & Cox, 1967). The administration of testosterone to 5-day-old females significantly reduces the predisposition for a sweet tasting saccharin solution (Wade & Zucker, 1969). Augmented preference for the sweet solution is shown by testicular feminized rats, which, if you recall, are genetic males lacking androgen-sensitive target tissue (Shapiro & Goldman, 1973). Androgen therefore suppresses the preference normally exhibited by females for salt and sweet tastes.

Brain Asymmetry and Associated Behaviors

It has been recognized for some time that the two cerebral hemispheres in humans are not mirror images of each other, as they differ functionally. This is seen in right-handed individuals for whom the left hemisphere coordinates most bodily movements, playing an especially important role in language production and comprehension. The right hemisphere appears to be involved with emotion, as manifested in music, art, and abstract thought. Such differences in function are known as *brain asymmetries.*

A good deal of evidence has accrued showing that brain asymmetries are not peculiar to humans but are seen in a variety of other species as well (Harnad, Doty, Goldstein, Jaynes, & Krauthamer, 1977). They include the canary in which asymmetry is found for song production, the rat with regard to side preference for turning, and chicks' discrimination, attack, and copulatory behaviors (Glick, Jerussi, & Zimmerberg, 1977; Howard, Rogers, & Boura, 1980; Nottebohm, 1977; Rogers & Anson, 1979).

It has been proposed by Geschwind (Geschwind & Behan, 1982) that brain asymmetries might be related to the presence of testosterone during the embryonic period of development. The hormone either slows the growth of the left hemisphere, thereby favoring development of the right hemisphere or, according to others (Galaburda, Corsiglia, Rosen, & Sherman, 1987), directly promotes the growth of the right hemisphere. That is why, according to Geschwind, males experience more learning disorders than females, who have less asymmetry (less embryonic exposure to testosterone and hence less right hemisphere dominance).

Studies with nonhuman subjects provide both indirect and direct support for the hypothesis that testosterone promotes brain asymmetries. Indirect support comes from the demonstration of sex differences in asymmetry. As examples, Andrew, Mench, and Rainey (1982) reported that female chicks do not exhibit asymmetry in visual discrimination tasks (the left hemisphere dominates in the male), whereas Denenberg et al. (1982) showed greater postural asymmetry in females than male rats (females are more biased toward the left). These indirect studies are complemented by one involving manipulation of the early hormonal milieu. Rosen, Berrebi, Yutzey, and Denenberg (1983) administered testosterone propionate to pregnant rats and found that the neonatal females display a rightward rather than the normal leftward bias in postural asymmetry.

Human Personality

Potentially important findings in the study of hormones and behavior concerns the possible involvement of the endocrine system in human behavioral development. Before examining the data, two methodological issues regarding the research are considered. An appreciation of these issues is requisite for understanding and properly evaluating the research.

One question concerns the *dependent measure,* that is, what are being used as data. Unlike research with animals in which direct observation of the behavior in question is possible, direct observation of human behavior most often cannot be accomplished. The reason is that what is frequently meant by behavior is really *personality,* a set of relatively stable dispositions that characterize the manner in which individuals react toward particular environmental stimuli and events. Although personality ideally is assessed by systematically observing the behavior of individuals in a variety of settings, such a tactic has obvious practical disadvantages that prohibit its use in most personality-related research. Instead, personality tests or interviews are used. This method poses a problem, then, in that hypotheses are tested and conclusions drawn about the role of hormones in the development of certain behavioral dispositions without ever actually observing the behavior.

Another problem concerns the *independent variable,* that is, what is being studied. Because direct manipulations of the endocrine system for experimental purposes cannot be performed in humans, other strategies must be used. These alternate strategies are problematical, however. One is simply to compare females with males. A difference between them with respect to the dependent measure in question would be attributed to their disparate hormone milieux. The problem here is obvious; differences need not be attributable to hormones but, rather, to the fact that parents and society in general treat girls and boys differently beginning right at birth. Hence early training (viz., the environment) can play an important role in the creation of sex differences in behavior.

Another approach is to study individuals who, at an early age, suffered from an endocrine disorder. A difference between the experimental and control subjects thus can be attributed to the endocrine disorder, that is, to disparities in the early endocrine environment. However, because the disorders are of a genetic origin, any differences between the affected subjects and controls could be as easily ascribed to genes as to the hormones. Furthermore, differences in the severity of a given disorder yield a nonhomogeneous treatment condition. A third approach is to examine people who during their embryonic period were exposed to hormones administered by physicians to their mothers, often to prevent threatened abortion. Although many more individuals have been exposed as embryos to hormones of exogenous origin than have suffered from a hormonal disorder (thereby permitting the formation of larger experimental groups), this procedure also poses a problem, i.e., lack of control of the independent variable. As stated previously (Gandelman, 1986a), "Because perinatal hormone exposure is neither performed by nor under the auspices of the investigator, a given experiment frequently contains an experimental group consisting of subjects exposed to different types and combinations of synthetic steroids for various lengths of time commencing at varying phases of perinatal development" (p. 495). A fourth and last approach involves the correlation of particular behaviors of children with the levels of hormones found in blood obtained from their umbilical cord soon after it was severed. This newer method incorporates both direct observation of behavior and direct assessment of endocrine state. Its drawback is that because blood sampling occurs at only a single point in time a restricted view of the prenatal hormonal milieu is provided.

Now that you have been alerted to some of the methodological concerns, we are ready to consider the data, beginning with a genetically based endocrine disorder that results in the exposure of embryonic females to elevated levels of androgen. The disorder, congenital adrenal hyperplasia (CAH), has a frequency of occurrence of 1:20,000 births. Briefly, the embryonic adrenal gland, instead of normally secreting cortisol and small amounts of androgen, secretes little if any cortisol but large amounts of androgen. The resulting masculinized genitalia (labial fusion and enlarged clitoris) (see Figure 3.7) permit early diagnosis. The genital abnormalities are surgically corrected, and cortisone treatment is given. The ability to reproduce is retained.

Ehrhardt, Epstein, and Money (1968) studied 15 CAH females ranging in age from 5 to 16 years. Each was matched to a control subject of the same race and about the same age, IQ, and socioeconomic background. The data emerged from interviews with both the children and their mothers. Although gender identity in all cases was female, differences between the experimental and control girls appeared with respect to a number of factors. The findings are summarized in Table 3.4, which gives the data of the CAH subjects relative to those of the controls. The authors did not subject the data to statistical analysis. I analyzed the data using chi-square tests, and only those differences that attained statistical significance are included in the table.

The profile of differences suggested to the investigators that the CAH females were masculinized; CAH girls showed more interest in physical activity, more interest in careers, and less interest in children and marriage. Indeed, most of the CAH females were described by themselves and their mothers as being tomboys throughout all of their childhood.

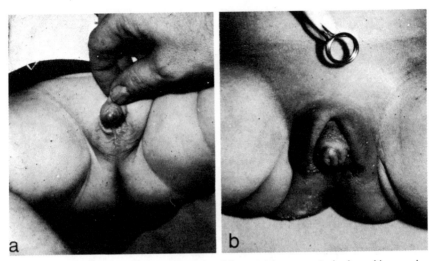

Figure 3.7 External genitalia of female siblings with congenital adrenal hyperplasia. (Courtesy of Dr. Charles Hammond, Duke University.)

Although the differences between the prenatally androgen-exposed and control females agree with data obtained from nonhuman animals with respect to the masculinizing action of perinatal androgen exposure, caution must be exercised when attributing the differences found in the CAH girls exclusively or even partially to the endocrine system. As Ehrhardt et al. stated:

> It is not possible to estimate on the basis of present data, whether individual differences of tomboyism may have reflected differences in parental attitude. Each parent knew of the child's genital masculinization at birth. This may have insidiously influ-

Table 3.4 Marriage, maternalism, physical energy, and tomboyism of congenital adrenal hyperplasia and control females

Parameter	Experimental Group (N = 15)	Control Group (N = 15)
Anticipation of marriage in fantasy and imagery	9	15
Marriage preferred to career	1	10
Preference for doll play	2	8
Great interest in infant care	1	7
Boys' clothes (e.g., slacks, shirts) strongly preferred	9	0
Engages in intense outdoor activities	11	5
Always thought of by mother and self as tomboy	11	6

Source: Based on the data of Ehrhardt et al. (1968).

enced their expectancies and reactions regarding the child's behavioral development and interests, but in a way not the same from parent to parent. Whereas one parent might accept, or even reward tomboyism and justify its appearance, another might try to suppress it. Attempted suppression might itself intensify the behavior it tries to abolish, should it elicit a reaction-formation and determination not to relinquish tomboyism. (p. 166)

Ehrhardt and Baker (1977), using another sample of 17 CAH females, essentially replicated the findings of Ehrhardt et al. (1968). A follow-up study of 13 of these now adolescent subjects revealed that, although about half of them became interested in dressing attractively, the low interest in becoming a parent persisted (Baker & Ehrhardt, 1976, as cited in Baker, 1980). Furthermore, 11 of 30 (37%) other women with a history of CAH rated themselves as being either bisexual or homosexual in contrast to 2 of 27 (7%) controls (Money, Schwartz, & Lewis, 1984).

Other data, using individuals exposed prior to birth to hormones of exogenous origin, tend to support the findings obtained from CAH females. The earliest study of that type was performed by Ehrhardt and Money (1967), who examined the offspring of women treated with synthetic progestational hormones (progestins) to prevent threatened abortion. It subsequently was discovered that some of those progestins had masculinizing properties, causing partial virilization of the genitalia. Ehrhardt and Money examined 10 progestin-exposed girls using procedures similar to those employed in the study of the CAH sample, except that a control group was not included. The results were virtually identical to those obtained from the CAH sample, including descriptions of the girls preferring to engage in physically demanding sporting activities. However, a follow-up study performed when the girls were between the ages of 16 and 27 years revealed that none of them pursued sports as a career or even as a major pastime (Money & Mathews, 1982). Lastly, Reinisch (1981) reported that females and males prenatally exposed to synthetic progestins having androgenic properties score higher than their same-sex sibling controls on a paper-and-pencil test designed to assess the potential for aggressive behavior.

Whereas some progestins have androgenic properties, naturally occurring progesterone blocks the action of androgens. Thus one would predict that prenatal exposure to progesterone should reduce masculinization. No such effect was reported for males, and only a minimal effect was observed in females (Ehrhardt, Grisanti, & Meyer-Bahlburg, 1977; Ehrhardt, Meyer-Bahlburg, Feldman, & Ince, 1984). With regard to the latter finding, the only difference between progesterone-exposed and control girls is that the former report a greater interest in feminine clothing styles. In later reports (Kester, 1984; Meyer-Bahlburg & Ehrhardt, 1982) virtually no effect of prenatal progesterone exposure was observed concerning the aggressive behavior of either males or females or the recreational and psychosexual development of males.

The administration of combinations of hormones, most notably estrogen and progestin, is common practice for the prevention of pregnancy complications. Yalom, Green, and Fisk (1973), the first to study children exposed prenatally to estrogen and progesterone, reported diminished masculinization in both 6- and

16-year-old boys. However, their findings must be viewed with some skepticism because the study contained a serious methodological flaw: The hormone-exposed subjects were born of diabetic mothers, whereas most of the unexposed control boys were born of healthy mothers. Reinisch and Karow (1977) also studied the offspring of estrogen- and progestin-treated women. Thirty-four children, averaging 12 years of age, were given the Cattell personality questionnaire. The offspring of mothers given high amounts of progestin relative to estrogen (some mothers were not given any estrogen) differed from those of mothers given high amounts of estrogen relative to progestin on various personality factors. The high-progestin-exposed children were more independent, sensitive, individualistic, self-assured, and self-sufficient. The high-estrogen subjects were more group-oriented and group-dependent. Similar results were obtained when the hormone-exposed children were compared to their unexposed siblings. Reinisch and Karow characterized the children exposed to high levels of progestin as more inner- or self-directed in contrast to those exposed to estrogen who are outer- or other-directed.

A different approach to the issue of endocrines and human behavioral development consists in correlating hormone levels at birth with various behaviors of young children. The initial study was carried out by Jacklin, Maccoby, and Doering (1982), who took blood from the umbilical cord as soon as it was severed and assayed the samples for five hormones. At 6, 9, 12, and 18 months the childrens' reactions to the presentation of various toys were observed. Some of the toys (e.g., a wind-up animal) were known to evoke fear. On the basis of their reactions, each child was assigned a timidity score. For boys, timidity scores were negatively correlated with levels of testosterone and progesterone (the higher their levels, the lower the timidity score) and positively correlated with the estradiol level. No significant correlations were found for females.

A later study (Marcus, Maccoby, Jacklin, & Doering, 1985) correlated hormone levels at birth with mood states throughout the first 2 years of life. Mood states were obtained from written observations made by the mothers. From those reports mood scores were derived by computing the proportion of time the child was in a happy/excited, quiet/calm, or negative mood. The results are similar to those reported for timidity in that statistically significant correlations between behavior and hormone levels are found only for males. The data are summarized in Table 3.5. An additional analysis, providing the "all-hormone" entry in the table, reveals that the relation between hormones and mood derives not from specific effects of a given hormone but from a component the hormones have in common. In other words, higher levels of hormones in general are associated with a happy/excited mood, whereas lower levels of hormones are related to a quiet/calm mood. This generalized effect makes interpretation of the data difficult. "We recognize that this is an anomalous finding from the standpoint of most thinking about biochemical processes and their effects upon behavior. Specific hormones have distinct chemical properties and distinct receptor sites and function in distinct ways in organizing the brain. An 'all-hormone' component does not seem to be biologically meaningful, however statistically valid it may be" (Marcus et al., 1985, p. 338).

Taken alone, the findings to date concerning hormones and human devel-

Table 3.5 Correlations between across-age mood scores and neonatal hormone levels (n = 104: 53 boys, 51 girls)

	Happy/Excited		Quiet/Calm		Negative	
Hormone	Boys	Girls	Boys	Girls	Boys	Girls
Androstenedione	.25***	−.18	−.27*	.24***	.03	−.16
Testosterone	.03	−.07	−.09	.15	.15	−.19
Esterone	.32*	−.11	−.34*	.18	.05	−.18
Estradiol	.19	−.08	−.23***	.11	.08	−.08
Progesterone	.30*	.05	−.36**	.04	.16	−.22
"All-hormone" component	.28*	−.11	−.32*	.18	.10	−.19

*$p \leq .05$.

**$p \leq .01$.

***$p \leq .10$.

Source: Marcus et al. Individual differences in mood in early childhood: Their relations to gender and neonatal sex steroids. *Developmental Psychobiology, 18,* 327–340.

opment are at most suggestive of a role of the endocrine system in the establishment of particular personality characteristics. Because data analyses often involved many comparisons between hormone-exposed and unexposed subjects (Ehrhardt, Meyer-Bahlburg, Feldman, & Ince, 1984; Kester, 1984; Meyer-Bahlburg & Erhardt, 1982; Reinisch & Karow, 1977), a proportion of the few reported statistically reliable differences may have occurred by chance. Furthermore, some of the positive results may have been mediated by the parents' behavior toward their children, rather than by prenatal exposure to hormones. (Most investigators do not mention this possibility.) These problems coupled with the occasional lack of appropriate control groups as well as the difficulties already described with regard to establishing the independent and dependent variables make it difficult to draw overall conclusions from the data. If we consider the data in light of the information derived from nonhuman subjects, however, the case for endocrine involvement in human behavioral development is strengthened. The less than robust findings from humans may be attributable to their greater complexity, which, among other things, is related to a diminished reliance on any single system with respect to the development of behavior.

HORMONES AND NEUROANATOMICAL BRAIN DIMORPHISM

The fact that the endocrine system influences behavioral development implies, of course, that hormones modify the central nervous system. Furthermore, differences between particular neuroanatomical features of the female and male brain should be governed by the endocrine system in a manner similar to the way in which it regulates the development of sexually dimorphic behavior.

Raisman and Field's (1971) discovery of a sex difference in the anatomy of the preoptic area of the rat brain gave impetus to what has become a major focus of inquiry, the influence of hormones on brain development. They found that most neurons from brain regions other than the amygdala make contact with preoptic neurons of the *male brain* by synapsing on a particular portion of the dendrite, the *shaft*. In contrast, preoptic neurons of the *female brain* contain a larger proportion of synapses on dendritic *spines*. As stated by Raisman and Field, "The fact that sexual dimorphism occurs in a part of the brain does not, of course, prove that such dimorphism is related to sexually differentiated functions such as the ability to produce an ovulatory surge of gonadotrophins or sexual behavior. However, the location of the anatomical difference in the preoptic area, which has been shown to be essential for these functions, is persuasive circumstantial evidence" (p. 733). A later experiment established that the sex difference is regulated by hormones (Raisman & Field, 1973); males castrated at birth exhibit a female pattern of synapses on dendritic spines, whereas females given testosterone propionate on day 4 (but not day 16) display a reduction in spine synapses.

In addition to the subtle morphological sex difference reported by Raisman and Field observable only with electron microscopy, Nottebohm and Arnold (1976) reported a gross disparity between the female and male brain that can be seen simply with the aid of a light microscope. Male canaries and zebra finches vocalize more than do females. The brains of males and females were removed, sectioned, and stained so particular brain regions, especially those involved in vocalization, would be discernible. These investigators found that for both species the three vocal control areas are larger in males than in females. Gorski, Gordon, Shryne, and Southam (1978) reported that the medial preoptic nucleus of the male rat is of larger volume than that of the female. Neonatal, in contrast to adult, castration of males leads to reduction of the volume, whereas exposure of the neonatal female to testosterone augments the volume.

Other studies, many more than can be reviewed in detail here, also have shown sex differences in brain and even spinal cord morphology (Breedlove, 1985; Breedlove & Arnold, 1980), differences which in most cases are amenable in a predictable manner to neonatal hormone manipulations. Examples include the ventromedial nucleus of the hypothalamus, which is of a greater volume in males (Matsumoto & Arai, 1983); the medial and central amygdala, having a greater volume in females (Staudt & Dorner, 1976); the hippocampus, which evidences more axonal sprouting in the female (Loy & Milner, 1980); and the arcuate nucleus, which contains more synapses on dendritic spines in the female (Matsumoto & Arai, 1980). Whereas most of the research is performed with rats, sex differences have been reported in many other species including the toad (Schmidt, 1982) and human (Hofman & Swaab, 1989).

Like behavioral development, then, physical development of the central nervous system (CNS) is in part controlled by the endocrine system. Androgen leads to the elaboration of male-typical patterns of behavior as well as to the development of a CNS distinct from that of the female. In the absence of sufficient androgenic stimulation, both behavior and nervous system morphology take a female course. This relation between behavior and morphology makes a good deal of sense; behavioral dimorphisms should be related to CNS dimorphisms.

However, it is not known just what these morphological distinctions between males and females have to do with behavior. What does a difference in volume of medial preoptic neurons mean? Moreover, how does the sexual dimorphism in the proportion of preoptic synapses on dendritic spines and shafts mediate behavioral differences? Answers to these difficult questions are necessary in order for research in the area of hormone–brain–behavior interactions to move beyond the present stage, which is essentially one of cataloging the differences in the CNS of females and males and then confirming that those differences can be altered predictably by early hormonal intervention.

WITHIN-SEX VARIABILITY

Although the disparate hormonal milieux of the male and female lead to the elaboration of a host of behavioral dimorphisms, one must not overlook the fact that differences exist *within a sex* with regard to the display of all sexually dimorphic behaviors. For example, though most males tend to exhibit higher levels of spontaneous fighting behavior than do females, some males fight little, whereas some females are highly aggressive. What is the cause of such variability? Because the development of the propensity to fight is hormonally mediated, is variability in the display of the behavior related to variability in early exposure to hormones? If so, one should be able to account for and thereby predict *individual differences.* Many factors may account for individual variation in hormone-mediated behaviors; three are considered here: temperature, uterine position, and maternal stress.

Temperature

A discovery with potentially far-reaching implications with regard to the genesis of individual differences has been reported by Roffi et al. (1987), who observed a marked effect of ambient temperature on testosterone levels in the newborn. A sharp rise in serum testosterone, seen in male rats about 2 hours after birth, has been implicated in both masculinization and defeminization. In one experiment rats were delivered surgically and the males immediately exposed to an ambient temperature of either 30°, 24°, 21°, or 18°C. Two hours later blood was withdrawn and assayed for testosterone. The data are summarized in Figure 3.8. It is apparent that testosterone levels are low in pups exposed to temperatures of 18° and 21°C.

Another experiment was performed to determine if the lowered testosterone levels seen after cooling can be increased by exposure to a normal temperature. After a 2-hour exposure to a temperature of 18°C, newborn male pups were placed with a lactating female. (The temperature underneath the mother is about 35°C.) Blood was drawn 2, 4, or 6 hours later when the pups were 4, 6, or 8 hours of age, respectively. Cooling for the first 2 hours of life delays the testosterone surge by 2 hours; the peak occurs at 4 hours of age. A third experiment revealed

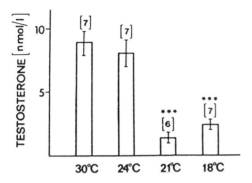

Figure 3.8 Influence of environmental temperature on the serum testosterone levels in neonatal male rats. Animals were delivered by cesarean section on day 22 of gestation and were exposed to an ambient temperature of either 30°, 24°, 21°, or 18°C. Blood was collected 2 hours later for testosterone assay. [*n*] = number of plasma pools assayed. * = significantly different means compared with pups placed at 24°C. (From Roffi et al., "Influence of the environmental temperature on the post-partum testosterone surge in the rat." *Acta Endocrinologica (Copenhagen), 115*, 478–82. © 1987 by *Acta Endocrinologica*. Reprinted by permission.)

that cooling does *not* influence serum testosterone levels in 1-day old rats. Roffi et al. concluded the following:

> Not all mothers warm their litters immediately after parturition. Intervals of one hour or more may separate the time of birth of a newborn and the onset of retrieving, licking, and nesting behaviours which promote pup warming. If the environmental temperature is 21°C or lower, the failure to warm pups could prevent or attenuate the testosterone surge which normally occurs in male rat pups during the first 2 hours after birth. . . . We speculate, however, that at least some of the variability between normal males with respect to their potential for male and female sexual behaviour as adults may be due to environmental variation affecting body temperature during the early postnatal period. (p. 481)

Matuszczyk, Silverin, and Larsson (1990) have in fact reported that male rats subjected to cooling soon after birth take longer to exhibit penile insertion relative to controls. They do not, however, display heightened levels of female sex behavior. It also should be noted that in some nonmammalian species, e.g., turtles and fish, temperature interacts with genotype to determine the sex of the organism (Bull & Vogt, 1979; Conover & Kynard, 1981).

Uterine Position

Pregnancies of many mammalian species almost always involve more than one embryo. Data have revealed that for some of these multibirth (polytocous) species sexual differentiation of the young is in part determined by their position within the uterus relative to other embryos. The relation between development and uterine position was first described by Clemens in 1974. He reported that adult female rats that had been situated in the uterus between two male embryos (referred to as m*F*m females) exhibited higher levels of male sex behavior in response to the administration of androgen treatment than did females that had not been located contiguous to males. (A pregnant rat uterus is illustrated in Figure 3.9.) Also, m*F*m females looked more like males at birth; they had a relatively long space between the anus and genitals, which is typical of males. The data suggested to Clemens that embryonic testicular secretions reach the female fetus, perhaps by diffusing across amniotic membranes. He and his colleagues (Clemens, Gladue, & Coniglio, 1978) verified the proposal by demonstrating that the administration of an antiandrogenic drug blocks the effect of uterine position. Moreover, m*F*m embryonic mice and gerbils have higher amniotic fluid testosterone levels than do females that are not adjacent to a male (Clark, Crews, & Galef, 1991; vom Saal & Bronson, 1980a).

The uterine position phenomenon has since been studied by others using a variety of behavioral measures, and with few exceptions (e.g., Simon & Cologer-Clifford, in press) the data have both verified and extended Clemens' discovery. Gandelman and associates (1977) found that m*F*m female mice fought more quickly following the initiation of testosterone treatment than did females having been located contiguous to no male embryos. (Remember that perinatal exposure of females to exogenously introduced testosterone reduces the duration of androgen stimulation required to induce fighting behavior.) Females

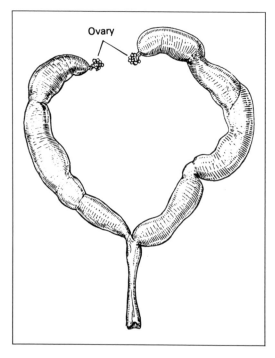

Figure 3.9 Uterus of a pregnant rat.

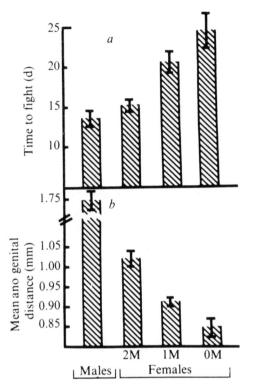

Figure 3.10 Number of days to fight following (A) the start of testosterone exposure of male and female mice and (B) anogenital distance at delivery. Females were located in the uterus either between two male fetuses (2M), next to one male fetus (1M), or contiguous to no male fetuses (0M). All animals were delivered prematurely and gonadectomized at that time (From Gandelman et al., "Contiguity to male foetuses affects morphology and behaviour of female mice." *Nature, 266,* 722–24. © 1977 by Macmillan Magazines. Reprinted by permission.)

contiguous to a single male were intermediate. Moreover, as seen in Figure 3.10, these differences in latency to exhibit male-like fighting behavior were paralleled by anogenital distance measures.

Female mice located between two male embryos also exhibit longer ovulatory cycles, reach puberty later, are less sexually attractive, and are less active than are females that did not reside between males (Kinsley, Miele, Konen, Ghiraldi, & Svare, 1986; McDermott, Gandelman, & Reinisch, 1978; vom Saal & Bronson, 1980b). Furthermore, mFm females exhibit a level of active avoidance responding similar to that found in males (Hauser & Gandelman, 1983). These data are consonant with the idea that androgen from embryonic males is conveyed in some manner to the female. However, males too are affected by uterine position. Those situated between two female embryos later exhibit reduced levels of parental behavior and a concomitant increase in infanticidal (pup-killing) behavior (vom Saal, 1983b). They also show enhanced amounts of sexual behavior and lower levels of aggression (vom Saal et al., 1983).

Whereas most investigators agree that the sexual differentiation of a given embryo may be influenced by other embryos, or "wombmates" as Clemens called them, there is disagreement as to the mechanism through which the effect is mediated. Some investigators, especially those using mice as subjects (vom Saal, 1983a), have argued that the mechanism is passive diffusion of gonadal secretions across adjacent amniotic membranes. Others have asserted, based on information gathered from rats, that gonadal secretions are transmitted not passively through amniotic diffusion but actively through the maternal circulatory system (Houtsmuller & Slob, 1990; Meisel & Ward, 1981; Richmond & Sachs, 1984). For the guinea pig, both diffusion and the circulatory system may be involved (Gandelman, 1986b). The mechanism responsible for the transmission of gonadal secretions from one embryo to another seems to be species-dependent.

Does the presence of a male embryo have any bearing on sexual differentiation of the human female? The fetal human testis begins to produce testosterone between days 70 and 90 of gestation, causing testosterone levels to rise in the amniotic fluid surrounding the male (Carson et al., 1982). This augmented amniotic testosterone coupled with the significant rise in maternal serum testosterone levels normally found during pregnancy (Zondek & Zondek, 1979) may cause female members of male–female twin sets to develop in a somewhat masculine direction. This intriguing possibility has yet to be explored.

Prenatal Stress

Because the pregnant animal's internal environment constitutes much of the embryo's external environment, it is reasonable to conjecture that major perturbations of the former may deleteriously affect development. The relation of maternal stress, known also as prenatal stress, to the later expression of sexually dimorphic behavior was first considered by Ward (1972). She applied stress to pregnant rats by placing them into small plastic tubes illuminated with bright and hot light on days 14 through 21 (the last week) of gestation. The manipulation produced piloerection, urination, and defecation—all indicators of stress. Following delivery the infants remained with their own mothers, although it would have been a better procedure to have fostered them (as well as the offspring of the nonstressed controls) to recently parturient, undisturbed mothers. That would have ruled out the possibility that an effect observed in the offspring of stressed females was mediated *postnatally* by stress-induced alteration of maternal behavior, milk composition, or the like (Moore & Power, 1986). In any event, when tested at about 3 months of age, a reduction was seen in the percentage of males that copulated: 73% of the controls versus 26% of the experimental animals. After these copulation tests, the males were castrated, injected with estrogen and progesterone, and placed with a sexually experienced male. Male offspring of stressed mothers exhibited more than three times more lordotic responses[2] than did control males. Males born of stressed females thus displayed a decrement in male and an increment in female sex behavior; they were demasculinized and feminized. Early postnatal stress was totally without effect.

---

[2]The *lordotic response,* exhibited by sexually receptive females of various species, consists in arching the back while concomitantly raising the rump. The posture facilitates intromission.

Later work by Ward and Weisz (1980, 1984) was designed to specify the mechanism through which maternal stress exerts its influence. They found that levels of testosterone differ between female and male embryos after day 17 of gestation. Between days 17 and 18 the males, unlike females, exhibit a precipitous elevation of testosterone that lasts 2 days. Testosterone levels then fall to a point only a bit higher than those of the female. This pattern of embryonic testosterone secretion is markedly altered as a consequence of maternal stress. Males of stressed mothers exhibit the rise in testosterone levels on day 17 followed by a decline on days 18 and 19. Therefore when testosterone levels are supposed to be low, they are high; and when they are expected to be high (day 18), they are low. Other data show that maternal stress causes this altered pattern of hormone secretion by directly interfering with testicular production of testosterone (Orth, Weisz, Ward, & Ward, 1983).

After publication of Ward's (1972) seminal experiment, many reports have appeared attesting to the influence of maternal stress (induced by social crowding, presentation of a stimulus that had been paired with pain, or malnutrition, as well as restraint and light plus heat) on various aspects of male behavior. Briefly summarizing the research, prenatal stress leads to a reduction of the following by males: killing of young (vom Saal, 1983b [mice]), intermale fighting (Kinsley & Svare, 1986 [mice]), asymmetries in the thickness of cerebral cortex (Fleming, Anderson, Rhees, Klinghorn, & Bakaitis, 1986 [rats], and latencies to exhibit maternal-like behavior (Kinsley & Bridges, 1988 [rats]. Moreover, it demasculinizes anatomically dimorphic regions of the preoptic area of rat brain (Anderson, Rhees, & Fleming, 1985). Maternal stress also affects the female. It lengthens anogenital distance, retards vaginal opening, causes longer estrous cycles, and augments sexual receptivity in mice (Politch & Herrenkohl, 1984; Zielinski, Vandenbergh, & Montano, 1991).

Research in the area of maternal stress is not without controversy, however. It is debatable as to whether maternal stress affects reproduction in the female rat (Beckhardt & Ward, 1982; Herrenkohl & Scott, 1984) and whether it reduces or augments postpartum aggressive behavior of lactating mice (Kinsley & Svare, 1988; Politch & Herrenkohl, 1979). Furthermore, the longevity of the stress-produced deficits are questionable. Masterpasqua, Chapman, and Lore (1976) reported that although maternal stress does lower levels of copulatory behavior in male rats as reported by Ward, it does so only when sex behavior is assessed in a series of *brief* tests. Of 41 prenatally stressed male rats, 39 successfully impregnated females when left with them continuously for 18 days.

Dörner and colleagues (1980, 1983) attempted to extend the findings on maternal stress from animals to man by asking if stress is related to male homosexuality. Because German and later East German authorities required that homosexuals seeking treatment for sexually transmitted disease be registered by the attending physician, Dörner et al. (1980) were able to obtain the identity and birth dates of homosexuals born between the years 1932 and 1953. They found that more of them were born during World War II and the immediate postwar period (1941 to 1947) than were born prior to and after that time, suggesting "a possible relationship between prenatal stress due to bomb attacks and other stressful war or early post-war events and sexual differentiation of the foetal brain" (p. 368).

In a second study (Dörner et al., 1983) heterosexual, bisexual, and homosexual men who were born prior to, during, and subsequent to the war were asked to consult their parents about stressful events that may have befallen their mothers during pregnancy. The reported stressful events were judged as being severe (e.g., father died during midpregnancy, mother raped at midpregnancy, father in fighting zone) or moderate (e.g., undesired pregnancy, bombardments during pregnancy, divorced during pregnancy). The data are presented in Figure 3.11. It is obvious that heterosexuals reported few prenatal stressful events, whereas the incidence of stressful events involving the mothers of homosexuals was high and that for bisexuals intermediate. The authors concluded that:

> prenatal stress may be regarded as a risk factor for the aetiogenesis of genuine, i.e., inborn bi- and homosexuality in men. . . . Moreover, in more than 50% of male homosexuals interviewed in this study prenatal stressful events were found which were based either on influences of war (in 33%) or on undesired pregnancies (in 23%). These findings indicate that prevention of war and undesired pregnancies may render possible a partial prevention of the development of sexual deviations. (pp. 86–87)

A report by Ellis, Ames, Peckham, and Burke (1988) presented similar findings. A total of 283 mothers (ranging in age from 36 to 77 years) and their offspring (ages 19 to 50 years) were asked to complete questionaires. Mothers were requested, in part, to provide information about the incidence, severity, and timing of stress that may have occurred during pregnancy. Their children were asked about their sexual orientation. The major finding was that, on average,

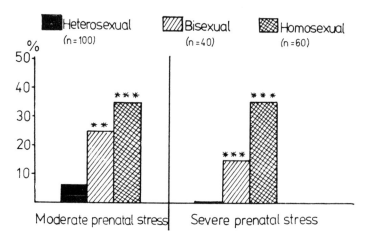

Figure 3.11 Percentage of prenatal stress in heterosexual, bisexual, and homosexual men. (Compared to heterosexual men: ** $p < .01$; *** $p < .001$.) (From Dörner et al., "Stressful events in prenatal life of bi- and homosexual men." *Endokrinologie, 81, 83–87.* © 1983 by Experimental Clinical Endocrinology. Reprinted by permission.)

stress experienced during the second trimester by mothers of homosexual males was nearly twice as severe as that reported by the mothers of heterosexuals. Mothers of bisexual males produced intermediate stress severity scores. Mothers of hetero- and homosexual females did not differ with regard to any aspect of prenatal stress.

This work on maternal stress and human sexual differentiation depends for data on the remembrances of past events. In the Ellis et al. (1988) study the average recall spanned a period of 25 years. Given the vagaries of memory, the use of such a *retrospective* technique is risky. Moreover, it is possible that differences in the reports of stress among mothers of homosexual, bisexual, and heterosexual men as described by Dörner et al. (1983) may be an artifact. Suppose, for example, that the homosexual and bisexual subjects took the task of interviewing their parents about stressful events more seriously than did the heterosexuals, thereby probing more persistently. Alternatively, perhaps the parents of homosexuals and bisexuals, attempting to "explain" the sexual orientation of their sons, are more apt to report unusual events, real or imagined, surrounding their pregnancies. In any event, although the work described above is certainly interesting and provocative, research pertaining to maternal stress and human sexuality must include *prospective* research, i.e., studies that actually follow pregnant women, documenting any stressful challenges and then observing the psychosexual development of their offspring.

CONCLUDING COMMENTS

A vast amount of information showing a relation between hormones and behavioral development has appeared since the 1970s. This information explosion is due, in great measure, to the establishment of techniques that permit precise quantification of both hormones and hormone-related structures such as intracellular receptor complexes. It now is known that hormones enter certain neurons, are bound to particular receptors, and are transported into cell nuclei where they ostensibly affect protein synthesis. However, the link between the molecular biology of the endocrine system and the display of behavior awaits explication. Precisely how is an alteration in protein synthesis translated into a change in behavior? Until such questions are answered, we cannot understand why animals exposed to relatively high levels of androgen during early development later choose a female as a sexual partner and why those spared from early androgen exposure show an enhanced preference for the taste of salt.

REFERENCES

Abbott, D. B., and Hearn, J. P. (1979). The effect of neonatal exposure to testosterone on the development of behavior in female marmoset monkeys. In *Sex, hormones and behavior: CIBA Foundation symposium 62* (pp. 346–65). New York: Excerpta Medica.

Anderson, D. K., Rhees, R. W., and Fleming, D. E. (1985). Effects of prenatal stress on differentiation of the sexually dimorphic nucleus of the preoptic area (SDN-POA) of the rat brain. *Brain Research, 332,* 113–18.

Andrew, R. J., Mench, J., and Rainey, C. (1982). Right-left asymmetry of response to visual stimuli in the domestic chick. In D. J. Ingle, M. A. Goodale, and R. J. W. Mansfield (Eds.), *Analysis of visual behaviour* (pp. 197–209). Cambridge, MA: MIT Press.

Baker, S. W. (1980). Psychosexual differentiation in the human. *Biology of Reproduction, 22,* 61–72.

Bardin, C. W., Bullock, L., and Blackburn, R. (1971). Testosterone metabolism in the androgen-insensitive rat: A model for testicular feminization. In D. Bergsma (Ed.), *The endocrine system,* vol. 7 (pp. 185–92). Baltimore: Williams & Wilkins.

Beatty, W. W., and Beatty, P. A. (1970). Hormonal determinants of sex differences in avoidance behavior and reactivity to electric shock in the rat. *Journal of Comparative and Physiological Psychology, 73,* 446–55.

Beckhardt, S., and Ward, I. L. (1982). Reproductive functioning in the prenatally stressed female rat. *Developmental Psychobiology, 16,* 111–18.

Beeman, E. A. (1947). The effect of male hormone on aggressive behavior in mice. *Physiological Zoology, 20,* 373–405.

Berthold, A. A. (1849). Transplantation der Hoden. *Archives of Anatomy and Physiology, 16,* 42–46.

Blizzard, D. A., Lippman, H. R., and Chen, J. J. (1975). Sex differences in openfield behavior in the rat: The inductive and activational role of gonadal hormones. *Physiology and Behavior, 14,* 601–08.

Bloch, E. (1979). Fetal gonadal endocrine activity and reproductive tract differentiation. *Contributions to Gynecology and Obstetrics, 5,* 21–37.

Breedlove, S. M. (1985). Hormonal control of the anatomical specificity of motoneuron-to-muscle innervation in rats. *Science, 277,* 1357–59.

Breedlove, S. M., and Arnold, A. P. (1980). Hormone accumulation in a sexually dimorphic motor nucleus of the rat spinal cord. *Science, 210,* 564–66.

Broadhurst, P. L. (1958). Determinants of emotionality in the rat: III. Strain differences. *Journal of Comparative and Physiological Psychology, 51,* 51–59.

Broida, J., and Svare, B. (1984). Sex differences in the activity of mice: Modulation by postnatal gonadal hormones. *Hormones and Behavior, 18,* 65–78.

Bull, J. J., and Vogt, R. C. (1979). Temperature-dependent sex determination in turtles. *Science, 206,* 1186–188.

Burns, R. K. (1961). Role of hormones in the differentiation of sex. In *Sex and internal secretions,* vol. 1 (pp. 76–158). Baltimore: Williams & Wilkins.

Carter, C. S., Clemens, L. G., and Hoekema, D. J. (1972). Neonatal androgen and adult sexual behavior in the golden hamster. *Physiology and Behavior, 9,* 89–95.

Carson, D. J., Okuno, A., Lee, P. A., Stetten, G., Didolkar, S. M., and Migeon, C. J. (1982). Amniotic fluid steroid levels. *American Journal of Diseases of Childhood, 136,* 218–22.

Clark, G., and Birch, H. G. (1945). Hormonal modifications of social behavior; the effect of sex-hormone administration on the social status of a male-castrate chimpanzee. *Psychosomatic Medicine, 7,* 321–29.

Clark, M. M., Crewes, D., and Galif, B. G. (1991). Concentrations of sex steroid hormones in pregnant and fetal Mongolian gerbils. *Physiology and Behavior, 49,* 239–43.

Clemens, L. G. (1974). Neurohormonal control of male sexual behavior. In W. Montagna and W. A. Sadler (Eds.), *Reproductive behavior* (pp. 23–53). New York: Plenum Press.

Clemens, L. G., Gladue, B. A., and Coniglio, L. P. (1978). Prenatal endogenous influences on masculine sexual behavior and genital morphology in male and female rats. *Hormones and Behavior, 20,* 40–53.

Conover, D. O., and Kynard, B. E. (1981). Environmental sex determination: Interaction of temperature and genotype in a fish. *Science, 213,* 577–79.

Dantchakoff, V. (1938a). Role des hormones dans la manifestation des instincts sexuels. *Comptes Rendus Academie des Sciences [D] (Paris), 206,* 945–47.

Dantchakoff, V. (1938b). Sur les effects de l'hormone male dans une jeune cobaye femelle traite' depuis un state embryonnaire (inversions sexcielles). *Comptes Rendus Societe de Biologie (Paris), 127,* 1255–268.

Dawson, J. L. M., Cheung, Y. M., and Lau, R. T. S. (1975). Developmental effects of neonatal sex hormones on spatial and activity skills in the white rat. *Biological Psychology, 3,* 213–29.

Denenberg, V. H., and Morton, J. R. C. (1962). Effects of environmental complexity and social groupings upon modification of emotional behavior. *Journal of Comparative and Physiological Psychology, 55,* 242–46.

Denenberg, V. H., Rosen, G. D., Hofmann, M., Gall, J., Stockler, J., and Yutzey, D. A. (1982). Neonatal postural asymmetry and sex differences in the rat. *Developmental Brain Research, 2,* 417–19.

Denti, A., and Negroni, J. A. (1975). Activity and learning in neonatally hormone treated rats. *Acta Physiologica Latino Americana, 25,* 99–106.

Dohler, K. D., Hancke, J. L., Srivastava, S. S., Hofmann, C., Shryne, J. E., and Gorski, R. A. (1984). Participation of estrogens in female sexual differentiation of the brain; neuroanatomical, neuroendocrine and behavioral evidence. *Progress in Brain Research, 61,* 99–117.

Donahoe, P. K., Budzik, G. P., Trelstad, R., Mudgett-Hunter, M., Fuller, M., Hutson, J. M., Ikawa, H., Hayashi, A., and MacLaughlin, D. (1982). *Recent Progress in Hormone Research, 38,* 279–330.

Dörner, G., Geier, Th., Ahrens, L., Krell, L., Munx, G., Sieler, H., Kittner, E., and Muller, H. (1980). Prenatal stress as possible aetiogenetic factor of homosexuality in human males. *Endokrinologie, 75,* 365–68.

Dörner, G., Schenk, B., Schmiedel, B., and Ahrens, L. (1983). Stressful events in prenatal life of bi- and homosexual men. *Endokrinologie, 81,* 83–87.

Dunlop, J. L., Gerall, A. A., and Carlton, S. F. (1978). Evaluation of prenatal androgen and ovarian secretions on receptivity in female and male rats. *Journal of Comparative and Physiological Psychology, 92,* 280–88.

Edwards, D. A. (1968). Fighting by neonatally androgenized females. *Science, 161,* 1027–28.

Edwards, D. A.,(1969). Early androgen stimulation and aggressive behavior in male and female mice. *Physiology and Behavior, 4,* 333–38.

Edwards, D. A., and Burge, K. G. (1971). Early hormone treatment and male and female sexual behavior in mice. *Hormones and Behavior, 2,* 49–58.

Edwards, D. A., and Herndon, J. (1970). Neonatal estrogen stimulation and aggressive behavior in female mice. *Physiology and Behavior, 5,* 993–95.

Ehrhardt, A. A., and Baker, S. W. (1977). Males and females with congenital adrenal hyperplasia: A family study of intelligence and gender-related behavior. In P. A. Lee, L. P. Plotnick, A. A. Kowarski, and C. J. Migeon (Eds.), *Congenital adrenal hyperplasia* (pp. 447–61). Baltimore: University Park Press.

Ehrhardt, A. A., and Money, J. (1967). Progestin-induced hermaphroditism: IQ and psychosexual identity in a study of ten girls. *Journal of Sex Research, 3,* 83–100.

Ehrhardt, A. A., Epstein, R., and Money, J. (1968). Fetal androgens and female gender identity in the early-treated adrenogenital syndrome. *Johns Hopkins Medical Journal, 123,* 160–67.

Ehrhardt, A. A., Grisanti, G. C., and Meyer-Bahlburg, H. F. L. (1977). Prenatal effects of sex hormones on human male behavior: Medroxyprogesterone acetate (MPA). *Psychoneuroendocrinology, 2,* 383–90.

Ehrhardt, A. A., Meyer-Bahlburg, F. H. L., Feldman, J. F., and Ince, S. E. (1984). Sex-dimorphic behavior in childhood subsequent to prenatal exposure to exogenous progestogens and estrogens. *Archives of Sexual Behavior, 13,* 457–77.

Ellis, L., Ames, M. A., Peckham, W., and Burke, D. (1988). Sexual orientation of human offspring may be altered by severe maternal stress during pregnancy. *Journal of Sex Research, 25,* 152–57.

Feder, H. (1981). Hormonal actions on the sexual differentiation of the genitalia and the gonadotrophin-regulating systems. In N. T. Adler (Ed.), *Neuroendocrinology of reproduction* (pp. 89–126). New York: Plenum Press.

Fleming, D. E., Anderson, R. H., Rhees, R. W., Klinghorn, E., and Bakaitis, J. (1986). Effects of prenatal stress on sexually dimorphic asymmetries in the cerebral cortex of the male rat. *Brain Research Bulletin, 16,* 395–98.

Forbes, R. T. (1949). A. A. Berthold and the first endocrine experiment: Some speculation as to its origin. *Bulletin of the History of Medicine, 23,* 263–67.

Galaburda, A. M., Corsiglia, J., Rosen, G. D., and Sherman, G. F. (1987). Planum temporale asymmetry, reappraisal since Geshwind and Levitsky. *Neuropsychologia, 25,* 853–68.

Gandelman, R. (1980). Gonadal hormones and the induction of intraspecific fighting in mice. *Neuroscience and Biobehavioral Reviews, 4,* 133–40.

Gandelman, R. (1984). Relative contributions of aggression and reproduction to behavioral endocrinology. *Aggressive Behavior, 10,* 123–33.

Gandelman, R. (1986a). Behavioral teratogenicity of gonadal and adrenal steroids. In E. P. Riley and C. V. Vithees (Eds.), *Handbook of behavioral teratology* (pp. 487–507). New York: Plenum Press.

Gandelman, R. (1986b). Uterine position and the activation of male sexual activity in testosterone propionate-treated female guinea pigs. *Hormones and Behavior, 20,* 287–93.

Gandelman, R., vom Saal, F. S., and Reinisch, J. M. (1977). Contiguity to male foetuses affects morphology and behavior of female mice. *Nature, 266,* 722–24.

Gentry, R. T., and Wade, G. N. (1976). Sex differences in sensitivity of food intake, body weight and running-wheel activity to ovarian steroids in rats. *Journal of Comparative and Physiological Psychology, 90,* 755–64.

Gerall, A. A. (1967). Effects of early postnatal androgen and estrogen injections on the estrous activity cycles and mating behavior of rats. *Anatomical Record, 157,* 97–104.

Gerall, A. A., Dunlop, J. L., and Hendricks, S. E. (1972). Effect of ovarian secretions on female behavioral potentiality in the rat. *Journal of Comparative and Physiological Psychology, 82,* 449–65.

Gerall, A. A., Hendricks, S. E., Johnson, L. L., and Bounds, T. W. (1967). Effects of early castration in male rats on adult sexual behavior. *Journal of Comparative and Physiological Psychology, 64,* 206–12.

Geshwind, N., and Behan, P. (1982). Left-handedness: Association with immune disease, migraine, and developmental learning disorder. *Proceedings of the National Academy of Science of the United States of America, 79,* 5097–100.

Glick, S. D., Jerussi, T. P., and Zimmerberg, B. (1977). Behavioral and neuropharmacological correlates of nigrostriatal asymmetry in rat. In S. Harnod, R. Doty, L. Gold-stein, L. Jaynes, and G. Krauthamer (Eds.), *Lateralization in the nervous system* (pp. 216–49). Orlando, FL: Academic Press.

Goldman, A. S., Shapiro, B. S., and Neumann, F. (1976). Role of testosterone and its metabolites in the differentiation of the mammary gland in rats. *Endocrinology, 99,* 1490–495.

Gorski, R. A., and Barraclough, C. A. (1963). Effect of low doses of androgen on the dif-ferentiation of hypothalamic regulatory control of ovulation in the rat. *Endocri-nology, 73,* 210–16.

Gorski, R. A., Gordon, J. H., Shryne, J. E., and Southam, A. M. (1978). Evidence for a morphological sex difference within the medial preoptic area of the rat brain. *Brain Research, 148,* 333–46.

Goy, R. (1970). Early hormonal influences on the development of sexual and sex-related behavior. In T. Melrechuck and G. Adelman (Eds.), *The neurosciences second study program* (pp. 165–83). New York: Rockefeller University Press.

Goy, R. W., Bridson, W. E., and Young, W. C. (1964). Period of maximal susceptibility of the prenatal guinea pig to masculinizing actions of testosterone propionate. *Journal of Comparative and Physiological Psychology, 57,* 166–74.

Goy, R. W., and Phoenix, C. H. (1971). The effects of testosterone propionate adminis-tered before birth on the development of behavior in genetic female rhesus mon-keys. In C. S. Sawyer and R. Gorski (Eds.), *Steroid hormones and brain function* (pp. 193–202). Berkeley: University of California Press.

Grady, K. L., Phoenix, C. H., and Young, W. C. (1965). Role of the developing rat testis in differentiation of the neural tissues mediating mating behavior. *Journal of Com-parative and Physiological Psychology, 59,* 176–82.

Grumbach, M. M., and Van Wyk, J. J. (1974). Disorders of sex differentiation. In R. H. Williams (Ed.), *Textbook of Endocrinology* (pp. 423–501). Philadelphia: Saun-ders.

Harnod, S., Doty, R., Goldstein, L., Jaynes, L., and Krauthamer, G. (Eds.). *Lateralization in the nervous system.* Orlando, FL: Academic Press, 1977.

Harris, G. W., and Jacobsohn, D. (1952). Functional grafts of the anterior pituitary. *Pro-ceedings of the Royal Society of London, 139,* 263–69.

Hauser, H., and Gandelman, R. (1983). In utero contiguity to males affects levels of avoid-ance responding in adult female mice. *Science, 220,* 437–38.

Hayashi, S., and Gorski, R. A. (1974). Critical exposure time for androgenization by intra-cranial crystals of testosterone propionate in neonatal female rats. *Endocrinology, 94,* 1161–169.

Hendricks, S. E., and Duffy, J. A. (1974). Ovarian influence on the development of sexual behavior in neonatally androgenized rats. *Developmental Psychobiology, 7,* 297–303.

Herrenkohl, L. R., and Scott, S. (1984). Prenatal stress and postnatal androgen: Effects on reproduction in female rats. *Experientia, 40,* 101–3.

Herschler, M. S., and Fechheimer, N. S. (1967). The role of sex chromosome chimerism in altering sexual development of mammals. *Cytogenetics, 6,* 204–11.

Hines, M. (1982). Prenatal gonadal hormones and sex differences in human behavior. *Psychological Bulletin, 92,* 56–80.

Hines, M., and Goy, R. W. (1985). Estrogens before birth and development of sex-related reproductive traits in the female guinea pig. *Hormones and Behavior, 19,* 331–47.

Hitchcock, F. A. (1925). Studies in vigor: V. The comparative activity of male and female albino rats. *American Journal of Physiology, 75,* 205–10.

Hofman, M. A., and Swaab, D. F. (1989). The sexually dimorphic nucleus of the preoptic area in the human brain: a comparative morphometric study. *Journal of Anatomy, 164,* 55–72.

Houtsmuller, E. J., and Slob, A. K. (1990). Masculinization and defeminization of female rats by males located caudally in the uterus. *Physiology and Behavior, 48,* 238–43.

Howard, K. J., Rogers, L. J., and Boura, A. L. A. (1980). Functional lateralisation of the chick forebrain revealed by use of intracranial glutamate. *Brain Research, 188,* 369–82.

Jacklin, C. N., Maccoby, E. E., and Doering, C. H. (1982). Neonatal sex-steroid hormones and timidity in 6–18-month old boys and girls. *Developmental Psychobiology, 16,* 163–68.

Josso, N., Picard, J-Y., and Tran, D. (1977). The antimüllerian hormone. *Recent Progress in Hormone Research, 33,* 117–67.

Jost, A. (1953). Problems of fetal endocrinology: The gonadal and hypophyseal hormones. *Recent Progress in Hormone Research, 8,* 379–418.

Jost, A., Chodkiewicz, M., and Mauleon, P. (1963). Intersexualite du foetus de veau produite par des androgenes comparaison entre l'hormone foetale responsable du freemartinisme et l'hormone testiculaire adulte. *Comptes Rendus Acadamie des Sciences [D] (Paris), 256,* 274–79.

Keller, K., and Tandler, J. (1916). Uber des Verhalten der Eihaute bei der Zwillingsstrachtigkeit des Rindes: Untersuchungen uber die Enstenhungsursache der geschlechtlichen Unterentwicklung von weiblichen Zwillingskalbern, welche neben einem mannlichen Kalbe zur Entwicklung gelangen. *Wien Teirartz Wochenschraft, 3,* 513–26.

Kester, P. A. (1984). Effects of prenatally administered 17α-hydroxyprogesterone caproate on adolescent males. *Archives of Sexual Behavior, 13,* 441–55.

Kinsley, C. H., and Bridges, R. S. (1988). Prenatal stress and maternal behavior in intact virgin rats: Response latencies are decreased in males and increased in females. *Hormones and Behavior, 22,* 76–89.

Kinsley, C., and Svare, B. (1986). Prenatal stress reduces intermale aggression in mice. *Physiology and Behavior, 36,* 783–86.

Kinsley, C., and Svare, B. (1988). Prenatal stress alters maternal aggression in mice. *Physiology and Behavior, 42,* 7–13.

Kinsley, C., Miele, J., Konen, C., Ghiraldi, L., and Svare, B. Intrauterine contiguity influences regulatory activity in adult female and male mice. *Hormones and Behavior, 20,* 7–12.

Krecek, J. (1973). Sex differences in salt taste: The effect of testosterone. *Physiology and Behavior, 10,* 683–88.

Krecek, J., Novakova, V., and Stilbral, K. (1972). Sex differences in the taste preference for a salt solution in the rat. *Physiology and Behavior, 8,* 183–88.

Lillie, F. R. (1916). The theory of the free-martin. *Science, 43,* 611–13.

Lillie, F. R. (1917). The free-martin: a study of the action of sex hormones in the foetal life of cattle. *Journal of Experimental Zoology, 23,* 371–452.

Lisk, R. D. (1980). Masculinized female hamsters do not require steroid treatment when adult for activation of the male copulatory response. *Psychoneuroendocrinology, 5,* 305–17.

Loy, R., and Milner, T. A. (1980). Sexual dimorphism in extent of axonal sprouting in rat hippocampus. *Science, 208,* 1282–283.

Manning, A., and McGill, T. E. (1974). Neonatal androgen and sexual behavior in female house mice. *Hormones and Behavior, 5,* 19–31.

Marcus, J., Maccoby, E. E., Jacklin, C. N., and Doering, C. H. (1985). Individual differences in mood in early childhood: Their relations to gender and neonatal sex steroids. *Developmental Psychobiology, 18,* 327–40.

Martinez, C., and Bittner, J. J. (1956). A non-hypophyseal sex difference in estrous behaviour of mice bearing pituitary grafts. *Proceedings of the Society for Experimental Biology and Medicine, 91,* 506–09.

Masterpasqua, F., Chapman, R. H., and Lore, R. L. (1976). The effects of prenatal psychological stress on the sexual behavior and reactivity of male rats. *Developmental Psychobiology, 9,* 403–11.

Matsumoto, A., and Arai, Y. (1980). Sexual dimorphism in "wiring pattern" in the hypothalamic arcuate nucleus and its modification by neonatal hormonal environment. *Brain Research, 190,* 238–42.

Matsumoto, A., and Arai, Y. (1983). Sex differences in volume of the ventromedial nucleus of the hypothalamus in the rat. *Endocrinologica Japonica, 30,* 277–80.

Matuszczyk, J. V., Silverin, B., and Larsson, K. (1990). Influence of environmental events immediately after birth on postnatal testosterone secretion and adult sexual behavior in the male rat. *Hormones and Behavior, 24,* 450–58.

McDermott, N. J., Gandelman, R., and Reinisch, J. M. (1978). Contiguity to male fetuses influences ano-genital distance and time of vaginal opening in mice. *Physiology and Behavior, 20,* 661–63.

McEwen, B. S., Lieberburg, I., Chaptal, C., and Krey, L. C. (1977). Aromatization: Important for sexual differentiation of the neonatal rat brain. *Hormones and Behavior, 9,* 249–63.

Meisel, R. L., and Ward, I. L. (1981). Fetal female rats are masculinized by male littermates located caudally in the uterus. *Science, 213,* 239–42.

Meyer-Bahlburg, H. F. L., and Ehrhardt, A. A. (1982). Prenatal sex hormones and human aggression: A review, and new data on progestogen effects. *Aggressive Behavior, 8,* 39–62.

Money, J., and Mathews, D. (1982). Prenatal exposure to virilizing progestins: An adult follow-up study on twelve women. *Archives of Sexual Behavior, 11,* 73–79.

Money, J., Schwartz, M., and Lewis, V. G. (1984). Adult erotosexual status and fetal hormonal masculinization and demasculinization: 46,XX congenital virilizing adrenal hyperplasia and 46,XY androgen-insensitivity syndrome compared. *Psychoneuroendocrinology, 9,* 405–14.

Moore, C. L., and Power, K. L. (1986). Prenatal stress affects mother–young interaction in Norway rats. *Developmental Psychobiology, 19,* 235–45.

Nadler, R. D. (1972). Intrahypothalamic exploration of androgen-sensitive brain loci in neonatal female rats. *Transactions of the New York Academy of Sciences, 34,* 572–81.

Nadler, R. D. (1973). Further evidence on the intrahypothalamic locus for androgenization of female rats. *Neuroendocrinology, 12,* 110–16.

Nathanielsz, P. W. (1976). *Fetal Endocrinology: An Experimental Approach.* Amsterdam: Elsevier/North Holland.

Nottebohm, F. (1977). Asymmetries in neural control of vocalisation in the canary. In S. Harnod, R. Doty, L. Goldstein, L. Jaynes, and G. Krauthamer (Eds.), *Lateralization in the nervous system* (pp. 23–44). Orlando, FL: Academic Press.

Nottebohm, F., and Arnold, A. P. (1976). Sexual dimorphism in vocal control areas of the songbird brain. *Science, 194,* 211–13.

Olioff, M., and Stewart, J. (1978). Sex differences in the play behavior of prepubescent rats. *Physiology and Behavior, 20,* 113–15.

Orth, J. M., Weisz, J., Ward, O. B., and Ward, I. L. (1983). Environmental stress alters Δ^5-3β hydroxysteroid dehydrogenase activity in the Leydig cells of fetal rats: A quantitative cytochemical study. *Biology of Reproduction, 28,* 625–31.

Payne, A. P. (1976). A comparison of the effects of neonatally administered testosterone, testosterone propionate and dihydrotestosterone on aggressive and sexual behavior in the female golden hamster. *Journal of Endocrinology, 69,* 23–31.

Pfeiffer, C. A. (1936). Sexual differences of the hypophysis and their determination by the gonads. *American Journal of Anatomy, 58,* 195–225.

Phoenix, C. H., Goy, R. W., Gerall, A. A., and Young, W. C. (1959). Organizing action of prenatally administered testosterone propionate on the tissues mediating mating behavior in the female guinea pig. *Endocrinology, 65,* 369–82.

Politch, J. A., and Herrenkohl, L. R. (1979). Prenatal stress reduces maternal aggression by mice offspring. *Physiology and Behavior, 23,* 415–18.

Politch, J. A., and Herrenkohl, L. R. (1984). Effects of prenatal stress on reproduction in male and female mice. *Physiology and Behavior, 32,* 95–99.

Pomerantz, S. M., Goy, R. W., and Roy, M. M. (1986). Expression of male-typical behavior in adult female pseudohermaphroditic rhesus: Comparisons with normal males and females. *Hormones and Behavior, 20,* 483–500.

Price, D. (1970). In vitro studies on differentiation of the reproductive tract. *Philosophical Transactions of the Royal Society of London (Biology), 259,* 309–36.

Price, D. (1972). Mammalian conception, sex differentiation, and hermaphroditism as viewed in historical perspective. *American Zoologist, 12,* 179–91.

Raisman, G., and Field, P. M. (1971). Sexual dimorphism in the preoptic area of the rat. *Science, 173,* 731–33.

Raisman, G., and Field, P. M. (1973). Sexual dimorphism in the neuropil of the preoptic area of the rat and its dependence on neonatal androgen. *Brain Research, 54,* 1–29.

Reddy, V. R., Naftolin, F., and Ryan, K. J. (1974). Conversion of androstenedione to estrone by neural tissues from fetal and neonatal rats. *Endocrinology, 94,* 117–21.

Reinisch, J. M. (1981). Prenatal exposure to synthetic progestins increases potential for aggression in humans. *Science, 211,* 1171–173.

Reinisch, J. M., and Karow, G. K. (1977). Prenatal exposure to synthetic progestins and estrogens: Effects on human development. *Archives of Sexual Behavior, 6,* 257–86.

Richmond, G., and Sachs, B. D. (1984). Further evidence for masculinization of female rats by males located caudally in utero. *Hormones and Behavior, 18,* 484–90.

Roffi, J., Chami, F., Corbier, P., and Edwards, D. A. (1987). Influence of the environmental temperature on the post-partum testosterone surge in the rat. *Acta Endocrinologica (Copenhagen), 115,* 478–82.

Rogers, L. J., and Anson, J. M. (1979). Lateralisation of function in the chicken forebrain. *Pharmacology, Biochemistry and Behavior, 10,* 679–86.

Rosen, G. D., Berrebi, A. S., Yutzey, D. A., and Denenberg, V. H. (1983). Prenatal testosterone causes shifts of asymmetry in neonatal tail posture of the rat. *Developmental Brain Research, 9,* 99–101.

Schmidt, R. S. (1982). Masculinization of toad pretrigeminal nucleus by androgens. *Brain Research, 244,* 190–92.

Scouten, C. W., Grotelueschen, L. K., and Beatty, W. W. (1975). Androgens and the organization of sex differences in active avoidance behavior in the rat. *Journal of Comparative and Physiological Psychology, 88,* 264–70.

Shapiro, B. H., and Goldman, A. S. (1973). Feminine saccharin preference in the genetically androgen insensitive male rat pseudohermaphrodite. *Hormones and Behavior, 4,* 371–75.

Short, R. V. (1970). The bovine freemartin: a new look at an old problem. *Philosophical Transactions of the Royal Society of London (Biology), 259,* 141–47.

Short, R. V. (1974). Sexual differences of the brain of the sheep. In M. G. Forest and J. Bertrand (Eds.), *Endocrinologie sexuele de la periode perinatale* (pp. 121–42). Paris: INSERM.

Simon, N. G., and Cologer-Clifford, A. (in press). *Hormones and Behavior.*

Simon, N. G., and Gandelman, R. (1978). The estrogenic arousal of aggressive behavior in female mice. *Hormones and Behavior, 10,* 118–27.

Simon, N. G., and Whalen, R. E. (1987). Sexual differentiation of androgen-sensitive and estrogen-sensitive regulatory systems for aggressive behavior. *Hormones and Behavior, 21,* 493–500.

Sines, J. O. (1961). Behavioral correlates of genesis of enhanced susceptibility to stomach lesion development. *Journal of Psychosomatic Research, 5,* 120–26.

Sodersten, P. (1973). Increased mounting behavior in the female rat following a single neonatal injection of testosterone propionate. *Hormones and Behavior, 4,* 1–17.

Staudt, J., and Dörner, G. (1976). Structural changes in the medial and central amygdala of the male rat, following neonatal castration and androgen treatment. *Endokrinologie, 67,* 296–300.

Stevens, R., and Goldstein, R. (1981). Effect of neonatal testosterone and estrogen on open-field behavior in rats. *Physiology and Behavior, 26,* 551–53.

Stewart, J., Skvarenina, A., and Pottier, J. (1975). Effects of neonatal androgens on open-field behavior and maze learning in the prepubescent and adult rat. *Physiology and Behavior, 14,* 291–95.

Svare, B., Davis, P. G., and Gandelman, R. (1974). Induction of fighting behavior in female mice following chronic androgen treatment during adulthood. *Physiology and Behavior, 12,* 339–403.

Tobet, S. A., and Baum, M. J. (1987). Role of prenatal estrogen in the development of masculine sexual behavior in the male ferret. *Hormones and Behavior, 21,* 419–29.

Tokuyama, K., Saito, M., and Okuda, H. (1982). Effects of wheel running on food intake and weight gain of male and female rats. *Physiology and Behavior, 28,* 899–903.

Vale, J. R., Ray, D., and Vale, C. A. (1972). The interactions of genotype and exogenous neonatal androgen: Agonistic behavior in female mice. *Behavioral Biology, 7,* 321–34.

Valenstein, E. S., Kakoluski, J. W., and Cox, V. C. (1967). Sex differences in taste preferences for glucose and saccharin solutions. *Science, 156,* 942–43.

vom Saal, F. S. (1983a). Models of early hormonal effects on intrasex aggression in mice. In B. B. Svare (Ed.), *Hormones and behavior* (pp. 197–222). New York: Plenum Press,

vom Saal, F. S. (1983b). Variation in infanticide and parental behavior in male mice due to prior intrauterine proximity to female fetuses: Elimination by prenatal stress. *Physiology and Behavior, 30,* 675–81.

vom Saal, F. S., and Bronson, F. H. (1980a). Sexual characteristics of adult female mice are correlated with their blood testosterone levels during prenatal development. *Science, 208,* 597–99.

vom Saal, F. S., and Bronson, F. H. (1980b). Variation in length of the estrous cycle in mice is due to former intrauterine proximity to male fetuses. *Biology of Reproduction, 22,* 777–80.

vom Saal, F. S., Grant, W. M., McMullen, C. W., and Laves, K. S. (1983). High fetal estrogen concentrations: Correlation with increased adult sexual activity and decreased aggression. *Science, 220,* 1306–308.

vom Saal, F. S., Svare, B., and Gandelman, R. (1976). Time of neonatal androgen exposure influences length of testosterone treatment required to induce aggression in adult male and female mice. *Behavioral Biology, 17,* 391–97.

Wade, G. N., and Zucker, I. (1969). Taste preferences of female rats: Modification by neonatal hormones, food deprivation and prior experience. *Physiology and Behavior, 4,* 935–43.

Ward, I. L. (1972). Prenatal stress feminizes and demasculinizes the behavior of males. *Science, 175,* 82–84.

Ward, I. L., and Weisz, J. (1980). Maternal stress alters plasma testosterone in fetal males. *Science, 207,* 328–29.

Ward, I. L., and Weisz, J. (1984). Differentential effects of maternal stress on circulating levels of corticosterone, progesterone, and testosterone in male and female rat fetuses and their mothers. *Endocrinology, 114,* 1635–644.

Whalen, R. E., and Etgen, A. (1978). Masculinization and defeminization induced in female hamsters by neonatal treatment with estadiol benzoate and RU-2858. *Hormones and Behavior, 10,* 170–77.

Whalen, R. E., and Nadler, R. D. (1963). Suppression of the development of female mating behavior by estrogen administration in infancy. *Science, 141,* 273–74.

Williams, R. H. (1974). *Testbook of endocrinology.* Philadelphia: Saunders.

Wilson, J. D., and Gloyna, R. E. (1970). The intranuclear metabolism of testosterone in the accessory organs of reproduction. *Recent Progress in Hormone Research, 26,* 309–36.

Yalom, I. D., Green, R., and Fisk, S. (1973). Prenatal exposure to female hormones: Effect on psychosexual development in boys. *Archives of Sexual Behavior, 28,* 554–61.

Zielinski, W., Vandenbergh, J. G., and Montano, M. M. (1991). Effects of social stress and intrauterine position on sexual phenotype in wild-type house mice (*Mus musculus*). *Physiology and Behavior, 49,* 117–23.

Zondek, L. H., and Zondek, T. (1979). Observations on the determination of fetal sex in early pregnancy. *Contributions to Gynecology and Obstetrics, 5,* 91–108.

4

Some Threats to Development

Heredity must be held accountable for all influences which have affected the male or female element up to the time when an intermixture of the two have taken place. Heredity established what may be called the "potential capacity" of the embryo. After fertilization every condition affecting the mother's health must have its influence, however small, upon the fetus. Remembering then its many factors which may be brought into play, we can understand how the original "potential" may be greatly modified, these modifications varying from beneficial constructive processes, through degrees of degeneracy, even to the absolute destruction of the pre-natal life.   J. M. Tompkins, 1915

We have seen that behavioral development is not an invariant outcome of nervous system maturation but that it results from interactions between neurological growth and reactivity to a host of stimulative events. We also have observed that much of the research designed to delineate factors responsible for normal development often informs us about the etiology of abnormal development. Thus the prevention of embryonic motility can lead to the abnormal development of joints, which in turn adversely affects movement. Similarly, the elimination of androgenic stimulation during early development can demasculinize and feminize the genetic male, whereas application of such stimulation can defeminize and masculinize the genetic female. Other factors that can adversely affect development are considered in the succeeding chapters, again within the context of the study of normal development. This chapter is different, however, as it deals with work designed expressly to study abnormal development.

Werboff and Gottlieb, in 1963, briefly reviewed research pertaining to the adverse effects on postnatal behavior of prenatal exposure to drugs. They called this research endeavor *behavioral teratology*. Behavioral teratology, now an important research specialty in psychology and pharmacology, also includes the study of nondrug agents such as x-irradiation and viruses.

Werboff and Gottlieb's definition of teratology leads to the question of what is meant by "adverse." Some outcomes, such as a lack of development of reproductive behavior, are clearly adverse. However, what of a small but reliable alteration of open field activity, a decline in response rate on a reinforcement schedule, or an increment in the ingestion of salt? According to Fein, Schwartz,

Jacobson, and Jacobson (1983), these more subtle effects must not be dismissed for the following reasons: (1) should the effects appear early, they may progress to more debilitating symptomatology with advancing age; (2) an agent that produces subtle behavioral changes in a population may cause major impairment in certain more susceptible individuals; and (3) a subtle behavioral perturbation may affect parent–infant interaction, which may lead to significant problems. The term *adverse*, then, should apply to *any* reliable deviation from normative behavior.

Owing to limitations of space, it is not possible to consider all of the identified behavioral teratogens. The list is long, and only some of the more pervasive and powerful items are considered here.

DRUGS

Before we commence the discussion of teratogenic drugs, a few words must be said about the placenta, the structure through which the embryo is provided not only with nutrients and oxygen but also with substances of exogenous origin. With few exceptions, drugs cross the placenta by passive diffusion. The facility with which a drug diffuses across placental tissue is governed by factors such as dosage, protein binding (protein-bound drugs cannot diffuse across placental membranes), half-life of the drug, mode of maternal administration, pH gradient across the membrane, and metabolism of the drug by the placenta itself. Molecular weight also is critical. With regard to the human placenta, water-soluble compounds cross the placenta only if of a molecular weight of less than 100 daltons. However, lipid-soluble compounds of a molecular weight of 1000 daltons or less (e.g., barbiturates, anticonvulsants, alcohol, narcotics, local anesthetics) also can diffuse readily, eventually being distributed widely in embryonic peripheral and central nervous system tissues (Waddell & Marlowe, 1976). The relation between maternal and embryonic blood alcohol content is shown in Figure 4.1. As is the case with other drugs, maximum concentrations in the embryo are generally not as high as those in the adult and require a longer period of time to be attained. Because of the immaturity of the embryonic liver, however, drug levels eventually are greater in the embryo than in the adult. It should be clear, then, that the placenta cannot be viewed as it once was, a barrier protecting the embryo from substances found in the mother's circulatory system.

Before considering data pertaining to embryonic drug exposure and development, a few observations are in order concerning some methodological problems inherent in teratological research using human subjects. On the one hand, factors that covary with the potential teratogen under study may be responsible, at least in part, for deficits seen in the offspring. For example, because a greater proportion of drinkers than nondrinkers smoke cigarettes, nicotine acting alone or in concert with alcohol may be the agent responsible for the observed deficits in the offspring of alcoholics. Similarly, the reduction of food intake often associated with cocaine abuse, rather than or in addition to the drug itself, may be responsible for the deficits in the offspring. Obstetrical care is another factor that

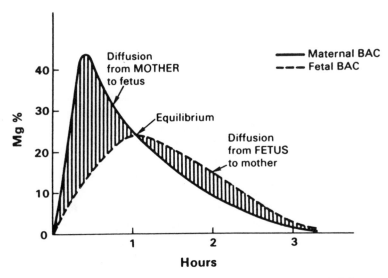

Figure 4.1 Maternal and fetal blood alcohol content (BAC) following a single drink. (From Rosett and Weiner, *Alcohol and the Fetus,* © 1984 by Oxford University Press. Reprinted by permission.)

often covaries with drug use; drug abusers tend to receive less medical attention. Therefore one would expect more health problems among the offspring of drug abusers even if the drug in question is benign. Lastly we have the postnatal environment, which may also place the offspring of mothers who use drugs during pregnancy at risk; neglect and abuse often characterize the behavior of drug abusers toward their children.

Even in cases in which the agent itself does not directly alter the behavior of the mother, its influence on the offspring's behavior may in turn adversely affect the mother's reaction to the infant. In other words, the effect of a drug may result from the synergy between a direct effect on the offspring and an altered reaction of the mother toward that infant. Brazelton (1961a) described a situation in which an infant displaying abnormal behaviors so demoralized its mother that she became depressed and, as a consequence, totally ineffectual in her interaction with the baby.

Two other factors also make interpretation of the data difficult. First, retrospective techniques often are used to determine the amount of drug taken during pregnancy. Because this technique depends on the memory and veracity of the respondents, information concerning dosage may not always be reliable (Day & Robles, 1989). Second, if a biological factor such as a gene is responsible for predisposing an adult toward substance abuse, that same factor may *independently* produce the developmental defects in her offspring.

Some of the problems found with human subjects are obviated by testing nonhumans. Animal subjects permit a degree of control impossible with humans while, of course, allowing one to test hypotheses by performing experimental manipulations that for ethical reasons cannot otherwise be accomplished. Three major methodological advantages are afforded by nonhuman subjects. One is that the amount of drug exposure can be rigidly controlled. A second is that they permit the use of a *cross-fostering* design in which offspring of mothers administered a drug during pregnancy can be reared by normal mothers, and others born of normal mothers can be reared by drug-exposed adults. This technique allows one to distinguish pre- from postnatal influences of the drug. Should a drug influence development by altering the mothers' behavior toward her young, the effect of the drug should be observed in *non*prenatally drug-exposed young reared by mothers administered the drug during pregnancy. Conversely, should the agent exert a direct effect on the embryo, permitting prenatally drug-exposed young to be raised by normal mothers should not mitigate the effects of the drug. Third, the use of nonhuman subjects eliminates most of the factors that covary with drug usage in humans. For example, because many drugs affect food intake, the non-drug-exposed pregnant animals can be maintained on diets that provide calories equivalent to those consumed by the drug-exposed animals, thereby accounting for the possibility that observed effects in the offspring are caused by a dietary factor rather than the drug. The use of nonhuman subjects also eliminates, of course, multiple drug use and poor obstetrical care.

Experimentation with animals is not without problems, however, principal among which is the selection of the species: rats, mice, hamsters, rabbits, guinea pigs, monkeys. The choice of an animal model often is governed by practical concerns relating to space and budget. However, the choice of subject may be crucial, in some cases determining whether a teratological effect will be observed. A well known example of this problem occurred with the drug thalidomide; although it is benign when given to pregnant rats, the offspring of treated rabbits exhibit anomalies similar to those shown by humans. Unfortunately and tragically, the drug was originally tested in rats.

The mode of drug administration is another problem facing the researcher. The various procedures used to administer drugs to pregnant animals (intraperitoneal and subcutaneous injection, intubation, placement of the drug in food or water), which of necessity often differ from the way they are self-administered by humans, at times yield divergent effects. Moreover, in some cases the method of administration produces adverse consequences not found in humans. Cocaine treatment is a prime example. It is usually administered by subcutaneous injection even though its vasoconstrictive properties cause painful necrosis of tissue surrounding the injection site. The problem is compounded by the fact that the subjects are injected on multiple gestation days. Therefore effects of this manipulation on the offspring may be related to maternal stress rather than to cocaine per se.

Another problem concerns dosage. The use of a wide variety of dosages and administration periods not only make comparisons among animal experiments difficult but make it hard to draw comparisons between the results of an animal experiment and information derived from humans. Lastly, it is often difficult, if not impossible, to select a behavior even somewhat analogous to one shown to be adversely affected in humans. What behavioral endpoints can be used with the laboratory rat that correspond to the cognitive deficits exhibited by individuals exposed prenatally to alcohol?

Now that we have considered some of the methodological issues surrounding the use of human and animal subjects, let us turn to the data.

Alcohol

Although the notion that maternal ingestion of alcohol can harm the embryo has been articulated since antiquity (see Plant [1985] for an interesting historical account), it was not until the report of Lemoine, Harousseau, Bortegru, and Menuet in 1968 that the issue began to receive serious attention from the scientific community. These investigators described similarities in growth retardation, facial features, and psychomotor disturbances among a group of 127 children of alcoholic mothers. The similarities were so marked that the authors claimed they could diagnose maternal alcoholism by simply examining the children. Five years later, Jones, Smith, and co-workers (Jones & Smith, 1973; Jones, Smith, Ulleland, & Streissguth, 1973) reported a number abnormalities in 11 offspring of alcoholic mothers ranging in age from newborn to 48 months. These abnormalities comprise what they called the *fetal alcohol syndrome* (FAS). Their publications were pivotal, leading to an avalanche of research in the form of case reports and studies involving human and nonhuman subjects.

According to Smith and Jones and their colleagues, FAS consists of three categories of anomaly: growth retardation, dysmorphic characteristics, and CNS abnormalities. Growth retardation in weight, height, or both commences prenatally as evidenced by low birth weight. The major dysmorphic features are craniofacial, including low nasal bridge, drooping eyelids, epicanthic folds, and thin upper lip (see Fig. 4.2A,B). Other dysmorphic features involve anomalies of the

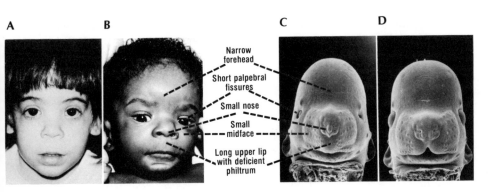

Figure 4.2 (A & B) Children with FAS. (C & D) Two 14-day-old mouse fetuses from ethanol-treated (C) and control (D) mothers. (From Sulik et al., "Fetal alcohol syndrome: Embryogenesis in a mouse model." *Science, 214,* 936–38. © 1981 by The American Association for the Advancement of Science. Reprinted by permission.)

joints, such as hip dislocation and the inability to completely extend the elbows. Problems involving the CNS include microcephaly, seizures, hyperactivity, attentional deficits, and learning/performance problems. Regarding the latter and based on their original sample of 11 children, IQ scores ranged from 50 to 83. It has been estimated that FAS occurs 0.4 to 3.5 times per 1000 births in the United States (Abel, 1985).

Most investigators agree that to be diagnosed as having FAS one must exhibit symptoms from each of the three categories. Individuals who do not meet that criterion but who do exhibit deficits are said to be suffering from *fetal alcohol effects* (FAE). Although the prevalence of FAE has not been estimated, it would be expected to be much higher than that of FAS.

Streissguth, Herman, and Smith (1978) categorized 20 offspring of alcoholic mothers ranging in age from 9 months to 20 years as to the severity of their dysmorphic symptomatology. Afterward, the children were administered standardized intelligence tests, and their caretakers were interviewed. The children's scores ranged from 15 to 105, with an average IQ of 65, a score indicative of retardation. Many of the children were described as being hyperactive and having attentional deficits, both of which probably accounted, in part, for problems observed in school. Interestingly, intelligence test performance was inversely related to the severity of facial dysmorphia. The average IQ scores, according to their dysmorphia ratings, were as follows: mildly dysmorphic 82; moderately dysmorphic 68; moderately severely dysmorphic 58; and most severely dysmorphic 55.

Although children of alcoholic mothers generally perform poorly on intelligence tests (Olegard et al., 1979), low IQ scores are not requisite for the appearance of behavioral and learning deficits. Shaywitz, Cohen, and Shaywitz (1980) studied 15 children who had been referred to a learning disorders clinic. All of the 15 displayed the morphological anomalies associated with FAS, and all exhibited failure in the school environment. According to the investigators, "Inability to function without intensive one-to-one or small group instruction, short attention span and distractability were shared by the patient population uniformly" (p. 980). Nevertheless, the IQ scores ranged from 80 to 113 with an average of 98.2.

The data described above as well as those of others (Clarren & Smith, 1978; Hrbek, Iversen, & Olsson, 1982; Steinhausen, Nestler, & Spohr, 1982) demonstrate that children of alcoholic mothers are at risk for a variety of physiological and behavioral abnormalities. Is it the case, then, that *only* chronic exposure to exceedingly high doses of the drug produces FAS? This question is important, as most women who drink when pregnant are not alcoholic. Streissguth, Barr, Sampson, and Martin (1989a) carefully examined this issue by performing a longitudinal study on more than 400 children. Pregnant women kept records of alcohol consumption beginning during the fifth month, and the offspring were given standardized intelligence tests when they were 4 years 3 months old. When analyzing their data the investigators statistically eliminated 30 covariates, e.g., smoking, prenatal antibiotic exposure, maternal education level, and race, that could have been related to test performance. The results revealed that the use of more than 1.5 oz of alcohol a day (about three drinks) during pregnancy is associated with an average IQ decrement of approximately five points, which according to Streissguth et al. (1989a) tripled "the risk of subnormal intelligence (i.e., IQ < 85) for a child of 'average background' in our sample" (p. 10).

Streissguth, Sampson, and Barr (1989b) interviewed an additional 1500 pregnant women regarding their alcohol, caffeine, cigarette, and other drug use. This sample was characterized as exhibiting light to moderate levels of alcohol consumption. Offspring were assessed on days 1 and 2, at 8 and 18 months, and at 4 and 7 years. The data are summarized in Table 4.1. Again we see that prenatal exposure to low to moderate levels of alcohol produces long-lasting behavioral effects. It thus is not solely the children of alcoholics who are at risk as a consequence of maternal alcohol consumption.

Returning to the alcoholic, we arrive at the obvious prescription of abstinence. However, does abstinence for part or all of pregnancy prevent the appearance of FAS? Two studies suggest that the answer is *no*. Olegard et al. (1979) identified five alcoholic women for whom sobriety could be induced commencing between weeks 5 and 12 of gestation. Eight other women abstained from drinking starting at weeks 20 to 25. Whereas size at birth was depressed in the offspring of the "late-sober" group relative to a nondrinking reference group, the children of the group of women who abstained beginning from early pregnancy exhibited no such decrement. However, the offspring of both the late- and early-sober groups displayed abnormal patterns of brain electrical activity. Little, Streissguth, Barr, and Herman (1980) reported that abstinence throughout the *entire* pregnancy did not even prevent lowered birth weight. This study suggests that chronic prefertilization exposure to high levels of alcohol produces long-term, if not permanent, effects on reproductive outcome. In contrast to the above, Autti-Rämö and Granström (1991) found a relation between degree of cognitive impairment and duration of heavy maternal alcohol consumption. If consumption did not extend beyond the first trimester, cognitive development was normal. Impaired development was observed if maternal drinking continued through the second trimester.

Many of the effects associated with prenatal alcohol exposure in humans have been produced experimentally in animals including nonhuman primates (Clarren, Astley, & Bowden, 1988; Ellis & Pick, 1976; McLain & Roe, 1984; Papara-Nicholson & Telford, 1957; Tze & Lee, 1975). As noted by Driscoll, Streissguth, and Riley (1990), even the dosages that produce effects in animals are comparable to those found in humans. Sulik, Johnston, and Webb (1981) injected pregnant mice with a relatively low dose of alcohol only twice, both times on day 7 of the 19-day gestation period. The resemblance between these subjects and human FAS children is striking (Fig. 4.2A–D). These authors concluded that alcohol "has a major effect in the mouse at a time corresponding to the third month of human gestation. Many women are not aware of their pregnancy at this stage. Those who are aware may not realize that social or binge drinking so early in pregnancy may be as deleterious to the embryo as constant heavy drinking" (p. 938).

As found in humans (Martin, Martin, Streissguth, & Lund, 1979a; Ouellette,

Table 4.1 Major behavioral findings of the Seattle longitudinal study on alcohol and pregnancy to date

Outcome	Test Procedure	R	F Test for Alcohol[a] F (df)	p
AT DAY 1				
Habituation	Brazelton	0.32	7.07(1323)	0.008
Low arousal		0.27	6.75(1297)	0.010
Opened eyes	Naturalistic		4.15(1115)	0.044
Body tremors	observations		4.21(1115)	0.042
Head to left			4.00(1115)	0.048
High level body activity			5.43(1115)	0.022
Hand to face			5.16(1115)	0.025
AT DAY 2				
Sucking pressure	Pressure	0.25	4.62(1147)	0.033
Latency to suck	transducer	0.23	2.90(1147)	0.091
AT 8 MONTHS				
Mental Dev. Index	Bayley scales	0.33	3.22(2452)	0.041
Psychomotor Dev. Index		0.28	5.15(1453)	0.024
AT 4 YEARS				
Attention				
Errors of omission	Vigilance task with	0.23	6.32(1351)	0.012
Errors of commission	microcomputer	0.26	5.35(1351)	0.021
Ratio correct		0.33	7.98(1351)	0.005
Trials oriented		0.23	.01(1276)	0.936
Reaction time		0.57	11.71(1066)	0.001
Time in movement	Motion detector	0.15	.00(1362)	0.984
Balance	Gross motor	0.27	5.00(1434)	0.026
Errors	Fine motor	0.34	6.47(1415)	0.011
Latency to correct		0.42	15.25(1415)	0.000
Time to complete		0.32	5.68(1437)	0.018
IQ	WPPSI	0.62	7.02(1408)	0.008
AT 7 YEARS				
Word reading	Stroop	0.80	4.59(1216)	0.033
Color naming		0.51	4.08(1216)	0.045
Attention				
Errors of omission-X task	Vigilance task with	0.27	5.09(1444)	0.025
Errors of omission-AX task	microcomputer	0.32	4.35(1443)	0.037
Errors of commission-X task		0.40	4.06(1444)	0.044
Errors of commission-AX task		0.45	9.68(1442)	0.002
Reaction time		0.38	7.22(1443)	0.007

[a]The F statistic presented here is for the effect of alcohol after adjusting for all the other variables in the multiple regression model.

Regression models were developed individually for each set of outcomes: nicotine is adjusted for in each analysis. All models except the sucking variables and naturalistic observations also adjust for caffeine, mother's diet during pregnancy, and mother's education. Other covariates were included as appropriate for each set of outcomes.

Source: Adapted from Streissguth et al. Neurobehavioral dose-response effects of prenatal alcohol exposure in humans from infancy to adulthood. Annals of the New York Academy of Sciences 562, 145–58. © 1989 by The New York Academy of Sciences. By permission.

Rosett, Rosman, & Weiner, 1977; Ulleland, 1972), the behavioral effects of embryonic alcohol exposure manifest early in a decrement of suckling behavior. Rockwood and Riley (1986), studying rats, reported that prenatally alcohol-exposed neonates exert significantly less pressure on the nipple when suckling, spend less time suckling, and display an altered suckling pattern relative to nonexposed controls. With regard to the latter, the experimental animals made fewer groups of normal short, rhythmic sucks. Alcohol-exposed neonates also take longer to acquire a response that brings them to the mother (Anandam & Stern, 1980) and, once there, take longer to commence suckling (Chen, Driscoll, & Riley, 1982).

Sensorimotor maturation was assessed by Molina, Hoffman, and Spear (1987), who found that prenatally alcohol-exposed rats are retarded on three indices. They exhibit a delay in attaining criterion in the righting reflex (returning to a prone position from a supine position) and in the horizontal screen test (grasping a mesh floor and offering resistance with the forelimbs while being gently pulled backward by the tail). They also exhibit a delay in auditory maturation as assessed by the day that both auditory canals fully open.

Prenatal alcohol exposure increases activity levels, another finding consistent with what is known from human studies. Branchey and Friedhoff (1976) and Fernandez, Caul, Osborne, and Henderson (1983), among others, reported increased movement of rats in the open field test; an increase in running wheel activity also has been found (Martin, Martin, Sigman, & Radow, 1978). This enhancement of activity probably is related in some manner to decrements observed in situations involving response inhibition. Alcohol-exposed rats require more trials to master a passive avoidance task in which the avoidance of punishment is made contingent on the withholding of movement (Driscoll, Chen, & Riley, 1982; Riley, Lochry, & Shapiro, 1979). Meyer and Riley (1986) argued that the preponderance of evidence, including deficits in reversal learning (Riley et al., 1979) and spontaneous alternation (Abel, 1982), support the contention that "animals exposed to alcohol prenatally have difficulty withholding prepotent responses" (p. 131).

Decrements by alcohol-exposed animals are observed in other conditioning and learning tasks. Conditioned taste aversion is one such example. The progeny of alcohol-treated mothers exhibit a decrement relative to controls in the subsequent avoidance of a substance that had been ingested prior to becoming ill (Riley et al. 1979). Gianoulakis (1990) reported a deficiency in the acquisition of the Morris swim maze, a device that requires a rat to learn the location of a submerged platform, allowing it to lift itself from the water. It is claimed that the water-filled maze provides a test of spatial memory. Alcohol-exposed subjects displayed longer latencies to perform the task and swam longer distances prior to locating the platform. Furthermore, when the platform was removed, the exposed animals searched for it in areas where it had not been located.

The development of sexually dimorphic behavior also is affected by uterine alcohol exposure. McGivern, Clancy, Hill, and Noble (1984) examined two behaviors that tend to differentiate females from males: saccharin preference and maze learning. Females normally consume a greater amount of a solution of saccharin and water than do males, and males require fewer trials than females to learn to negotiate a complicated maze. Neither sexual dimorphism was apparent in rats exposed to alcohol prior to birth: Males exhibited an increment of saccharin intake relative to that of controls, females consumed less of the sweet solution, and males made more and females fewer errors in the complex maze.

The play behavior of juvenile rats also is sexually dimorphic, exhibited at higher levels by males. Prenatal alcohol exposure reverses this male–female difference (Meyer & Riley, 1986). Lastly, male rats exposed to alcohol from gestation day 12 to postpartum day 10 exhibited a significant reduction in both the latency to mount a receptive female and the number of times they intromitted (Parker, Udani, Gavalu, & Van Thiel, 1984).

The fact that uterine exposure to alcohol disrupts the normal development of sexually dimorphic behaviors suggests that the drug alters the early hormonal milieu. McGivern, Raum, Salido, and Redei (1988) addressed this possibility directly by assessing levels of testosterone in normal and alcohol-exposed male rat embryos. In contrast to normal embryos, which show a precipitous elevation of testosterone on day 18, alcohol-exposed embryos exhibited no such surge. This finding is similar to that of Ward and Weisz (1980), who, as noted in Chapter 3, demonstrated the lack of a normal testosterone surge in embryos of dams exposed to stress during pregnancy, suggesting, then, that alcohol shares certain as yet unspecified properties with stressors in general.

Given the wide range of behavioral deficits resulting from embryonic alcohol exposure, it is not surprising that such exposure alters the course of brain development. Eighteen-day-old mouse embryos of mothers administered the drug from days 11 to 17 of gestation display a decrease in the number of cells per gram of cerebrum (cerebrum = an entire hemisphere less olfactory lobes, basal ganglia, hippocampus, and meninges) and in the number of cells per gram of cerebral protein. Alcohol exposure also decreases the ability of cerebral cells to grow in a culture, suggesting cellular dysfunction (Blakley & Fedoroff, 1985). West, Hodges, and Black (1981) reported that alcohol exposure disrupts the cellular organization of the hippocampus. Apropos the findings regarding elimination of behavioral sexual dimorphisms, the sexually dimorphic nucleus of the preoptic area, a brain structure normally larger in males than females, is smaller in prenatally alcohol-exposed males (Barron, Bliss-Tieman, & Riley, 1988). Furthermore, the sexually dimorphic nucleus is of reduced size in prenatally alcohol-exposed females relative to control females (Ahmed, Shryne, Gorski, Branch, & Taylor, 1991).

It is apparent that in utero alcohol exposure can alter the course of morphological and behavioral development. The critical issue, and one that awaits explication, is the mechanism of action of the drug. What does alcohol do to the embryo? As reviewed by Hoyseth and Jones (1989), five nonmutually exclusive mechanisms of action have been proposed. One is that alcohol interferes with the placental transfer of nutrients to the embryo, causing an impairment of growth and morphological deformations. Second, the drug may produce abnormal muscle tissue by inhibiting cellular migration during early ontogenesis (which may account for the poor suckling seen in alcohol-exposed neonates). Oxygen deprivation may be another means by which alcohol produces terato-genic effects on behavior. It is known that the liver can consume up to 100% more oxygen than normal in order to metabolize alcohol. Moreover, alcohol causes vasoconstriction and, in large dosages, a transient collapse of the placental vasculature, both of which augment embryonic oxygen deprivation. A fourth possible mechanism of action of alcohol involves prostaglandins, oxygenated fatty acids implicated in a host of physiological functions. Alcohol increases the embryonic prostaglandin level, which in turn stimulates production of cyclic adenosine monophosphate, which slows the rate of cell division. Lastly, some of the teratogenic properties of the drug may result from its action on the endocrine system. In addition to affecting levels of testosterone, prenatal alcohol stimulation affects the functioning of the hypothalamic-pituitary-adrenal axis as seen in altered levels of adrenocorticotropic and growth hormone (Taylor, Branch, Cooley-Matthews, & Poland, 1982; Thadoni, 1982) and disrupts mechanisms that control the release of antidiuretic hormone (Dow-Edwards, Trachtman, Riley, Freed, & Milhorat, 1989).

In addition to the possibilities outlined above, the consequences of prenatal alcohol exposure may be due in part to its suppressive influence on embryonic behavior. As reported by Smotherman, Woodruff, Robinson, and Del Real (1986), rat fetuses of mothers given alcohol exhibited 51% less spontaneous activity than controls 4 hours after drug administration.

Another point is worth noting. Little et al. (1980) reported that in humans abstinence throughout the pregnancy did not prevent lowered birth weight, suggesting that alcohol produces long-term, possibly permanent effects on the reproductive outcome. Ledig et al. (1990) also reported long-term effects with rats. Maternal alcohol exposure before mating was associated with alterations of a number of biochemical parameters involved in alcohol metabolism and behavior. The offspring of alcohol-exposed females were more active in the open field and spent more time than controls in a novel environment—both findings suggestive of reduced emotionality. Ledig et al. concluded that "some effects on the embryo attributed by several authors to prenatal alcohol exposure in utero may be in fact related to prepregnancy alterations" (p. 285). This potentially important finding awaits verification and extension.

Cocaine

It is estimated that by 1986 almost 15% of the population of the United States had tried cocaine (Gavin & Ellinwood, 1988). Such an estimate makes it imperative to determine what the drug can do to the developing organism. Owing to the recency with which the scientific community has addressed the potential teratological influence of cocaine, much less is known about this drug than about some others, such as alcohol. There are, for example, no longitudinal studies of the behavioral development of prenatally cocaine-exposed children.

Water- and lipid-soluble and of low molecular weight, cocaine readily crosses the placenta. It can be detected in embryonic serum in less than a minute following maternal administration (see Fig. 4.3). Both the drug and its metabolite benzoylecgonine are found in the embryonic circulatory system and brain tissue at levels directly related to maternal dosage. Moreover, cocaine has as much affinity for embryonic brain tissue as it has for that of the adult brain (Spear, Kirstein, & Frambes, 1989b).

The adverse effects of cocaine on pregnancy outcome were initially reported by Acker, Sachs, Tracey, and Wise in 1983. Abruptio placentae (separation of the placenta from the uterine wall) occurred in two patients following cocaine administration. One of the neonates was stillborn and the other severely depressed. Similar findings have since been presented by others (e.g., Bingol, Fuchs, Diaz, Stoma, & Gromish, 1987; Ryan, Ehrlich, & Finnegan, 1987). Bingol et al. also reported some skull defects and unspecified major congenital malformations.

MacGregor et al. (1987) studied 70 women who had used cocaine during pregnancy. Control patients were matched to the study population on the basis of age, parity, socioeconomic group, tobacco use, and medical complications. The study population had a higher incidence of preterm (before week 37) labor and delivery, and the offspring not only exhibited lower birth weight—predictable owing to the high incidence of premature delivery—but also were small for their gestational age. Because cocaine is an anorexic, the reduction of body weight may have been produced indirectly by the action of the drug on maternal food intake. It should be noted, however, that the reduced body weight of cocaine-exposed neonates has not been found in all studies (Bingol et al., 1987; Chasnoff,

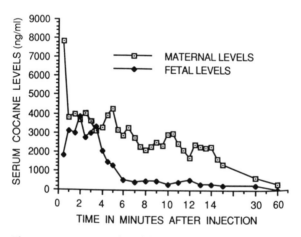

Figure 4.3 Maternal and fetal serum cocaine levels measured every 30 seconds to 1 minute for 15 minutes, then at 30 and 60 minutes after cocaine injection 2.0 mg/kg IV to pregnant sheep. (From Woods et al., "Prenatal cocaine exposure to the fetus: A sheep model for cardiovascular evaluation." *Annals of the New York Academy of Sciences, 562,* 267–79. © 1989 by The New York Academy of Sciences. Reprinted by permission.)

Hunt, Kletter, & Kaplan, 1986). Although it is possible that the results of MacGregor and co-workers might have been caused by other substances (most of the cocaine abusers also administered other drugs), the fact that no differences in pregnancy outcome were found between women taking only cocaine and those taking cocaine and other drugs makes the possibility unlikely. Similar results were obtained by LeBlanc, Parekh, Naso, and Glass (1987) and Cherukuri, Minkoff, Feldman, Parekh, and Glass (1988), who studied the children of women who had taken alkaloidal cocaine ("crack").

Other work with human subjects focuses, in part, on behavior and neurophysiology. Chasnoff, Burns, Schnall, & Burns (1985) and Chasnoff, Burns, and Burns (1987) administered the Brazelton Neonatal Behavioral Assessment Scale (NBAS) on postnatal day 3. Infants born to cocaine-using mothers scored higher on tremulousness, irritability, and state lability than controls. These behavioral states "interfere with the ability of the infant to interact with or respond to the caretaker. As this occurs, the caretaker becomes more passive in his or her attempts at interaction, thus setting up a cycle of increasing passivity on the part of both infant and caretaker" (Chasnoff et al., 1987, p. 293). Cohen, Anday, and Leitner (1989) also reported hyperreactivity of cocaine-exposed infants to sensory stimulation more than a week after birth. In contrast to these reports, Neuspiel, Hamel, Hochberg, Greene, and Campbell (1991) found little effect of prenatal cocaine exposure on the NBAS. Because most of the cocaine-exposed newborns they encountered in their hospital were full term and relatively healthy, Neuspiel et al. speculated that the greatest risk for these children may derive from the social environment, specifically from their drug-abusing parents.

Regarding brain electrical activity, Doberczak, Shanzy, Sonie, and Kandall (1988) recorded the electroencephalograms (EEGs) of 38 neonates who had been exposed to cocaine but to no other known drugs of abuse during embryonic development. When recorded during the first week of life, 17 children exhibited abnormalities characterized by cerebral irritation with bursts of sharp waves and spikes. Of these 17, five children displayed normalized EEGs when retested between days 8 and 19. All but one of the remaining abnormal EEGs normalized between 3 and 12 months of age. (One child had yet to be retested.) The neurophysiological abnormalities tend to normalize as cocaine metabolites disappear from the neonates' urine.

Let us now turn to the research with nonhuman subjects. As expected, the administration of cocaine to pregnant animals affects pregnancy outcome. Fantel and MacPhail (1982), for example, reported decreased weights of cocaine-exposed rat and mouse embryos in comparison to embryos of non-drug-exposed mothers. The latter were fed food in amounts consumed by the cocaine-treated adults (known as a *pair-fed* control group). Maternal drug treatment also led to elevated rates of uterine resorption. Similar findings, including abruptio placentae, were reported by Church, Dintcheff, and Gessner (1988), and Mahalik, Gautieri, and Mann (1980) found skeletal defects (delayed ossification of skull and paws, malformed sterum, extra ribs) and eye defects (malformed and missing lenses). Woods, Plessinger, and Clark (1987) reported that prenatal cocaine causes a decrease in uterine blood flow, thereby reducing oxygen flow to the fetus. Hypoxia may thus be involved in some of the abnormalities observed as a consequence of embryonic cocaine exposure.

Metabolic activity of the brain also appears to be adversely affected by embryonic cocaine exposure. Dow-Edwards, Freed, and Fico (1990) exposed rats to the drug on days 8 through 22 of pregnancy via stomach intubation at a dosage that did not influence embryonic brain or body size. Intubation was used in place of daily subcutaneous injections (the procedure generally employed with nonhuman subjects) because, as stated previously, the latter produce substantial tissue destruction around the injection sites, creating a potentially stressful situation that in itself could affect postnatal development. Of 45 brain structures examined, 2 cortical and 14 subcortical regions exhibited decreases in metabolic activity. They included motor and somatosensory cortices, hypothalamus, septum, hippocampus, and amygdala. It is interesting that postnatal exposure produces effects different from those seen with prenatal exposure; the administration of cocaine on postnatal days 1 through 10 had virtually no effect on males and produced *increased* cerebral metabolism in females (Dow-Edwards, Freed, & Milhorat, 1988).

Because prenatal exposure to cocaine affects brain development, it should come as no surprise that it also influences sleep patterns. Burchfield, Graham, Abrams, and Gerhardt (1990) attached electrodes to fetal sheep, which enabled them to determine electrical activity of the cortex, eye movement, and neck muscle activity. Fetuses then received direct intravenous infusion of cocaine or saline. The percentage of time spent in rapid-eye-movement (REM) sleep declined significantly during the period of cocaine administration but not during saline infusion. This finding is of potential developmental import in that REM sleep is hypothesized to be a factor that fosters cerebral maturation. Furthermore, the authors drew a comparison between the irritability exhibited by prenatally cocaine-exposed infants and adults who have undergone REM sleep deprivation.

Male sexual differentiation also has been reported to be affected by prenatal exposure to cocaine (Raum, McGivern, Peterson, Shryne, & Gorski, 1990). First it was demonstrated that the administration of cocaine to cesarean-delivered rat pups reduces the hypothalamic uptake of radioactively labeled testosterone that was injected directly into the ventricles 30 minutes after cocaine treatment. Uptake of testosterone and of its estradiol derivative were reduced by about 50%. In a second experiment, male rats born of mothers administered the drug on days 15 through 20 of gestation exhibited less scent marking on days 60 and 80 of life than unexposed controls. They also displayed deficits in copulatory behavior when tested between 90 and 120 of age. Prenatally exposed animals took almost five times as long to mount a sexually receptive female as did controls. Furthermore, once sexual behavior commenced, the exposed subjects ejaculated after fewer intromissions. It is unclear, however, if the deficit in sexual behavior was observed on all or only the final test (tests were administered once a week for 4 weeks).

Spear et al. (1989a) administered cocaine daily to gestating rats on days 8 through 20 and evaluated its influence on various behaviors. Male and female drug-exposed offspring were compared to the young of both pair-fed control mothers and mothers maintained on a free feeding regimen. No differences were observed with regard to body weight at birth and at weaning, data that complement some findings with human subjects. Also, the attainment of various criteria of sensorimotor maturation did not distinguish between the cocaine-exposed and control offspring. A difference did appear, however, in the formation of an odor/taste association. On postnatal day 7 some animals were removed from their mothers and were presented with two odorants 5 hours later. During 3-minute presentations of one olfactory stimulus, milk was infused directly into the mouth through an indwelling cannula. Nothing accompanied the presentations of the other stimulus. Afterward the young were given an odor preference test in which the two olfactory stimuli were emitted from opposite ends of a test chamber. Time spent on either side of the chamber was recorded. In contrast to the behavior of the two control groups of non–drug-exposed young, the cocaine-exposed rats did not display a preference for the odor that had been paired with milk.

Other young were tested for their responsiveness to a painful stimulus: electrical shock delivered through the metal grids that comprised the cage floor. Animals normally exhibit two types of response to such stimulation: movement and wall-climbing (alternate forelimb treading against the walls of the apparatus with the body held in a near vertical plane). Tests were given on days 8, 10, 12, 14, and 16. On each day the cocaine-exposed rat pups exhibited more movement and less wall-climbing than did the nonexposed animals. Nonetheless, the groups did not differ in overall sensitivity to the electric shock.

Two other studies, though also demonstrating effects of prenatal cocaine exposure on postnatal behavior, presented data much less clear than those of Spear et al. (1989a). Hutchings, Fico, and Dow-Edwards (1989) examined the influence of prenatal cocaine exposure on the development of locomotor activity in the rat. Rats were tested daily from days 1 through 32 of life. The only differences were found on days 20 and 23, at which time the offspring of mothers administered cocaine 60 mg/kg, but not those of mothers given 30 mg/kg, during the last 2 weeks of pregnancy were more active than the pair-fed controls.

In a second study Smith, Mattran, and Kurkjian (1989) found that cocaine-exposed males, but not females, show less spontaneous alternation (going first left and then right or vice versa in a choice situation such as a T maze) than controls when tested on days 25, 30, 35, 40, and 45. An uninterpretable third-order interaction (drug $\times$ age at testing $\times$ time period during a testing session) was found for males in the development of open field activity. Also, experimental males take longer to leave the start compartment of a water-filled maze, but only during the early trials on the initial day of testing.

It is obvious that much more research regarding prenatal cocaine exposure and development is needed. Longitudinal studies of human subjects are especially important. Until then we will have only a rudimentary understanding of cocaine's teratogenic properties and little idea as to the mechanisms through which it adversely affects development.

Diethylstilbestrol

Diethylstilbestrol (DES), a compound with estrogenic properties, has served various functions since its synthesis in 1938. It was prescribed to suppress lactation, alleviate menopausal symptoms, treat severe acne, prevent conception, and control carcinoma of the prostate and breast (Noller & Fish, 1974) in humans and to promote weight gain in cattle (McMartin et al., 1978). Of import to this discussion, DES also was used to prevent threatened abortion. It has been estimated (Weiss, 1975) that several million people alive today have been exposed to this estrogenic compound prenatally.

Diethylstilbestrol is no longer used, having been banned by the U.S. Food and Drug Administration because of its carcinogenic action on the female offspring of DES-treated mothers. Herbst, Ulfelder, and Poskanzer (1971) were the first to show the relation between prenatal DES exposure and adenocarcinoma of the vagina. Since then, various abnormalities have been shown to result from gestational exposure to the compound, the most prevalent being vaginal adenosis, an alteration of the cell structure of the vagina. According to one report this disorder occurs 18 times more often in exposed than in unexposed offspring (Johnson, Driscoll, Hertig, Cole, & Nickerson, 1979). DES exposure also is related to menstrual irregularities, hirsutism, and pregnancy problems (Barnes et al., 1980; Peress, Tsai, Morther, & Williamson, 1982). Regarding the latter, DES-exposed women have a higher incidence of premature delivery and perinatal death (Cousins, Karp, Lacey, & Lucas, 1980).

Aside from its adverse effects on physical development and pregnancy, DES also has been reported to affect behavior, presumably by acting on the embryonic brain. However, because DES is estrogenic and estrogen levels normally are high during the latter portion of pregnancy, why should the embryonic brain be adversely affected by DES but not maternal estrogen? Estrogen, a steroid hormone, has been shown in the rat to bind to a protein molecule (α-fetoprotein), which renders the hormone relatively inactive (Plapinger & McEwen, 1978). Because it is nonsteroidal, DES does not bind to α-fetoprotein and is thus biologically active when it reaches the embryonic brain. Estrogen, but not DES, also has been shown to be converted by the rhesus monkey placenta to a less potent hormone, estrone (Slikker, Hill, & Young, 1982).

Vessay, Fairweather, Norman-Smith, and Buckley (1983) conducted a follow-up study on the offspring of treated women given the drug to reduce the incidence of toxemia during their first pregnancy. The women, assigned randomly to a DES or a placebo group, were informed neither during the study nor after its completion as to whether they received DES. DES treatment generally commenced in the 12th week, with the average total amount of DES taken being 11.5 g. The children (138 DES sons, 121 DES daughters; 126 control sons, 145 control daughters) were between 24 and 30 years of age when the investigators obtained their medical records.

The nonexposed and DES-exposed women differed on only a single outcome variable—benign lesions of the cervix—whereas there were no differences at all between the exposed and the control men. Unexpectedly, however, almost twice as many of the DES-exposed (14%) than nonexposed (7%) offspring exhibited psychiatric disorders including depression, anxiety, and anorexia. Because neither the practitioners nor the subjects were aware of who had been exposed to DES and because their mothers had been assigned randomly to experimental and control groups, Vessey and co-workers excluded the possibility that the differences resulted from a procedural artifact. Rather, they suggested that in utero exposure to DES adversely affects psychological well-being. Ehrhardt et al. (1987), however, reported only a relatively slight elevation in depressive episodes of DES-exposed subjects.

A year after the publication by Vessey et al., Hines and Shipley (1984) reported that gestational exposure to DES affects cerebral lateralization, which, as noted in Chapter 3, is greater in men than women. The study population consisted of 25 daughters (14 to 29 years old) of mothers treated with DES for at least 5 months and who evidenced no drug-related malignancies. These daughters were compared to their unexposed sisters on various tasks that assess cognitive abilities and cerebral lateralization. They did not differ on cognitive abilities, but the exposed and unexposed females did diverge on a dichotic listening task in which two syllables are presented simultaneously, one to each ear. The subject is asked to report the sounds she heard. The DES-exposed women were much better able to identify sounds entering the right ear (viz., left cerebral hemisphere) than the left ear. Such right ear bias, which was not exhibited by their unexposed sisters, is typically shown by males, thereby suggesting that prenatal exposure to DES masculinizes the pattern of cerebral dominance.

Ehrhardt, Meyer-Bahlburg, and their associates conducted a comprehensive assessment of the sexuality of women exposed prenatally to DES (Ehrhardt et al., 1985; Meyer-Bahlburg et al., 1984, 1985). A moderately sized sample of 30 DES-exposed women aged 17 to 30 years, 27 of whom had vaginal adenosis, was compared to a non-hormone-exposed sample matched in age and socioeconomic background. The control women also underwent many of the same gynecological procedures as the DES-exposed subjects: The control women had a history of abnormal Papanicolaow smears, which placed them in a high risk group for cancer of the reproductive organs. In one instance a subsample of the DES women were also compared to their unexposed sisters.

The DES-exposed women did not differ from controls on the age of attainment of various indices of psychosexual development including first boyfriend, first necking, first intercourse, and first marriage. However, a difference did emerge on measures of sexual orientation. Relative to the matched controls, DES-exposed women exhibited higher levels of bisexual or homosexual responsiveness on various items relating to masturbation fantasies, sexual attractions, and sexual relations/sexual responsiveness (both current and lifelong) as judged by the Kinsey Rating Scale. Given these differences, it is not surprising that the exposed subjects had more homosexual and fewer heterosexual contacts than controls. However, even excluding all subjects with significant bi- or homosexuality scores, the remaining DES subjects still reported fewer heterosexual partners. When 15 of the experimental subjects were compared to their sisters, the former exhibited a higher level of bi- or homosexuality on items relating to current and lifelong sexual responsiveness.

Sexual activity level also differentiated the hormone-exposed from the matched controls. The DES females reported lower sex drives and lower frequency of sexual thoughts. They also experienced fewer orgasms during heterosexual encounters.

Masculinization of sexual behavior can be produced by early exposure to estrogen as well as androgen, as discussed in Chapter 3. Because testosterone, the principal androgen, is metabolically converted in the brain to estrogen, it has been suggested that estrogen may actually be the active agent in the masculinization process. Prenatal exposure to DES therefore may masculinize and defeminize human females, thus accounting for the data of Ehrhardt, Meyer-Bahlburg, and co-workers and those of Hines and Shipley (1984) on cerebral lateralization. This explanation is supported by the results of one of the few experiments with DES using animal subjects: Female guinea pigs exposed in utero to DES exhibit a reduction in female, and a concomitant increase in male, sexual behavior (Hines & Goy, 1985).

Phenobarbital

Barbiturates, in particular phenobarbital, have been prescribed to pregnant women to (1) treat insomnia, morning sickness, and epileptic seizures; (2) reduce stress associated with labor and delivery; and (3) reduce serum levels of bilirubin in the embryo. Because pregnant women may also take these drugs as therapy for a plethora of afflictions not directly related to pregnancy, embryonic exposure to barbiturates has been extensive. According to one estimate (Reinisch & Sanders, 1982), 25% of all women pregnant during the 1950s and 1960s and 10% of those pregnant during the 1970s were administered barbiturates. Not included in this estimate are women who used the drug for nonmedicinal, recreational purposes.

Relative to information derived from nonhuman subjects, little is known about the aversive consequences of prenatal barbiturate exposure in humans. The incidence of anomalies such as cleft palate, congenital heart disease, and abnormalities of fingers and toes has been reported to be about two to three times greater in the offspring of epileptics who took barbiturates for their anticonvulsive property (Smith, 1977; Smithalls, 1976). Because some data suggest that epileptics normally have greater difficulty with pregnancy than nonepileptics, Montouris, Fenichel, and McLain (1979) argued that the teratogenicity of barbiturates, at least with regard to the production of congenital anomalies, has not been firmly established.

Brazelton (1961b) reported behavioral differences between the offspring of mothers administered more than 150 mg of barbiturate during labor and those of mothers given doses not exceeding 60 mg. The data are summarized in Figure 4.4, in which it is readily apparent that the high-dose barbiturate-exposed group took longer to exhibit *responsive feedings* (defined by being awake and alert) than did the low-dose group. Consequently, the former required an additional day to start to gain weight. In a related finding, babies born of mothers exposed to 200 mg barbiturate just prior to delivery displayed a reduction in both sucking rate and the pressure exerted on the nipple for at least the first 4 days of life

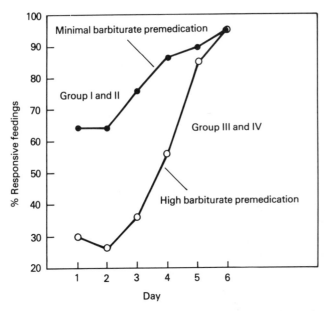

Figure 4.4 Percentage of feedings during which infants of mothers administered high and low levels of barbiturate were awake and alert (responsive feedings). (From Brazelton, "Psychophysiologic reactions in the neonate: II. Effect of maternal medication in the neonate and his behavior." *Journal of Pediatrics 58,* 513–18. © 1961 by Mosby-Year Book. Reprinted by permission.)

(Kron, Stein, & Goddard, 1966). Prenatal barbiturate exposure just prior to delivery also appears to reduce the amount of time infants spend looking at visual stimuli (Stechler, 1964) and causes transient abnormalities in brain electrical activity (Borgstedt & Rosen, 1968).

Data gathered from nonhuman subjects support the rather sparse findings from humans, portraying barbiturates as teratogens that produce alterations of behavior and the nervous system. The initial experiment was performed in 1952 by Armitage who administered a single injection of barbiturate to pregnant rats on day 19.5 of gestation, about 1.5 days prior to delivery. Drug-exposed animals, when adult, made more errors than the controls in three different mazes. Deficiencies also have been reported in the acquisition of the complex Hebb-Williams maze and the eight-arm radial maze (Kleinberger & Yanai, 1985; Mauri, 1966). Prenatal exposure also elevates open field activity (Middaugh, Simpson, Thomas, & Zemp, 1981a,b), retards acquisition of active and passive avoidance responding (Martin, Martin, LeMire, & Mackler, 1979b; Middaugh, Santos, & Zemp, 1975), and reduces operant responding on fixed ratio schedules of reinforcement (Martin et al., 1979b; Middaugh et al., 1975).

Embryonic barbiturate exposure also leads to reproductive dysfunction. Gupta and Yaffe (1981) administered phenobarbital to pregnant rats and monitored the sexual maturation of the female offspring. Drug-exposed animals attained puberty later than controls and exhibited higher incidences of abnormal estrous cycles and infertility. They also had higher-than-normal levels of plasma estrogen and uterine estrogen receptors. It was speculated that phenobarbital may act on the hypothalamus to inhibit the release of gonadotropins, hormones essential for the attainment of sexual maturation.

Prenatal phenobarbital exposure also produces reproductive dysfunction in male rats, causing a delay in testicular descent and infertility. Exposed males physically resemble females in that they have a shortened space between anus and genitals. These effects are most likely secondary to the reduction in testosterone synthesis observed in 1- and 3-day-old drug-exposed animals (Gupta, Yaffe, & Shapiro, 1982). The testosterone deficit, also manifest in brain levels of the hormone, probably accounts for the significant diminution of male, but not female, sexual behavior following pentobarbital treatment during the period of sexual differentiation (Clemens, Popham, & Ruppert, 1979).

The data from animals and the few that have thus far been obtained from human subjects demonstrate that early exposure to barbiturate leads to wide-ranging alterations of behavior. It should not be surprising, then, that in addition to affecting the endocrine system the drug also influences the development of CNS morphology and biochemistry. Two areas of the brain are particularly affected: hippocampus and cerebellum. In utero barbiturate exposure causes substantial reductions in the number of cerebellar Purkinje cells and hippocampal pyramidal cells, both of which normally develop prenatally (Yanai & Berman, 1981). Should drug treatment extend to the neonatal period, cells that normally form at that time (cerebellar and hippocampal granule cells) also are lost (Yanai, Berman, Shafer, Yedwab, & Tabakoff, 1981). Structures directly involved in neuronal transmission are affected as well; exposure to barbiturate on gestation days 18 to 20 in the rat reduces the length and number of branching points of hippocampal dendrites (Jacobson, Antolick, Scholey, & Uemura, 1988). Lastly, decreased hypothalamic levels of norepinephrine and dopamine, as well as alterations in dopamine receptor binding, are found in rats exposed to barbiturate in utero (Takagi, Alleva, Seth, & Balazs, 1986; Yanai, Sze, Iser, & Melamed, 1985).

X-IRRADIATION

Children of pregnant survivors of the atomic bombing of Hiroshima and Nagasaki testify to the detrimental consequences of prenatal exposure to x-irradiation. Although such exposure produced various effects including growth retardation, missing phalanges, cataracts, and malignancies, mental retardation was the principal manifestation of fetal irradiation (Mole, 1982). According to Mole, there is some evidence that the frequency of retardation (diagnosed if a child was "unable to perform simple calculations, to make simple conversation, to take care of himself or herself, or if he or she was completely unmanageable or had been institutionalised" (Wood, Johnson, & Omori, 1967) is positively related to radiation dosage. Dosage was estimated according to distance from the bomb hypocenter, taking into account the shielding of each individual. The prevalence of retardation also is related to gestational age at the time of exposure. Otake and Schull (1984) found that the period of maximum susceptibility was between weeks 8 and 15 postconception; no cases of retardation were observed if exposure occurred prior to the eighth week.

The offspring of pregnant atomic bomb survivors have provided investigators with dramatic examples of the pernicious influence of prenatal exposure to irradiation. However, precise delineation of the behavioral effects of prenatal irradiation requires laboratory experimentation, which for obvious reasons must be performed with nonhuman subjects. Results of these investigations demonstrate that irradiation affects motor activity, emotionality/arousal, and conditioning/ learning. Let us begin with motor activity.

The initial attempt to quantitatively assess the influence of irradiation on motor activity is that of Furchtgott and Echols (1958a,b), who placed 27-day-old rats on two parallel, narrow metal rods, left paws on one rod and right paws on the other. After completing a successful trial, one in which the subject made four successive steps with alternate hindlegs on the two rods, the distance between the rods was increased. Control animals were able to negotiate rods separated by greater distances than could prenatally irradiated subjects. Also, the higher the dosage of radiation, the shorter was the maximum distance between the rods that an animal could tolerate. Lastly, irradiation on gestation days 14 and 15 was more debilitating than treatment on days 16 and 17 or on day 18. According to Werboff, Goodman, Havlena, & Sikov (1961), prenatally irradiated 26- and 27-day-old rats have less motor strength (as measured by the length of time an animal can hang from a rod by its forepaws) than controls, and prenatally irradiated adults are inferior to controls in the ability to climb an inclined plane (Wechkin, Elder, & Furchtgott, 1961). They also are slower than controls in developing an upright posture (Werboff et al., 1961). Irradiated squirrel monkeys are deficient in the performance of reflexes and in neuromuscular coordination including nursing, tail-hanging, head-up orientation, and body-righting (Ordy, Brizzee, Dunlap, & Knight, 1982).

The result of uterine radiation exposure also has been studied by making long-term observations of the offspring. This procedure was used by Sikov, Resta, Lofstrom, and Meyer (1962), who observed the progeny of rats irradiated on day 10 or 15 of pregnancy. They described the symptomatology as follows:

> In some animals, evidence of altered behavior was first seen at birth, while others appeared normal until more mature. The resulting neurological syndrome was evidenced as various combinations of symptoms. Many animals lost the righting reflex or developed an impairment of placing reactions at some period during their life. Some displayed hypersensitivity to stimuli which manifested itself as exaggerated myoclonic jerks in response to sensory stimuli. Spasticity of the hindlimbs was found only in the 15-day, 185-r rats; at times this was accompanied by a hind-limb ataxia which was also noted in other groups. A number of animals displayed a convulsive disorder similar to the Jacksonian seizure of man. Other neurological deficits noted were gait defects, "backing-up," and forced circling. At the time of puberty, many males developed priapism [chronic penile tumescence] which persisted until death. (p. 131)

A major defect in the locomotor activity of prenatally irradiated rats is the development of "hopping," which occurs when paired fore- and hindlimbs move in unison instead of alternating. This symptom has been studied in detail in an attempt to specify its underlying neurological basis (D'Amato and Hicks, 1980; Mullinex, Norton, & Culver, 1975). Hicks and D'Amato (1980) provided data showing that the hopping gait is principally caused by damage to the dorsal horn of the spinal cord.

Irradiation also has been shown to influence a set of behaviors in a manner indicative of heightened emotionality or arousal. First, irradiated rats exhibit higher levels of both active and passive avoidance behavior than controls (Deagle & Furchtgott, 1968; Tamaki & Inouye, 1981). Second, animals that undergo prenatal irradiation more readily acquire a conditioned emotional response (suppression of instrumental responding by the concurrent presentation of a formerly neutral stimulus that had been paired repeatedly with an aversive stimulus). Sharp (1965) reported that the response–suppression property of a sound (click) can be established by pairing it with electric shock at intensities and durations below those required by normal subjects. Irradiated animals also are less likely than controls to voluntarily leave their home cage to enter unfamiliar territory (Furchtgott & Echols, 1958a) and less readily commence mating behavior (Furchtgott, Murphree, Pace, & Dees, 1959). Lastly, rats irradiated during the first half of gestation tend to show a decline in open-field activity, indicative of increased emotionality (Werboff, Havlena, & Sikov, 1962).

Conditioning/learning also is affected by irradiation. Prenatally exposed animals commit more errors than controls in tests with complex mazes (Fowler, Hicks, D'Amato, & Beach, 1962; Kiyono, Seo, & Shibagaki, 1981) and in the attainment of visual discriminations (Graham, Marks, & Ershoff, 1959; Ordy et al., 1982). Furthermore, irradiated animals are inferior to controls in the acquisition of a classically conditioned response (Walker & Furchtgott, 1970).

The evidence cited above and a good deal of other research attest to the adverse consequences of exposing pregnant animals to x-irradiation. In virtually all cases the negative outcomes are attributed to a direct effect of irradiation on the embryo. However, the cross-fostering design has been used in few experiments; the irradiated embryos subsequently are reared by their biological mothers, who also have been exposed to radiation. Two experiments that do provide for the fostering of prenatally irradiated animals to nonirradiated mothers and nonirradiated embryos to irradiated dams show that irradiated mothers themselves may influence development. Ader and Deitchman (1972) discovered that irradiated mothers spend less time with their young regardless of whether their young were prenatally irradiated. Furthermore, fewer prenatally irradiated rats reared by irradiated mothers survive beyond 30 days compared to those reared by nonirradiated dams. Offspring reared by irradiated mothers weigh less than those reared by control dams, are *less* emotional, and are more sensitive to subsequent irradiation. Sherrod, Meier, and Connor (1977) similarly reported that nonirradiated offspring reared by irradiated mice are less active than others nursed by nonexposed mothers. These data show, then, that the effects reported in most work on prenatal exposure to x-irradiation may be caused in part by an effect of radiation on the adult female.

It is generally agreed, however, that a direct effect of irradiation on the embryonic CNS is the major contributor to postnatal behavioral dysfunction.[1] Histological and biochemical alterations in various areas of the brain (including cerebellum, hippocampus, corpus callosum, and cerebral cortex) and spinal cord have been widely reported (e.g., Antal & Fulop, 1986; Cowen & Geller, 1960; Deroo, Gerber, & Maes, 1986; Hicks & D'Amato, 1980). Most researchers believe that the primary teratogenic mechanism is *cell loss,* which can occur in two ways: Irradiation kills neuroblasts (embryonic progenitors of nerve cells) and inhibits mitotic division. Rakic (1986) has suggested that irradiation also interferes with *neuronal migration,* the process by which a developing nerve cell reaches its final position and develops its appropriate synaptic contacts. Migration generally occurs after the final cell division of the blastocyst. Altered neuronal migratory patterns would modify the brain's circuitry, which in turn could lead to behavioral changes.

RUBELLA

Although rubella (or German measles) was first described early during the eighteenth century, it was not until 1941 that the disease was recognized as producing congenital defects. Gregg (1941) reported a high incidence of cataracts in infants of mothers who had contracted rubella early in pregnancy. Gregg (1945) also reported a relation between maternal rubella and congenital heart disease, uterine malformation, and renal abnormalities (Gregg, 1945). Not only were Gregg's observations momentous in terms of understanding a disease that theretofore had been considered benign but also for "exemplifying a new concept of infectious processes" (Forbes, 1969, p. 5), that of viral transmission from the gravid female to the embryo. Gregg's initial observations have been extended to encompass additional clinical manifestations, including deafness, glaucoma, and psychomotor defects. Collectively, these clinical sequelae are known as the *expanded rubella syndrome.*

The virus, present in maternal blood, is transmitted to the embryo by way of the placenta, where it is widely distributed, having been recovered from face, eye, liver, intestine, hands, and feet of therapeutically aborted embryos (Parkman, Hopps, & Meyer, 1973). It also has been located in infected children up to 18 months of age, attesting to the persistent nature of the infection (Blattner, 1966). The incidence of congenital defects is highest (estimated by some to be as high as 75 to 100%) when the disease in contracted within the first 2 months of pregnancy. The rate declines sharply if infection occurs after the third month (Alastair, 1969). There is no relation, however, between the severity of the infection in the mother and subsequent effects in the offspring; a pregnant women with no overt signs of the disease can give birth to a debilitated baby (Avery, Monif, Sever, & Leikin, 1965).

---

[1] Mole (1990) speculated that mental retardation in humans exposed prenatally to radiation may be caused by a reduction in oxygen transport to the brain rather than to a direct effect on the developing brain. This possibility may warrant appropriate experiments with nonhuman subjects.

According to Alastair (1969), rubella virus produces malformations directly by causing cell death and inhibiting mitosis. It apparently also causes vascular damage, which can produce deleterious effects, especially on brain tissue. Rorke and Spiro (1967) reported extensive vascular damage involving cerebral blood vessels, often taking the form of destruction of one or more layers of the vessel wall. Vascular degeneration was associated with necrosis of adjacent neural tissue.

Germane to this discussion is the fact that maternal rubella is associated not only with congenital malformations and enhanced susceptibility to other diseases but also with mental retardation and behavioral disturbances. As reviewed by Chess, Korn, and Fernandez (1971) the results of studies performed prior to the 1964 rubella epidemic in the United States were equivocal; some investigators reported that rubella children did not differ from normals, whereas others reported behavioral effects. Subsequent research that benefited from the large number of afflicted children revealed that the virus is indeed a behavioral teratogen.

One of the earliest postepidemic studies is that of Desmond and co-workers (Desmond et al., 1967, 1978), who examined 100 rubella children monthly for the first 3 months of life and then at 3-month intervals. The children exhibited a host of neurological abnormalities throughout the first year, and the symptoms persisted; 66% of the 64 children who survived to 18 months displayed "a wide range of motor deficits, hyperactivity, restlessness, convulsions, stereotyped movements and poor progress in adaptive behavior" (Desmond et al., 1967, p. 320) at 18 months of age. Four of them (7%) were classified as autistic. Of the 53 who survived to age 16 to 18 years, 11 had "cerebral dysfunction involving balance, fine and gross motor co-ordination, learning disabilities and disturbances of movement (Desmond et al., 1985, p. 723), and 17 exhibited behavior disturbances consisting in hyperkinesis, impulsivity, perseveration, low frustration thresholds, and attentional disorders. The latter is a prevalent symptom, described by others as an enhanced tendency toward distractibility and hyperactivity (Hicks, 1970; Vernon, 1969, cited by Chess et al., 1971). The four children classified by Desmond et al. (1978) as autistic at 18 months were severely retarded at 16 to 18 years.

The most comprehensive study of the behavioral consequences of congenital rubella has been performed by Chess and her associates, who studied 243 children enrolled in the Rubella Birth Defect Evaluation Project, which was established in response to the 1964 epidemic (Chess, 1977; Chess & Fernandez, 1980; Chess, Fernandez, & Korn, 1979; Chess et al., 1971). The children were 2.5 to 4.0 years of age at the start of the study. About 80% of the sample exhibited one or more rubella-associated physical defects, categorized as visual, auditory, neurological, or cardiac. As summarized in Table 4.2, 20% of the children having no associated physical defects exhibited some form of psychiatric disorder, compared to almost 60% of children with an associated physical defect. Furthermore, two relations between physical defects and mental disturbance were uncovered: (1) the greater the number of defects, the higher the probability that a child would suffer a psychiatric disorder; and (2) those with visual loss alone or in combination with hearing loss were most at risk.

Table 4.2 Number and percentage of rubella children who exhibited particular categories of mental disturbance

Category	No Physical Defect (n = 50)		With Physical Defect (n = 193)	
	No.	%	No.	%
No psychiatric disorder	40	80.0	78	40.4
Cerebral dysfunction	0	0	2	1.0
Cerebral dysfunction + mental retardation	0	0	3	1.6
Reactive behavior disorder	8	16.0	22	11.4
Autism	0	0	1	0.5
Partial syndrome of autism	0	0	1	0.5
Mental retardation				
Unspecified	0	0	1	0.5
Borderline	1	2.0	6	3.1
Mild	0	0	7	3.6
Moderate	0	0	13	6.7
Severe	0	0	26	13.5
Profound	0	0	11	5.7
Reactive behavior disorder				
+ Cerebral dysfunction + mental retardation	0	0	2	1.0
+ Mental retardation—borderline	0	0	2	1.0
+ Mental retardation–moderate	1	2.0	1	0.5
+ Mental retardation—severe	0	0	1	0.5
Mental retardation				
Unspecified + autism	0	0	2	1.0
Borderline + autism	0	0	2	1.0
Moderate + autism	0	0	1	0.5
Severe + autism	0	0	3	1.6
Profound + autism	0	0	1	0.5
Unspecified + partial syndrome of autism	0	0	3	1.6
Moderate + partial syndrome of autism	0	0	3	1.6
Cerebral dysfunction + mental retardation + partial syndrome of autism	0	0	1	0.5

Note: Some of the children had rubella-associated physical defects and others did not. Modified from Chess et al. *Psychiatric Disorders of Children with Congenital Rubella.* © 1971 by Bruner/Mazel. By permission.

The investigators also went beyond the diagnostic categories in an attempt to characterize patterns of behavioral disturbance. The most frequent difficulty (occurring in 74% of the children) involved *mood,* specifically temper tantrums, withdrawn behavior, and separation anxiety. Sixty-four percent of the sample exhibited *discipline* problems, often taking the form of disruptive and destructive activities. It is not surprising, then, that more than half had problems in the area of *social relations,* exhibiting hitting, kicking, and biting of other children. Close to half of the children also had *sleep* problems, and more than 50% experienced difficulty *feeding* and *eating.* Parents reported that their children frequently refused to learn to eat. Two thirds of the sample displayed odd *habits* and *rituals,* including the smelling of all objects, rocking, and arm flapping. In contrast to the low prevalence rate in the general population (3.1 cases per 10,000 children), 10 of the 243 children were diagnosed as being autistic, and 8 others displayed many of the symptoms associated with the disorder. Although exceptions were not infrequent, children with physical defects tended to exhibit more behavioral disturbances than nondamaged children.

Intellectual development also was assessed with standard intelligence tests. The results are summarized in Table 4.3. As Chess and co-workers remarked, although 2 to 3% of children in a random population are expected to be classified as retarded, 23% of the rubella children were so classified. Performance on the tests was related to physical condition. "the children's cognitive abilities decrease as the number of physical defects increases. Nevertheless, it is interesting to note that even among those children with no apparent physical defects there was a higher percentage of retardation than is normally encountered (6% against 3%)" (Chess et al., 1971, p. 78).

When reexamined between the ages of 8 and 9, a large proportion of the sample continued to exhibit retardation, psychiatric disorders, and behavioral pathology. Three of the original ten children diagnosed as autistic recovered, and four new cases of the disorder were uncovered. That some children recovered and others were later diagnosed as being autistic led Chess to conclude that autism runs a course similar to that of a viral infection such as rubella, "in which recovery, chronicity, improvement, worsening, and delayed effects can all occur" (Chess, 1977, p. 81). It led her to speculate that autism, the etiology of which theretofore had been considered by many to be environmental, may be organically based.

The development of the rubella vaccine has dramatically reduced the incidence of the disease but has not eliminated congenital rubella. On one hand, the

Table 4.3 Evaluation of intelligence of children with congenital rubella

Intellectual Level	No.	%
Superior	4	2.3
Above average	17	9.9
Average	53	31.0
Dull normal	23	13.5
Borderline	17	9.9
Mild retardation	6	3.5
Moderate retardation	11	6.4
Severe retardation	15	8.8
Profound retardation	7	4.1
No estimate possible	18	10.5
Total	171	99.9

Source: From Chess et al. *Psychiatric Disorders of Children with Congenital Rubella.* © 1971 by Bruner/Mazel. Reprinted by permission.

vaccine, although remarkably effective, fails to prevent rubella in about 5 to 7% of the cases. Moreover, because the vaccine consists of live rubella virus, it places embryos at risk if it is administered to a pregnant woman within 3 months of conception or, of course, if it is given to a woman who is unaware of her pregnancy. Lastly, some individuals simply are not inoculated.

CONCLUDING COMMENTS

As stated at the outset, this discussion was not intended as a comprehensive examination of all documented behavioral teratogenic agents, as such an effort would easily exceed the space limitations of this volume. Instead, its purpose was to acquaint the reader with some pervasive teratogens of differing types and to describe a number of important methodological issues that constrain behavioral teratogenic research.

Four generalizations can be made about laboratory research in behavioral teratology. (1) Most experiments examine the influence of a single agent. (2) The dependent measures always involve postnatal behavior. (3) An effect of an agent on behavior is assumed to be produced by its ability to interfere with embryonic development. (4) The data are considered almost exclusively from the standpoint of the affected subjects. Let us briefly consider each of these generalizations.

Although experiments that consider the influence of a single agent yield important information, in the world outside the laboratory a given agent frequently acts in concert, and often in synergy, with others. This situation certainly is the case with drugs; multiple drug users comprise a large proportion of the population of drug abusers. It is important, then, to examine the influence of simultaneous and sequential exposure to two or more teratogens. Furthermore, given the relation between embryonic and postembryonic behavior, teratological research would likely benefit from assessment of an agent's potential influence on prenatal as well as postnatal behavior.

Next is the issue of attribution. Although the effect of a teratogen is almost always attributed, at least implicitly, to its interference with embryonic development, in only some cases is such a conclusion warranted. It is because the cross-fostering experimental design, which permits one to distinguish prenatal from postnatal effects, is infrequently used. Therefore the possibility that the effect of a teratogen is caused by alteration of an aspect of the postnatal environment, such as maternal behavior, is rarely considered.

Lastly, the focus of the research, as reflected in both the design of experiments and the discussion sections of the written reports, is almost exclusively on the effectiveness of the agent in question. Thus attention is paid almost exclusively to the subjects who exhibit behavioral anomalies. Little thought is given those who for some reason are immune to the teratogen except to consider them as manifesting the expected variation as found in all experiments. However, an understanding of why particular subjects are spared could provide important information about the mechanisms through which an agent produces its adverse effects and perhaps suggestions as to how the effects of a teratogen may be prevented.

REFERENCES

Abel, E. L. (1982). In utero alcohol exposure and developmental delay of response inhibition. *Alcoholism: Clinical and Experimental Research, 6,* 369–76.

Abel, E. L. (1985). *Fetal alcohol exposure and effects. A comprehensive bibliography.* Westport, CT: Greenwood Press.

Acker, D., Sachs, B. P., Tracey, K. J., and Wise, W. E. (1983). Abruptio placentae associated with cocaine use. *American Journal of Obstetrics and Gynecology, 146,* 220–21.

Ader, R., and Deitchman, R. (1972). Prenatal maternal x-irradiation: Maternal and offspring effects. *Journal of Comparative and Physiological Psychology, 78,* 202–9.

Ahmed, I. I., Shryne, J. E., Gorski, R. A., Branch, B. J., and Taylor, A. N. (1991). Prenatal ethanol and the prepubertal sexually dimorphic nucleus of the preoptic. *Physiology and Behavior, 49,* 427–32.

Alastair, J. (1969). Congenital rubella. *American Journal of Diseases of Children, 118,* 35–44.

Anandam, N., and Stern, J. M. (1980). Alcohol in utero: Effects on preweaning appetitive learning. *Neurobehavioral Toxicology, 2,* 199–205.

Antal, S., and Fulop, Z. (1986). Histological studies in developing brain after 0.5 gy neutron irradiation in utero. In H. Kriegel, W. Schmahl, G. B. Gerber, and F. E. Stieve (Eds.), *Radiation risks to the developing nervous system* (pp. 141–53). New York: Gustav Fischer.

Armitage, S. G. (1952). The effects of barbiturates on the behavior of rat offspring as measured in learning and reasoning situations. *Journal of Comparative and Physiological Psychology, 45,* 146–52.

Autti-Rämö, I., and Granström, M. -L. (1991). The psychomotor development during the first year of life of infants exposed to intrauterine alcohol of various duration. *Neuropediatrics, 22,* 59–64.

Avery, G. B., Monif, G.R.G., Sever, J. L., and Leikin, S. L. (1965). Rubella syndrome after inapparent maternal illness. *American Journal of Diseases of Children, 110,* 444–46.

Barnes, A. B., Calton, T., Gundersen, J., Noller, K. L., Tilley, B. C., Strama, T., Townsend, D. E., Hatab, P., and O'Brien, P. C. (1980). Fertility and outcome of pregnancy in women exposed in utero to diethylstilbestrol. *New England Journal of Medicine, 302,* 609–13.

Barron, S., Bliss-Tieman, S., and Riley, E. P. (1988). Effects of prenatal alcohol exposure on the sexually dimorphic nucleus of the preoptic area of the hypothalamus in male and female rats. *Alcoholism: Clinical and Experimental Research, 12,* 59–64.

Bingol, N., Fuchs, M., Diaz, V., Stone, R. K., and Gromish, D. S. (1987). Teratogenicity of cocaine in humans. *Journal of Pediatrics, 110,* 93–96.

Blakley, P. M., and Fedoroff, S. (1985). Effects of prenatal alcohol exposure on neural cells in mice. *International Journal of Developmental Neuroscience, 3,* 69–76.

Blattner, R. J. (1966). Congenital rubella: Persistent infection of brain and liver. *Journal of Pediatrics, 68,* 997–99.

Borgstedt, A. D., and Rosen, M. G. (1968). Medication during labor correlated with behavior and EEG of the newborn. *American Journal of Diseases of Children, 115,* 21–24.

Branchey, L., and Friedhoff, A. J. (1976). Biochemical and behavioral changes in rats exposed to ethanol in utero. *Annals of the New York Academy of Sciences, 273,* 328–30.

Brazelton, T. B. (1961a). Psychophysiologic reactions in the neonate. I. The value of observation of the neonate. *Journal of Pediatrics, 58,* 508–12.

Brazelton, T. B. (1961b). Psychophysiologic reactions in the neonate. II. Effect of maternal medication in the neonate and his behavior. *Journal of Pediatrics, 58,* 513–18.

Burchfield, D. J., Graham, E. M., Abrams, R. M., and Gerhardt, K. J. (1990). Cocaine alters behavioral states in fetal sheep. *Developmental Brain Research, 56,* 41–45.

Chasnoff, I. J., Burns, K. A., and Burns, W. J. (1987). Cocaine use in pregnancy: Perinatal morbidity and mortality. *Neurotoxicology and Teratology, 9,* 291–93.

Chasnoff, I. J., Burns, W. J., Schnall, S. H., and Burns, K. A. (1985). Cocaine use in pregnancy. *New England Journal of Medicine, 313,* 666–69.

Chasnoff, I., Hunt, C., Kletter R., and Kaplan, D. (1986). Increased risk of SIDS and respiratory pattern anomalies in cocaine-exposed infants. *Pediatric Research, 20,* 425A.

Chen, J. S., Driscoll, C. D., and Riley, E. P. (1982). Ontogeny of suckling behavior in rats prenatally exposed to alcohol. *Teratology, 26,* 145–53.

Cherukuri, R., Minkoff, H., Feldman, J., Parekh, A., and Glass, A. (1988). Cohort study of alkaloidal cocaine ("crack") in pregnancy. *Obstetrics and Gynecology, 72,* 147–51.

Chess, S. (1977). Follow-up report on autism in congenital rubella. *Journal of Autism and Childhood Schizophrenia, 7,* 69–81.

Chess, S., Korn, S. J., and Fernandez, P. B. (1971). *Psychiatric disorders of children with congenital rubella.* New York: Brunner/Mazel, 1971.

Chess, S., and Fernandez, P. (1980). Impulsivity in rubella deaf children: A longitudinal study. *American Annals of the Deaf, 125,* 505–9.

Chess, S., Fernandez, P., and Korn, S. (1979). Behavioral consequences of congenital rubella. *Progress in Child Psychiatry and Child Development, 32,* 467–75.

Church, M. W., Dintcheff, B. A., and Gessner, P. K. (1988). Dose-dependent consequences of cocaine on pregnancy outcome in the Long-Evans rat. *Neurotoxicology and Teratology, 10,* 51–58.

Clarren, S. K., Astley, S. J., and Bowden, D. M. (1988). Physical anomalies and developmental delays in nonhuman primate infants exposed to weekly doses of ethanol during gestation. *Teratology, 37,* 561–69.

Clarren, S. K., and Smith, D. W. (1978). The fetal alcohol syndrome. *New England Journal of Medicine, 298,* 1063–67.

Clemens, L. G., Popham, T. V., and Ruppert, P. H. (1979). Neonatal treatment of hamsters with barbiturate alters adult sexual behavior. *Developmental Psychobiology, 12,* 49–59.

Cohen, N. E., Anday, E. K., and Leitner, D. S. (1989). Effects of in-utero cocaine exposure on sensorineural reactivity. *Annals of the New York Academy of Sciences, 562,* 344–48.

Cousins, L., Karp, W., Lacey, C., and Lucas, W. E. (1980). Reproductive outcome of women exposed to diethylstilbestrol in utero. *Obstetrics and Gynecology, 56,* 70–76.

Cowen, D., and Geller, L. M. (1960). Long-term pathological effects of prenatal x-irradiation on the central nervous system of the rat. *Journal of Neuropathology and Experimental Neurology, 1,* 488–527.

D'Amato, C. J., and Hicks, S. P. (1980). Development of the motor system: Effects of radiation on developing corticospinal neurons and locomotor function. *Experimental Neurology, 70,* 1–23.

Day, N. L., and Robles, N. (1989). Methodological issues in the measurements of substance use. *Annals of the New York Academy of Sciences, 562,* 8–13.

Deagle, J., and Furchtgatt, E. (1968). Passive avoidance in prenatally x-irradiated rats. *Developmental Psychobiology, 1,* 90–92.

Deroo, J., Gerber, G. B., and Maes, J. (1986). Biogenic amines: Amino acids and regional blood flow in rat brain after prenatal irradiation. In H. Kriegel, W. Schmahl, G. B. Gerber, and F. E. Stieve (Eds.), *Radiation risks to the developing nervous system* (pp. 211–20). New York: Gustav Fischer.

Desmond, M. M., Fisher, E., Vorderman, A., Schaffer, H., Andrew, L., and Catlin, F. (1978). The longitudinal course of congenital rubella encephalitis in non-retarded children. *Journal of Pediatrics, 93,* 584–91.

Desmond, M. M., Wilson, G. S., Melnick, J. L., Singer, D. B., Zion, T. E., Rudolph, A. J., Pineda, R. G., Ziai, M. H., and Blattner, R. J. (1967). Congenital rubella encephalitis. *Journal of Pediatrics, 71,* 311–31.

Desmond, M. M., Wilson, G. S., Vorderman, A. L., Murphy, M. A., Thurber, S., Fisher, E. S., and Kroulik, E. M. (1985). The health and educational status of adolescents with congenital rubella syndrome. *Developmental Medicine and Child Neurology, 27,* 721–29.

Doberczak, T. M., Shanzy, S., Sonie, R. T., and Kandall, S. R. (1988). Neonatal neurologic and electroencephalographic effects of intrauterine cocaine exposure. *Journal of Pediatrics, 113,* 354–58.

Dow-Edwards, D. L., Freed, L. A., and Fico, T. A. (1990). Structural and functional effects of prenatal cocaine exposure in adult rat brain. *Developmental Brain Research, 57,* 263–68.

Dow-Edwards, D. L., Freed, L. A., and Milhorat, T. H. Stimulation of brain metabolism by perinatal cocaine exposure. (1988). *Developmental Brain Research, 42,* 137–41.

Dow-Edwards, D. L., Trachtman, H., Riley, E. P., Freed, L. A., and Milhorat, T. H. (1989). Arginine vasopressin and body fluid homeostasis in the fetal alcohol exposed rat. *Alcohol, 6,* 193–98.

Driscoll, C. D., Chen, J. S., and Riley, E. P. (1982). Passive avoidance performance in rats prenatally exposed to alcohol during various periods of gestation. *Neurobehavioral Toxicology and Teratology, 4,* 99–103.

Driscoll, C. D., Streissguth, A. P., and Riley, E. P. (1990). Prenatal alcohol exposure: comparability of effects in humans and animal models. *Neurotoxicology and Teratology, 12,* 231–37.

Ehrhardt, A. A., Feldman, J. F., Rosen, L. R., Meyer-Bahlburg, H.F.L., Gruen, R., Veridiano, N. P., Endicott, J., and Cohen, P. (1987). Psychopathology in prenatally DES-exposed females: Current and lifetime adjustment. *Psychosomatic Medicine, 49,* 183–96.

Ehrhardt, A. A., Meyer-Bahlburg, H.F.L., Rosen, L. R., Feldman, J. F., Veridiano, N. P., Zimmerman, I., and McEwen, B. S. (1985). *Archives of Sexual Behavior, 14,* 57–75.

Ellis, F. W., and Pick, J. R. (1976). Beagle model of the fetal alcohol syndrome. *The Pharmacologist, 18,* 190.

Fantel, A. G., and MacPhail, B. J. (1982). The teratogenicity of cocaine. *Teratology, 26,* 17–19.

Fein, G. G., Schwartz, P. M., Jacobson, S. W., and Jacobson, J. L. (1983). Environmental toxins and behavioral development. *American Psychologist,* 1188–197.

Fernandez, K., Caul, W. F., Osborne, G. L., and Henderson, G. I. (1983). Effects of chronic alcohol exposure on offspring activity in rats. *Neurobehavioral Toxicology and Teratology, 5,* 135–37.

Forbes, J. A. (1969). Rubella: Historical aspects. *American Journal of Diseases of Children, 118,* 5–11.

Fowler, H., Hicks, S. P., D'Amato, C. J., and Beach, F. A. (1962). Effects of fetal irradiation on behavior in the albino rat. *Journal of Comparative and Physiological Psychology, 55,* 309–14.

Furchtgatt, E., and Echols, M. (1958a). Activity and emotionality in pre- and neonatally x-irradiated rats. *Journal of Comparative and Physiological Psychology, 51,* 541–45.

Furchtgatt, E., and Echols, M. (1958b). Locomotion coordination following pre- and neonatal X irradiation. *Journal of Comparative and Physiological Psychology, 51,* 292–94.

Furchtgatt, E., Murphree, R. L., Pace, H. B., and Dees, J. W. (1959). Mating activity in fetally irradiated male swine and rats. *Psychological Reports, 5,* 545–48.

Gavin, F. H., and Ellinwood, E. H. (1988). Cocaine and other stimulants. *New England Journal of Medicine, 318,* 1173–182.

Gianoulakis, C. (1990). Rats exposed prenatally to alcohol exhibit impairment in spatial navigation. *Behavioural Brain Research, 36,* 217–28.

Graham, T. M., Marks, A., and Ershoff, B. H. (1959). Effects of prenatal x-irradiation on discrimination learning in the rat. *Proceedings of the Society for Experimental Biology and Medicine, 100,* 74–81.

Gregg, N. M. (1941). Congenital cataract following German measles in the mother. *Transactions of the Ophthalmological Society of Australia, 3,* 35–46.

Gregg, N. M. (1945). Rubella during pregnancy in the mother, with its sequelae of congenital defects in the child. *Medical Journal of Australia, 1,* 313–15.

Gupta, C., and Yaffe, S. J. (1981). Reproductive dysfunctions in female offspring after prenatal exposure to phenobarbital: Critical period of action. *Pediatric Research, 15,* 1488–491.

Gupta, C., Yaffee, S. J., and Shapiro, B. H. (1982). Prenatal exposure to phenobarbital permanently decreases testosterone and causes reproductive dysfunctions. *Science, 216,* 640–42.

Herbst, A. I., Ulfelder, H., and Poskanzer, D. C. (1971). Adenocarcinoma of the vagina. *New England Journal of Medicine, 284,* 878–81.

Hicks, D. E. (1970). Comparison profiles of rubella and non-rubella deaf children. *American Annals of the Deaf, 115,* 86–92.

Hicks, S. P., and D'Amato, C. J. (1980). Development of the motor system: Hopping rats produced by prenatal irradiation. *Experimental Neurology, 70,* 24–39.

Hines, M., and Goy, R. W. (1985). Estrogens before birth and development of sex-related reproductive traits in the female guinea pig. *Hormones and Behavior, 19,* 331–47.

Hines, M., and Shipley, C. (1984). Prenatal exposure to diethylstilbestrol (DES) and the development of sexually dimorphic cognitive abilities and cerebral lateralization. *Developmental Psychology, 20,* 81–94.

Hoyseth, K. S., and Jones, P.J.H. (1989). Ethanol induced teratogenesis: Characterization, mechanisms and diagnostic approaches. *Life Sciences, 44,* 643–49.

Hrbek, A., Iversen, K., and Olsson, T. (1982). Evaluation of cerebral function in newborn infants with fetal growth retardation. In J. Courjon and F. Mauguiere (Eds.), *Clinical applications of evoked potential in neurology* (pp. 89–95). New York: Raven Press.

Hutchings, D. E., Fico, T. A., and Dow-Edwards, D. L. (1989). Prenatal cocaine: Maternal toxicity, fetal effects and locomotor activity in rat offspring. *Neurotoxicology and Teratology, 11,* 65–69.

Jacobson, C. D., Antolick, L. L., Scholey, R., and Uemura, E. (1988). The influence of prenatal phenobarbital exposure on the growth of dendrites in the rat hippocampus. *Developmental Brain Research, 44,* 233–39.

Johnson, L. D., Driscoll, S. G., Hertig, A. T., Cole, P. T., and Nickerson, R. J. (1979). Vaginal adenosis in stillborns and neonates exposed to diethylstilbestrol and steroidal estrogens and progestins. *Obstetrics and Gynecology, 53,* 671–79.

Jones, K. L., and Smith, D. W. (1973). Recognition of the fetal alcohol syndrome in early infancy. *Lancet, 2,* 999–1001.

Jones, K. L., Smith, D. W., Ulleland, C. N., and Streissguth, P. (1973). Pattern of malformations in offspring of chronic alcoholic mothers. *Lancet, 1,* 1267–271.

Kiyono, S., Seo, M., and Shibagaki, M. (1981). Effects of environmental enrichment upon maze performance in rats with microcephaly induced by prenatal x-irradiation. *Japanese Journal of Physiology, 31,* 769–73.

Kleinberger, N., and Yanai, J. (1985). Early phenobarbital-induced alterations in hippocampal acetylcholinesterase activity and behavior. *Developmental Brain Research, 22,* 113–23.

Kron, R. E., Stein, M., and Goddard, K. E. (1966). Newborn sucking behavior affected by obstetric sedation. *Pediatrics, 37,* 1012–16.

LeBlanc, P. E., Parekh, A. J., Naso, B., and Glass, L. (1987). Effect of intrauterine exposure to alkaloidal cocaine ("crack"). *American Journal of Diseases of Children, 141,* 937–38.

Ledig, M., Misslin, R., Kopp, P., Vogel, E., Tholey, G., and Mandel, P. (1990). Alcohol exposure before pregnancy: Biochemical effects on the offspring of rats. *Pharmacology, Biochemistry and Behavior, 36,* 279–85.

Lemoine, P., Harousseau, H., Bortegru, J. P., and Menuet, J. C. (1968). Les enfants de parents a' propos de 127 cas. *Quest Medicine, 25,* 476–82.

Little, R. E., Streissguth, A. P., Barr, H. M., and Herman, C. S. (1980). Decreased birth weight in infants of alcoholic women who abstained during pregnancy. *Journal of Pediatrics, 96,* 974–77.

MacGregor, S. N., Keith, L. G., Chasnoff, I. J., Rosner, M. A., Chisum, G. M., Shaw, P., and Minogue, J. P. (1987). Cocaine use during pregnancy: Adverse perinatal outcome. *American Journal of Obstetrics and Gynecology, 157,* 686–90.

Mahalik, M. P., Gautieri, R. F., and Mann, D. E. (1980). Teratogenic potential of cocaine hydrochloride in CF-1 mice. *Journal of Pharmaceutical Sciences, 69,* 703–6.

Martin, J. C., Martin, D. C., Sigman, G., and Radow, B. (1978). Maternal ethanol consumption and hyperactivity in cross-fostered offspring. *Physiology and Behavior, 6,* 362–65.

Martin, D. C., Martin, J. C., Streissguth, A. P., and Lund, C. A. (1979a). Sucking frequency and amplitude in newborns as a function of maternal drinking and smoking. In M. Gallenter (Ed.), *Currents in alcoholism,* vol. 5 (pp. 203–39). Orlando, FL: Grune & Stratton.

Martin, J. C., Martin, D. C., LeMire, R., and Mackler, B. (1979b). Effects of maternal absorption of phenobarbital upon rat offspring development and function. *Neurobehavioral Toxicology, 1,* 49–55.

Mauri, N. (1966). Effect of maternal medication during pregnancy upon behavioral development in offspring. *Tohuku Journal of Experimental Medicine, 89,* 265–73.

McGivern, R. F., Clancy, A. N., Hill, M. A., and Noble, E. P. (1984). Prenatal alcohol exposure alters adult expression of sexually dimorphic behavior in the rat. *Science, 224,* 896–98.

McGivern, R. F., Raum, W. J., Salido, E., and Redei, E. (1988). Lack of prenatal testosterone surge in fetal rats exposed to alcohol: Alterations in testicular morphology and physiology. *Alcoholism: Clinical and Experimental Research, 12,* 243–47.

McLain, D. E., and Roe, D. A. (1984). Fetal alcohol syndrome in the ferret *(Mustela putorius). Teratology, 30,* 203–10.

McMartin, K. E., Kennedy, K. A., Greenspan, P., Alam, S. N., Greiner, P., and Yam, J. (1978). Diethylstilbestrol: A review of its toxicity and use as a growth promotant in food-producing animals. *Journal of Environmental Pathology and Toxicology, 1,* 279–313.

Meyer, L. S., and Riley, E. P. (1986). Social play in juvenile rats prenatally exposed to alcohol. *Teratology, 34,* 1–7.

Meyer-Bahlburg, H.F.L., Ehrhardt, A. A., Feldman, J. F., Rosen, L. R., Veridiano, N. P., and Zimmerman, I. (1985). Sexual activity level and sexual functioning in women exposed to diethylstilbestrol. *Psychosomatic Medicine, 47,* 497–511.

Meyer-Bahlburg, H.F.L., Ehrhardt, A. A., Rosen, L. R., Feldman, J. F., Veridiano, N. P., Zimmerman, I., and McEwen, B. S. (1984). Psychosexual milestones in women prenatally exposed to diethylstilbestrol. *Hormones and Behavior, 18,* 359–66.

Middaugh, L. D., Santos, C. A., and Zemp, J. W. (1975). Phenobarbital during pregnancy alters operant behavior of offspring in C57 BL/6J mice. *Pharmacology, Biochemistry and Behavior, 3,* 1137–139.

Middaugh, L. D., Simpson, L. W., Thomas, T. N., and Zemp, J. W. (1981a). Prenatal maternal phenobarbital increases reactivity and retards habituation of mature offspring to environmental stimuli. *Psychopharmacology, 74,* 349–52.

Middaugh, L. D., Thomas, T. N., Simpson, L. W., and Zemp, J. W. (1981b). Effects of prenatal maternal injections of phenobarbital on brain neurotransmitters and behavior of young C57 mice. *Neurobehavioral Toxicology and Teratology, 3,* 271–75.

Mole, R. H. (1982). Consequences of pre-natal radiation exposure for post-natal development: A review. *International Journal of Radiation Biology, 42,* 1–12.

Mole, R. H. (1990). Severe mental retardation after large prenatal exposures to bomb irradiation: Reduction in oxygen transport to fetal brain: a possible abscopal mechanism. *International Journal of Radiation Biology, 58,* 705–11.

Molina, J. C., Hoffman, H., and Spear, L. P. (1987). Sensorimotor maturation and alcohol responsiveness in rats prenatally exposed to alcohol during gestation day 8. *Neurotoxicology and Teratology, 9,* 121–28.

Montouris, G. D., Fenichel, G. M., and McLain, L. W. (1979). The pregnant epileptic. *Archives of Neurology, 36,* 601–3.

Mullinex, P., Nortin, S., and Culver, B. (1975). Locomotor damage in rats after x-irradiation in utero. *Experimental Neurology, 48,* 310–24.

Neuspiel, D. R., Hamel, S. C., Hochberg, E., Greene, J., and Campbell, D. (1991). Maternal cocaine use and infant behavior. *Neurotoxicology and Teratology, 13,* 229–33.

Noller, K. L., and Fish, C. R. (1974). Diethylstilbestrol usage: its interesting past, important present, and questionable future. *Medical Clinics of North America, 58,* 793–810.

Olegard, R., Sabel, K-G., Aronsson, M., Sandin, B., Johansson, P. R., Carlsson, C., Kyllerman, M., Iverson, K., and Hrbek, A. (1979). Effects on the child of alcohol abuse during pregnancy. *Acta Paediatrica Scandinavica, 275*(suppl.), 112–21.

Ordy, J. M., Brizzee, K. R., Dunlap, W. P., and Knight, C. (1982). Effects of prenatal ^{60}Co irradiation on postnatal neural, learning, and hormonal development of the squirrel monkey. *Radiation Research, 89,* 309–24.

Otake, M., and Schull, W. J. (1984). In utero exposure to A-bomb radiation and mental retardation; a reassessment. *British Journal of Radiology, 57,* 409–14.

Ouellette, E. M., Rosett, H. L., Rosman, N. P., and Weiner, L. (1977). Adverse effects on offspring of maternal alcohol abuse during pregnancy. *New England Journal of Medicine, 297,* 528–30.

Papara-Nicholson, D., and Telford, I. R. (1957). Effects of alcohol on reproduction and fetal development in the guinea pig. *Anatomical Record, 127,* 438.

Parker, S., Udani, M., Gavalu, J. S., and Van Thiel, D. H. (1984). Adverse effects of ethanol upon the adult sexual behavior of male rats exposed in utero. *Neurobehavioral Toxicology and Teratology, 6,* 289–93.

Parkman, P. D., Hopps, H. E., and Meyer, H. M. (1973). Virus isolation procedures. In H. Friedman and J. E. Prier (Eds.), *Rubella* (pp. 33–50). Springfield, IL: Charles C Thomas.

Peress, N. R., Tsai, C. C., Morther, R. S., and Williamson, H. O. (1982). Hirsutism and menstrual patterns in women exposed to diethylstilbestrol in utero. *American Journal of Obstetrics and Gynecology, 144,* 135–40.

Plant, M. (1985). *Women, drinking and pregnancy.* London: Tavistock Publications.

Plapinger, L., and McEwen, B. S. (1978). Gonadal steroid-brain interactions in sexual differentiation. In J. B. Hutchinson (Ed.), *Biological determinants of sexual behavior* (pp. 153–218). New York: John Wiley & Sons.

Rakic, P. (1986). Normal and abnormal neuronal migration during brain development. In H. Kriegel, W. Schmahl, G. B. Gerber, and F. E. Stieve (Eds.), *Radiation risks to the developing nervous system* (pp. 35–44). New York: Gustav Fischer.

Raum, W. J., McGivern, R. F., Peterson, M. A., Shryne, J. H., and Gorski, R. A. (1990). Prenatal inhibition of of hypothalamic sex steroid uptake by cocaine: effects on neurobehavioral sexual differentiation in male rats. *Developmental Brain Research, 53,* 230–36.

Reinisch, J. M., and Sanders, S. A. (1982). Early barbiturate exposure: The brain, sexually dimorphic behavior and learning. *Neuroscience and Biobehavioral Reviews, 6,* 311–19.

Riley, E. P., Lochry, E. A., and Shapiro, N. R. (1979). Lack of response inhibition in rats prenatally exposed to alcohol. *Psychopharmacology, 62,* 47–52.

Rockwood, G. A., and Riley, E. P. (1986). Suckling deficits in rat pups exposed to alcohol in utero. *Teratology, 33,* 145–51.

Rorke, L. B., and Spiro, A. J. (1967). Cerebral lesions in congenital rubella syndrome. *Journal of Pediatrics, 70,* 243–55.

Rosett, H. L., and Weiner, L. (1984). *Alcohol and the fetus.* New York: Oxford University Press.

Ryan, L., Ehrlich, S., and Finnegan, L. (1987). Cocaine abuse in pregnancy: Effects on the fetus and newborn. *Neurotoxicology and Teratology, 9,* 295–99.

Sharp, J. C. (1965). The effects of prenatal x-irradiation on acquisition, retention, and extinction of a conditioned emotional response. *Radiation Research, 24,* 154–57.

Shaywitz, S. E., Cohen, D. J., and Shaywitz, B. A. (1980). Behavior and learning difficulties in children of normal intelligence born to alcoholic mothers. *Journal of Pediatrics, 96,* 978–82.

Sherrod, K. B., Meier, G. W., and Connor, W. H. (1977). Open-field behavior of prenatally irradiated and/or postnatally handled C57 BL/6 mice. *Developmental Psychobiology, 10,* 195–202.

Sikov, M. R., Resta, C. F., Lofstrom, J. E., and Meyer, J. S. (1962). Neurological deficits in the rat resulting from x-irradiation in utero. *Experimental Neurology, 5,* 131–38.

Slikker, W., Hill, D. E., and Young, J. F. (1982). Comparison of the transplacental pharmacokinetics of 17β-estradiol and diethylstilbestrol in the subhuman primate. *Journal of Pharmacology and Experimental Therapeutics, 221,* 173–82.

Smith, D. W. (1977). Teratogenicity of anticonvulsive medications. *American Journal of Diseases of Children, 131,* 1337–339.

Smith, R. F., Mattran, K. M., and Kurkjian, M. F. (1989). Alterations in offspring behavior induced by chronic prenatal cocaine dosing. *Neurotoxicology and Teratology, 11,* 35–38.

Smithalls, R. W. (1976). Environmental teratogens of man. *British Medical Bulletin, 32,* 27–33.

Smotherman, W. P., Woodruff, K. S., Robinson, S. R., and Del Real, C. (1986). Spontaneous fetal behavior after maternal exposure to ethanol. *Pharmacology, Biochemistry and Behavior, 24,* 165–70.

Spear, L. P., Kirstein, C. L., Bell, J., Yoottanasumpun, V., Greenbaum, R., O'Shea, J., and Spear, N. E. (1989a). Effects of prenatal cocaine exposure on behavior during the early postnatal period. *Neurotoxicology and Teratology, 11,* 57–63.

Spear, L. P., Kirstein, C. L., and Frambes, N. A. (1989b). Cocaine effects on the developing central nervous system: Behavioral, psychopharmacological, and neurochemical studies. *Annals of the New York Academy of Sciences, 562,* 291–307.

Stechler, G. (1964). Newborn attention as affected by medication during labor. *Science, 144,* 315–17.

Steinhausen, H. C., Nestler, V., and Spohr, H-L. (1982). Development and psychopathology of children with the fetal alcohol syndrome. *Developmental and Behavioral Pediatrics, 3,* 49–54.

Streissguth, A. P., Barr, H. M., Sampson, P. D., and Martin, D. C. 91989a). IQ at age 4 in relation to maternal alcohol use and smoking during pregnancy. *Developmental Psychology, 25,* 3–11.

Streissguth, A. P., Herman, C. S., and Smith, D. W. (1978). Intelligence, behavior, and dysmorphogenesis in the fetal alcohol syndrome: A report on 20 patients. *Journal of Pediatrics, 92,* 363–67.

Streissguth, A. P., Sampson, P. D., and Barr, H. M. (1989b). Neurobehavioral dose-response effects of prenatal alcohol exposure in humans from infancy to adulthood. *Annals of the New York Academy of Sciences, 562,* 145–58.

Sulik, K. K., Johnston, M. C., and Webb, M. A. (1981). Fetal alcohol syndrome: Embryogenesis in a mouse model. *Science, 214,* 936–38.

Takagi, S., Alleva, F. R., Seth, P. K., and Balazs, T. (1986). Delayed development of reproductive functions and alteration of dopamine receptor binding in hypothalamus of rats exposed prenatally to phenyltrin and phenobarbital. *Toxicology Letters, 34,* 107–13.

Tamaki, Y., and Inouye, M. (1981). Avoidance learning under delayed shock termination in prenatally x-irradiated rats. *Developmental Psychobiology, 14,* 95–99.

Taylor, A. N., Branch, B. J., Cooley-Matthews, B., and Poland, R. E. (1982). Effects of maternal alcohol consumption in rats on brain and rhythmic pituitary-adrenal function in neonatal offspring. *Psychoneuroendocrinology, 3,* 49–58.

Thadoni, P. V. (1982). Fetal alcohol syndrome: neurochemical and endocrinological abnormalities. *Progress in Biochemical Pharmacology, 16,* 585–89.

Tze, W. J., and Lee, M. (1975). Adverse effects of maternal alcohol consumption on pregnancy and foetal growth in rats. *Nature, 257,* 479–80.

Ulleland, C. N. (1972). The offspring of alcoholic mothers. *Annals of the New York Academy of Sciences, 197,* 167–69.

Vessey, M. P., Fairweather, D. V. I., Norman-Smith, B., and Buckley, J. (1983). A randomized double-blind controlled trial of the value of stilboestrol therapy in pregnancy: long-term follow-up of mothers and their offspring. *British Journal of Obstetrics and Gynaecology, 90,* 1007–17.

Waddell, W. J., and Marlowe, G. C. (1976). Disposition of drugs in the fetus. In B. L. Mirkin (Ed.), *Perinatal pharmacology and therapeutics* (pp. 119–268). Orlando, FL: Academic Press.

Walker, S., and Furchtgatt, E. (1970). Effects of prenatal x-irradiation on the acquisition, extinction, and discrimination of a classically conditioned response. *Radiation Research, 42,* 120–28.

Ward, I. L., and Weisz, J. (1980). Maternal stress alters plasma testosterone in fetal males. *Science, 207,* 328–29.

Wechkin, S., Elder, R. F., and Furchtgatt, E. (1961). Motor performance in the rat as a function of age and prenatal x irradiation. *Journal of Comparative and Physiological Psychology, 54,* 658–59.

Weiss, K. (1975). Vaginal cancer: An iatrogenic disease. *International Journal of Health Services, 5,* 235–51.

Werboff, J., Goodman, I., Havlena, J., and Sikov, M. R. (1961). Effects of prenatal x-irradiation on motor performance in the rat. *American Journal of Physiology, 201,* 703–6.

Werboff, J., and Gottlieb, J. S. (1963). Drugs in pregnancy: Behavioral teratology. *Obstetrics and Gynecologic Survey, 18,* 420–23.

Werboff, J., Havlena, J., and Sikov, M. R. (1962). Effects of prenatal x-irradiation on activity, emotionality, and maze-learning in the rat. *Radiation Research, 16,* 441–52.

West, J. R., Hodges, C. A., and Black, A. C. (1981). Prenatal exposure to ethanol alters the organization of hippocampal mossy fibers in rats. *Science, 211,* 957–59.

Wood, J. W., Johnson, K. G., and Omori, Y. (1967). In utero exposure to the Hiroshima atomic bomb: follow-up at 20 years. *Pediatrics, 39,* 385–92.

Woods, J. R., Plessinger, M. A., and Clark, K. E. (1987). Effect of cocaine on uterine blood flow and fetal oxygenation. *Journal of the American Medical Association, 257,* 957–60.

Woods, J. R., Plessinger, M. A., Scott, K., and Miller, R. K. (1989). Prenatal cocaine exposure to the fetus: A sheep model for cardiovascular evaluation. *Annals of the New York Academy of Sciences, 562,* 267–79.

Yanai, J., and Berman, A. (1981). Neuronal deficits in mice following neonatal exposure to barbiturates. *Experimental Neurology, 73,* 199–208.

Yanai, J., Berman, A., Shafer, R., Yedwab, J., and Tabakoff, B. (1981). Audiogenic seizures and neuronal deficits following early exposure to barbiturate. *Developmental Neuroscience, 4,* 345–50.

Yanai, J., Sze, P. Y., Iser, C., and Melamed, E. (1985). Studies on brain monoamine neurotransmitters in mice after prenatal exposure to barbiturate. *Pharmacology, Biochemistry and Behavior, 23,* 215–19.

5

Postnatal Maternal Influences

Thus it is easy but fallacious to jump from the observation that psychopathic or affectionless characters in a clinical setting commonly have experienced severe, prolonged and early maternal deprivation to the conviction that severe, early and prolonged maternal deprivation commonly produces psychopathic or affectionless character. M. D. Ainsworth, 1962

Prior to the twentieth century, Western culture placed virtually no emphasis on the child's early psychological environment as a determinant of later behavior. That early emotional experiences influence, if not determine, the course of human behavioral development was initially systematized by Freud. Based on interpretation of his own early recollections and those of his patients, Freud constructed a theory of psychosexual development that set forth the bases for normal and abnormal personality development, a theory that constitutes the bedrock of psychoanalytic thinking. It is believed that certain parental behaviors channel the infants' physiological drives, drives related principally to sucking, excretion, and genital stimulation, thereby promoting the evolution of particular personality typologies.

However, the highly theoretical nature of psychoanalytic thinking and the fact that it deals with the controversial issue of infantile sexuality precluded it from exerting a major influence on traditional views of development. The role of infantile events remained virtually ignored. It appears to have been the general opinion that if infants are properly fed and protected against cold and infection, their abilities and personality develop as fully as their heredity and native endowment warrant. It seems to have been assumed that the emotional and social characteristics are essentially genetically determined (Ribble, 1944).

The situation began to change, however, as a consequence of observations of infants separated from their mothers, the principal study being that of Ribble (1944), who described 600 newborns residing in three maternity hospitals. Infants who were not "mothered" and those who received inadequate care exhibited symptoms, including lack of appetite, pallor, loss of muscle tone, vomiting, diarrhea, and excessive sleep. Calling this condition *marasmus,* or wasting away, Ribble wrote:

> The present indications are that this malady was not due primarily to inappropriate feeding or digestive disturbance, nor, as some investigators have thought, to some

basic biological defect of circulation. It has instead the nature of a general disorga-
nization of functions and a deterioration of primary body reflexes due in large measure to lack of "mothering" or stimulation. (p. 634)

Supporting this interpretation were observations of additional marasmic infants
that revealed a significant improvement in health following the introduction of
substitute mothering.

Riddle's work provoked a good deal of criticism, some of which bordered on
the vitriolic. As Orlansky (1949), for one, stated, "One gets the general impression that every infant hovers on the border of death, and that the balance in the
direction of life must be tipped by adequate 'mothering' and sucking. After a
while, one wonders how it is that babies who are not fondled and sung to ever
manage to survive at all" (p. 12). Such criticism notwithstanding, the idea that
development can be shaped by early life experiences took hold. Numerous
research programs were established in an attempt to carefully delineate those
early experiences and to identify the mechanisms through which they affect
development. Initially, efforts were made to expand on Ribble's observations of
the importance of mothering. It was accomplished by systematically examining
the impact of maternal separation on both humans and animals, the idea being
that the extent to which the mother contributes to normal development can be
inferred from the degree of abnormality seen as a function of her removal.

As a life event that unfortunately befalls human infants and as a manipulation
deliberately used with animal subjects, maternal separation can occur either
soon after birth or sometime thereafter. If it takes place soon after birth, the offspring can be thought of as experiencing a lack of mothering, or *maternal privation.* If, on the other hand, mothers and infants are separated at a later time,
loss of mothering, or *maternal deprivation,* ensues. Maternal deprivation, then,
results from a discontinuity in an already formed child–mother relationship,
whereas maternal privation refers to the complete absence of such a relationship.

Two caveats are in order, however. First, the distinction between maternal
privation and deprivation may be unclear. Is an infant separated from its
mother, for example, at the age of 1 week undergoing maternal privation or
deprivation? In other words, had a significant mother–infant relationship been
established within the initial week of the infant's life such that loss of the mother
evokes a state of deprivation? Second, even distinguishing maternal privation
from maternal deprivation on the basis of an operational definition (time of separation) does not necessarily mean that they are indeed distinct events having
differing behavioral consequences.

Another technique used to determine the extent to which the mother influences the course of her offspring's development also involves her removal.
Despite this condition, however, the young are not even briefly orphaned, as a
foster mother is immediately provided. The key to this procedure is that the foster mother is a member of another species. Does being raised by an alien mother
alter the outcome of behavioral development? This research strategy is known
as *cross-species fostering.*

MATERNAL PRIVATION

Data from Humans

It had been known for years that infants living in institutions such as foundling homes experienced an exceptionally high mortality rate. As reviewed by Spitz (1945), 90% of infants institutionalized in the Baltimore area died within the first year of life; a similar finding of 71% was reported for a major foundling home in Germany. According to Kesson (1965), only 45 of 10,272 children admitted to a foundling home in Dublin between 1775 and 1800 survived. As a consequence of the introduction of better methods of hygiene, mortality rates began to decline until, by the late 1930s, they did not differ from those of children in the general population. However, the increased longevity of institutionalized children unmasked another problem: Investigators such as Ribble reported a high incidence of psychological disturbance.

The first major investigation of the psychological consequences of institutional rearing was performed by Spitz (1945), who compared 61 infants living in a foundling home to 69 infants living in a nursery. All of the children were less than a year old. The foundling home contained children of unwed mothers who gave up their babies because they could not be supported, whereas the nursery was for the children of delinquent girls. The foundling home and nursery environments differed markedly. Children living in the foundling home interacted with adult caretakers only briefly, usually while being fed; they were provided with few play things and spent a good deal of time lying on their backs in cots, the sides of which were draped with sheets, which severely limited visual stimulation. They spent so much time in their cots, in fact, that a hollow was formed in the mattress deep enough to prevent them from turning in any direction. In contrast, infants residing in the nursery were given toys, were cared for by their own mothers or foster mothers, and spent time in cribs that allowed them to see what was happening around them.

A number of differences were observed between the two groups of institutionalized infants. Using an overall index of development, The Developmental Quotient, Spitz found that the score dropped markedly in the foundling home subjects, attaining an average level of 72 by the end of the first year. Children in the nursery, however, attained an average score of 105, comparable to that of two control groups of noninstitutionalized infants. The difference between the foundling home and nursery subjects appears even more pronounced, considering that when initially tested between 2 and 3 months of age, the former had scored higher (over 130) than subjects residing in the nursery (less than 100). Moreover, despite what Spitz called excellent hygienic conditions and medical care, the orphaned infants were highly susceptible to disease and resistant to treatment; 26% of the children up to the age of 2.5 died from measles during the course of Spitz's study.

Spitz (1946) performed a follow-up study on 21 children who had not been adopted and had to remain in the foundling home, the youngest being 2 years and the oldest 4 years 1 month. A summary of the findings is given in Table 5.1. Spitz noted that "the mental development of these 21 children is extraordinarily retarded compared to that of normal children between the ages of two and four, who move, climb, and babble all day long, and who conform to or struggle against the educational demands of the environment" (p. 113). Physical retardation also was observed; whereas all of the institutionalized children were over 2 years of age, only three fell into the height and weight range of normal 2-year-olds.

The foundling home provided an environment deficient in stimulation, few playthings were available, and most time was spent in sheet-enclosed cots. Yet Spitz did not believe that inadequate perceptual experience per se was responsible for the developmental deficits. He argued instead that the retardation was caused by the lack of the mother or a mother-substitute. Perceptual experience, according to Spitz, *is* important for normal development but can become influential only when it is obtained by interacting emotionally with the mother.

> The child learns to grasp by nursing at the mother's breast and by combining the emotional satisfaction of that experience with tactile perceptions. He learns to distinguish animate objects from inanimate ones by the spectacle provided by his mother's face in situations fraught with emotional satisfaction. (Spitz, 1945, p. 68)

Table 5.1   Development of 21 children[a] who remained in a foundling home

Parameter	No.
Bodily development	
Incapable of any locomotion	5
Sit up unassisted (without walking)	3
Walk assisted	8
Walk unassisted	5
Handling materials	
Cannot eat alone with spoon	12
Eat alone with spoon	9
Cannot dress alone	20
Dresses alone	1
Adaptation to demands of environment	
Not toilet trained in any way	6
Toilet trained, partially	15
Speech development	
Cannot talk at all	6
Vocabulary: 2 words	5
Vocabulary: 3–5 words	8
Vocabulary: a dozen words	1
Uses sentences	1

[a]Ages 2 years to 4 years 1 month.

Source: Adapted from Spitz. Hospitalism: A follow-up report on investigation described in Volume 1, 1945. *Psychoanalytical Study of the Child, 2,* 113–17. © 1946 by International Universities Press. By permission.

The research was roundly criticised by Pinneau (1955), who stated, among other things, that Spitz failed to mention whether the foundling home infants suffered from any congenital abnormalities that might have accounted for the reported deficits in development. Pinneau also questioned the validity and the predictive value of the Hertzer-Wolf Baby Test, which Spitz used to provide quantitative assessment of development.

Provence and Lipton (1962), in their later study of institutionalized infants, responded to the issue of congenital abnormalities by establishing a strict set of criteria for the inclusion of subjects. Infants with an obvious handicap of any kind, prematurely born infants, and any who had a severe illness or operation were excluded. Regarding the question of infant tests, in conjunction with the disputed Hertzer-Wolf Baby Test, Provence and Lipton also used the Gesell Developmental Examination. Moreover, they pointed out that the tests, in addition to permitting the comparison of infants of a particular age with normative standards, are of value because they provide a structured situation within which to observe the children behave.

They examined 75 institutionalized infants during the first year of life and compared them to an equal number of family-reared infants. Although the institution was much less spartan than Spitz's foundling home in that toys were available and the infants were kept in cribs and thus were able to see the world around them, there were similarities. In both environments the infants were not encouraged to be motorically active, sensory stimulation was minimal, and interaction with the adult caretakers was limited.

Retardation of motor behavior was apparent. The initial deficit, observed at 2 months, involved the way in which they responded to being held. "They did not adapt their bodies well to the arms of the adult, they were not cuddly . . . they felt something like sawdust dolls; they moved, they bent easily at the proper joints, but they felt stiff or wooden" (p. 56). At 3 and 4 months less than normal kicking activity was observed. Delays were exhibited in head control, pulling themselves to a standing position, walking with support, and walking unaided.

The institutionalized infant was generally inactive and took little interest in investigating objects in its environment. Also, the infant did not try to escape from unpleasant stimuli but, rather, cried forlornly. The only type of motoric behavior that did increase in frequency was rocking, which initially appeared at about 5.5 months as side-to-side head movement.

Deficits also were observed in the infants' emotional reactivity. By the second month they displayed little vocalization in response to the presence of people, and there was a concomitant absence of playful activities with others, such as engaging in a peek-a-boo game. The children exhibited fewer affective expressions and failed to seek the adult when in distress. "There were no signs that they anticipated or expected that a need would be met" (p. 82).

Impairment of both qualitative and quantitative aspects of sound production was observed early. By the end of the year not one of the infants uttered a single word, and they rarely cried. When they did cry, it was poorly differentiated, lacked vigor, and was devoid of the expressions found in the crying of normal infants.

These areas are just some of the differences observed by Provence and Lipton between institutionalized and family-reared infants. Others involve reactions to inanimate objects and discovery of the body and sense of self. Follow-up observations were made on some of the children after they had been placed in foster homes, which generally occurred between the ages of 1 and 2 years. Although dramatic gains were made, deficits were noted in the areas of emotional relationships, impulse control, play, and flexibility in thought and action. These long-term consequences of institutional rearing are similar to those reported earlier by Goldfarb (1943, 1944), who compared infants placed immediately into foster homes with others whose placement occurred after they had been institutionalized for 3 years. Data were obtained when the children were between 10 and 14 years old. The children who had been institutionalized were deficient in language, conceptual ability, and forming social relations. They also were aggressive and unrepentant when confronted with their misdeeds.

Provence and Lipton argued, as did Spitz, that the deficits observed in institutionalized children are caused by a lack of maternal care. However, they viewed the role of the mother more objectively than did Spitz. Not dependent on any special emotional linkage or bond, the mother is primarily seen as an instructor, teaching her infant how to adapt to its environment and how to master the developmental tasks that occur during the initial year of life.

There can be little doubt that institutions such as those described in the research considered here do not foster normal development. However, to what extent do the data implicate maternal privation per se as causing retarded development? Because the foundling homes provided their charges with minimal levels of stimulation—in extreme cases infants were virtually prisoners kept in solitary confinement—perceptual deprivation may have been responsible for the deficits. This possibility has been supported experimentally. Casler (1965) administered the Gesell Development Schedule to 16 institutionalized infants and formed eight approximately matched pairs as determined by their scores. One member of each pair was provided with extra tactile stimulation by stroking their skin (except for hands, mouths, and genitals) 20 minutes a day for 50 days. The Gesell test then was readministered. Although the scores of both groups declined, infants given extra tactile stimulation declined significantly less than did their nonstimulated counterparts. Casler commented:

> If the correct amount of tactile stimulation can be given to the institutionalized child, and if the other forms of perceptual stimulation that future experimentation finds to be important are also obtainable within an institutional setting, then there is reason to ask whether mother love remains a variable of importance in infant development. (p. 170)

In another study, Dennis and Najarian (1957), using the Cattell Infant Scale, found that institutionalized infants ostensibly exhibit intellectual retardation between the ages of 3 and 12 months. However, because most of the items on the scale require that the infant be tested in a sitting position on the tester's lap and because the infants had had little experience in sitting positions (they were not held while being fed and they were swaddled until 4 months of age, which severely limited movement of legs and arms), the investigators suggested that their poor performance was caused by "a lack of learning opportunities in situations comparable to the test situations" (p. 12). This supposition is supported by the significant increments in developmental test scores seen in institutionalized infants having been afforded experience in sitting upright and in observing and manipulating objects (Dennis & Sayegh, 1965). Even the administration of 20 minutes of extra rocking a day between days 6 and 36 of life increased the amount of time institutionalized infants spent visually exploring their environments (White & Castle, 1964).

It is possible, then, that deficits seen in the development of institutionalized children may be attributed to an overall lack of perceptual experience and, extrapolating, that an important function of the mother is to provide such stimulation. This view certainly does not minimize the maternal role but would divorce it from explanations based on concepts such as mother–infant attachment, emotional satisfaction, and mother love.

It is also possible that the findings attesting to the adverse effects of institutional rearing may in some measure be artifactual. As pointed out by Thompson and Grusec (1970), children placed in foundling homes do not represent a random sample of the general infant population. Mothers who gave up their babies probably were at the low end of the socioeconomic scale and often unwed. It is likely, then, that because of economic hardship and the fact that many of the pregnancies were unwanted, the medical care received during pregnancy was less than that normally obtained by women who maintained their babies. Therefore unlike most noninstitutionalized infants, the orphaned infants were at risk even before birth. Institutional living with its attendant disadvantages may have exacerbated already existing deficits. It is difficult to imagine, however, that prenatal health problems would have been experienced by so many institutionalized infants to account for all of the differences found between them and maternally reared children.

Data from Animals

The individual most closely associated with the laboratory study of maternal privation is Harlow. During the course of his early work with macaque monkeys, which consisted in part of separating infants from mothers 6 to 12 hours after delivery and bottle feeding them, Harlow noticed that they appeared to be "attached" to the gauze pads that covered the wire cage floor. The infants clung to them and became emotional when the pads were removed for sanitary reasons. This observation prompted Harlow to initiate the now reknowned surrogate mother investigations (Harlow, 1958) from which generalizations were made regarding the nature of the infant's responsiveness to the mother.

Two surrogate mothers were constructed. One was made from wood, covered with sponge rubber and then with terry cloth, and the other was constructed from wire mesh and left uncovered (see Figure 5.1). Both surrogates were made available to eight infant monkeys. For four monkeys, only the cloth-covered surrogate lactated (a bottle was attached to it), and the wire mesh mother provided

Figure 5.1 Bare and cloth-covered surrogate mothers. (From Harlow, "The nature of love." *American Psychologist, 13*, 673–85. © 1958 by The American Psychological Association. Reprinted by permission.)

milk to the other four infants. Figure 5.2 shows the total time spent by the infants on each artificial mother. It is readily apparent that nursing is not the factor responsible for what Harlow has called "affectional responding"; the cloth-covered surrogate was preferred regardless of its lactational state. Rather, it was thought that the infant derives "contact-comfort" from clinging to the soft, cloth-covered surrogate as it normally would receive from the mother.

Differential responding to the surrogates was also demonstrated when the young were presented with stimuli assumed to provoke fear, such as a wind-up drum-beating teddy bear. Again, the variable of nursing was without effect; infants overwhelmingly rushed to the cloth-covered mother when confronted with the toy. Moreover, when given the opportunity to press a lever that resulted in the opening of a window and a chance to see what was outside of the dimly lit test chamber, monkeys responded at higher rates when they were able to view the cloth-covered surrogate than when the wire mother was stationed outside. Again, the results are independent of which surrogate provided milk.

> We were not surprised to discover that contact comfort was an important basic affectional or love variable, but we did not expect it to overshadow so completely the variable of nursing; indeed, the disparity is so great as to suggest that the primary function of nursing as an affectional variable is that of insuring frequent and intimate body contact of the infant with the mother. (Harlow, 1958, p. 677)

Although the primate infant exhibits behaviors toward the cloth-covered surrogate that have been interpreted as attachment, separation from the surrogate

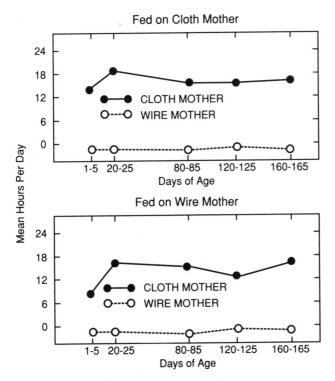

Figure 5.2 Long-term contact time on cloth and wire surrogate mothers. (From Harlow, "The nature of love." *American Psychologist, 13,* 673–85. © 1958 by The American Psychological Association. Reprinted by permission.)

yields fewer and less severe physiological changes than those observed following separation from the mother. Reite and co-workers (Reite & Short, 1978; Reite, Short, Kaufman, & Stynes, 1978a; Reite, Short, Seiler, & Pauley, 1981) reported significant decreases in heart rate and body temperature, as well as sleep disturbances, in infant monkeys separated from their mothers. However, infants separated from surrogates display no significant heart rate and temperature changes with a much less pronounced disturbance of sleep than that observed in subjects separated from mothers (Reite, Short, & Seiler, 1978b). Hennessy and Kaplan (1982) presented a similar finding; whereas a significant elevation of cortisol was seen 0.5 hour after maternal separation (Coe, Mendoza, Smotherman, & Levine, 1978), infants separated from surrogates exhibited no such elevation, suggesting, then, that separation from the surrogate is less arousing or distressing than is separation from the mother. This idea, in turn, implies that attachment to the surrogate is less intense than to the mother.

Germane to this discussion, of course, are the behavioral consequences of maternal privation. It cannot be emphasized too strongly, however, that Harlow's methodology and that of others often involves separation not only from the mother but from additional sources of social stimulation: peers and other adults. The importance of those extramaternal sources of social stimulation has been underscored by the fact that the mother's presence *alone* in some cases may not be sufficient to support normal behavioral development (Harlow & Harlow, 1962). Therefore although it often is assumed that maternal privation has produced an adverse effect on the infant, in many cases no such conclusion is warranted. With this important qualification in mind, let us proceed with a description of the research.

Monkeys isolated from birth, regardless of whether a cloth-covered surrogate is available, exhibit various behavioral abnormalities including self-clutching, stereotyped body rocking, and deficiencies in social behavior (Harlow & Harlow, 1962; Harlow, Joslyn, Senko, & Dopp, 1966; Harlow & Suomi, 1971). With regard to the latter, they neither initiate nor reciprocate the grooming and play behaviors of peers and exhibit abnormalities in sexual behavior. Although males are sexually motivated and able to perform most of the individual behaviors that comprise copulation, they are incapable of integrating them into a cohesive and thus successful copulatory act. Females, on the other hand, show little if any interest in sex. If forced to copulate, the ensuing pregnancy is normal. However, the parturient females either ignore their young or subject them to physical abuse, occasionally leading to their death.

Some of the behavioral deficits seen as a consequence of isolation rearing can be overcome by either changing a particular characteristic of the surrogate mother or by confronting isolation-reared animals with social stimuli. Mason and Berkson (1975) provided one of two groups of isolated rhesus monkeys with fur-covered, lactating, surrogate mothers. The other group was given identical surrogates except they were mobile, suspended from a mechanism that moved the surrogate up and down in a circular excursion about the cage. Whereas 9 of 10 monkeys raised with stationary surrogates developed the stereotyped body-rocking, none of the nine subjects kept with mobile surrogates did so. According to Mason and Berkson, the alleviation of rocking was due to either the reception of proprioceptive-kinesthetic stimulation provided by the movement of the surrogate or to the development of more mature forms of behaviors incompatible with rocking. The latter was suggested by the fact that infants with mobile surrogates spent more time playing than did the other infants. It is worth noting that Berkson (1967), in a review of the literature, found that the absence of maternal stimulation may be related to the development of rocking in human infants.

Regarding the beneficial effects of social stimulation, Harlow and Suomi (1971) reported that isolation-reared parturient females that initially ignored their babies eventually responded positively to the persistent attempts by the infants over the course of months to make physical contact and nurse. In fact, from the fourth month onward those persistent infants received lesser amounts of punishment and more nipple contact than did the offspring of normal mothers. The authors also found that when 6-month-old isolates were allowed to interact with a normal adolescent for 2 hours a day, 3 days per week for a month and then in pairs with two normals for the next 5 months, dramatic rehabilitation was observed. At 1 year it was barely possible to distinguish the isolates from the normal monkeys in terms of exploratory, locomotive, and play behavior.

Moreover, a marked decline of huddling and self-clasping was observed. Similar findings were obtained with monkeys after 12 months of isolation (Novak & Harlow, 1974).

We have seen, then, that unless certain remedial action is taken, isolation rearing produces ostensibly permanent adverse effects on behavioral development. However, not all primates are as affected by isolation rearing as are rhesus monkeys. Squirrel monkeys, separated from their mothers at birth and placed into social groups at either 4 or 12 months, although exhibiting abnormal self-directed behaviors such as excessive digit sucking, displayed normal sexual, maternal, and social behaviors (Rosenblum, 1968). The author speculated that the effects of isolation are attenuated in squirrel monkeys because they normally receive much less maternally initiated stimulation such as grooming and carrying than do young macaque and rhesus monkeys. Furthermore, unlike isolation-reared male rhesus monkeys, most isolated chimpanzees eventually exhibit copulatory behavior (Rogers & Davenport, 1970).

Dogs too are adversely affected by maternal privation. Fox and Stelzner (1967) found that hand-reared puppies separated from their mothers and littermates from day 3 of life until testing at week 12 were deficient relative to dogs reared by their mothers and then isolated from peers at 3.5 weeks and to dogs reared with peers by their mothers until testing. The experimenter-reared animals were the least reactive toward other dogs; they were nonvocal, nonoral, and initially nonaggressive. After a period of social contact, however, they soon became overaggressive and rarely engaged in play behavior.

The difficulty with sustaining rats apart from the mother (they cannot be bottle-fed) was surmounted by Thoman (Thoman & Arnold, 1968), who designed a catheter to deliver milk formula directly into the stomach. That was the easy part, as she then undertook the herculean task of intubating the infants once every 3 hours for the first 3 days of life and every 4 hours thereafter until day 15 when they could feed themselves. The young were kept in incubators with a warm, pulsating piece of plastic tubing that presumably served as a surrogate mother.

Thoman and Arnold found that maternal privation alone or in combination with isolation from littermates does not affect sexual behavior and the ensuing pregnancy. Also, it has virtually no effect on the display of overt maternal activities; motherless animals build nests, clean the young, and retrieve and nurse them. Nevertheless, the offspring of motherless rats exhibit a significant maturational delay; eye-opening occurs later than expected. Because other work (Levine, 1962) has shown retarded eye-opening to be related to low levels of maternal stimulation, it was surmised that maternal privation causes females to provide their own young with less than optimal levels of stimulation. Thoman and Arnold also found that the offspring of motherless rats are less likely to survive, again indicating some type of abnormality in maternal behavior. Lastly, young reared by totally isolated mothers weigh less than those nurtured by mothers who had themselves been reared by a mother. They also weigh less than the offspring of motherless rats raised in an incubator with littermates present, attesting to the importance of extramaternal social stimulation to development.

The attenuated maturational and survival rates of the offspring of motherless females notwithstanding, Thoman and Arnold were struck by the modest effect of maternal privation in rats relative to that observed in monkeys. Although they did not speculate as to the cause of the disparity, one possibility comes readily to mind. Unlike infant monkeys, which can be fed by either fastening a bottle to a surrogate mother or by holding it for them, infant rats had to be picked up and a catheter placed in their stomachs a total of 90 times between birth and day 15. The feeding procedure may have provided stimulation that to some degree replaced that normally derived from the mother, thereby attenuating the adverse effect of maternal privation.

Finally, the emotional reactivity of rats also has been shown to be affected by maternal privation. Thoman, Levine, and Arnold (1968) reported that incubator-reared animals, with or without littermates present, have both higher basal levels of corticosterone (rodent adrenals produce corticosterone instead of cortisol) and higher corticosterone levels in response to stress than do mother-reared rats. They also display lower levels of activity in an open-field test and higher heart rate responses to auditory stimulation and electric shock (Koch & Arnold, 1972).

MATERNAL DEPRIVATION

Data from Humans

That separation from the mother at some time after a significant period of mother–infant interaction has transpired adversely affects psychological development was forcefully articulated by the influential psychoanalytically oriented theorist Bowlby. According to Newcombe and Lerner (1982), Bowlby's ideas may have evolved, in part, from his clinical experience in Britain with adults who exhibited neurotic and psychotic symptomatology as a consequence of the loss of a loved one during World War I. These adverse effects of bereavement underscored the need to appraise a patient's relationships with others when seeking to establish the etiology of particular psychological disorders. The importance of this idea coupled with the psychoanalytic postulate that many adult disorders have roots in early life probably led Bowlby to concentrate on the impact of early loss on personality development.

Bowlby (1944) compared 44 juvenile delinquents (all had been caught stealing) sent to a child guidance clinic to a like number of juveniles who did not steal but were referred to the clinic for other reasons. He found that 17 of the former ("thieves") had been separated from their mothers for 6 months or more within the first 5 years of life, whereas only two of the "nonthieves" experienced such separation. Moreover, of 14 thieves diagnosed as being of Affectionless Character (inability to form and maintain loving relationships), 12 had experienced maternal separation; it was true of only 5 of the remaining 30 delinquents.

Bowlby's study has been criticized by a number of individuals (e.g., Ainsworth, 1962) who found it highly unlikely that maternal deprivation itself can lead to delinquency. Rather, some type of early dysfunctional parent–child interaction is thought to be the true antecedent that either acts by itself to predispose a child to delinquency or synergizes with maternal deprivation. This notion is based on data showing that juvenile delinquency is related to parental neglect (e.g., Lewis, 1954).

In another study, cited frequently over the years, Bowlby and co-workers (Bowlby, Ainsworth, Boston, & Rosenbluth, 1956) examined a group of 60 children who had been placed in a sanatorium for varying periods prior to the age of 4 years to receive treatment for tuberculosis. Upon their arrival they underwent 10 days of quarantine. They then were confined to cots for the next 3 months with parental visits permitted only once a week for 3 hours. Substitute mothering was not provided. The study was carried out after the children had been released and returned to their homes and school. Each child was compared to three control classmates matched for age and sex. The data consisted of three components: a description of each quartet of children as gleaned from the teachers' responses to a multiple choice questionaire, the childrens' performance on an IQ test, and psychologists' comments on the behavior of the children during administration of the IQ test.

Although the IQ scores of the two groups were similar, one half of the sanatorium children were judged to have responded adequately during the administration of the test compared to three fourths of the controls, a statistically significant difference. Inadequate responding consisted in a failure to respond at all or an overanxiety to please the tester. With regard to the teachers' reports, no reliable differences emerged between the formerly hospitalized and control children. However, Bowlby and his co-workers went on to perform an additional analysis of those teachers' reports. That reanalysis prompted a spate of criticism because it relied on the post hoc elimination of data deemed "unreliable" (more than 40% of the data were discarded). An analysis of the remaining "reliable" data revealed that on some of the items a significant proportion of the hospitalized children had ratings indicative of maladjustment; the children tended to be withdrawn and apathetic, their tempers were easily lost, and they were given toward roughness. Bowlby et al. did note that the differences observed between the maternally deprived and control subjects were not as great as had been expected and that "of those who are damaged only a small minority develop those very serious disabilities of personality which first drew attention to the pathogenic nature of the experience" (p. 240). However, had the questionable reanalysis of the data not been performed, no differences whatsoever would have emerged from the teachers' observations of the children.

Although some of Bowlby's well known and highly influential findings may be questioned, he and his collegues are not alone in attesting to the adverse effects produced by maternal deprivation. Additional support has come from many quarters (see reviews by Ainsworth, 1962, and Lebovici, 1962). Nonetheless, some studies have revealed no negative effects. Some of those inconsistencies undoubtedly are due to the disparate research strategies that have been developed to deal with the difficult tasks of identifying and studying maternally deprived children. However, the discrepant findings also may be attributed, at least in part, to the fact that the data are as much a reflection of the particular institutions within which the children reside as they are to the independent variable. In other words, the investigations of necessity have studied the institutions as well as, or perhaps instead of, maternal deprivation. Because institutional practices differ markedly, so must the data. Wootton (1962) went so far as to contend that the matter of institutionalization is a social rather than a psychological issue. This criticism is also applicable, of course, to the maternal privation studies discussed earlier.

Assuming that maternal deprivation does indeed produce adverse psychological consequences, the issue becomes that of identifying those consequences. Deprivation appears to have both immediate and long-term effects. Spitz and Wolf (1946) called the immediate impact of deprivation *anaclitic depression.* The syndrome, affecting about one third of their sample population, is comprised of weepiness, withdrawal, dejection, stupor, loss of appetite, and insomnia. Recovery is rapid and usually complete if the infant is returned to its mother within 3 months, after which permanent effects are observed. Bowlby (1961) described a similar temporal reaction to maternal separation: protest, despair, and detachment. During the protest phase the child cries a good deal of time. This period is followed by a despair reaction during which behavior becomes disorganized. The final phase, detachment, is the adjustment the child eventually makes to maternal loss. Detachment is evident following reunion, as the child often exhibits indifference or even hostility toward its mother (Bowlby, 1973). Maternal deprivation also has been implicated in the failure of hospitalized infants to thrive, referred to, if you recall, as marasmus, or "hospitalism." One of the most striking aspects of the syndrome is growth retardation (Patton & Gardner, 1962), which may be caused by a decline in the release of growth hormone by the pituitary (Powell, Brasel, Raiti, & Blizzard, 1967). More is said about that subject later.

Bowlby's (1944; Bowlby et al., 1956) description of what he believed are the long-term consequences of maternal deprivation is, as expected, psychoanalytically based. Loss of the mother engenders frustration, which increases sexual and aggressive impulses while inhibiting normal superego development. Because the superego is believed to constrain sexual and aggressive tendencies, one can expect difficulties in those areas later in life, as seen, for example, in the delinquent children of Bowlby's (1944) study. Bowlby also believed that maternal loss prevents the establishment of close interpersonal relationships with others.

Loss of the mother has been linked to severe psychological depression. Beck, Sethi, and Tuthill (1963) reported a significantly higher rate of maternal loss in adults judged to be severely depressed than those rated mildly depressed. Similarly, Munro (1966) found that almost twice as many severe depressives relative to normals experienced the death of their mothers during childhood. Moderately depressed individuals and normals did not differ. According to Arbel and Stravynski's (1991) findings, however, maternal loss is *not* associated with what is now diagnosed as "avoidant personality disorder," the avoidance of relationships with others despite a strong desire to foster such relationships.

Data from Animals

The use of nonhuman subjects understandably permits more precise analysis of the effects of maternal deprivation than is possible with humans. In an early study, Seay, Hansen, and Harlow (1962) observed the behavior of 6-month-old rhesus monkeys during a 3-week period of maternal deprivation. Initially, the infants exhibited excessive vocalizations and disoriented locomotor behavior. They also attempted to break through the clear plastic barrier that separated them from their mothers. Those behaviors were followed within a few days by lethargy and withdrawal. The observations of Seay et al., which were later confirmed by others (e.g., Hinde, Spencer-Booth, and &, 1966; Kaufman & Rosenblum, 1967; Singh, 1975), are similar to the protest and despair reactions of human children in response to maternal loss as described by Bowlby (1961). The detachment reaction, active avoidance of the mother during the initial portion of the reunion period, also has been reported (e.g., Codner & Nadler, 1984; Rosenblum, 1978). However, others such as Spencer-Booth and Hinde (1971a) found that infant rhesus monkeys and their mothers make immediate contact upon reunion. It has been suggested (Nadler & Codner, 1983) that the detachment reaction might be obscured in some species by the mother's rapid retrieval of her infant.

In contrast to the views of Spitz and Bowlby, who defined the immediate responses of humans to separation as negative or debilitating, Kaufman (1973) proposed that for nonhuman primates the reactions may be beneficial. Put simply, the agitated behavior (vocalization and excessive locomotion) seen initially upon separation may serve to call attention to the infant, thereby facilitating the mother's search for it. With the mother's continued absence, however, it is to the infant's advantage to become inactive; inactivity would help conserve the infant's energy and prevent it from being found by predators. Becoming inactive corresponds to the despair phase of the separation reaction.

Reite, Short, Seiler, & Pauley (1981) presented a detailed analysis of the behavior of eight pigtailed monkeys prior to and during a 10-day period of maternal separation and throughout the first 4 days of reunion. The young were raised in social groups containing one male and four to eight females, some with young. The behavioral variables are summarized in Table 5.2 and the findings are presented in Figure 5.3. It is apparent that the frequency with which many behaviors are exhibited changes markedly during separation and returns to baseline following reunion. Various aspects of mother–infant interaction also change in frequency throughout the course of the reunion period (see Figure 5.3e).

How long do the effects of maternal deprivation last? Rhesus monkeys separated from their mothers for either one or two 6-day periods when 21 to 32 weeks old and nonseparated controls were observed at 12 and 30 months of age (Spencer-Booth & Hinde, 1971b). At 12 months, about 5 months after the infants were reunited with their mothers, the separated animals tended to spend less time away from their mothers and exhibited less locomotor activity. They also were less likely to approach strange objects such as mirrors and balls when the tests

Table 5.2 Behavioral variables studied in pigtailed monkeys prior to, during, and after maternal separation

Behaviors	Type[a]	Description
Activity		
Activity count	F	A measure of the infant's activity
Motion	D	Locomotion—walking, running, or climbing
Rest	D	At rest—no visible movement; eyes may be open or closed
Slouch	D	Characteristic posture of depression in which the infant sits hunched over, often with the head down, and yet is awake
Social contact		
Play	D	Social play (with other animals)
Contact other	D	Physical contact with another animal (other than mother)
Initiate groom	D	Grooming another animal
Receive groom	D	Receives groom from another animal
Receive threat	F	Receives a threat from another animal
Environmental contact		
Oral obx	D	Exploration of inanimate object with mouth
Obx	D	Visual examination of inanimate objects usually while manually manipulating them
Obs	D	Exploring sawdust or woodchip bedding on pen floor
Self-directed		
Oral self	D	Self-mouthing and self-licking
Chew	D	Chewing of foodstuffs, e.g., biscuits or fruit
Auto groom	D	Animal grooms itself
Auto play	D	Playing alone
Auto gen	D	Self-directed genital exploration
Mother–infant		
Physical contact	D	All times the infant was physically in contact with the mother
Off	D	All times the infant was not in physical contact with the mother
Other level	D	Infant is on a different vertical level from the mother
Away	D	All times the infant was on another level from the mother and/or more than 60 cm from her
Nipple	D	Infant holding the mother's nipple in its mouth
Wean	F	Nipple withdrawal; mother removes nipple from infant's mouth
Punish	F	Infant punished by mother or other adult

[a]F = frequency items; D = duration items.

Source: Adapted from Reite et al. Attachment, loss and depression. *Journal of Child Psychology and Psychiatry, 22,* 141–69. © 1981 by Pergamon Press. By permission.

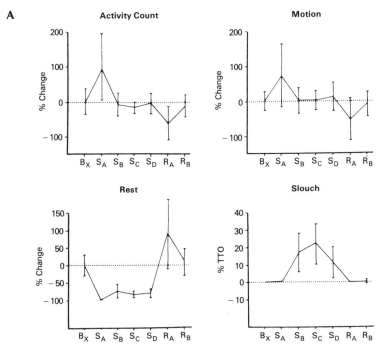

Figure 5.3 (A) Changes in scores for activity group variables during separation (S_A–S_D) and reunion (R_A and R_B). Baseline mean values (B_X) are represented by the dotted lines. The vertical brackets for separation and reunion represent 95% confidence intervals for change (%) from baseline. For B_X the brackets indicate the 95% confidence interval across animals converted to percent of baseline. (These explanations pertain to Figure 5.3A–E.)

were held in a novel environment. Thus a single 6-day period of isolation was effective in establishing the differences between experimentals and controls. At 30 months, about 2 years after the separation experience, differences still were apparent; maternally separated monkeys, especially those that had experienced two periods of separation, were less active and less ready to approach strange objects. Thus maternal deprivation of a relatively short duration produces long-term, perhaps permanent, effects on behavior.

Spencer-Booth and Hinde (1971b) also noted that although protest and despair reactions characterize behavior during separation, individuals differ markedly in the degree to which they respond to separation and in the rate at which the effects of separation subside after reunion. Lewis, McKinney, Young, and Kraemer (1976), comparing the results of five experiments, found so much variability they cautioned against the use of the maternally deprived animal as an experimental model of human depression. Their conclusion is not surprising in view of Spitz and Wolf's (1946) finding that some human infants appear to be totally immune to the depressive effects of maternal separation.

According to Spencer-Booth and Hinde (1971a), neither age at the time of

B

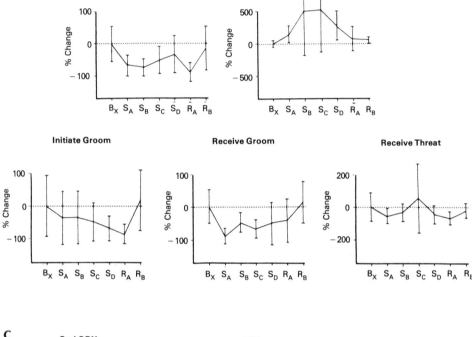

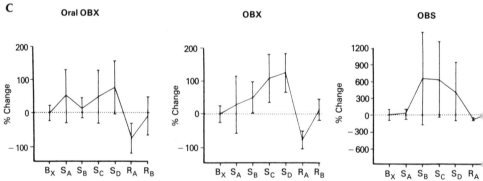

Figure 5.3 *(Continued)* Changes in behaviors during separation and reunions: (B) social contact group behaviors; (C) environmental contact behaviors (OBX = visual examination of inanimate objects; OBS = exploring bedding on cage floor); and (D) (facing page) self-directed behaviors (auto gen = self-directed genital exploration). (E) *(facing)* Changes in mother–infant behaviors during the reunion period after 10 days of separation. (From Reite et al., "Attachment, loss and depression." *Journal of Child Psychology and Psychiatry, 22,* 141–69. © 1981 by Pergamon Press. Reprinted by permission.)

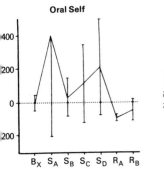

Oral Self

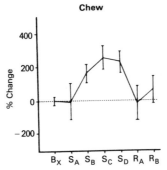

Chew

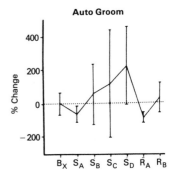

Auto Groom

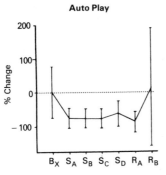

Auto Play

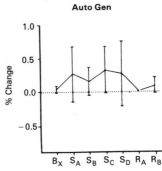

Auto Gen

E

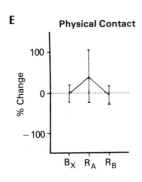

Physical Contact

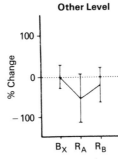

Other Level

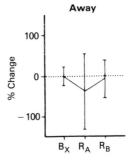

Away

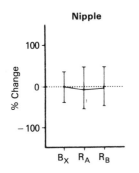

Nipple

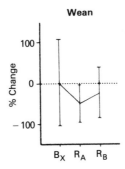

Wean

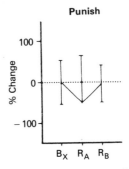

Punish

145

separation, sex, nor amount of contact with other group members during the separation period contribute significantly to the individual differences. They surmised, therefore, that the differences must derive from physiological factors intrinsic to the infant and from its relationship with the mother prior to separation. Regarding the latter, Hinde and McGinnis (1977) contended that variation in postseparation behavior is attributable, in part, to the mother–infant interaction seen prior to separation; infants from "tense" mother–infant dyads (those in which the infant is primarily responsible for maintaining proximity with the mother and those in which the infant suffers a relatively large number of rejected nipple contacts) exhibit the most distress. However, the causes of differential responsiveness to maternal deprivation and reunion have as yet to be elucidated with any degree of certainty. The issue of individual variability is important; understanding why certain individuals are immune to or only marginally affected by maternal loss might well shed light on the question of *how* maternal deprivation produces its adverse consequences.

Infraprimates, as well as primates, are responsive to maternal deprivation. The oft-cited study of Seitz (1959) described a host of changes in the behavior of adult cats that underwent separation commencing at 2 weeks of age. Whereas control animals, which stayed with their mothers for the first 3 months, and others separated at 6 weeks did not differ, cats separated at 2 weeks:

> were the most anxious in novel situations. They were the most disturbed by, and slowest to recover from, intense stimulation. They were the most persistent, but also most disorganized, in their efforts to get food when hungry and frustrated. They were the most aggressive, but least successful, in feeding competitions. . . . Throughout their lives [they] were more suspicious, fearful and aggressive both toward other cats and toward the experimenters. (p. 364)

Impressive as Seitz's results appear to be, a methodological factor renders them virtually uninterpretable. At 2 weeks of age, the cats were unable to feed themselves by lapping milk. Therefore the animals maternally deprived at 2 weeks had to be fed by hand using a medicine dropper until they became capable of feeding themselves. (Seitz failed to mention when that occurred.) Hence the findings may not have been due to maternal deprivation per se but, rather, to a nutritional factor associated with the hand-rearing procedure. Unfortunately, neither a description of the diet fed the kittens nor their growth rate relative to that of the controls was provided.

Nutrition plays a much more subtle role than simply permitting the young to survive. It also serves as a physiological regulator. This point was demonstrated by Hofer (1970), who reported a decline in heart and respiratory rates of 2-week-old maternally deprived rats, decreasing by more than 40% by 12 to 16 hours after separation. The results were dependent on neither the method of separation (infants could be removed from the mother or vice versa) nor a loss of body temperature. Moreover, the decline in heart rate can be temporarily but completely reversed within a matter of minutes by placing as little as 0.5 ml of a milk formula (bovine milk plus water), but not a nonnutritive solution, directly into the stomach (Hofer, 1971). Respiratory rates could not be so reversed.

The rapidity with which the nutrient accelerates heart rate following its placement into the stomach indicates that it acts prior to being absorbed into the circulatory system. That the effect of the nutrient is eliminated by the β-adrenergic blocker propanolol (Hofer, 1971) and by spinal cord transection at level T_4 (Hofer & Weiner, 1975) suggested that the efferent portion of the pathway involves an increase in neuronal activity along the spinal cardioacceleratory pathways to the β-adrenergic synapses of the myocardium. The afferent limb of the pathway may involve a change in α-adrenergic vasoconstrictor tone (Hofer, 1983).

Hofer's research emphasizes the need to distinguish between maternal and nutritional factors when using maternal deprivation to isolate the mother's role in development. Not only is such a distinction made infrequently, even basic information pertaining to the infant's nutritional status prior to and during separation is rarely provided, especially in primate research; one is often not even informed if weaning was completed prior to separation.

Even with the best of intentions, however, separating maternal from nutritional factors can lead to inconclusive data. Novakova (1966), for example, in a study of the effect of maternal deprivation on the acquisition and retention of a conditioned response separated one group of rats from their mothers on day 15, about 10 to 15 days prior to normal weaning but at a time when the young begin to ingest solid food. Another group of subjects also was weaned prematurely on day 15. However, instead of removing the mothers, they were prevented from providing milk by cauterizing their teats, a procedure that does not affect the display of maternal behaviors. The nonlactating females were separated from their young on day 30 as were the mothers of a third group of rats who nursed their young normally throughout the entire 30-day period. This experimental design ostensibly allows one to distinguish between a nutritional factor associated with early weaning and a maternal factor; if the prematurely weaned rats kept with their nonlactating mothers perform better than the prematurely weaned animals deprived of their mothers, one can attribute the enhanced performance to the mothers' presence *irrespective of lactation.*

At 8 months of age the animals that were weaned early and deprived of their mothers acquired a conditioned response (associating a stimulus with the offset of electric shock) more slowly than did the prematurely weaned subjects that were allowed to remain with their nonlactating mothers or the normally weaned controls. The former also exhibited poorer retention of the response when retested 12 weeks later. *However,* the rats that lived with nonlactating mothers consumed more solid food between days 16 and 20 of life than did the maternally deprived animals. All that can be concluded from Novakova's clever attempt to disentangle maternal from nutritional influences in prematurely weaned animals is that maternal presence enhances the intake of solid food. Thus differences in the later acquisition and retention of a conditioned response may have been mediated by differences in food intake during early life.

Hofer (1973) presented data indicating that certain behaviors are affected by the absence of the mother independent of her role in governing the nutritional status of the young. Although infusion of milk into the stomach, as expected, prevented the decline in heart rate caused by maternal separation, differences were not observed between intubated and unfed infants in terms of locomotion and defecation/urination rates; these parameters increased in both groups.

Vocalization also is affected by separation. Young rats emit high-frequency vocalizations (30 to 50 kHz) in response to separation (Sales & Pye, 1974), which during the first few days of life are mainly associated with a decline in the infant's body temperature (Allin & Banks, 1971). Infant rats are poikilothermic; that is, they are unable to maintain their body temperature, which falls markedly in the absence of the heat provided by the mother. Thus warming of the isolation chamber to about 36°C prevents vocalization (Okon, 1971). Later, at about 14 days, vocalizations are influenced by social factors. Normally, 2-week-old rats

Table 5.3 Physiological variables studied in pigtailed monkeys prior to, during, and after maternal separation

Variable	Brief Description
Mean day heart rate (HR)	Mean of all heart rate samples obtained between 1000 and 1600 hours
Mean night HR	Mean of all heart rate samples obtained between 2200 and 0400 hours
Mean day body temp. (BT)	Mean of all body temperature samples obtained between 1000 and 1600 hours
Mean night BT	Mean of all body temperature samples obtained between 2200 and 0400 hours
Sleep latency	Time between lights out and sleep onset
Awake	Time awake after sleep onset and before final arousal preceding lights on in the morning
No arousals	Number of awakenings between sleep onset and final morning arousal
Total sleep time (TST)	Minutes of total sleep (combination of drowsy, stages 1, stages 3 + 4, REM)
Drowsy	See Reite, Pauley, Kaufman, Stynes, & Marker (1974) for description
Stage 2	Stage 2 sleep
Stage 3–4	Stages 3 and 4 are combined
Slow wave sleep (SWS)	Drowsy, stage 2, and stages 3–4 combined
REM time	Minutes of REM sleep
No. REM periods	Number of REM periods during the night
Mean REM length	Mean length of REM periods for a given night
REM latency	Time from sleep onset to beginning of first REM period
Inter-REM interval (IRI)	Mean interval between REM period onset times
Alpha frequency	Mean frequency of EEG alpha activity as determined from power spectral analysis (see Reite & Short, 1980, for details)
Alpha ratio	Ratio of the EEG spectral power in the 6- to 10-Hz frequency band divided by the power in the 3- to 6-Hz band

Source: Adapted from Reite et al. Attachment, loss and depression. *Journal of Child Psychology and Psychiatry, 22,* 141–69. © 1981 by Pergamon Press. By permission.

produce little ultrasound except in response to the comings and goings of the mother, which lead to the emission of ultrasound at a rate of approximately 1 pulse per minute. The rate increases to about 12/minute when a pup is separated from its mother and littermates and left in its home cage and to 25/minute when a pup is placed alone in an unfamiliar environment (Hofer & Shair, 1978). Furthermore, if the latter is permitted contact with either its anesthetized mother or an anesthetized littermate, vocalization markedly declines. Contact with a warm clay object is without effect. Because the rat mother normally leaves her 2-week-old young 15 to 20 times a day, Hofer and Shair suggested that littermates function to prevent "separation distress" during her absence.

Hofer, Shair, and Murowchick (1989) went on to show that 2-week-old rats reared alone from the day of birth (intubated and kept in cups floating in a warm waterbath) also display an increased rate of vocalization when placed in a novel environment. They exhibit a reduction in vocalization when confronted with an anesthetized dam. These data demonstrate that neither vocalization, presumed by Hofer et al. (1989) and by others to be indicative of separation distress, nor its reduction by the mother's presence develops as a function of the infant's early interaction with the mother, unless of course it is acquired within hours of delivery. "What appears to have taken place in our experiments is that the [artifically reared] infants have come to identify the composite stimulus pattern of their cups as familiar, so the cup has become, in essence, a social surrogate" (p. 562). This explanation accounts for the increased vocalization following removal from the cups but does not explain its reduction in the presence of the anesthetized dam.

As we have seen, much has been learned about the behavioral correlates of maternal deprivation. Complementing those findings are data pertaining to the physiological consequences of deprivation. A careful analysis was presented by Reite et al. (1981), who monitored the heart rate, body temperature, and sleep patterns of young pigtailed monkeys (see Table 5.3). The data are shown in Figure 5.4. It is apparent that the young undergo marked changes following removal of the mother (she was removed during the day). Heart rate and night body temperature declined and the animals slept less. Also, varying degrees of recovery occurred both during the course of the deprivation period and following reunion.

Figure 5.4 (*overleaf*) Percent change (from baseline) during separation and reunion in: (A) mean day heart rate (HR) and mean night HR; (B) mean day body temperature (BT) and mean night BT; (C) sleep latency, awake time, number of arousals, and total sleep time; and (D) drowsy, stage 2, and stages 3 and 4 sleep. (E) Percent changes (from baseline) in rapid-eye-movement (REM) sleep including the inter-REM interval (IRI). (N) = number of animals for whom data were available. Baseline mean values (B_x) are represented by the dotted lines. The vertical brackets for separation and reunion represent 95% confidence intervals for change (%) from baseline. For B_x the brackets indicate the 95% confidence interval across animals converted to percent of baseline. (From Reite et al., "Attachment, loss and depression ." *Journal of Child Psychology and Psychiatry, 22,* 141–69. © 1981 by Pergamon Press. Reprinted by permission.)

A

Mean Day HR

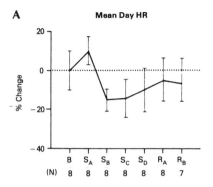

	B	S_A	S_B	S_C	S_D	R_A	R_B
(N)	8	8	8	8	8	8	7

Mean Night HR

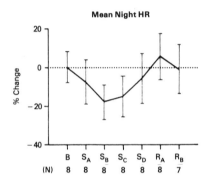

	B	S_A	S_B	S_C	S_D	R_A	R_B
(N)	8	8	8	8	8	8	7

B

Mean Day BT

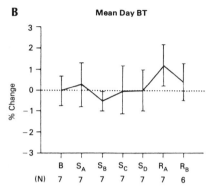

	B	S_A	S_B	S_C	S_D	R_A	R_B
(N)	7	7	7	7	7	7	6

Mean Night BT

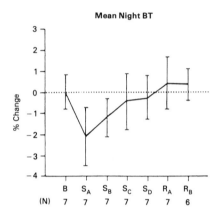

	B	S_A	S_B	S_C	S_D	R_A	R_B
(N)	7	7	7	7	7	7	6

C

Sleep Latency

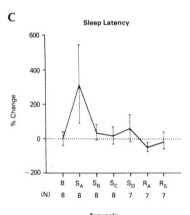

	B	S_A	S_B	S_C	S_D	R_A	R_S
(N)	8	8	8	8	7	7	7

Awake

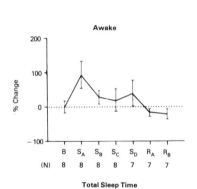

	B	S_A	S_B	S_C	S_D	R_A	R_B
(N)	8	8	8	8	7	7	7

Arousals

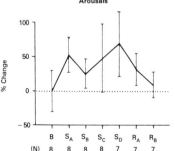

	B	S_A	S_B	S_C	S_D	R_A	R_B
(N)	8	8	8	8	7	7	7

Total Sleep Time

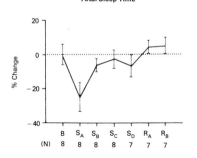

	B	S_A	S_B	S_C	S_D	R_A	R_B
(N)	8	8	8	8	7	7	7

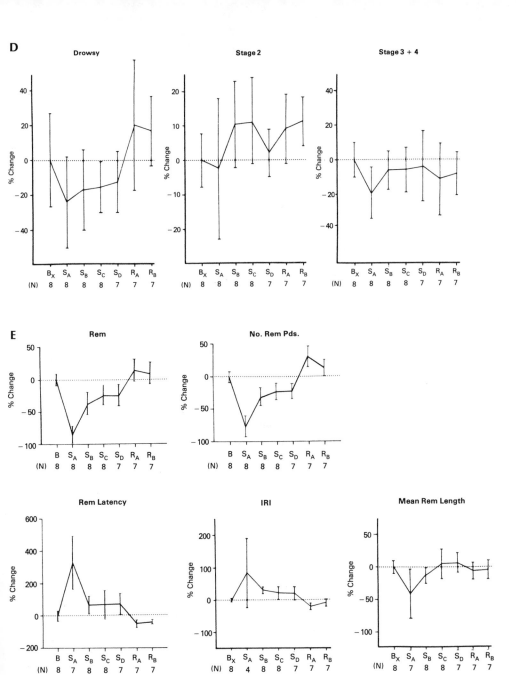

Figure 5.4 A–E (*caption on p. 149*)

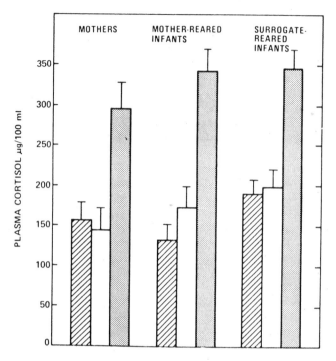

Figure 5.5 Plasma cortisol concentrations (mean ± SE) for mother and infant squirrel monkeys for each experimental condition (cross-hatched bars = base; clear bars = separation–reunion; dotted bars = separated). (From Mendoza et al., "Pituitary-adrenal response to separation in mother and infant squirrel monkeys." *Developmental Psychobiology, 11,* 169–75. © 1978 by John Wiley & Sons. Reprinted by permission.

Reite et al. then correlated behavioral data collected prior to separation with the data obtained during separation to determine if one can predict the degree of an infant's physiological reaction to maternal loss from knowledge of certain aspects of its preseparation behavior, such as activity and mother–infant interactions. The results of the analysis led Reite et al. to conclude that the correlation "is not clear cut, suggesting that even knowing a good bit about a given infant's early behavioral development, it is difficult to predict that infant's physiological reaction to separation, especially early in separation" (p. 163).

The endocrine system, in particular the pituitary-adrenal axis, also is reactive to maternal separation. Mendoza, Smotherman, Miner, Kaplan, and Levine (1978) assessed levels of cortisol in the plasma of infant squirrel monkeys prior to the mothers' removal, 30 minutes after her removal, and during a separate removal-reunion session. The data are shown in Figure 5.5. Wiener, Bayart, Faull, and Levine (1990) also found that the degree of elevation is dependent on the conditions of separation. Monkeys placed in a strange cage away from their mothers exhibited a greater rise in cortisol levels than those placed in a cage adjacent to their mothers. Monkeys left in familiar social groups (three or four mother–infant pairs) in their home cages after removal of their mothers displayed the smallest elevation. Familiar conspecifics, familiar surroundings, or both appear then to ameliorate the effect of maternal separation.

Rats also exhibit a rise in levels of cortisocosterone when separated from their mothers (Hennessy & Weinberg, 1990). Furthermore, it appears that the duration of the separation experience required to elicit the increase declines with advancing age. Whereas Hennessy and Weinberg found an elevation in 18-day-olds after 30 minutes of separation, elevations are exhibited by 10-day-olds after at least 120 minutes of separation (Kuhn & Schanberg, 1988).

Because cortisol and corticosterone are hormones that facilitate the organism's ability to cope with stressful situations and because their levels rise during separation, maternal deprivation has been viewed as a stressor. Such an assumption is buttressed by the observation that increased cortisol production is usually associated with the display of separation-elicited distress vocalizations and agitated movement (Coe, Wiener, Rosenberg, & Levine, 1985). Interestingly, however, there is a discontinuity between hormonal and behaviorial manifestations of stress following the initial period of maternal separation and after multiple separations. Coe, Wiener, and Levine (1983) reported frequency of distress vocalizations and plasma cortisol levels in squirrel monkey infants across a 6-hour separation period. As seen in Figure 5.6, although vocalizations decline, cortisol output increases. Hennessy (1986) found that young continue to respond to separation hormonally but not vocally, even after having been separated *80 times* previously. Behavior, then, particularly vocalization, may be a less sensitive index of the distress caused by long-term maternal deprivation than endocrine reactivity.

Coe et al. (1985) reported data causally relating the initial cortisol elevation to the display of behavior. Prior to being separated from their mothers, infant squirrel monkeys were injected with metapyrone, a drug that blocks the adrenal response to separation. The infants did not display the pacing and stereotyped movements typically observed in response to separation. Rather, they spent most of the observation periods being inactive. It was concluded that short-term adrenal activation may mobilize or shape the coping behavior of the maternally separated animal.

The well documented relation between chronic stress and illness and the fact that for humans separations and losses not only are rated as highly stressful events but have been associated with increased morbidity and mortality (e.g., Hurst, Jenkins, & Rose, 1976) imply that maternal deprivation should adversely affect physical health. Although this condition has been generally described in humans as "failure to thrive," more specific information has been obtained from animals. Ackerman, Hofer, and Weiner (1975, 1978) reported that rats separated from their mothers at 15 days of age are 85% more prone to develop gastric ulceration in response to the application of stress (food deprivation and physical restraint) on day 30 than are animals separated from their mothers on day 21 or later. The increase in ulceration rate is related causally to a fall in body temperature, which accompanies stress in 15-day-old separated young. Prevention of hypothermia prevents the formation of ulcers.

As mentioned earlier, data suggest that maternally deprived humans suffer from abnormally low levels of growth hormone. This relation has been substan-

Table 5.4   Concentration of growth hormone in serum of
10-day-old rat pups under various conditions

Experimental Conditions[a]	Growth Hormone	
	No.	Percent of Control ± SEM
Nondeprived controls	30	100 ± 3
Deprived		
1 Hour	10	53 ± 8*
2 Hours	16	60 ± 6*
6 Hours	5	59 ± 12*
Deprived and returned		
15 Minutes	5	155 ± 32
1 Hour	8	99 ± 7
2 Hours	13	94 ± 7
4 Hours	5	100 ± 4

[a]Maternally deprived and killed immediately or maternally deprived and returned to the mother for the indicated times before being killed.

*Statistically different from control ($p < .05$, Student's t-test).

Source: Adapted from Kuhn et al. Selective depression of growth hormone during maternal deprivation in rat pups. *Science, 201,* 1034–36. © 1978 by The American Association for the Advancement of Science. By permission.

tiated with nonhuman subjects. Kuhn, Butler, and Schanberg (1978) removed 10-day-old rats from their mothers and took blood samples 1, 2, or 6 hours later. Blood was obtained from other subjects either 15 minutes or 1, 2, or 4 hours after being returned to their mothers following a 2-hour separation period. Other young, not separated from their mothers, provided baseline data. As seen in Table 5.4, the serum concentration of growth hormone exhibited a significant decline throughout the entire deprivation period and returned to normal within as little as 15 minutes after the young were returned to their mothers. Because other pituitary hormones (prolactin, thyroid-stimulating hormone, and adrenocorticotrophic hormone) were not affected by maternal separation, the reduction of growth hormone results from specific rather than general suppression of pituitary function. Furthermore, because the decline in serum growth hormone is seen 1 hour after the onset of maternal deprivation and the level of the hormone is normal 15 minutes after the termination of deprivation, it is unlikely that the findings are mediated by a nutritional factor.

Evoniuk, Kuhn, and Schanberg (1979) went on to show that growth hormone level may be regulated by specific tactile stimuli provided by the mother. In an effort to mimic the mothers' grooming activity, some 8-day-old maternally separated rats were given 10 to 20 short, fairly heavy strokes on the head and back area with a moistened camel hair brush once every 5 minutes for 2 hours. Others either were stroked more gently, given a tail pinch once every 5 minutes, or left alone. A fifth group of young was not maternally deprived. Blood was obtained at the end of the 2-hour period and serum growth hormone levels determined. The data are shown in Figure 5.6. It is apparent that heavy stroking, designed to imitate the mothers' grooming behavior, prevented the decline in growth hor-

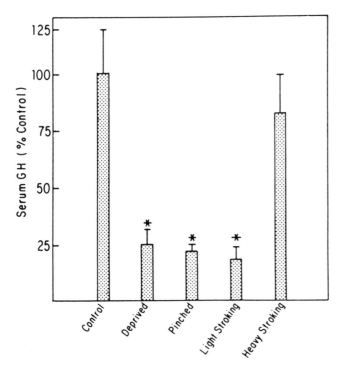

Figure 5.6   Serum growth hormone (GH) expressed as percent of that of control subjects (* = $p < .002$ or better compared to controls). (From Evoniuk et al., "The effect of tactile stimulation on serum growth hormone and tissue ornithine decarboxylase activity during maternal deprivation in rat pups." *Communications in Psychopharmacology, 3,* 363–70. © 1979 by Pergamon Press. Reprinted by permission.)

mone. It also was shown that stroking returns the hormone level to normal after it is lowered by 2 hours of maternal deprivation. The neural connection between the tactile stimulus and the endocrine response has not as yet been specified.

Lastly, the immune system also appears to be affected by maternal separation. Two young bonnet monkeys, separated from their mothers for 2 weeks, showed suppressed lymphocyte proliferation in response to mitogens relative to their preseparation baseline levels (Laudenslager, Reite, & Harbeck, 1982). Coe et al. (1985) similarly reported lower levels of antibody production in response to antigen challenge in seven separated squirrel monkeys compared to six nondeprived controls. This alteration in antibody production is apparently related to the magnitude of the behavioral response (vocalization and time spent in slouched postures) seen as a consequence of maternal separation (Laudenslager, Held, Boccia, Reite, & Cohen, 1990).

In addition to studies that focus on the physiological correlates of maternal deprivation, other research has attempted to identify neurochemical substrates that might underlie separation and the accompanying reactions. In other words, what causes an animal to become distressed? Panksepp made the interesting suggestion that endogenous brain opioids (endorphins) are involved in reactivity to separation, contending that opioids normally *inhibit* those areas of the brain that mediate separation distress. During periods of separation, opioid levels decline, the inhibition is lifted, and the organism experiences distress and behaves accordingly. It was predicted, therefore, that the administration of opioids should reduce distress in a manner similar to that of social reunion. The prediction has been supported; isolation-induced vocalization in young dogs (Panksepp, Herman, Conner, Bishop, & Scott, 1978), guinea pigs (Herman & Panksepp, 1978), chicks (Panksepp, Bean, Bishop, Vilberg, & Sakley, 1980a), rats (Carden & Hofer, 1990), and nonhuman primates (Kalin, Shelton, & Barksdale, 1988) is reduced following the administration of a relatively low dose of the opiate morphine sulfate. Conversely, opiate antagonists should exacerbate the distress reaction. The administration of naloxone, a substance that binds to opioid receptors and thus prevents opioid uptake, does increase distress vocalization (Herman & Panksepp, 1978; Panksepp, Meeker, & Bean, 1980b). However, the effect of the opiate antagonist is not reliable, seen by Panksepp in only about half of his experiments (Panksepp, Siviy, & Normansell, 1985). Its effectiveness appears to be influenced by various factors, including time of day, season, age, and level of social stimulation. Some of these factors may explain the lack of effect of naloxone and other opioid antagonists on distress vocalization reported by others (Cuomo et al., 1988; Winslow and Insel, 1991). The potential relation between the psychological effects of separation and brain opioids is an exciting possibility with obvious clinical implications, one clearly warranting continued investigation.

CROSS-SPECIES FOSTERING

Even if a nursing animal accepts young of a different species, a number of conditions must be met for cross-species fostering to be successful. On the one hand, the young must provide the adult with the requisite amount of tactile stimulation to cause milk letdown; they must be physically able to extract milk from an alien nipple; and they must be able to survive on milk that differs from that of its own species. On the other hand, the foster mother's maternal activities must be compatible with the needs of the infant. For example, infants of certain species require that the adult lick their anogenital region to stimulate urination and defecation. These conditions strictly limit the number of species between which cross-species fostering can be successfully implemented. In fact, with a single exception—dogs raised by cats—cross-species fostering in mammals has been performed in the laboratory only between mice and rats (mouse young raised by rat mothers).

The results of the initial experiment (Denenberg, Hudgens, & Zarrow, 1964) showed that single mouse pups reared by rats in rat litters and then housed with rats after weaning differ in various ways from mice having lived entirely with mice, from mice kept with rats after weaning, and from mice raised singly by mouse mothers. Mice reared by rats in the presence of rat young are less active, less aggressive, and prefer the rat as a social stimulus. Though showing that the behavior of the mouse can be modified by pre- and postweaning interaction with rats, the question remained as to whether the effects are caused by being raised by rat mothers or by living with rat young. Additional research addressed that issue.

Denenberg, Hudgens, and Zarrow (1966) fostered four male and two female 4-day-old mice to lactating rats whose own young had been removed. Other mice remained with their own mothers. Rat-reared mice are less active on the first of four daily open-field tests, fought less among themselves, and weighed more at weaning. It was later shown that rat-reared mice are a sufficient stimulus to evoke attack from other aggressive mice; as a consequence, these mice exhibit defensive behaviors (Hudgens, Denenberg, & Zarrow, 1967). Moreover, weanling mice that have been reared by rats exhibit lower plasma levels of corticosterone 30, 45, and 60 minutes after being placed in a novel environment (Denenberg, Rosenberg, Paschke, Hess, & Zarrow, 1968). The preference for rats as social stimuli, as reported in the initial experiment (Denenberg et al., 1964), however, is not caused by the rat mother but by being housed with rats after weaning (Hudgens, Denenberg, & Zarrow, 1968).

The rat mother, then, is somehow responsible for changes in behavior and adrenocortical activity of mouse young. How does she do it? Three explanations are possible. One is that the changes seen in the mice result from the ingestion of rat milk. Another is that the changes are induced passively by the rat mother's emission of particular stimuli, such as odors and sounds. Third, the changes may occur actively, a product of the behaviors directed by the rat toward the young.

The second possibility, a passive influence, was examined by housing mice reared by mouse mothers in a cage in which a double wire mesh partition separated them physically from an adult female rat (Denenberg, Paschke, Zarrow, & Rosenberg, 1969a). The young therefore were the recipients of olfactory, auditory, and visual stimuli from the rat but not behavior. This living arrangement had no effect on the weanling's corticosterone response to placement in a novel environment. Although neither open-field activity nor aggressive behavior were assessed, the data suggest that the rat mother's influence depends on either the provision of milk or behavior. Distinguishing between those possibilities required the use of a somewhat different preparation, one euphemistically called the "rat aunt," a nonlactating maternally behaving rat.

Capitalizing on the fact that nonlactating rats can be induced to behave maternally by simply maintaining them in the presence of young, Denenberg, Rosenberg, and Zarrow (1969b) placed each future rat aunt into a cage housing a rat mother and its litter. After 6 days the aunt was removed and immediately put into a cage containing a mouse mother and its 4-day-old pups and left there until weaning on day 21. As expected, the rat engaged in a variety of maternal behaviors, such as retrieving the young and hovering over them in a nursing posture while the lactating mouse managed to provide the nourishment. (I say "managed" because the rat aunt even mothered the mouse mother.) The offspring were weighed and their activity assessed in the open field when they were about 90 days old. Two weeks later blood was obtained for corticosterone analysis

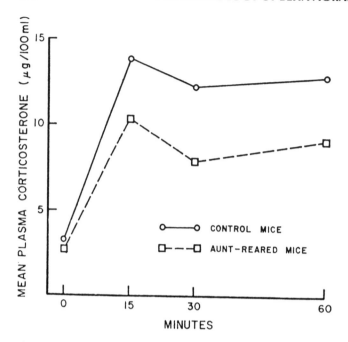

Figure 5.7 Mean plasma corticosterone as a function of amount of exposure to a novel environment for experimental and control mice. (From Denenberg et al., "Mice reared with rat aunts: Effects in adulthood upon plasma corticosterone and open-field activity." *Physiology and Behavior, 4,* 705–7. © 1969 by Pergamon Press. Reprinted by permission.)

either immediately or 15, 30, or 60 minutes after the offspring were placed in a novel environment. Relative to mice reared only by mouse mothers, animals exposed to the rat aunt weighed more, were less active, and, as shown in Figure 5.7, exhibited lower corticosterone levels after placement in a novel environment. With regard to aggressive behavior, the effectiveness of the rat aunt and, for that matter of the rat mother, depends on the strain of the mouse. Both rat mothers and aunts comparably reduce aggression of C57BL/10J mice, whereas neither mother nor aunt is effective in Swiss-Webster mice (Paschke, Denenberg, & Zarrow, 1971).

The rat aunt experiment strongly suggests that the changes observed in mice raised by rat mothers are caused by the latter's behavior toward the young rather than by their milk. This suggestion is supported by the results of an experiment that tested the prediction that rat aunts exhibiting high levels of maternal activities should produce more of a change in the mouse young than those displaying low levels of maternal behavior (Rosenberg, Denenberg, & Zarrow, 1970). Rats were prevented from giving milk by ligating and surgically removing the nipples, a procedure called *thelectomy*. Some of these rats then were mated; and within 12 hours of giving birth they were removed from their young and placed in a cage containing a mouse mother and its 3-day-old infants. Other rat aunts were thelectomized but not mated. Ratings revealed that aunts that had experienced pregnancy and brief interaction with their own young exhibited a higher degree of maternal responsiveness toward the mouse offspring than the nonmated aunts. As predicted, the former effected more of a change in the mouse offspring than did the latter; 21-day-old mice raised with the mated rat aunts exhibited the lowest plasma corticosterone level, those kept with the nonmated aunts exhibited an intermediate level, and mice raised without aunts exhibited the highest level after 30 minutes of exposure to a novel environment. Also, mice reared with mated rat aunts displayed the lowest level of open field activity. These data lend further support to the notion that the differences between mouse-reared and rat-reared mice are due to variations in pup-directed maternal activities, such as retrieval and licking. Perhaps they are performed at different rates or more vigorously by the adult rat, thereby providing the young with altered levels of stimulation. In this regard a relation has been reported between the rate a mother rat licks the anogenital region of her male offspring and their later sexual behavior; pups that are licked less often exhibit longer intervals between mounts (Birke & Sadler, 1987). It is not known, however, whether the difference in sexual behavior is caused by the differential licking or the mothers are differentially responsive to males that are already different.

Cross-species fostering also been performed between dogs and cats. Fox (1969) fostered four 25-day-old chihauhaus singly to lactating cats with four to six kittens. The puppies were accepted and within a few hours were suckling (see Fig. 5.8). Other puppies were raised by their own mothers. After weaning at 2 months, the cat-reared dogs were kept with cats, and the controls were housed with one another. Behavioral tests were conducted 2 months later.

One test consisted in the animals' reactions to their mirror images. Unlike control dogs, which appeared highly aroused, barking, tail wagging, and pawing and jumping at the mirror, the cat-raised dogs exhibited little reaction. They became much more reactive to their mirror images after being housed with other chihauhaus for 2 weeks. The cat-raised dogs also were submissive toward other dogs, although they were frequently observed to play with their cat peers. It appears, then, that species recognition is established in the chihauhua between the second and fourth months of life. However, the design of Fox's experiment precludes assessment of the relative contributions of the foster mother and cat peers to the modification of the dogs' socialization process. The findings of Hudgens et al. (1968) with cross-fostered mice suggest that it is the postweaning experience with cats that is the principal contributor to the altered species identification.

CONCLUDING COMMENTS

Overall, the data derived from humans and nonhumans agree that absence of the mother beginning immediately after birth (maternal privation) and her loss some time after having interacted with her infants (maternal deprivation) are related to significant modifications in the offspring's behavior and physiology. Some of those changes follow soon after the imposition of maternal separation and others transpire later in life, in some cases long after the offspring has been reunited with its mother. Generally, maternal privation is associated with more profound long-term consequences than is maternal deprivation.

Figure 5.8 Chihauhua being suckled by a foster mother cat at 20 days of age and another feeding with foster peers at 6 weeks of age. (From Fox, "Behavioural effects of rearing dogs with cats during the 'critical period of socialization'." *Behaviour, 35*, 274–80. © 1969 by E. J. Brill. Reprinted with permission.)

Although the research area of maternal separation has a long history commencing with observations of institutionalized human infants during the 1940s, a number of issues still require attention. These issues already have been addressed, but two of the most basic bear repeating. Paramount perhaps is the need to distinguish the influence of maternal separation from the effects of seclusion from other sources of social stimulation. This point is especially valid for nonhuman primate research in which maternal separation often is embedded within the larger experimental context of social isolation. It also is important to clarify the role of individual differences in reaction to maternal loss, as such information could explain how maternal separation causes developmental dysfunction and perhaps suggest ways to prevent or ameliorate such dysfunction.

Cross-species fostering research has demonstrated that fundamental changes in behavior and in reactivity of the pituitary/adrenal system occur when mice are raised by rats. Although it is known that those changes are *not* caused by rat milk or by visual, auditory, or olfactory cues emitted by the foster mother and that physical contact *must* transpire between rat and mouse infants, it is still not known how the changes are produced. Just what does the rat mother or aunt do to the mouse babies that is so unlike what is done to them by the mouse mother? Such information could inform us as to how the natural mother *normally* channels the development of aggressive behavior, activity, and reactivity to stressful events.

REFERENCES

Ackerman, S. H., Hofer, M. A., and Weiner, H. (1975). Age at maternal separation and gastric erosion susceptibility in the rat. *Psychosomatic Medicine, 37,* 180–84.

Ackerman, S. H., Hofer, M. A., and Weiner, H. (1978). Early maternal separation increases gastric ulcer risk in rats by producing a latent thermoregulatory disturbance. *Science, 201,* 373–76.

Ainsworth, M. D. (1962). The effects of maternal derivation: A review of findings and controversy in the context of research strategy. In *Deprivation of maternal care. A reassessment of its effects,* Geneva: World Health Organization.

Allin, J. T., and Banks, E. M. (1971). Effects of temperature on ultrasound production by infant albino rats. *Developmental Psychobiology, 4,* 149–56.

Arbel, N., and Stravynski, A. (1991). A retrospective study of separation in the development of adult avoidant personality disorder. *Acta Psychiatrica Scandinavica, 83,* 174–78.

Beck, A. T., Sethi, B. B., and Tuthill, R. W. (1963). Childhood bereavement and adult depression. *Archives of General Psychiatry, 9,* 295–302.

Berkson, G. (1967). Abnormal stereotyped motor acts. In J. Zubin and H. F. Hunt (Eds.), *Comparative psychopathology* (pp. 76–94). Orlando, FL: Grune & Stratton.

Birke, I. A., and Sadler, D. (1987). Differences in maternal behavior of rats and the sociosexual development of the offspring. *Developmental Psychobiology, 20,* 85–99.

Bowlby, J. (1944). Forty-four juvenile thieves: Their characters and home-life (II). *International Journal of Psychoanalysis, 25,* 107–27.

Bowlby, J. (1961). Processes of mourning. *International Journal of Psychoanalysis, 42,* 317–40.

Bowlby, J. (1973). *Separation: anxiety and anger.* New York: Basic Books.

Bowlby, J., Ainsworth, M., Boston, M., and Rosenbluth, D. (1956). The effects of motherchild separation: A follow-up study. *British Journal of Medical Psychology, 29,* 211–44.

Carden, S., and Hofer, M. (1990). Socially mediated reduction of isolation distress in rat pups is blocked by naltrexone but not by RO 15-1788. *Behavioral Neusorcience, 104,* 457–64.

Casler, L. (1965). The effect of extra-tactile stimulation on a group of institutionalized infants. *Genetic Psychology Monographs, 71,* 137–75.

Codner, M. A., and Nadler, R. D. (1984). Mother-infant separations and reunions in the great apes. *Primates, 25,* 204–17.

Coe, C. L., Mendoza, S. P., Smotherman, W. P., and Levine, S. (1978). Mother-infant attachment in the squirrel monkey: adrenal response to separation. *Behavioral Biology, 22,* 256–63.

Coe, C. L., Wiener, S. G., and Levine, S. (1983). Psychoendocrine responses of mother and infant monkeys to disturbance and separation. In L. A. Rosenblum and H. Moltz (Eds.), *Symbiosis in parent–offspring interactions* (pp. 189–214). New York: Plenum Press.

Coe, C. L., Wiener, S. G., Rosenberg, L. T., and Levine, S. (1985). Endocrine and immune responses to separation and maternal loss in nonhuman primates. In M. Reite and T. Field (Eds.), *The psychobiology of attachment and separation* (pp. 163–99). Orlando, FL: Academic Press.

Cuomo, V., Cagiano, R., DeSalvia, M. A., Restani, P., Galimberti, R., Racagni, G., and Galli, C. L. (1988). Ultrasonic vocalization in rat pups as a marker of behavioral development: An investigation of the effects of drugs influencing brain opioid system. *Neurotoxicology and Teratology, 10,* 465–69.

Denenberg, V. H., Hudgens, G. A., and Zarrow, M. X. (1964). Mice reared with rats: modification of behavior by early experience with another species. *Science, 143,* 380–81.

Denenberg, V. H., Hudgens, G. A., and Zarrow, M. X. (1966). Mice reared with rats: Effects of mother on adult behavior patterns. *Psychological Reports, 18,* 451–56.

Denenberg, V. H., Paschke, R., Zarrow, M. X., and Rosenberg, K. M. (1969a). Mice reared with rats: Elimination of odors, vision, and audition as significant stimulus sources. *Developmental Psychobiology, 2,* 26–28.

Denenberg, V. H., Rosenberg, K. M., and Zarrow, M. X. (1969b). Mice reared with rat aunts: Effects in adulthood upon plasma corticosterone and open-field activity. *Physiology and Behavior, 4,* 705–7.

Denenberg, V. H., Rosenberg, K. M., Paschke, R., Hess, J. L., and Zarrow, M. X. (1968). Plasma corticosterone levels as a function of cross-species fostering and species differences. *Endocrinology, 83,* 900–902.

Dennis, W., and Najarian, P. (1957). Infant development under environmental handicap. *Psychological Monographs: General & Applied, 71,* 1–13.

Dennis, W., and Sayegh, Y. (1965). The effect of supplementary experiences upon the behavioral development of infants in institutions. *Child Development, 36,* 81–90.

Evoniuk, G. E., Kuhn, C. M., and Schanberg, S. M. (1979). The effect of tactile stimulation on serum growth hormone and tissue ornithine decarboxylase activity during maternal deprivation in rat pups. *Communications in Psychopharmacology, 3,* 363–70.

Fox, M. W. (1969). Behavioural effects of rearing dogs with cats during the 'critical period of socialization.' *Behaviour, 35,* 274–80.

Fox, M. W., and Stelzner, D. (1967). The effects of early experience on the development of inter and intraspecies social relationships in the dog. *Animal Behaviour, 15,* 377–86.

Goldfarb, W. (1943). Effects of early institutional care on adolescent personality. *Journal of Experimental Education, 12,* 106–29.

Goldfarb, W. (1944). Effects of early institutional care on adolescent personality. *American Journal of Orthopsychiatry, 14,* 441–47.

Harlow, H. (1958). The nature of love. *American Psychologist, 13,* 673–85.

Harlow, H. F., and Harlow, M. K. (1962). Social deprivation in monkeys. *Scientific American, 207,* 137–46.

Harlow, H. F., Joslyn, W. D., Senko, M. G., and Dopp, A. (1966). Behavioral aspects of reproduction in primates. *Journal of Animal Science, 25,* 49–65.

Harlow, H. F., and Suomi, S. J. (1971). Social recovery by isolation-reared monkeys. *Proceedings of the National Academy of Science of the United States of America, 68,* 1534–538.

Hennessy, M. B. (1986). Multiple, brief maternal separations in the squirrel monkey: Changes in hormonal and behavioral responsiveness. *Physiology and Behavior, 36,* 245–50.

Hennessy, M. B., and Kaplan, J. N. (1982). Influence of the maternal surrogate on pituitary-adrenal activity and behavior of infant squirrel monkeys. *Developmental Psychobiology, 15,* 423–31.

Hennessy, M. B., and Weinberg, J. (1990). Adrenocortical activity during conditions of brief social separation in preweaning rats. *Behavioral and Neural Biology, 54,* 42–55.

Herman, B. H., and Panksepp, J. (1978). Effects of morphine and naloxone on separation distress and approach attachment: Evidence for opiate mediation of social affect. *Pharmacology, Biochemistry and Behavior, 9,* 213–20.

Hinde, R. A., and McGinnis, I. M. (1977). Some factors influencing the effects of temporary mother-infant separation—some experiments with rhesus monkeys. *Psychological Medicine, 7,* 197–212.

Hinde, R. A., Spencer-Booth, Y., and Bruce, M. (1966). Effects of 6-day maternal deprivation on rhesus monkey infants. *Nature, 210,* 1021–33.

Hofer, M. A. (1970). Physiological responses of infant rats to separation from their mothers. *Science, 168,* 871–73.

Hofer, M. A. (1971). Cardiac rate regulated by nutritional factor in young rats. *Science, 172,* 1039–41.

Hofer, M. A. (1973). The role of nutrition in the physiological and behavioral effects of early maternal separation on infant rats. *Psychosomatic Medicine, 35,* 350–59.

Hofer, M. A. (1983). The mother-infant interaction as a regulator of infant physiology and behavior. In L. A. Rosenblum and H. Moltz (Eds.), *Symbiosis in parent–offspring interactions* (pp. 61–75). New York: Plenum Press.

Hofer, M. A., and Shair, H. (1978). Ultrasonic vocalization during social interaction and isolation in 2-week old rats. *Developmental Psychobiology, 11,* 495–504.

Hofer, M. A., Shair, H. N., and Murowchick, E. (1989). Isolation distress and maternal comfort responses of two-week-old rat pups reared in social isolation. *Developmental Psychobiology, 22,* 553–66.

Hofer, M. A., and Weiner, H. (1975). Physiological mechanisms for cardiac control by nutritional intake after early maternal separation in the young rat. *Psychosomatic Medicine, 37,* 8–24.

Hudgens, G. A., Denenberg, V. H., and Zarrow, M. X. (1967). Mice reared with rats: Relations between mother's activity level and offsprings' behavior. *Journal of Comparative and Physiological Psychology, 63,* 304–8.

Hudgens, G. A., Denenberg, V. H., and Zarrow, M. X. (1968). Mice reared with rats: Effects of preweaning and postweaning social interactions upon adult behaviour. *Behavour, 30,* 259–74.

Hurst, M. J., Jenkins, D., and Rose, R. M. (1976). The relation of psychological stress to the onset of medical illness. *Annual Review of Medicine, 72,* 301–12.

Kalin, N. H., Shelton, S. E., and Barksdale, C. M. (1988). Opiate modulation of separation-induced distress in non-human primates. *Brain Research, 440,* 285–92.

Kaufman, I. C. (1973). Mother-infant separation in monkeys: An experimental model. In J. P. Scott and E. C. Senay (Eds.), *Separation and depression* (pp. 53–66). Washington, DC: American Association for the Advancement of Science.

Kaufman, I. C., and Rosenblum, L. A. (1967). The reaction to separation in infant monkeys: Anaclitic depression and conservation-withdrawal. *Psychosomatic Medicine, 29,* 648–75.

Kesson, W. (1965). *The child.* New York: John Wiley & Sons.

Koch, M. D., and Arnold, W. J. (1972). Effects of early social deprivation on emotionality in rats. *Journal of Comparative and Physiological Psychology, 78,* 391–99.

Kuhn, C. M., Butler, S. R., and Schanberg, S. M. (1978). Selective depression of growth hormone during maternal deprivation in rat pups. *Science, 201,* 1034–36.

Kuhn, C., and Schanberg, S. (1988). Growth hormone and corticosterone responses to maternal deprivation differ in sensory trigger and time course. Paper presented at the meeting of the International Society for Developmental Psychobiology, Toronto, Canada.

Laudenslager, M. L., Held, P. E., Boccia, M. L., Reite, M. L., and Cohen, J. J. (1990). Behavioral and immunological consequences of brief mother-infant separation: A species comparison. *Developmental Psychobiology, 23,* 247–64.

Laudenslager, M. L., Reite, M., and Harbeck, R. J. (1982). Suppressed immune response in infant monkeys associated with maternal separation. *Behavioral and Neural Biology, 36,* 40–48.

Lebovici, S. (1962). The concept of maternal deprivation: A review of research. In *Deprivation of maternal care: A reassessment of its effects* (pp. 75–95). Geneva: World Health Organization.

Levine, S. (1962). The effects of infantile experience on adult behavior. In A. J. Bachrach (Ed.), *Experimental foundations of clinical psychology* (pp. 118–69). New York: Basic Books.

Lewis, H. (1954). *Deprived children (the Mershal experiment. A social and clinical study.* London: Oxford University Press.

Lewis, J. K., McKinney, W. T., Young, L. D., and Kraemer, G. W. (1976). Mother-infant separation in rhesus monkeys as a model of human depression. *Archives of General Psychiatry, 33,* 699–705.

Mason, W. A., and Berkson, G. (1975). Effects of maternal mobility on the development of rocking and other behaviors in rhesus monkeys: A study with artificial mothers. *Developmental Psychobiology, 8,* 197–211.

Mendoza, S. P., Smotherman, W. P., Miner, M. T., Kaplan, J., and Levine, S. (1978). Pituitary-adrenal response to separation in mother and infant squirrel monkeys. *Developmental Psychobiology, 11,* 169–75.

Munro, A. (1966). Parental deprivation in depressive patients. *British Journal of Psychiatry, 112,* 443–57.

Nadler, R. D.,, and Codner, M. A. (1983). Maternal separation and reunion of an infant orangutan. *Primates, 24,* 67–76.

Newcombe, N., and Lerner, J. C. (1982). Britain between the wars: The historical context of Bowlby's theory of attachment. *Psychiatry, 45,* 1–13.

Novak, M. A., and Harlow, H. F. (1974). Social recovery for the first year of life: 1. Rehabilitation and therapy. *Developmental Psychology, 11,* 453–65.

Novakova, V. (1966). Role of the mother during the suckling period of newborn rats on subsequent adult learning. *Physiology and Behavior, 1,* 219–21.

Okon, E. E. (1971). The temperature of vocalization in infant golden hamsters and Wistar rats. *Journal of Zoology, London, 164,* 227–37.

Orlansky, H. (1949). Infant care and personality. *Psychological Bulletin, 46,* 1–48.

Panksepp, J., Bean, N. J., Bishop, P., Vilberg, T., and Sakley, T. L. (1980a). Opioid blockade and social comfort in chicks. *Pharmacology, Biochemistry and Behavior, 13,* 673–83.

Panksepp, J., Herman, B., Conner, R., Bishop, P., and Scott, J. P. (1978). The biology of social attachments: Opiates alleviate separation distress. *Biological Psychiatry, 13,* 607–18.

Panksepp, J., Meeker, R., and Bean, N. J. (1980b). The neurochemical control of aging. *Pharmacology, Biochemistry and Behavior, 12,* 437–43.

Panksepp, J., Siviy, S. M., and Normansell, L. A. (1985). Brain opioids and social emotions. In M. Reite and T. Field (Eds.), *The psychobiology of attachment and separation* (pp. 3–49). Orlando, FL: Academic Press.

Paschke, R. E., Denenberg, V. H., and Zarrow, M. X. (1971). Mice reared with rats: An interstrain comparison of mother and "aunt" effects. *Behaviour, 38,* 315–31.

Patton, R. G., and Gardner, I. I. (1962). *Growth failure in maternal deprivation.* Springfield, IL: Charles C Thomas.

Pinneau, S. R. (1955). The infantile disorders of hospitalism and anaclitic depression. *Psychological Bulletin, 52,* 429–53.

Powell, G. F., Brasel, J. A., Raiti, S., and Blizzard, R. M. (1967). Emotional deprivation and growth retardation simulating idiopathic hypopituitarism. *New England Journal of Medicine, 276,* 1279–283.

Provence, S., and Lipton, R. C. (1962). *Infants in institutions.* New York: International Universities Press.

Reite, M., and Short, R. (1978). Nocturnal sleep in separated monkey infants. *Archives of General Psychiatry, 35,* 1247–253.

Reite, M., Pauley, J. D., Kaufman, I. C., Stynes, A. J., and Marker, V. (1974). Normal physiological patterns and physiological behavioral correlations in unrestrained monkey infants. *Physiology and Behavior, 12,* 1021–33.

Reite, M., Short, R., and Kaufman, I. C., Stynes, A. J., and Pauley, J. D. (1978a). Heartrate and body temperature in separated monkey infants. *Biological Psychiatry, 13,* 91–105.

Reite, M., Short, R., and Seiler, C. (1978b). Physiological correlates of maternal separation in surrogate-reared infants: A study in altered attachment bonds. *Developmental Psychobiology, 11,* 427–35.

Reite, M., Short, R., Seiler, C., and Pauley, J. D. (1981). Attachment, loss and depression. *Journal of Child Psychology and Psychiatry, 22,* 141–69.

Ribble, M. A. (1944). Infantile experience in relation to personality development. In J. McV. Hunt (Ed.), *Personality and behavior disorders* (pp. 621–51). New York: Ronald Press.

Rogers, C. M., and Davenport, R. K. (1970). Chimpanzee maternal behavior. In G. H. Bourne (Ed.), *The chimpanzee* (pp. 361–68). Basel: S. Karger.

Rosenberg, K. M., Denenberg, V. H., and Zarrow, M. X. (1970). Mice *(Mus musculus)* reared with rat aunts: The role of rat-mouse contact in mediating behavioural and physiological changes in the mouse. *Animal Behaviour, 18,* 138–43.

Rosenblum, L. A. (1968). Mother-infant relations and early behavioral development in the squirrel monkey. In L. Rosenblum and R. W. Cooper (Eds.), *The Squirrel Monkey* (pp. 207–34). New York: Academic Press.

Rosenblum, L. A. (1978). Affective maturation and mother-infant relationship. In M. Lewis and L. A. Rosenblum (Eds.), *The development of affect* (pp. 275–292). New York: Plenum Press.

Sales, G. D., and Pye, D. (1974). *Ultrasonic communication by animals.* London: Chapman & Hall.

Seay, B. M., Hansen, E. W., and Harlow, H. F. (1962). Mother-infant separation in monkeys. *Journal of Child Psychology and Psychiatry, 3,* 123–32.

Seitz, P.F.D. (1959). Infantile experience and adult behavior in animal subjects: II. Age of separation from the mother and adult behavior in the cat. *Psychosomatic Medicine, 21,* 353–78.

Singh, M. E. (1975). Mother-infant separation in rhesus monkeys living in natural environments. *Primates, 16,* 471–76.

Spencer-Booth, Y., and Hinde, R. A. (1971a). Effects of 6 days of separation from mother on 18- to 32-week old rhesus monkeys. *Animal Behaviour, 19,* 174–91.

Spencer-Booth, Y., and Hinde, R. A. (1971b). Effects of brief separations from mothers during infancy on behaviour of rhesus monkeys 6–24 months later. *Journal of Child Psychology and Psychiatry, 12,* 157–72.

Spitz, R. A. (1945). Hospitalism. *Psychoanalytic Study of the Child, 1,* 53–74.

Spitz, R. A. (1946). Hospitalism: A follow-up report on investigation described in Volume 1, 1945. *Psychoanalytic Study of the Child, 2,* 113–17.

Spitz, R. A., and Wolf, K. A. (1946). Anaclitic depression: An inquiry into the genesis of psychiatric conditions in early childhood. *Psychoanalytic Study of the Child, 2,* 313–42.

Thoman, E. B., and Arnold, W. J. (1968). Effects of incubator rearing with social deprivation on maternal behavior in rats. *Journal of Comparative and Physiological Psychology, 65,* 441–46.

Thoman, E. B., Levine, S., and Arnold, W. J. (1968). Effect of maternal deprivation and incubator rearing on adrenocortical activity in the adult rat. *Developmental Psychobiology, 1,* 21–23.

Thompson, W. R., and Grusec, J. E. (1970). Studies of early experience. In P. H. Mussen (Ed.), *Carmichael's manual of child psychology* (pp. 565–654). New York: John Wiley & Sons.

White, B. L., and Castle, P. W. (1964). Visual exploratory behavior following postnatal handling of human infants. *Perception and Motor Skills, 18,* 497–502.

Wiener, S. G., Bayart, F., Faull, K. F., and Levine, S. (1990). Behavioral and physiological responses to maternal separation in squirrel monkeys *(Saimiri sciureus). Behavioral Neuroscience, 104,* 108–15.

Winslow, J. T., and Insel, T. R. (1991). Endogenous opioids: Do they modulate the rat pup's response to social isolation. *Behavioral Neuroscience, 105,* 253–63.

Wootton, B. (1962). A social scientist's approach to maternal deprivation. In *Deprivation of maternal care: A reassessment of its effects* (pp. 63–73). Geneva: World Health Organization.

6

Early Stimulation

Cerebral gymnastics are not capable of improving the organization of the brain by increasing the number of cells, because it is known that the nerve cells after the embryonic period have lost the property of proliferation; but it can be admitted as very probable that mental exercise leads to a greater development of the dendritic apparatus and of the system of axonal collaterals in the most utilized cerebral regions.　　S. Ramon y Cajal, 1894

That development is modified as a consequence of the young organism's interaction with its environment is an idea that has received a great deal of attention. The notion is conceptually straightforward; behavioral reactivity to certain kinds of stimulation alters brain function, which in turn alters brain development. An altered brain leads inevitably to altered behavior.

Three techniques have been used to manipulate the young animal's environment. One involves providing infants with restricted periods of supplemental stimulation. This manipulation is referred to as *handling* because it is commonly implemented by removing infants from their mothers and returning them a few minutes later. As a generic term, however, handling refers to any procedure that provides discrete periods of stimulation, from placing human infants into a rocking incubator to shaking a cage containing newborn animals. It is performed during the nursing period and is usually carried out over successive days.

A second technique also involves augmented levels of stimulation. In this case, however, the stimulation is provided not for fixed periods of time but chronically by enhancing the complexity of the young subjects' living environment. This procedure, usually initiated at weaning, is known as *environmental enrichment*. An enriched environment consists of a large cage containing a group of animals along with an array of stimulus objects that can be explored and manipulated.

A third type of procedure consists of confronting animals not with a large class of stimuli, as is the case with handling and environmental enrichment, but with exceedingly specific stimuli. Thus, for example, sometime between birth and weaning subjects may be exposed to particular visual stimuli or specific odors. For want of a better term, this manipulation is called *sensory/perceptual programming*.

HANDLING

Whereas handling as an experimental procedure using animals is performed prior to weaning and generally does not involve stroking the subject, its first appearances in the literature involved the stroking of weanling animals. Bernstein (1952) petted some rats for 10 minutes every day beginning on day 21 of life and, starting on day 60, tested them in a T maze with food reinforcement. The handled subjects required fewer trials to master the maze and made fewer errors than rats for which handling commenced on day 50 and than those not handled at all. Four years later Weininger (1956) reported both physiological and behavioral effects of 10 minutes of stroking from days 21 through 42. Handled rats were larger than the nonhandled controls; they weighed more between days 44 and 79 and had a greater skeletal length. They also were less adversely affected by the stress of 48 hours of immobilization coupled with food and water deprivation, having lighter adrenal glands and exhibiting fewer instances of heart damage. With regard to behavior, the handled animals were more active than controls when placed in a strange open field.

These early experiments were the precursors to a large body of research that explored the consequences of preweaning stimulation. Although we do not go into detail here, suffice it to say that ample evidence attests to the fact that handling before weaning is much more effective than its administration after weaning (Brookshire, Littman, & Stewart, 1961; Levine & Otis, 1958). In fact, some reports (Ader, 1959; Levine & Otis, 1958) have even failed to substantiate Weininger's (1956) early findings concerning postweaning handling.

The effects of handling are manifest in both physiological and behavioral changes. Let us begin by considering the influence of handling on physiology.

Physiological Effects of Handling

Rats and mice handled during infancy weigh more in adult life than nonhandled animals (Denenberg, 1962; Denenberg & Karas, 1959) and recover faster from early preweaning malnutrition (Anes & Winick, 1979). In addition, handling accelerates physiological development. Morton, Denenberg, and Zarrow (1963) reported that handled rats of both sexes exhibit earlier sexual maturation as assessed in the female by vaginal opening and first estrus and in the male by seminal vesicle and prostate gland weights. Handling also advances the time at which levels of brain cholesterol rise (Levine & Alpert, 1959) as well as causing the normal 24-hour rhythm of adrenal corticosterone secretion to appear by day 16 as opposed to between days 21 and 25 for nonhandled rats (Ader, 1969). Furthermore, stress-induced adrenocortical activity as well as the ability of adrenocorticotropic hormone (ACTH) to cause release of corticosterone from the adrenal gland is seen earlier in handled animals (Levine, 1968; Levine, Alpert, & Lewis, 1958).

Handling also appears to promote physical well-being. Diminished susceptibility to stress-induced gastric ulceration in both normal and lesion-susceptible rats has been reported (Ader, 1965, 1970), and Levine and Otis (1958) found fewer mortalities among handled rats in response to 120 hours of food and water deprivation. Resistance to cancer also is enhanced. Rats handled daily throughout the first 3 weeks of life exhibit a significant retardation in tumor development as adults following injections of Walker 256 carcinosarcoma (Ader & Friedman, 1965).

Because practically all of the research pertaining to handling and the later ability to survive severe insult has been performed with rats, the extent to which the saluatory effects of handling generalize to other species is virtually unknown. It is known, however, that the findings do not generalize to the mouse. Handled mice reportedly die sooner than controls following a leukemia injection and following terminal food and water deprivation (Denenberg & Karas, 1959; Levine & Cohen, 1959). Additional comparative data certainly are needed.

Beyond affecting the rats' ability to survive physical insult, handling also alters the central nervous system. This fact was first demonstrated by Altman, Das, and Anderson (1968), who handled rats for 15 minutes a day from days 2 through 11. In this case, handling consisted in removing the infants from the dam and rubbing them. The handled and control animals were injected on day 11 with thymidine-^{3}H, a precursor of DNA. Thymidine-^{3}H is incorporated only into the nuclei of cells about to multiply, thus providing a measure of cell proliferation. The counting of thymidine-^{3}H–labeled cells disclosed a higher rate of mitosis in the cerebellum, hippocampus, and neocortex of the handled subjects on days 11 and 41. These newly formed cells consist mainly of short-axoned neurons called "microneurons."

Altman et al. (1968) concluded that handling *delays* postnatal brain maturation. Cell proliferation in the nonhandled animals significantly declines by day 11, but because of the putative handling-induced maturational delay cell proliferation continues. Altman et al. applied their reasoning to the anthropological notion of "infantilization," which refers to an excessively prolonged period of postnatal development. They wrote:

> ... delay in the proliferation and migration of the precursors of microneurons extends the time available for the exertion of environmental modulatory influences on the organization of the brain ... that infantilization, which is a property shared by all altricial species, is not entirely genetically determined but is subject, during a critical period of development, to environmental influences, such as some factor inherent in the handling procedure. [Altman et al., 1968, p. 19]

The corpus callosum, a structure connecting the cerebral hemispheres, also is influenced by early handling experience (Berrebi et al., 1988). Adult male rats handled on days 1 to 20 have larger collosa in terms of both total area and width than nonhandled males and handled and nonhandled females. These findings may be related to the reported induction in males of specialized hemispheric functioning (lateralization) by handling. Denenberg, Garbanati, Sherman, Yutzey, and Kaplan (1978) found that whereas the ablation of either the right or left neocortex increased open-field activity of nonhandled male rats, *only* ablation of the right neocortex affected the activity of handled males. This finding is interpreted as induction of lateralization. Other findings that relate early handling experience to brain laterality were presented by Denenberg et al. (1980) and Garbanati et al. (1983).

Because handling alters the morphology of certain brain regions, it is not surprising that it also affects brain activity, specifically activation of the hippocampus. Brief but intense activation of hippocampal cells normally potentiates their subsequent activation. This potentiation, lasting up to several hours, is considered by some to be the basis of hippocampal involvement in learning and memory. The ability of the rat hippocampus to exhibit potentiation is not present at birth but develops gradually, reaching adult levels by the third week. Wilson, Willner, Kurz, and Nakel (1986) handled rats using a conventional handling procedure on days 4 to 8; on days 10 and 12 they were removed from the mother, placed in a box, and shaken gently for 5 minutes; and on days 9, 11, and 13 they were removed from the dam for 1 hour and left undisturbed. These handled rats exhibited greater potentiation than controls, as seen from electrophysiological recordings made between days 28 and 41. That is, the application of electrical stimulation to hippocampal cells 30 minutes after the initial application of a brief and intense electrical stimulus elicited a higher amplitude event than that found in nonhandled subjects.

Behavioral Effects of Handling

Handling has been reported to have two major behavioral outcomes. It is generally agreed that it influences the organism's reactivity to stressful stimuli—its "emotionality" as it is often called. Reactivity of this sort is frequently assessed by the amount of activity displayed in a novel environment such as the open field. It is believed that an inverse relation exists between such activity and emotionality (Denenberg, 1969), as rodents tend to freeze when frightened. A second effect of handling is that it directly influences an animal's ability to acquire new behaviors. The findings regarding this behavioral outcome are by no means clear.

Emotionality

Denenberg and Morton (1962) found that adult rats handled daily from birth to weaning were significantly more active in the open field (viz., less emotional) than controls. Also indicative of reduced emotionality was a significant decline in defecation. This finding of reduced emotionality in handled rats has been replicated many times (Denenberg & Whimbey, 1963; Levine, Haltmeyer, Karas, & Denenberg 1967) and in situations other than the open field (Weinberg, Krahn, & Levine, 1978). Table 6.1 presents some representative data. Other information reveals that handling need not be performed throughout the entire lactation period for emotionality to be affected. Denenberg, Morton, Kline, & Grota (1962), for example, reported that handling from birth to day 10 is sufficient. However, the greater the amount of early stimulation, the greater the attenuation of emotionality (Denenberg, 1964).

Rats are not the only species for which early handling reduces emotionality.

Table 6.1 Open-field activity and defecation scores for handled and nonhandled rats

Treatment During Infancy	Day 1	Day 2	Day 3	Day 4
Nonhandled				
Mean activity	12.36	4.90	4.10	5.75
Percent defecation	52.08	50.93	61.11	61.11
No.	144	108	72	36
Handled				
Mean activity	8.69	8.81	11.92	16.03
Percent defecation	38.89	31.48	27.78	36.11
No.	144	108	72	36
Activity (t)	1.94*	2.37†	3.87‡	3.36‡
Defecation (χ^2)	4.54†	7.64‡	14.88‡	3.56*

*$p < .10$
†$p < .05$
‡$p < .01$

Source: From Levine et al. Physiological and behavioral effects of infantile stimulation. *Physiology and Behavior* 2:55–59. © 1967 by Pergamon Press. Reprinted by permission.

Wyly, Denenberg, DeSantis, Burns, and Zarrow (1975) handled rabbits on days 1 to 10, 11 to 20, or 1 to 20 of life and tested them in the open field starting on day 31. Handled rabbits exhibited more activity than controls. Activity expressed as a function of handling is as follows: days 1 to 20 > days 11 to 20 > 1 to 10. We see, then, that 20 days of handling is more effective than 10 days, and that age determines the degree to which the animal is affected by the extra stimulation. Handling also increased the amount of time the rabbit spent near a cage containing a like-sex stimulus rabbit.

Meyer and McCormick (1978) placed handled and nonhandled mice into an apparatus in which various intensities of electrical shock were administered through the grid floor. Their reactivity to the shock was assessed by recording the number of instances of jumping, running, and squeaking. The findings are shown in Figure 6.1. It can be seen that handled mice reacted to the shock less intensely than nonhandled subjects; in other words, they appeared to be less emotional.

A set of experiments complementary to those that measure activity entail the assessment of levels of corticosterone, an adrenal hormone released in response to rising levels of ACTH, which is liberated by the pituitary in response to stress. Corticosterone performs various functions that facilitate an organism's responsiveness to stressful events such as the mobilization of glucose stores.

A report by Levine in 1962 provided the initial evidence linking handling to a modification of the pituitary-adrenal system. Handled and nonhandled rats were administered electrical shock on day 60, and blood samples were taken for corticosterone analysis from separate groups of animals at various times following shock termination.

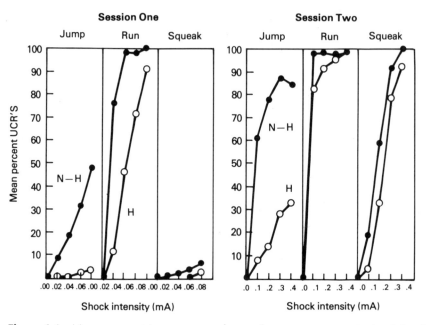

Figure 6.1 Mean percent jump, run, and squeak responses at each shock level for early handled (H) and nonhandled (N-H) groups of mice. (From Meyer and McCormick, "Unconditioned responding in mice as a function of early handling and shock intensity." *Psychological Record, 28,* 571–74. © 1978 by The Psychological Record. Reprinted with permission.)

Handling affected the rapidity with which corticosterone levels rose. Manipulated subjects exhibited a significant elevation as early as 15 seconds after shock termination, whereas the controls did not show a comparable rise until 300 seconds after shock offset. Similar results were obtained by Haltmeyer, Denenberg, and Zarrow (1967); they also found that whereas handled animals had a greater level of corticosterone in the plasma when measured at the time of shock offset, after its termination the hormone was released at a slower rate in handled animals. In other words, handled animals appear to recover from stress faster than nonhandled animals.

Although handling enhances responsiveness of the pituitary-adrenal system to painful electrical shock, Levine et al. (1967) found that handling *attenuates* pituitary-adrenal reactivity to the stress engendered by placement in a novel environment. This differential responsiveness of the pituitary-adrenal system and the fact that handled animals secrete less corticosterone than nonhandled subjects following cessation of electrical shock suggested to some (e.g., Levine et al., 1967) that early handling facilitates the rat's later adaptation to stress. The logic is as follows: First, because the adrenal gland contains a finite amount of corticosterone, its conservation in response to a situation such as a novel environment, which poses a questionable threat to the animal's well-being, as well as its conservation following the actual removal of a stressor make good sense. Second, it also is to the animal's distinct advantage to quickly secrete large amounts of corticosterone when faced with a situation that is obviously life-threatening, such as exposure to painful electrical shock.

Meaney et al. (1985) examined in detail the ability of handled animals to recover quickly from stress, as shown by the rapid return of corticosterone to baseline levels. Reduction of adrenal corticosterone secretion is accomplished through a negative feedback system; although high levels of ACTH cause corticosterone release, the ensuing elevated levels of corticosterone *inhibit* the release of additional ACTH. Handling therefore appears to promote the development of this negative feedback system. Because the feedback system is dependent, in part, on brain receptors that are sensitive to corticosterone, Meany et al. assessed the degree to which corticosterone binds to various areas of the brains of handled and nonhandled adult rats. Binding was found to be higher in the hippocampus and frontal cortex of handled animals. Therefore handled animals may recover from stress with greater rapidity than nonhandled animals because handling in some manner promotes the development of the corticosterone receptor system, enhancing the ability of corticosterone to dampen ACTH release.

According to Meaney, Aitken, van Berkel, Bhatnogar, and Sapolsky (1988), the enhanced negative feedback between corticosterone and ACTH has ramifications much later in life. Aged (2-year-old) rats that had been handled during infancy not only recover from stress faster but also have lower basal levels of corticosterone than controls. Furthermore, handled animals do not exhibit neuronal loss in the hippocampus or the cognitive deficits normally seen in elderly rats. Because of evidence causally relating neuronal loss and cognitive deficits to chronically elevated levels of corticosterone, Meaney et al. concluded that handling, by lowering basal corticosterone levels, prevents certain age-associated impairments.

Acquired Behavior

Unlike the general consensus regarding the inverse relation between handling and emotionality, the data directly relating handling to later acquisition of behavior are far from consistent. This point is readily apparent when considering avoidance conditioning, a task frequently employed within the context of early handling. As reviewed by Daly (1973), some studies have reported that handling facilitates avoidance conditioning, whereas others reported that it produces no effect. In a few cases handling has been found to retard avoidance conditioning. Even discounting the negative findings, one cannot conclude that avoidance conditioning was *directly* influenced by handling. As Daly (1973) and Denenberg (1964) pointed out, improved performance may be secondary to a reduction of emotionality. Because emotional reactivity often involves freezing, a response incompatible with active avoidance responding, a reduction in emotionality (viz., freezing) obviously is advantageous.

With regard to the influence of handling on approach (appetitive) conditioning, the data also are inconclusive. The results of some studies (Denenberg & Morton, 1962; Goldman, 1965) are in accord with Denenberg's (1964) hypothesis that handling should not affect conditioning situations that lack a major aversive element. Although other data suggest that handling facilitates appetitive conditioning (Wong, 1972; Wong & Judd, 1973), Wong and Wong (1978) concluded that the only definitive data demonstrating positive effects of handling on acquired behavior derive from aversive conditioning paradigms.

Weiner, Schnobel, Lubow, and Feldon (1985) examined the influence of handling on conditioning devoid not only of an aversive component but also of a positive component. It was accomplished with a *latent inhibition* paradigm in which the repeated presentation of stimuli that are not followed by reinforcing consequences renders them incapable of supporting future conditioning. It is as if this repeated nonreinforced preexposure causes subjects to learn to ignore the stimuli. Here, then, is a situation ostensibly lacking any motivational factor. "Consequently, any differences obtained between handled and nonhandled animals in their ability to develop latent inhibition cannot be attributed to motivation-emotional differences, but rather to differences in attentional processes underlying learning to ignore irrelevant stimuli" (Weiner et al., 1985). Handled and nonhandled rats were exposed to a series of tones that later served as the conditioned stimulus in avoidance conditioning. The results showed that whereas both the handled and nonhandled females exhibited latent inhibition, *only* the handled males exhibited it. The authors concluded that handling does affect at least one conditioning task that does not involve an emotional-motivational component, and it does so only in the male. In this case nonhandling produces a deleterious effect.

Handling as a Stressor

Juxtaposed against data demonstrating the salutory influence of handling on health, maturation rate, and the development of an organism's reactivity to stress are data showing that handling itself is a stressor. If true, early stress must be beneficial! This view is of course at odds with that of the psychoanalytic community, which insists that early trauma can lead to later psychological difficulties, and with that of physiologists, who contend that the myriad physiological reactions that accompany stress are harmful, particularly if they occur early in life. Let us look at those nonintuitive data relating handling to stress.

The association between handling and stress is supported by evidence of two sorts. First, handling and other manipulations that are unambiguously stressful exert similar effects on the infant. For example, the application of various stressors, such as cold, heat, and electrical shock, as well as handling, to 2-day-old rats elicit elevated levels of corticosterone (Denenberg, Brumaghin, Haltmeyer, & Zarrow, 1967; Zarrow, Denenberg, Haltmeyer, & Brumaghin, 1967). Parenthetically, the release of corticosterone in response to handling fails to appear if the pups are kept warm during the 3 minutes they are removed from the mother, thereby demonstrating that cold may be a factor critical to the handling phenomenon. (See also Russell, 1971, and Schaefer, 1978, for additional thoughts regarding the mediation of the handling phenomenon.)

The release of corticosterone by handling not only is used to argue that handling is a stressor, it also provides the basis for an explanation of how handling operates to affect later reactivity to stress (Denenberg & Zarrow, 1970; Levine & Mullins, 1966).

> We know that handling is effective only during early infancy and we also know that corticosterone is a steroid. The sex hormones, which are also steroids, are known to have their organizing effects during early infancy or even pre-natally. Thus . . . corticosterone may be performing a similar role with respect to emotional behavior as the sex steroids are performing with respect to maleness and femaleness. If this is so, then it follows that the corticosterone released from the adrenal gland must be localizing itself in the brain of the immature rat, presumably, in the hypothalamic region. [Denenberg & Zarrow, 1970, p. 131]

With regard to the latter point, radioactively labeled corticosterone, after being injected into 2-day-old rats, is indeed found in the hypothalamus (Zarrow, Philpott, Denenberg, & O'Connor, 1968).

A second line of evidence suggesting that handling is stressful is that both it and unequivocal stressors yield similar developmental effects. The data of Levine, Chevalier, and Korchin (1956) are often cited in this regard. These investigators administered electrical shock to one group of rats daily between birth and weaning, handled a second group, and left a third group alone. The avoidance performance of both the shocked and handled animals surpassed that of the undisturbed animals. Denenberg and Smith (1963) further reported that both handled and shocked rats display increased open field activity, and Ader (1969) found that handling and shock advance the age at which the 24-hour adrenocortical rhythm first appears. A final example is a study by Werboff and Havlena (1963), which consisted of inducing convulsions in some 3-day-old rats by exposing them to microwave diathermy, handling others, and leaving others undisturbed. At 30 days of age all animals were tested for seizure activity induced by exposure to sound (audiogenic seizure). Although 41% of the undisturbed animals exhibited seizures, none of the handled or convulsed animals did so.

Although these data and others do show similarities between handled animals and those subjected to indisputable stressors, two points must be noted. First, some data show that handling produces unique effects. Pfeifer, Rotundo, Myers, and Denenberg (1976) reported that rats handled for the first 5 days of life exhibit a smaller corticosterone release on day 37 in response to stress produced by the open field, electrical shock, or heat than do animals given electrical shock on days 1 to 5 of life (see also Denenberg, 1968). Second, many of the studies that report similarities between handled animals and those conventionally stressed have a methodological flaw owing to the fact that animals challenged with standard stressors usually are also handled. This problem is seen, for example, in the Levine et al. (1956) study in which the animals were removed from the mothers and placed on a grid floor. Those left undisturbed on the floor were designated the handled group, and those exposed to electricity through the grids comprised the shocked group. Thus one group was handled, and the second was shocked and handled. If handling is a unique form of stimulation producing singular developmental effects, both groups would be expected to develop in a similar manner. However, the similarity would be related to handling, not stress.

Moving from research with animals to humans, we find some additional and interesting evidence linking early stress to certain attributes of physical development. This work, inspired by the research reviewed above, well illustrates one important function of animal research that is often overlooked: the generation of hypotheses that can be tested with human subjects. The data are from anthropological studies of Landauer and Whiting (1964), who used the Human Relations Area Files (HRAF) at Harvard University to identify societies that engage in child rearing practices considered to be stressful. The practices are summarized in the following list in descending order of intuitively judged severity.

Circumcision

Piercing of nose, lips, or ears

Scarification by cutting or burning

Vaccination

Molding by forceful stretching or shaping (not passive pressure as in a headboard)

Extremes of temperature: hot or cold baths

Internal agents: emetics, irritants, enemas

Abrasion: rubbing with sand or scraping with shell or other hard object

Extraordinarily intense stimulation: massaging, annointing, exposure to loud noises

Binding: swaddling or other severe restriction of movement [Landauer & Whiting, 1981, p. 359]

Each of 62 societies was given a weighted score indicative of the amount of stress experienced during the first 2 weeks of life, and these scores were correlated with the average height of the adult males, information also contained in the HRAF. The positive correlation of .30 is statistically significant: the more stress, the taller the males.

A second study was undertaken in which societies were limited to those in which the HRAF reported heights of at least 25 males. Also, the definition of stress was restricted to the practice of circumcision, piercing, scarification, vaccination, and molding; and the age criterion was extended from 2 weeks to 2 years, as the latter represents the average age of weaning in the societies under study. The average height of adult males in 18 societies with stressful infant care practices was 65.2 inches in contrast to 62.7 inches in 17 societies in which those practices were not observed, a statistically reliable difference. The study was repeated with 30 different societies, and the results were similar: A difference of 2.6 inches favored societies with stressful practices. Landauer and Whiting (1981) also reported that adult stature is unaffected by stress commencing after the second year of life.

Landauer and Whiting then considered the possibility that a factor other than stress might have contributed to the findings. Suppose, for example, that societies that engaged in stressful infant care practices for some reason had more dietary protein available. Additional analyses not only ruled out a dietary factor as a cause of the enhanced stature of adult males stressed as infants but also eliminated climate, genetic, and geographic factors.

Regarding stressed females, Whiting (1965) reported that they are, on average, 4.0 inches taller than those from nonstressed societies. Furthermore, the average menarcheal age for stressed females is 12.8 years compared to 13.6 years for nonstressed females.

In most investigations, handling involves removing young animals from their mothers. Accordingly, Gunders and Whiting (1968) asked if maternal separation might itself constitute a source of stress that would also correlate with adult stature. In some societies infants remain in physical contact with the mother or other caretaker until weaning, whereas in others they are taken from the mother soon after birth and routinely spend long periods away from her. A significant positive correlation between maternal separation and stature of adult males was found. As before, neither a nutritional, genetic, nor geographic factor was related to the findings.

Lastly, Landauer and Whiting (1981) managed to perform one controlled experiment in an attempt to substantiate their findings regarding early stress and stature. Smallpox vaccinations are stressful because by introducing live virus they induce a mild case of the disease. Landauer and Whiting, using a group of 278 Kenyan children, randomly selected some to be vaccinated prior to 2 years of age (in some cases polio and DPT vaccinations were given as well) and others to be vaccinated after 2 years. Data were collected when the children were between 3 and 7 years old. Although the two groups apparently did not differ in terms of disease prevalence, the children vaccinated prior to the age of 2 had grown more during the intervening years than those vaccinated later. Differences were found for height, leg length, and head circumference.

Landauer and Whiting's work provide evidence linking early stress to the enhancement of physical growth in males and females and to the acceleration of puberty in females, findings similar to those obtained from handled animals. It would be of great interest to carry the research a step further by ascertaining whether stress influences human psychological development, especially with regard to indices of emotionality.

Handling and the Premature Infant

As a consequence of being deprived of a significant period of in utero development, premature infants suffer far more neurological, social, motor, and psychological deficits than do full-term infants. Accordingly, attempts have been made to identify interventions that reduce infant mortality and the risk of developmental problems after premature birth. Because of the salutary influence of early handling on the development of animals, it was logical to ask if the application of extra stimulation would benefit the premature infant. It should be noted, however, that because the preterm infant usually spends its first weeks of life in an incubator, which buffers it from most of the stimulation normally impinging on the full-term infant, the additional stimulation may actually be compensatory rather than supplementary.

Two forms of stimulation, tactile and vestibular, have been generally used. In one of the earliest studies, Solkoff, Yaffe, Weintraub, and Blase (1969) provided five premature infants with tactile stimulation 5 minutes per hour every hour for the first 10 days; each infant's neck, back, and arms were gently rubbed. Five other infants, given tactile stimulation only in association with feeding and diaper changes, served as controls. The experimental infants were more active and regained their initial birth weight faster than the controls. Moreover, as assessed by the Bayley Test of Mental and Motor Development given 7 to 8 months after discharge from the nursery, all of the handled infants were rated as being active and physically healthy. In contrast, three of the controls were rated as more than two standard deviations below the growth mean for their age. Finally, four of the controls were deficient in motor development for their ages compared to only a single experimental subject.

A number of researchers (e.g., Barnard & Bee, 1983; Rausch, 1981; Scott, Cole, Lucas, & Richards, 1983) subsequently examined the influence of supplemental tactile stimulation on the development of premature infants, and their data generally confirm the earlier findings. Scafidi et al. (1986) provided 20 preterm infants with tactile/kinesthetic stimulation consisting of stroking and passive movement of the arms and legs during three 15-minute sessions a day for 10 consecutive days. Twenty additional infants served as controls. The stimulated infants exhibited an average of 47% more weight gain per day than controls and spent more time awake and active. They also scored higher on the Brazelton scale of development. These results of supplemental tactile/kinesthetic stimulation permitted the infants to be discharged from the hospital 6 days earlier than controls at a hospital cost savings of $3,000 per infant! Similar findings were later reported by Scafidi et al. (1990). Kuhn et al. (1991) also reported that tactile/vestibular stimulation increases premature infants' levels of norepinephrine and epinephrine, but their levels of dopamine, cortisol, and growth hormone do not differ from those of controls. This finding suggests that the early stimulation has specific effects on the maturation or activity of the sympathetic nervous system.

Vestibular stimulation was dispensed by Clark, Cordero, Goss, and Manos (1989) by placing 15 premature subjects into a specially designed incubator that provided side-to-side rocking (see Figure 6.2). Infants were rocked 15 minutes three times a day for 2 weeks. The results are shown in Figure 6.3. Relative to 11 controls, the handled infants scored significantly higher on the Dubowitz Neurological Assessment Test of neuromuscular development given at the end of the 2-week treatment period and again 2 weeks later. The test measures muscle tone, movement, habituation, reflexes, and neurobehavioral reactions such as alertness. The groups, however, did not differ on habituation and weight gain. A somewhat similar study using a combination of tactile, visual, vestibular, and auditory stimulation also reported a facilitation of motor and mental development (Lieb, Renfield, & Guidubaldi, 1980). Again weight gain was unaffected.

Scarr-Salapatek and Williams (1973) not only gave a combination of visual, tactile, and vestibular stimulation to 15 preterm infants during their 6-week stay

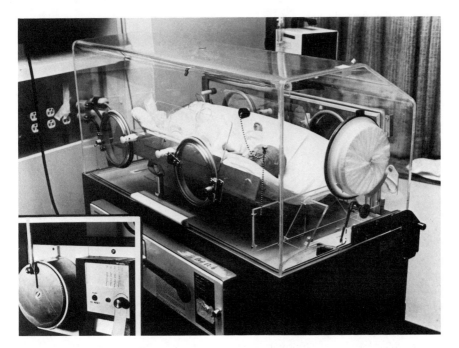

Figure 6.2   Isolette modified to provide side-to-side rocking of infants. Motion is provided by a pushrod connected eccentrically to a motorized rotating wheel located in the base of the isolette (inset). (From Clark et al., "Effects of rocking on neuromuscular development in the premature." *Biology of the Neonate, 56,* 306–14. © 1989 by Karger AG. Reprinted by permission.)

in the hospital but also trained their mothers to maintain the enhanced levels of stimulation for the first year of life. At 4 weeks of age the experimental infants exhibited a higher developmental status than controls, including a greater gain in weight. At 1 year, they scored an average of 10 points higher on the Cattell Infant Intelligence Scale. "The experimental treatment that began in the premature nursery and continued through the first year of life had brought the [experimental] group to nearly normal levels of behavioral development" (Scarr-Salapatek & Williams, 1973).

Premature infants also benefit from treatment commencing after the infants' release from the hospital. Rice (1977) trained the mothers of 15 preterm infants to administer a combination of tactile (stroking) and vestibular (rocking and cuddling) stimulation for 30 days following their release. Tactile stimulation was given for 15 minutes and vestibular stimulation for 5 minutes four times a day. Fourteen infants served as controls. When examined at 4 months of age, the handled group significantly exceeded the controls in neurological and mental development as assessed by the Baley Scales.

Based on the data reviewed here and elsewhere (Cornell & Gottfried, 1976; Field, 1980), it is safe to conclude that the provision of extra stimulation pro-

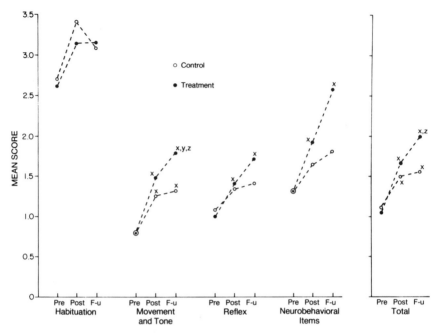

Figure 6.3 Results of Dubowitz Comprehensive Examination at pretest (Pre), posttest (Post), and follow-up (F-u). Experimental infants were exposed to 15-minute rocking sessions three times a day between the pretesting and posttesting (14 days) (x = $p < 0.05$ compared with the same group at pretest; y = $p < 0.05$ compared with the same group at posttest; z = $p < 0.05$ compared with control group at the same test). (From Clark et al., "Effects of rocking on neuromuscular development in the premature." *Biology of the Neonate, 56,* 306–14. © 1989 by Karger AG. Reprinted by permission.)

motes neurological and psychological development of the premature infant. Data that relate such stimulation to weight gain, however, are ambiguous.

Various issues relating to handling and development of the premature infant remain to be considered. One, of course, is how stimulation produces its beneficial effects. A second, related issue concerns the extent to which the parents might augment the effectiveness of the handling regimen. If extra stimulation enhances the infant's responsiveness to its environment, might it not in turn enhance the parents' reactions to the infant? According to Solkoff et al. (1969), it might:

> In general, the homes of the handled infants were found to offer the child more stimulation (e.g., more toys, greater mother–infant interaction, etc.) than was the case in the homes of the nonhandled babies. It is tantalizing to speculate whether the handling procedures may have more positively affected the infants' behavior, thereby resulting in a more positive attidude on the part of the mother toward her infant. [p. 767]

A similar observation was made by Siqueland (1970), who provided supplemental stimulation in the form of extra "mothering" and stroking to one member of a set of premature twins. Ten sets of twins were used in all.

> . . . the comments of some of our mothers of the twins suggested the possibility that differences in the behavior of the twins . . . may have programmed the mother to interact with the twins differentially. When mothers were asked to indicate the similarities and differences in early behavior patterns of the twins, it was not uncommon for the mother to emphasize initial differences with such statements as "this one is content to be by himself while the other one is always demanding my attention" or "I always feed the one first because the other likes to be played with and will wait." [pp. 12–13]

A third issue concerns the endurance of the handling phenomenon. How long do the effects of supplemental stimulation last? To answer this question, long-term follow-up studies of handled and nonhandled premature infants must be performed. This writer is unaware of any such studies.

Lastly, one may ask if supplemental stimulation also benefits full-term infants. An experiment by Clark, Kreutzberg, and Chee (1977) suggests that it does. Thirteen full-term infants between the ages of 3 and 13 months were given vestibular stimulation by spinning them at 16.7 revolutions per minute in a rotating chair while being held in the lap of an adult. Each child was given 16 sessions consisting of 10 spins per session. Two sessions, separated by 30 minutes, were given twice a week for 4 weeks. Two control groups were used; one was treated identically except for the rotation, and the other was left undisturbed. All subjects were given a reflex and motor test prior and subsequent to the treatment period. The former assessed 17 reflexes, and the motor tests evaluated skills in lying, sitting, creeping, standing, and walking. Taking into account each child's pretreatment level of performance, it was found that the stimulated children scored significantly higher than controls on both tests, improving 12.2% on the reflex test and 27.4% on the motor skills test. The two control groups combined improved only 3.8% and 6.7%, respectively. It was suggested that the vestibular stimulation may have promoted the maturation of the vestibuloocular reflex, which "provided the visual system a more stable retinal image against which motor involvement with the environment developed more rapidly" (Clark et al., 1977). Clearly, additional research on stimulation and the development of the full-term infant is warranted.

ENVIRONMENTAL ENRICHMENT

Early stimulation also is provided by allowing weanling animals to live in *enriched environments*. As mentioned previously, such an environment usually consists in keeping a group of animals in a large cage containing objects that the animals can explore and manipulate. The length of stay in the enriched environment varies, but it usually is on the order of 2 months. Living arrangements of this sort are of course antithetical to the standard laboratory housing condition, which is often referred to as an *impoverished environment* (see Figure 6.4).

Figure 6.4 Enriched (top) and impoverished (bottom) environments. (From Renner and Rosenzweig, *Enriched And Impoverished Environments.* © 1987 by Springer-Verlag. Reprinted by permission.)

The rationale behind this experimental strategy is that the augmented stimulation provided by the enriched environment enhances brain activity, which eventually manifests in physiological and behavioral change. Therefore differences should be apparent between the brains and behavior of subjects from enriched and impoverished environments. That the brain responds to "exercise" is not at all a new concept. Phrenologists used it to explain localized brain growth and, according to Renner and Rosenzweig (1987), the Italian scientist Malacarne (1744–1816) demonstrated with birds that enriched experience enhances brain growth.

Modern study of environmental enrichment was given impetus by Hebb (1949), who proposed that enriched experiences occurring early in life lead to alterations of the brain, which in turn improve an animal's problem-solving ability. This proposal led a number of researchers, including Hebb's own students, to test the effects of environmental enrichment. Although more than four decades have elapsed since the publication of Hebb's book, interest in environmental enrichment continues. This enduring attention is probably due in large measure to the marked changes in the brain that have been reported to result from exposure to what appears to be a rather innocuous manipulation. However, prior to commencing our exploration of the findings, let us first consider a theoretical issue related to the nature of environmental enrichment research.

What Is Really Being Studied?

As implied by the term "environmental enrichment research," one would surmise that the endeavor is designed to study the impact of living in an environment that provides enhanced levels of stimulation. Moreover, the methodology supports this supposition; subjects from enriched environments are compared to control animals having resided in impoverished environments. However, aside from those living in laboratories and, unfortunately, in some zoos, animals do *not* live in impoverished environments. Rather, their natural environments constantly provide them with multitudinous forms of stimulation. In fact, relative to the natural environment, the experimenter-imposed enriched environment is impoverished. One can argue, then, that the research logically should be viewed from a converse perspective—that of the impoverished environment. Instead of studying, for example, the influence of environmental enrichment on brain growth, one should examine the effect of environmental impoverishment on brain retardation. In other words, the enriched environment should be considered the control condition and the impoverished environment the experimental condition. This change in perspective might have some effect upon the conduct of research in the field, but more importantly would alter the way in which investigators view the role of the environment.

Environmental Enrichment and Problem-Solving Behavior

A preliminary report by Hebb (1947), noting the enhanced problem-solving ability of rats reared as pets with much of their time spent outside their cages, represents the first demonstration of the effects of enrichment on learned behavior. Five years later Hebb's observation was confirmed by Forgays and Forgays (1952), who demonstrated that rats raised in groups in large cages with playthings present from day 26 throughout the testing period, which commenced on day 90, made fewer errors in the Hebb-Williams maze[1] across a series of 24 problems than animals kept in groups in similar cages but without playthings. Animals housed in the latter condition were superior to others kept in small cages with or without playthings. Thus both cage size and stimulus objects are influential. Forgays and Read (1962) further showed that rats exhibit a period of maximal sensitivity to the enrichment procedure; 3 weeks of enrichment commencing immediately after weaning on day 22 was more effective than enrichment from birth to weaning and from days 88 to 109. In fact, animals that experienced the latter did not differ from those given no enrichment experience.

Many experiments have been performed to assess the influence of enrichment on acquired behavior. Most that involved relatively difficult spatial learning tasks, such as the Hebb-Williams maze, the older Lashley III maze, and the more recently developed and difficult 17-unit radial arm maze, have found that environmental enrichment leads to superior performance by the rat (Bennett, Rosenzweig, & Diamond, 1970; Conwell & Overman, 1981;; Denenberg, Woodcock, & Rosenberg, 1968; Greenough, Yuwiler, & Dollinger, 1973; Juraska, Henderson, & Muller, 1984). Using an enlarged version of the Hebb-Williams maze, Wilson, Warren, and Abbott (1965) reported that cats placed in a large room containing other cats, toys, a scratching post, and so forth for 5 hours a day from days 46 through 90 made fewer errors than controls. Mogensen (1991) reported that enriched animals exhibit enhanced performance on a delayed alternation task that consists in reinforcing a subject for entering the arm of a maze it had *not* visited on the preceding trial. Mogensen concluded that environmental enrichment may initially bias the rat "towards applications of spatial hypotheses during problem solving behaviour."

The enhanced performance of enriched animals on spatial learning tasks may be due to the fact that they make better use of extra-maze cues. In other words, they use stimuli from outside the maze, such as the position of an overhead light or window, to help them navigate to the goal. This point is surmised because rats kept in enriched environments are more disrupted by rotation of the maze than are nonenriched subjects (Brown, 1968; Forgays & Forgays, 1952). Because enriched environments are large cages that contain objects (groups of animals and playthings), the greater use of extra-maze cues may arise from the enriched animals' experience in observing those objects from a distance.

In contrast to the differences between enriched and control animals generally found with relatively complicated learning tasks, it is often the case that enriched and control subjects cannot be differentiated when simple tasks such as visual

---

[1] The *Hebb-Williams maze,* billed as an intelligence test for rats (Rabinovitch & Rosvald, 1951), consists of a box containing movable partitions. The food-deprived rat is required to navigate from the start section to the goal section, which contains food. By reconfiguring the partitions, each subject is given a series of different spatial learning problems differing in complexity. The device became a popular assessment instrument for examining the influence of enriched environments and other types of early experience.

discriminations (Sjoden, 1976), acquired taste aversions (Domjan, Schorr, & Best, 1977), active avoidance (Freeman & Ray, 1972), and conditioned heart rate suppression (Caul, Freeman, & Buchanon, 1974) are used.

Environmental Enrichment and the Brain

Commencing with the pioneering work of Bennett, Diamond, Krech, and Rosenzweig, it has been shown that the brains of animals from enriched environments differ from those of animals kept under standard laboratory conditions. The differences involve three major parameters: size, neuroanatomy, and neurochemistry.

Size

The initial data concerning brain size and environment were obtained by dissecting the brains of enriched and control rats and comparing the weight of various regions of the cortex. Bennett, Rosenzweig, and Diamond (1969), in one of their many studies involving brain weight, placed 25-day-old rats into enriched or standard laboratory cages. Thirty days later the animals were killed and their brains removed and dissected according to the scheme shown in Figure 6.5. The

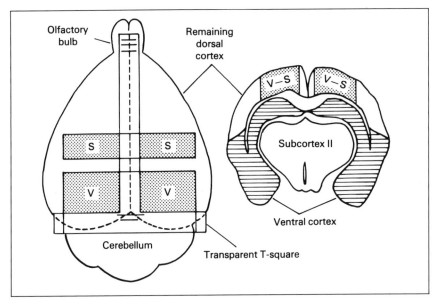

Figure 6.5 (Left) Dorsal aspect of the rat brain, showing how the samples of the visual (occipital) area (V) and the somesthetic area (S) were dissected, guided by a small transparent T square. (Right) Sagittal section of the rat brain. Total cortex is comprised of the V and S sections plus the remaining dorsal cortex. (From Rosenzweig et al., "Effects of environmental complexity and training on brain chemistry and anatomy: a replication and extension." *Journal of Comparative Physiological Psychology, 55,* 429–37. © 1962 by The American Psychological Association. Reprinted by permission.)

occipital and somesthetic cortices were separated, leaving the remaining dorsal cortex, ventral cortex (including hippocampus), cerebellum plus medulla, and the remainder of the subcortex. The results are summarized in Table 6.2. With the exception of the ventral cortex, the somesthetic, occipital, and dorsal cortices of enriched animals were significantly heavier than those of controls. Differences were not found for the subcortex. The greatest effect is seen in the occipital cortex (12.7% increase). That the occipital cortex, although primarily involved in visual functioning, does serve other functions explains why increases in occipital weight are found with blind rats and when the experiment is conducted in the dark (Rosenzweig et al., 1969). Also, animals housed singly in wire cages within the enriched environment (in other words, animals that can see but not interact with the enriched environment) do not exhibit altered cerebral weights (Ferchmin et al., 1975) (see Figure 6.6). Therefore the effects of the enriched environment on the occipital cortex are not mediated by augmented levels of visual stimulation. It also has been demonstrated that the effects of environmental enrichment on brain weight are not permanent. Bennett, Rosenzweig, Diamond, Morimoto, and Hebert (1974) found that the increase in occipital cortex weight is no longer apparent 32 days after rats from enriched environments are

Table 6.2 Wet weights of brain sections of rats from enriched and impoverished conditions

Sample Source	Mean weights (mg)				Dry/Wet Ratio		Percent Differences	
	Wet		Dry					
	EC	IC	EC	IC	EC	IC	Wet	Dry
	Cortex							
Occipital	72.7	64.5	15.7	14.0	0.216	0.217	12.7‡	12.5†
Somesthetic	56.8	54.0	12.6	12.0	.222	.222	5.0*	4.8*
Remaining dorsal	292	270	61.9	57.1	.212	.212	8.4†	8.5‡
Ventral	278	274	59.8	58.9	.215	.215	1.6	1.5
Total	700	662	150.0	142.0	.214	.214	5.7‡	5.7‡
	Rest of brain							
Cerebellum, pons, medulla	384	384	93.0	93.4	.242	.243	−0.1	−0.4
Remainder	490	484	109.2	108.0	.223	.223	1.2	1.0
Total subcortex	874	869	202.0	201.5	.231	.232	0.6	0.3
	Total brain							
	1574	1530	352.2	343.4	.224	.224	2.8*	2.6
	Ratio of cortex to rest of brain							
	0.801	0.763	0.742	0.705			5.0‡	5.3‡

EC = enriched condition; IC = impoverished condition.

Included are the percentage differences between the condition (100 × [EC − IC]/IC) and the statistical significance of the differences.

*$p < .05$.

†$p < .01$.

‡$p < .001$.

Source: Adapted from Bennett et al. Rat brain: effects of environmental enrichment on wet and dry weights. *Science* 163:825–26. © 1969 by The American Association for the Advancement of Science. Reprinted by permission.

Figure 6.6 Three small observer cages inside an enriched environment (From Ferchmin et al., "Direct contact with enriched environment is required to alter cerebral weights in rats." *Journal of Comparative Physiological Psychology, 88,* 360–67. © 1975 by The American Psychological Association. Reprinted by permission.)

housed under standard laboratory conditions. Similar though less complete reversals have been reported by Katz and Davies (1984).

The increase in rat cerebral cortex weight has been reported by numerous investigators in addition to Rosenzweig et al. (e.g., Cummins et al., 1973; Ferchmin, Eterovic, & Caputto, 1970). Similar effects also have been found in other species (mouse: LaTorre, 1968; gerbil: Rosenzweig & Bennett, 1969; ground squirrel: Rosenzweig, Bennett, Alberti, Morimato, & Renner, 1982).

Not only does the cerebral cortex get heavier after exposure to an enriched environment, it also gets longer. This fact was initially reported by Altman, Wallace, Anderson, and Das (1968) who kept rats in enriched environments for 90 days beginning at weaning. Walsh and co-workers (Walsh, Budtz-Olsen, Torok, & Cummins, 1970; Walsh, Cummins, & Budtz-Olsen, 1973) found graded effects depending on the length of enrichment exposure; 30 days of exposure yielded cortices that on average were 1.2% longer than those of controls, whereas exposure for 80 days produced an average increase of 2.5%. Cortical thickness, too, increases as a function of enrichment, with the greatest effect found in the occipital cortex (Diamond et al., 1966).

And two other differences between the brains of enriched and control animals should be noted. Occipital cortices of enriched rats contain more glial cells (Diamond, Ingham, Johnson, Bennett, & Rosenzweig, 1976). Also, occipital nuclei of both the enriched rat and cat comprise a larger area than those of controls (Beaulieu & Colonnier, 1985; Diamond, Lindner, & Raymond, 1967).

Neuroanatomy

Holloway (1966) provided preliminary evidence linking environmental enrichment to neuroanatomical changes, specifically to alterations in dendritic branching. His data suggested that after about 85 days in the enriched environment rats exhibit higher levels of dendritic branching in occipital cortex than did control littermates. This preliminary finding was confirmed by Volkmar and Greenough (1972) and again by Greenough and Volkmar (1973), who reported that the largest effects are seen in basal rather than apical dendrites (see Figure 6.7). Basal dendrites receive synaptic input from nearby neurons, and the latter receive input from neurons located farther away. Furthermore, Globus, Rosenzweig, Bennett, and Diamond (1973) found that basal dendrites from enriched animals have a greater density of spines, projections from the dendrite that form the synapse (see inset in Figure 6.7).

Synapses within the visual cortex can be differentiated with regard to shape of the synaptic vesicles (synaptic vesicles contain neurotransmitter substance). Beaulieu and Colonnier (1987) reported that the number of synapses associated with flat synaptic vesicles differs between enriched and control cats. Furthermore, the difference may be related to the fact that the electrical activity of cortical neurons in response to certain visual stimuli are altered by environmental enrichment (Beaulieu & Cyander, 1990a,b).

It must be noted that not all cell types within a particular cortical region exhibit dendritic plasticity (Juraska, Greenough, Elliot, Mark, & Berkowitz, 1980), and not all animals exhibit the same degree of plasticity. In addition to anticipated individual differences, Juraska (1984a,b) reported that female rats manifest a smaller degree of branching than males in response to environmental enrichment. An assessment of the influence of androgen would be of interest here.

Furthermore, dendritic plasticity is not restricted to cells of the occipital cortex. Greenough, Volkmar, and Juraska (1973) demonstrated that after 30 days of enrichment exposure increased branching is seen in rat temporal cortex. For the monkey, enrichment affects only the motor cortex (Stell & Riesen, 1987). Plasticity is not even restricted to cortical tissue. Greenough and associates (Black, Sirevaag, Wallace, Savin, & Greenough, 1989; Floeter and Greenough 1978, 1979) reported that a noncortical structure, the cerebellum, also undergoes changes, including enhanced dendritic branching, as a consequence of enrichment experience.

Volkmar and Greenough (1972) have proposed that "the increased branching presumably provides increased surface for synaptic contacts, and this greater potential for interneuronal interaction suggests a greater capacity for information processing, loosely defined, in the brain of the animal reared in a more stimulating environment." A test of the proposal requires that synapses themselves be directly assessed. Turner and Greenough (1985), using electron micrography, found an increase of about 20% in the number of synapses per neuron in occip-

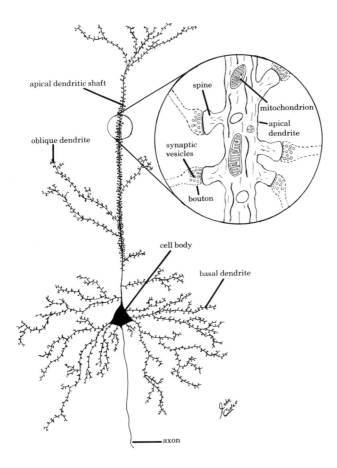

Figure 6.7 Typical Golgi-stained pyramidal neuron whose cell body is in layer 5 of the cortex. The dendrites (apical, oblique, basal) receive synaptic input from other nerve cells. (Inset) Enlargement of a segment of the apical shaft. The projections from the dendrites are called spines, which form synapses with axon terminals from other neurons. (From Greenough, "Experimental modification of the developing brain." *American Scientist, 63,* 37–46. © 1975 by Sigma Xi, The Scientific Research Society. Reprinted by permission.)

ital cortices of enriched rats. Whether the number of synapses is at all related to information processing, however, is another matter, one awaiting resolution.

Neurochemistry

Attempts have been made to determine if neurochemical changes occur as a consequence of environmental enrichment. One such effort involved neurotransmitters. If the brains of animals exposed to an enriched environment are more active (i.e., if they exhibit heightened synaptic transmission), greater levels of a neurotransmitter such as acetylcholine should be present as well as of the enzyme required to break down the transmitter. With regard to acetylcholine, the enzyme is acetylcholinesterase (AChE). According to Rosenzweig, Bennett, and Diamond (1972b), only a trend exists in the direction of a greater absolute level of AChE activity in both the cortex and subcortex of enriched rats. However, because the cortex of enriched animals is larger, AChE should be expressed as a function of unit weight. When this measurement is used, the activity of the enzyme is slightly lower in the cortex and slightly higher in the subcortex of the enriched subject (Rosenzweig, Bennett, & Diamond, 1972a). All that can be concluded from this finding is that cortical weight increases at a faster rate than does the level of AChE and, presumably, acetylcholine. Data relating to other neurotransmitters such as serotonin, dopamine, and norepinephrine are inconclusive.

Because protein synthesis had been implicated in information processing and because the enriched environment has been thought of as providing more stimuli or information to process, quantitative or qualitative differences in brain protein synthesis (or both) have been predicted between enriched and control animals. RNA level in the occipital cortex per unit weight is higher while DNA per unit weight is lower in enriched rats (Rosenzweig & Bennett, 1978). Here then we have a quantitative change. With regard to a qualitative change, Uphouse and Bonner (1975) and Grouse, Schrier, Bennett, Rosenzweig, and Nelson (1978) reported that RNA is more diverse following a period of environmental enrichment. Others, however, failed to find such a difference (Mushynski, Levitan, & Ramirez, 1973).

Application of Environmental Enrichment

Environmental enrichment may have therapeutic applications. First, enriched environments have been shown to attenuate behavioral deficits caused by damage to certain regions of the brain. Will, Rosenzweig, Bennett, Hebert, and Morimoto (1977), for example, show that enrichment ameliorates the adverse effect of occipital cortex lesions on performance in the Hebb-Williams maze. As little as 2 hours a day of enrichment exposure for 60 days is sufficient to markedly reduce the number of errors. Also facilitated are performance of a complex motor task following lesions of the motor cortex (Held, Gordon, & Gentile, 1985) and conditioning following damage to the dorsal hippocampus (Dalrymple-Alford & Kelche, 1987). Furthermore, enrichment facilitates maze learning and retention in rats' brain damaged by the perinatal induction of hypothyroidism and by the perinatal administration of monosodium glutamate (Davenport, Gonzalez, Carey, Bishop, & Hagquist, 1976; Saari, Fong, Shiuji, & Armstrong, 1990). However, only damage to particular brain structures is ameliorated by enrichment; damage to the septum, entorhinal cortex, or fimbria-fornix is not affected (Dalrymple-Alford & Kelche, 1987). For additional information on the influence of postoperative housing on recovery of function see Dalrymple-Alford and Kelche (1985).

Environmental enrichment also appears to counteract some of the deficits associated with aging. Unlike handling, which loses its effectiveness as the animal matures, environmental enrichment retains its ability to alter the brain even when the subject in question is elderly. Cummins et al. (1973) reported an increase in whole brain weight of 509-day-old rats given 15 to 30 minutes of enrichment experience a day for 3 weeks, and Black, Parnisari, Eichbaum, and Greenough (1986) found that 26-month-old rats respond to 80 days of enrichment with an increase in dendritic material in the occipital cortex. Dendritic loss in the cerebellum can be partially offset by enrichment experience (Greenough, McDonald, Parnisari, & Camel, 1986). Generally, the brain changes seen in old animals in response to environmental enrichment, significant though they are, are of a lesser magnitude than those observed in younger subjects.

Regarding behavior, certain results suggest that environmental enrichment provides some protection against age-related behavioral decline. Doty (1972) reported that rats given enrichment experience from days 300 to 660 were superior on a reversal learning task. Enrichment also improves the performance of elderly mice on a passive avoidance and food-seeking task (Kubanis, Zornetzer, & Freund, 1982; Warren, Zerweck, & Anthony, 1982).

What Causes the Enrichment Phenomenon?

A number of hypotheses have been offered to explain how environmental enrichment produces its effects. Three of the major hypotheses are briefly considered here.

One involves the endocrine system. Environmental enrichment causes alterations in hormone levels, which in turn act on the brain. This idea calls upon data showing that certain hormones such as those produced by the thyroid, pituitary, and gonads are involved in brain development *and* are affected by conditions of housing.

Another explanation is that the effects observed in differential housing experiments essentially are caused by the *control* condition rather than by environmental enrichment. It is claimed that the control condition, which differs drastically from the environment that would be encountered under natural conditions, is so *abnormal* that it creates a state of chronic stress. It is known that certain stress-related hormones adversely affect brain development. (As mentioned previously, animals housed under control conditions may be thought of as comprising the experimental group, whereas those maintained in enriched environments, those more akin to the nonlaboratory environment, comprise the control group.) Because the control condition is usually the standard laboratory housing arrangement, most laboratory animals are, by implication, abnormal; and, presumably, so may be the data derived from them.

Lastly, it has been argued that the differences between enriched and impoverished animals are caused by the fact that the former have a greater opportunity to engage in information processing, that is, to store information about their environment. This experience may result in brain changes associated with the formation of synapses.

Tests of both the hormonal and stress hypotheses were conducted by Black et al. (1989). Regarding the former they reasoned thusly: Because the hormones that modify brain development (and that are affected by housing conditions) are also known to influence other organs, an enriched environment should modify nonbrain tissue in a manner similar to the way it modifies the brain. This prediction was not supported. Rats kept in an enriched environment from the time of weaning exhibit a *slower* rate of skeletal and visceral (liver, kidney, spleen, thymus) growth despite the fact that, as we have seen, certain portions of the brain are enlarged. Moreover, somatic growth of adult rats is slow and not particularly sensitive to an enriched environment, whereas effects on the brain are readily produced.

The stress hypothesis involves a different prediction. If the stress engendered by the control condition causes retardation of brain development, it must be demonstrated that control subjects are consistently more stressed than enriched subjects. Using the weight of the adrenal gland as an index of chronic stress (the heavier the gland, the more stress), Black et al. reported that there was no effect of the housing condition on adrenal weight in the young animals, whereas the adrenal weights of rats exposed to the enriched environment as adults were *heavier* than controls. Thus it does not appear that animals housed under impoverished conditions are subject to chronic stress, although assessment of adrenal hormone output would have been preferable to the determination of adrenal gland weight.

By the process of elimination, then, Black et al. inferred that brain development is modulated by degree of information processing. They stated:

> Learning remains the best explanation of the brain effects of environmental complexity. Complex experience provides abdundant opportunities for learning new information, and synapses and associated tissue elements are then formed in brain regions linked to learning and memory. [pp. 747–748]

This idea awaits direct confirmation, which, given the considerable interest in the neuronal changes accompanying learning, may be forthcoming in the near future.

SENSORY/PERCEPTUAL PROGRAMMING

Unlike handling and environmental enrichment, which provide the organism with stimulation rather broad in scope, sensory/perceptual programming allows the young organism to experience only specific stimuli. Although experience with discrete stimuli in practically all sensory modalities has been examined (Mistretta & Bradley, 1978), research has tended to focus on the visual and olfactory systems.

Visual Stimulation

Individual neurons of the visual system, specifically cells of the lateral geniculate nucleus and that portion of the visual cortex known as the striate cortex (see Figure 6.8) are selectively activated by certain features of a visual stimulus. The pattern of retinal stimulation that activates a cell is called the cell's *receptive field.*

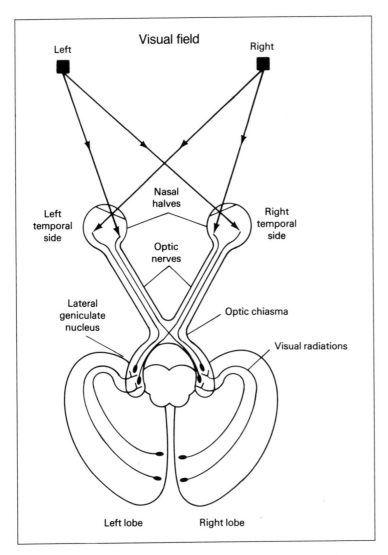

Figure 6.8 Human visual system (highly simplified) showing the projection of the visual fields through the system. Observe that fibers originating in the inner or nasal halves of the retinas cross at the optic chiasma, whereas fibers originating in the outer or temporal halves of the retinas do not cross. Observe also that the right half of the visual field projects on the left half of each retina (and to the left hemisphere of the brain). Similarly, the left half of the visual field projects on the right half of each retina (and to the right hemisphere). (Adapted from Schiffman, *Sensation and Perception.* © 1990 by John Wiley & Sons. With permission.)

Kuffler (1953) showed that the receptive fields of ganglion cells have concentric "on" and "off" regions; a spot of light falling on the "on" region of the retina increases the firing rate of the cell, whereas stimulation to the surrounding "off" region inhibits the cell's activity. For other cells the receptive field is reversed; the "on" region surrounds the "off" region.

The Nobel Prize-winning research of Hubel and Wiesel (1959, 1962) consisted, in part, of identifying three classes of cells of the cat striate cortex that differ in terms of receptive field. *Simple cells* respond to a feature such as a line, bar, or edge having a specific orientation (see Figure 6.9A). *Complex cells* (Figure 6.9B) are similar except that the location of the particular feature within the visual field is not critical and they respond to movement. *Hypercomplex cells* (Figure 6.9C) exhibit the properties of complex cells, but in addition they respond selectively to stimuli of particular lengths. A pattern of striate cortical organization similar to that discovered in the cat has been observed in sheep (Kendrick & Baldwin, 1987) and monkeys (Gross, Rocha-Miranda, & Bender, 1972; Hubel & Wiesel, 1968).

Wiesel and Hubel (1963) also examined the influence of early visual deprivation. It was accomplished by preventing visual stimulation from reaching one eye of the kitten by suturing the eyelid so it would not open at the time of eye-opening or by severely restricting visual input with translucent goggles. After about 3 months of monocular deprivation, the sutures or goggles were removed and the deprived and normal eyes examined. Almost all of the cells of the striate cortex could be activated *only* by providing stimulation to the normal eye. Also, the few cells that could be activated by stimulating the deprived eye had abnormal receptive fields. Our concern, however, is not with early visual deprivation per se but, rather, with the effect of restricted visual experience on receptive field organization. Nevertheless, bear in mind that by restricting visual experience to certain types of stimuli, one is by definition depriving the organism of many other forms of visual stimulation.

The initial discovery that early visual experience can modify receptive fields of cells in the striate cortex was made by Hirsch and Spinelli (1970). Beginning at 3 weeks of age the total visual experience of kittens consisted in viewing a white field containing three black vertical lines with one eye and a white field containing three black horizontal lines with the other. The stimuli were contained in a mask which was placed on the kittens for about 8 hours a day for 7 to 9 weeks. When not wearing the mask the kittens were kept in a darkened room. The electrical activity of single cells of the striate cortex was monitored while the kittens viewed a screen upon which was projected a black spot moving across a white field. Unlike normal kittens, which have cells activated by elongated stimuli (elongated receptive fields) in various orientations including oblique and diagonal, the receptive fields of these kittens were oriented either horizontally or vertically. Furthermore and importantly, cells with horizontal receptive fields were activated *only* by appropriately stimulating the eye that had been exposed to the horizontal lines. Conversely, cells with vertical receptive fields responded *only* when the appropriate stimulus was given to the eye that had experienced the vertical lines.

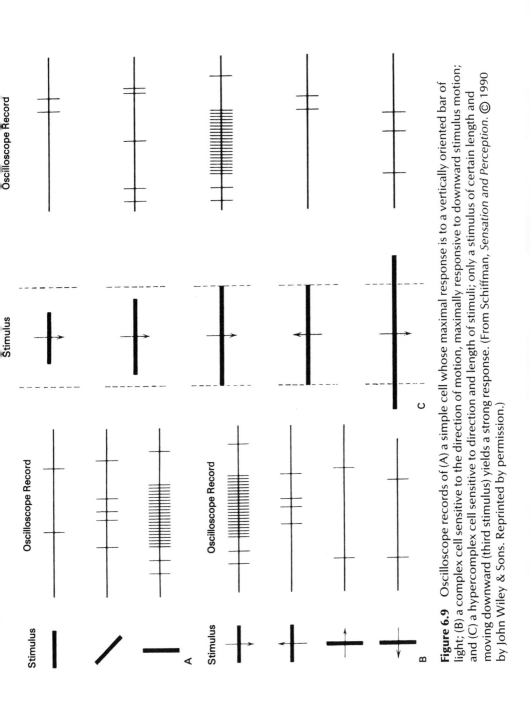

Figure 6.9 Oscilloscope records of (A) a simple cell whose maximal response is to a vertically oriented bar of light; (B) a complex cell sensitive to the direction of motion, maximally responsive to downward stimulus motion; and (C) a hypercomplex cell sensitive to direction and length of stimuli; only a stimulus of certain length and moving downward (third stimulus) yields a strong response. (From Schiffman, *Sensation and Perception.* © 1990 by John Wiley & Sons. Reprinted by permission.)

The change in the distribution of orientations of cortical unit receptive fields that we found when kittens were raised with both eyes viewing different patterns demonstrates that functional neural connections can be selectively and predictably modified by environmental stimulation. [Hirsch & Spinelli, 1970, p. 871]

Six months after the publication of Hirsch and Spinelli's findings, Blakemore and Cooper (1970) reported almost identical results. Beginning at 2 weeks of age kittens were placed in the apparatus shown in Figure 6.10 for 5 hours each day for 4.5 months. One kitten viewed vertical lines as depicted in Figure 6.10, and another viewed horizontal lines. At all other times they were kept in a darkened room. Two and half months later, after the kittens had had some limited exposure to a normally lit environment, electrical recordings were made from single cells of the striate cortex. Of 125 cells tested, 124 responded selectively; that is, those of the kitten that had been exposed to horizontal lines responded only to a horizontal stimulus, and those of the subject exposed to vertical lines only fired when a vertical stimulus impinged on the retina. The authors stated that

the visual cortex may adjust itself during maturation to the nature of its visual experience. Cells may even change their preferred orientation towards that of the com-

Figure 6.10 Apparatus used to provide visual stimulation to kittens for 5.5 hours a day for 4.5 months. (From Blakemore and Cooper, "Development of the brain depends on the visual environment." *Nature, 228,* 477–78. © 1970 by Macmillan Magazines, Ltd. Reprinted by permission.)

monest type of stimulus; so perhaps the nervous system adapts to match the probability of occurrence of features in its visual input. [p. 478]

Because early visual stimulation reduces the number of stimuli that can activate particular striatal neurons—in other words, because the visual system in a sense has been simplified—Hirsch (1972) referred to such early experience as "environmental surgery."

Although some studies have not been confirmatory (Carlson, Hubel, & Wiesel, 1986; see also review by Fregnac & Imbert, 1984), most have substantiated and extended the findings that early visual experience modifies receptive field development (Levanthal & Hirsch, 1975; Rauschecker & Singer, 1981). Pettigrew and Freeman (1973) found, for example, that unlike those of normal cats, cortical cells of kittens that experienced an environment lacking straight line contours were maximally activated by spots of light but not straight lines. Other biases also have been reported. Thus animals exposed to stimuli moving in only a single direction appear to have more complex cortical cells that are selective to stimuli moving in that particular direction (Tretter, Cynoder, & Singer, 1975). What must be ascertained is whether early visual experience modifies cells having already established receptive fields or alters cells that, at least initially, are uncommitted.

Although the biasing of receptive field development of cortical neurons by early visual experience is important in its own right, it is especially relevant to this discussion with regard to its ability to modify behavior. Does receptive field alteration bias visually guided behavior? Unfortunately, little research has been addressed to this issue. Blakemore and Cooper (1970) did note that their cats were behaviorally responsive to only the contour to which they had been exposed as kittens. When, for example, a sheet of plastic covered with either horizontal or vertical lines was thrust at them, they exhibited a startle reaction only to the stimulus they had experienced. When a black rod was held vertically, only the cat that had been exposed to vertical black lines attempted to play with it. The other cat was attracted only to the rod held horizontally.

Muir and Mitchell (1973) performed an experiment designed expressly to assess the impact of early visual experience on later behavior. Using the procedure of Blakemore and Cooper (see Figure 6.8), one kitten was exposed to horizontal lines and the other to vertical lines for 5 hours a day beginning on day 20 of life and continuing through the 4th month. They were subsequently kept in a normally lighted environment from 3 to 6 months and then tested. One other cat also was exposed to vertical lines but for only 2 weeks beginning at week 3. Afterward the animals were trained to press one of two panels with their noses. One of the panels was dark and blank, and the other contained a series of black parallel lines called a grating. The distance between the lines (spatial frequency) could be varied. The greater the spatial frequency (i.e., the closer together the lines), the more difficult it was to distinguish the panel with the grating from the blank panel. The cats were trained to discriminate between the panels; each time it pressed the panel with the grating the cat was reinforced with food.

The ability of the subjects to discriminate between the grating and blank panel was found to be influenced by early visual experience. The cats that had been exposed to the vertical lines (including the one that received only 2 weeks of such exposure) were better able to discriminate between a vertically oriented grating of high spatial frequency and the blank panel than between a horizontally oriented grating of high spatial frequency and the blank panel. The converse was true for the subject exposed to the horizontal lines. Normally reared cats, in contrast, exhibited no such preferential discriminative abilities.

Man's ability to resolve contours also may be influenced by early experience. Freeman, Mitchell, and Millodot (1972) reported that individuals suffering from astigmatism (a refractive defect of the lens that causes blurred vision) continue to exhibit differences in the resolution of vertical and horizontal gratings even though their vision has been corrected with glasses. Moreover, individuals who are better able to resolve a horizontal grating when wearing their glasses exhibit more blurring to the vertical than to the horizontal grating when their glasses are removed and vice versa. Because astigmatism generally is present from an early age, Freeman et al. asserted that the defect produces a biasing similar to that produced by exposing young animals to vertical or horizontal lines.

> Suppose that the retinal image of a developing visual system suffers from astigmatism that causes extensive blur along the horizontal, but not the vertical, axis. The visual cortex could adapt to the discordant input from the retina by "tuning" itself to the features clearly imaged along the vertical axis. [p. 1385]

Annis and Frost (1975) conducted a clever study designed to determine whether individuals with normal visual accuity are also influenced by selective early visual experience. One group of subjects were adult Euro-Canadians who grew up in an environment consisting of "typical North American houses and buildings, which provide a visual environment with marked predominance of vertical and horizontal contours." Other subjects were Cree Indians who had been raised in traditional housing: tents during the warm weather and a lodge in the winter. These structures as well as the forest within which they were located contained contours of all orientations, with none predominating. Subjects were tested by presenting them with a gradient of a fixed spatial frequency that was rotated to one of four orientations: vertical, horizontal, left oblique, right oblique. They were asked to adjust a pointer so that it corresponded to the orientation of the grating. Acuity was assessed by placing the gradient at varying distances from the subject. The acuity scores of the Euro-Canadian sample varied as a function of grating orientation; acuity was greater for vertical and horizontal gratings than for those in oblique orientations. The Cree sample, however, did not exhibit higher resolution for vertically and horizontally oriented gratings.

The most parsimonious explanation, according to Annis and Frost, is that the disparity between the two groups is caused by differing amounts of early visual exposure to vertical and horizontal contours. Although it seems reasonable, it must be regarded as highly tentative, nonetheless, as surely the developmental histories of the Euro-Canadian and Cree samples differed in other respects as well. Until such other factors (nutrition being one) are eliminated, the difference in acuity cannot be ascribed to visual experiences with any degree of certainty.

Olfactory Stimulation

Olfactory deprivation adversely affects the olfactory bulb, that portion of the brain which receives input from olfactory receptors. Frazier and Brunjes (1988) reported a 25% decrease in the size of the olfactory bulb of 30-day-old rats subjected to the surgical closure of one nostril on day 1 of life. Restricting early olfactory experience also has been accomplished by continuously exposing young rats or mice to a stream of unchanging, highly concentrated, synthetically odorized air that presumably masks other odors. Studies employing this technique report degeneration of certain cells (mitral cells) of the olfactory bulb (see review by Reasner, 1987). Unlike those studies on the visual system that report enhanced acuity for the visual stimulus to which the young animals were exposed, animals exposed to a single intense olfactory stimulus do not exhibit altered acuity for that stimulus (Laing & Panhuber, 1980), although they may be deficient in the detection of other odors (Laing & Panhuber, 1978).

Instead of exposing animals to a single olfactory stimulus, Rosselli-Austin and Williams (1990) exposed rats from days 1 to 21 of life to a different odor every 24 hours. Only natural odors, such as those from banana peel, onion, garlic, pine needles, and decayed bark, were used. The odorants were placed in bottles and suspended from the cage tops. Histological analysis on day 31 revealed that the olfactory bulbs of the odor-exposed animals contained 35% more mitral cells and 40% more granule cells than those of nonexposed controls. Furthermore, the mitral cells of the experimental subjects contained significantly larger nuclei.

Developing organisms, however, are not normally found in situations that either limit olfactory experience or enhance it by providing a different stimulus every 24 hours. Rather, they are exposed to specific odors in addition to those that normally comprise their olfactory milieu. The question, of course, is the extent to which this type of experience influences olfactory-related physiology and behavior.

Leon and co-workers have conducted a series of experiments illustrating that such early olfactory experience does affect neuronal activity in response to the later presentation of that now familiar odor. In the initial experiment (Coopersmith & Leon, 1984) some rat pups were exposed to peppermint-odorized air for 10 minutes each day from birth through day 18. At the same time, the pups' perineal region was stimulated to mimic the licking they receive from the rat mothers. Because the level of glucose found in a cell is considered to be directly related to the cell's activity, the dependent measure was the amount of glucose (2-deoxy-D-glucose [2DG]) in the olfactory bulb. Radioactively labeled 2DG was injected on day 19 and its uptake in olfactory bulb cells determined after 45 minutes of exposure to the peppermint odor. The animals that had previously experienced the peppermint stimulus had 64% more uptake of labeled 2DG in spatially distinct regions of the glomerular layer of the bulb than controls. (The glomerulus receives information directly from the olfactory receptor cells and conveys it to other brain areas.) In addition, those regions of high 2DG uptake undergo a morphological change, increasing in width by about 30% while the cross-section of individual cells increase by 21% (Woo, Coopersmith, & Leon, 1987). Coopersmith and Leon (1986) later demonstrated that the enhanced activity of olfactory bulb cells caused by early olfactory experience persists into adult life.

Additional experiments were performed to clarify the results of the initial report. First, because *only* the familiar peppermint stimulus was presented in conjunction with the assessment 2DG uptake, the specificity of the effect was left in doubt. That is, perhaps early experience with a novel odor leads to enhanced 2DG uptake in response to all types of odors. Coopersmith, Henderson, and Leon (1986), however, reported that the response is specific to the familiar odor. Rats exposed to peppermint displayed increased uptake of 2DG in response to the odor of peppermint but not to the unfamiliar odor of cyclohexanone and vice versa. Moreover, regions of the glomerulus showing enhanced uptake of 2DG in response to peppermint were different from those showing enhanced uptake in response to cyclohexanone.

Another issue concerns perineal stimulation, which is presented in conjunction with the odor. To what extent does it contribute to the enhancement of 2DG uptake? According to Sullivan and Leon (1986), it plays a necessary role, as they found no enhancement of 2DG uptake when the familiar olfactory stimulus was presented without the tactile stimulus. They stated:

> This limitation on olfactory-based behavioral and neural plasticity may be of profound functional significance to the pup. Within the confines of the pup's environment, the primary source of tactile stimulation is the mother. Thus, the development of early olfactory neural and behavioral changes may only occur to those odors experienced in conjunction with the mother's presence, such as maternal and nest odors. [p. 281]

Sullivan and Leon (1987) also reported that even a *single* exposure to an odor on day 6 in conjunction with tactile stimulation can enhance 2DG uptake in response to that odor, when assessed the following day.

Having seen that early olfactory experience alters neuronal activity of the olfactory system, we must now inquire as to its behavioral influence. The results of many experiments reveal that early exposure to an odor leads to a later *preference* for that odor. Olfactory preference tests typically consist in monitoring the amount of time a subject spends in the presence of each of two or more odors. Should significantly more time be spent sampling one of the stimuli, it is stated that that odor is preferred. Note that preference assessed in this manner should not be construed as a demonstration of acquired positive affect. In other words, spending more time in the presence of a familiar odor may not mean that the subject "likes it more" but, perhaps, that it is perceived as less aversive than a novel odor.

The initial research consisted in providing young animals with a rather lengthy exposure period to the artificial odorants. Brunjes and Alberts (1979), for example, showed that if a rat spends the first 14 days of its life with a mother or a nest that is scented, it prefers to huddle with conspecifics that are similarly scented. A comparable finding has been presented for the guinea pig (Carter &

Marr, 1970). In an interesting study having implications for adult sexuality, Fillion and Blass (1986) kept male rat pups with mothers whose nipples and vaginal areas were coated with the lemon scent of citral throughout the entire nursing period. When tested for sexual behavior on about day 100, the subjects ejaculated more quickly when presented with a female whose vaginal area was coated with citral than when given a normal female. "These findings suggests that, at least for this mammal, the degree to which a feminine feature is sexually arousing to adult males can be established in the context of suckling" (Fillion & Blass, 1986).

Early olfactory experience also influences human odor preference. Cernoch and Porter (1985) conducted a series of experiments in which 12- to 18-day-old infants were presented with two gauze pads. One contained odor from the underarms of their mothers, and the other contained odor from other adults. The results are summarized in Table 6.3. Breast-feeding, but not bottle-feeding, infants preferred their mothers' axillary odors to those of unfamiliar nursing mothers, nonparturient females, and their fathers (Cernoch & Porter, 1985). In contrast, bottle-feeding infants do not discriminate between odors of their own mothers and those of other females. The investigators speculate that breast-feeding relative to bottle-feeding infants spend greater amounts of time in close proximity to the mothers' skin, thereby providing them with a greater amount of experience with maternal odor.

In a study more akin to those conducted with animals, Balogh and Porter (1986) exposed some 5.0- to 21.3-hour-old infants to the odor of cherry and oth-

Table 6.3 Mean durations of orientation to the simultaneously presented olfactory stimuli

Experiment and Olfactory Stimulus	Mean Seconds Oriented Toward Each Odor Stimulus	*t*-Test for Correlated Samples
Breast-feeding infants (*n* = 13)		
Mother's axillary odor *vs.*	62.5	2.65, df = 12, p < .05
Nonparturient female's axillary odor	42.0	
Breast-feeding infants (*n* = 16)		
Mother's axillary odor *vs.*	72.9	3.16, df = 15, p < .01
Unfamiliar lactating female's axillary odor	37.1	
Bottle-feeding infant (*n* = 15)		
Mother's axillary odor *vs.*	53.5	.26, df = 14, N.S.
Axillary odor of unfamiliar bottle-feeding female	57.4	
Bottle-feeding infants (*n* = 15)		
Mother's axillary odor *vs.*	49.3	.26, df = 14, N.S.
Nonparturient female's axillary odor	51.3	

Source: Adapted from Cernoch and Porter. Recognition of maternal axillary odors by infants. *Child Development* 56:1593–1598. © 1985 by The University of Chicago Press. By permission.

ers to the odor of ginger. The odorants, placed in nylon bags, were secured to the inside of the infants' bassinet and left there for an average of 23 hours. When the infants were tested with both odors (within 70 minutes after the initial exposure), females, but not males, displayed a preference for the familiar odor.

Although the studies reviewed above and many others involve relatively long exposures, other work shows that preferences can develop after much briefer exposures. This point was first demonstrated by Caza and Spear (1984), who exposed 10- and 15-day-old male rats to either lemon oil or methylsalicylate for 3, 9, or 27 minutes. When given both odors immediately after the initial exposure phase, pups of either age who had as little as 3 minutes of exposure preferred the familiar odor. The preference was still evident when the animals were tested 24 hours after the exposure period.

In their 2DG experiments, which involved 10 minutes of exposure a day, Leon and co-workers also showed that in a two-choice test in which the rats were permitted to hover near the source of either the familiar odor or an unfamiliar one, they spent more time near the former. As was the case with 2DG uptake, the effect was observed *only* for animals that received tactile stimulation while experiencing the odor (Sullivan & Leon, 1986). The requirement that tactile stimuli accompany the presentation of the odor in order for the preference to be acquired is at variance with Caza and Spear's (1984) report in which tactile stimulation was not provided.

We have seen that early olfactory experience produces brain and behavioral changes. The former are similar to those caused by early visual stimulation in that they both involve the alteration of selective groups of neurons. Behaviorally, however, visual experience has been shown to affect acuity, whereas olfactory experience influences preference. This difference probably derives, in part, from the fact that vision researchers usually assess acuity, whereas those concerned with olfaction test for preference. It would be instructive to reverse the conventional methodology; does olfactory acuity change for a particular stimulus to which the young animals have been exposed, and do animals spend more time viewing visual stimuli to which they have been previously exposed?

CONCLUDING COMMENTS

The findings are clear; handling, environmental enrichment (or, depending on your perspective, environmental impoverishment), and sensory/perceptual programming exert significant, at times dramatic, and often what may be considered beneficial effects on development. Yet two obvious and critical issues remain unresolved. First, by what manner does early stimulation affect the central nervous system? Just how does early experience with horizontal lines modify receptive fields? Through what mechanism does an enriched environment cause dendritic branching? How does a familiar odor enhance levels of glucose within cells of the olfactory bulbs? And second, is there a *causal* relation between those brain alterations and behavioral development?

REFERENCES

Ader, R. (1959). The effects of early experience on subsequent emotionality and resistance to stress. *Psychological Monographs, 73,* whole no. 472.

Ader, R. (1965). Effects of early experience and differential housing on behavior and susceptibility to gastric erosions in the rat. *Journal of Comparative and Physiological Psychology, 60,* 233–38.

Ader, R. (1969). Early experiences accelerate maturation of the 24-hour adrenocortical rhythm. *Science, 163,* 1225–26.

Ader, R. (1970). Effects of early experience and differential housing on susceptibility to gastric erosions in lesion-susceptible rats. *Psychosomatic Medicine, 32,* 569–80.

Ader, R., and Friedman, S. B. (1965). Differential early experience and susceptibility to transplanted tumors in the rat. *Journal of Comparative and Physiological Psychology, 59,* 361–64.

Altman, J., Das, G. D., and Anderson, W. J. (1968). Effects of infantile handling on morphological development of the rat brain: An exploratory study. *Developmental Psychobiology, 1,* 10–20.

Altman, J., Wallace, R. B., Anderson, W. J., and Das, G. D. (1968). Behaviorally induced changes in length of cerebrum in rats. *Developmental Psychobiology, 1,* 112–17.

Anes, B. M., and Winick, M. (1979). Behavioral and physiological effects of early handling and early malnutrition in rats. *Developmental Psychobiology, 12,* 381–89.

Annis, R. C., and Frost, B. (1973). Human visual ecology and orientation anistropies in acuity. *Science, 182,* 729–31.

Balogh, R. D., and Porter, R. H. (1986). Olfactory preferences resulting from mere exposure in human neonates. *Infant Behavior and Development, 9,* 395–401.

Barnard, K. E., and Bee, H. L. (1983). The impact of temporally patterned stimulation on the development of preterm infants. *Child Development, 54,* 1156–67.

Beaulieu, C., and Colonnier, M. (1985). The effects of environmental complexity on the numerical density of neurons and on the size of their nuclei in the visual cortex of cat. *Society for Neuroscience Abstracts, 11,* 225.

Beaulieu, C., and Colonnier, M. (1987). The effect of the richness of the environment on cat visual cortex. *Journal of Comparative Neurology, 266,* 478–94.

Beaulieu, C., and Cynader, M. (1990a). Effect of the richness of the environment on cat visual cortex. I. Receptive field properties. *Developmental Brain Research, 53,* 71–81.

Beaulieu, C., and Cynader, M. (1990b). Effect of the richness of the environment on neurons in cat visual cortex. II. Spatial and temporal frequency characteristics. *Developmental Brain Research, 53,* 82–88.

Bennett, E. L., Rosenzweig, M. R., and Diamond, M. C. (1969). Rat brain: Effects of environmental enrichment on wet and dry weights. *Science, 163,* 825–26.

Bennett, E. L., Rosenzweig, M. R., and Diamond, M. C. (1970). Time courses of effects of differential experience on brain measures and behavior of rats. In W. L. Byrne (Ed.), *Molecular approaches to learning and memory* (pp. 55–89). Orlando, FL: Academic Press.

Bennett, E. L., Rosenzweig, M. R., Diamond, M. C., Morimoto, H., and Hebert, H. (1974). Effects of successive environments on brain measures. *Physiology and Behavior, 12,* 621–31.

Bernstein, L. (1952). A note on Christie's "Experimental naivete and experiential naivete." *Psychological Bulletin, 49,* 38–40.

Berrebi, A. S., Fitch, R. H., Ralphe, D. L., Denenberg, J. O., Friedrich, V. L., and Denenberg, V. H. (1988). Corpus callosum: Region-specific effects of sex, early experience and age. *Brain Research, 438,* 216–24.

Black, J. E., Parnisari, R., Eichbaum, E., and Greenough, W. T. (1986). Morphological effects of housing environment and voluntary exercise on cerebral cortex and cerebellum of old rats. *Society for Neuroscience Abstracts, 12,* 1579.

Black, J. E., Sirevaag, A. M., Wallace, C. S., Savin, M. H., and Greenough, W. T. (1989). Effects of complex experience on somatic growth and organ development. *Developmental Psychobiology, 22,* 727–52.

Blakemore, C., and Cooper, G. F. (1970). Development of the brain depends on the visual environment. *Nature, 228,* 477–78.

Brookshire, K. H., Littman, R. A., and Stewart, C. N. (1961). Residue of shock trauma in the white rat: A three-factory theory. *Psychological Monographs, 75,* whole no. 514.

Brown, R. T. (1968). Early experience and problem-solving ability. *Journal of Comparative and Physiological Psychology, 65,* 433–40.

Brunjes, P. C., and Alberts, J. R. (1979). Olfactory stimulation induces filial preferences for huddling in rat pups. *Journal of Comparative and Physiological Psychology, 93,* 548–55.

Carlson, M., Hubel, D. H., and Wiesel, T. N. (1986). Effects of monocular exposure to oriented lines on monkey striate cortex. *Developmental Brain Research, 25,* 71–81.

Carter, C. S., and Marr, J. N. (1970). Olfactory imprinting and age variables in the guinea pig. *Animal Behaviour, 18,* 238–44.

Caul, W. F., Freeman, B. J., and Buchanon, D. C. (1974). Effects of differential rearing condition on heart rate conditioning and response suppression. *Developmental Psychobiology, 8,* 63–68.

Caza, P. A., and Spear, N. E. (1984). Short-term exposure to an odor increases its subsequent preference in preweanling rats: A descriptive profile of the phenomenon. *Developmental Psychobiology, 17,* 407–22.

Cernoch, J. M., and Porter, R. H. (1985). Recognition of maternal axillary odors by infants. *Child Development, 56,* 1593–598.

Clark, D. L., Cordero, L., Goss, K. C., and Manos, D. (1989). Effects of rocking on neuromuscular development in the premature. *Biology of the Neonate, 56,* 306–14.

Clark, D. L., Kreutzberg, J. R., and Chee, F.K.W. (1977). Vestibular stimulation influence on motor development in infants. *Science, 196,* 1228–229.

Coopersmith, R., Henderson, S. R., and Leon, M. (1986). Odor specificity of the enhanced neural response following early odor experience in rats. *Developmental Brain Research, 27,* 191–97.

Coopersmith, R., and Leon, M. (1984). Enhanced neural response to familiar olfactory cues. *Science, 225,* 849–51.

Coopersmith, R., and Leon, M. (1986). Enhanced neural response by adult rats to odors experienced early in life. *Brain Research, 371,* 400–403.

Cornell, E. H., and Gottfried, A. W. (1976). Intervention with premature human infants. *Child Development, 47,* 32–39.

Cornwell, P., and Overman, W. (1981). Behavioral effects of early rearing conditions and neonatal lesions on the visual cortex in kittens. *Journal of Comparative and Physiological Psychology, 95,* 848–62.

Cummins, R. A., Walsh, R. N., Budtz-Olsen, O. E., Konstantinos, T., and Horsfall, C. R. (1973). Environmentally induced changes in the brains of elderly rats. *Nature, 243,* 516–18.

Dalrymple-Alford, J. C., and Kelche, C. R. (1985). Behavioural effects of preoperative and postoperative differential housing in rats with brain lesions: A review. In B. E. Will, P. Schmitt, and J. C. Dalrymple-Alford (Eds.), *Brain plasticity, learning, and memory* (pp. 441–58). New York: Plenum Press.

Dalrymple-Alford, J. C., and Kelche, C. R. (1987). Behavioral effects of differential postoperative housing after septal lesions made in weanling rats. *Psychobiology, 15,* 255–60.

Daly, M. (1973). Early stimulation of rodents: A critical review of present interpretations. *British Journal of Psychology, 64,* 435–60.

Davenport, J. W., Gonzalez, L. M., Carey, J. C., Bishop, S. B., and Hagquist, W. W. (1976). Environmental stimulation reduces learning deficits in experimental cretinism. *Science, 191,* 578–79.

Denenberg, V. H. (1962). An attempt to isolate critical periods of development in the rat. *Journal of Comparative and Physiological Psychology, 55,* 813–15.

Denenberg, V. H. (1964). Critical periods, stimulus input, and emotional reactivity. *Psychological Review, 71,* 335–51.

Denenberg, V. H. (1968). A consideration of the usefulness of the critical period hypothesis as applied to the stimulation of rodents in infancy. In G. Newton and S. Levine (Eds.), *Early experience and behavior.* Springfield, IL: Charles C Thomas.

Denenberg, V. H. (1969). Open-field behavior in the rat: What does it mean? *Annals of the New York Academy of Sciences, 159,* 852–59.

Denenberg, V. H., Brumaghin, J. T., Haltmeyer, G. C., and Zarrow, M. X. (1967). Increased adrenocortical activity in the neonatal rat following handling. *Endocrinology, 81,* 1047–52.

Denenberg, V. H., Garbanati, J., Sherman, G. F., Yutzey, D. A., and Kaplan, R. (1978). Infantile stimulation induces brain laterality in rats. *Science, 201,* 1150–151.

Denenberg, V. H., Hofmann, M., Garbanati, J., Sherman, G. F., Rosen, G. D., and Yutzey, D. A. (1980). Handling in infancy, taste aversion, and brain laterality in rats. *Brain Research, 20,* 123–33.

Denenberg, V. H., and Karas, G. G. (1959). Effects of differential infantile handling upon weight gain and mortality in the rat and mouse. *Science, 190,* 381–89.

Denenberg, V. H., and Morton, J.R.C. (1962). Effects of preweaning and postweaning manipulations upon problem-solving behavior. *Journal of Comparative and Physiological Psychology, 55,* 1096–98.

Denenberg, V. H., Morton, J.R.C., Kline, N. J., and Grota, L. J. (1962). Effects of duration of infantile stimulation upon emotionality. *Canadian Journal of Psychology, 16,* 72–76.

Denenberg, V. H., and Smith, S. A. (1963). Effects of infantile stimulation and age upon behavior. *Journal of Comparative and Physiological Psychology, 56,* 307–12.

Denenberg, V. H., and Whimbey, A. E. (1963). Infantile stimulation and animal husbandry: A methodological study. *Journal of Comparative and Physiological Psychology, 56,* 877–78.

Denenberg, V. H., Woodcock, J. M., and Rosenberg, K. M. (1968). Long-term effects of preweaning and postweaning free-environment experience on rats' problem-solving behavior. *Journal of Comparative and Physiological Psychology, 66,* 533–35.

Denenberg, V. H., and Zarrow, M. X. (1970). Infantile stimulation, adult behaviour and adrenocortical activity. In S. Kazda and V. H. Denenberg (Eds.), *The postnatal development of phenotype* (pp. 123–32). Prague: Academia.

Diamond, M. C., Ingham, C. A., Johnson, R. E., Bennett, E. L., and Rosenzweig, M. R. (1976). Effects of environment on morphology of rat cerebral cortex and hippocampus. *Journal of Neurobiology, 7,* 75–85.

Diamond, M. C., Law, F., Rhodes, H., Lindner, B., Rosenzweig, M. R., Krech, D., and Bennett, E. L. (1966). Increases in cortical depth and glia numbers in rats subjected to enriched environments. *Journal of Comparative Neurology, 128,* 117–25.

Diamond, M. C., Lindner, B., and Raymond, A. (1967). Extensive cortical depth measurements and neuron size increases in the cortex of environmentally enriched rats. *Journal of Comparative Neurology, 131,* 357–64.

Domjan, M., Schorr, R., and Best, M. (1977). Early environmental influences on conditioned and unconditioned ingestional and locomotor behavior. *Developmental Psychobiology, 10,* 499–506.

Doty, B. A. (1972). The effects of cage environment upon avoidance responding of aged rats. *Journal of Comparative and Physiological Psychology, 27,* 358–60.

Ferchmin, P. A., Eterovic, V. A., and Caputto, R. (1970). Studies of brain weight and RNA content after short periods of exposure to environmental complexity. *Brain Research, 20,* 49–57.

Ferchmin, P. A., Bennett, E. L., and Rosenzweig, M. R. (1975). Direct contact with enriched environment is required to alter cerebral weights in rats. *Journal of Comparative and Physiological Psychology, 88, 360–67.*

Field, T. (1980). Supplemental stimulation of preterm neonates. *Early Human Development, 3/4,* 301–14.

Fillion, T. J., and Blass, E. M. (1986). Infantile experience with suckling odors determines adult sexual behavior in male rats. *Science, 231,* 729–31.

Floeter, M. K., and Greenough, W. T. (1978). Cerebellar plasticity: Modification of dendritic branching by differential rearing in monkeys. *Society for Neuroscience Abstracts, 4,* 471.

Floeter, M. K., and Greenough, W. T. (1979). Cerebellar plasticity: modification of Purkinje cell structure by differential rearing in monkeys. *Science, 206,* 227–29.

Forgays, D. G., and Forgays, J. W. (1952). The nature of the effect of free-environmental experience in the rat. *Journal of Comparative and Physiological Psychology, 45,* 322–28.

Forgays, D. G., and Read, J. M. (1962). Critical periods for free-environmental experience in the rat. *Journal of Comparative and Physiological Psychology, 55,* 816–18.

Frazier, L. I., and Brunjes, P. C. (1988). Unilateral odor deprivation: Early postnatal changes in olfactory bulb cell density and number. *Journal of Comparative Neurology, 269,* 355–70.

Freeman, R. D., Mitchell, D. E., and Millidot, M. (1972). A neural effect of partial visual deprivation in humans. *Science, 175,* 1384–386.

Freeman, B. J., and Ray, O. S. (1972). Strain, sex, and environmental effects on appetitively and adversively motivated tasks. *Developmental Psychobiology, 5,* 101–9.

Fregnac, Y., and Imbert, M. (1984). Development of neuronal selectivity in primary visual cortex of cat. *Physiological Review, 64,* 325–434.

Garbanati, J. A., Sherman, G. F., Rosen, G. D., Hofmann, M., Yutzey, D. A., and Denenberg, V. H. (1983). Handling in infancy, brain laterality and muricide in rats. *Behavioral Brain Research, 7,* 351–59.

Globus, A., Rosenzweig, M. R., Bennett, E. L., and Diamond, M. C. (1973). Effects of differential experience on dendritic spine counts in rat cerebral cortex. *Journal of Comparative and Physiological Psychology, 82,* 175–81.

Goldman, P. S. (1965). Conditioned emotionality in the rat as a function of stress in infancy. *Animal Behaviour, 13,* 434–42.

Greenough, W. T. (1975). Experimental modification of the developing brain. *American Scientist, 63,* 37–46.

Greenough, W. T., McDonald, J. W., Parnisari, R. M., and Camel, J. E. (1986). Environmental conditions modulate degeneration and new dendrite growth in cerebellum of senescent rats. *Brain Research, 308,* 136–43.

Greenough, W. T., and Volkmar, F. R. (1973). Pattern of dendritic branching in occipital cortex of rats reared in complex environments. *Experimental Neurology, 40,* 491–504.

Greenough, W. T., Volkmar, F. R., and Juraska, J. M. (1973). Effects of rearing complexity on dendritic branching in frontolateral and temporal cortex of the rat. *Experimental Neurology, 41,* 371–78.

Greenough, W. T., Yuwiler, A., and Dollinger, M. (1973). Effects of post-trial eserine administration on learning in "enriched"- and "impoverished"-reared rats. *Behavioral Biology, 8,* 261–72.

Gross, C. G., Rocha-Miranda, C. E., and Bender, D. B. (1972). Visual properties of neurons in inferotemporal cortex of macaque. *Journal of Neurophysiology, 35,* 96–111.

Grouse, L. D., Schrier, B. K., Bennett, E. L., Rosenzweig, M. R., and Nelson, P. G. (1978). Sequence diversity studies of rat brain RNA: Effects of environmental complexity on rat brain RNA diversity. *Journal of Neurochemistry, 30,* 191–203.

Gunders, S. M., and Whiting, J.M.W. (1968). Mother-infant separation and physical growth. *Ethnology, 2,* 196–206.

Haltmeyer, G. C., Denenberg, V. H., and Zarrow, M. X. (1967). Modification of the plasma corticosterone response as a function of infantile stimulation and electric shock parameters. *Physiology and Behavior, 2,* 61–63.

Hebb, D. O. (1947). The effects of early experience on problem solving at maturity. *American Psychologist, 2,* 206–7.

Hebb, D. O. (1949). *The organization of behavior.* New York: John Wiley & Sons.

Held, J. M., Gordon, J., and Gentile, A. M. (1985). Environmental influences on locomotor recovery following cortical lesions in rats. *Behavioral Neuroscience, 99,* 678–90.

Hirsch, H.V.B. (1972). Visual perception in cats after environmental surgery. *Experimental Brain Research, 15,* 405–23.

Hirsch, H.V.B., and Spinelli, D. N. (1970). Visual experience modifies distribution of horizontally and vertically oriented receptive fields in cats. *Science, 168,* 869–71.

Holloway, R. L. (1966). Dendritic branching: Some preliminary results of training and complexity in rat visual cortex. *Brain Research, 2,* 393–96.

Hubel, D. H., and Wiesel, T. N. (1959). Receptive fields of single neurons in the cat's striate cortex. *Journal of Physiology, 148,* 574–91.

Hubel, D. H., and Wiesel, T. N. (1962). Receptive fields, binocular interaction and functional architecture of the cat's visual cortex. *Journal of Physiology, 160,* 106–54.

Hubel, D. H., and Wiesel, T. N. (1968). Receptive fields and functional architecture of monkey striate cortex. *Journal of Physiology, 195,* 215–43.

Juraska, J. M. (1984a). Sex differences in dendritic response to differential experience in the rat visual cortex. *Brain Research, 295,* 27–34.

Juraska, J. M. (1984b). Sex differences in developmental plasticity in the visual cortex and hippocampal dentate gyrus. *Progress in Brain Research, 61,* 205–14.

Juraska, J. M., Greenough, W. T., Elliot, C., Mark, K. J., and Berkowitz, R. (1980). Plasticity in adult visual cortex: An examination of several cell populations after differential rearing. *Behavioral and Neural Biology, 29,* 157–67.

Juraska, J. M., Henderson, C., and Muller, J. (1984). Differential rearing experience, gender, and radial maze performance. *Developmental Psychobiology, 17,* 209–15.

Katz, H. B., and Davies, C. A. (1984). Effects of differential environments on the cerebral anatomy of rats as a function of previous and subsequent housing conditions. *Experimental Neurology, 83,* 274–87.

Kendrick, K. M., and Baldwin, B. A. (1987). Cells in temporal cortex of conscious sheep can respond preferentially to the sight of faces. *Science, 236,* 448–50.

Kubonis, P., Zornetzer, S. F., and Freund, G. (1982). Memory and postsynaptic cholinergic receptors in aging mice. *Pharmacology, Biochemistry and Behavior, 17,* 313–22.

Kuffler, S. W. (1953). Discharge patterns and functional organization of mammalian retina. *Neurophysiology, 16,* 37–68.

Kuhn, C. M., Schanberg, S. M., Field, T., Symanski, R., Zimmerman, E., Scafidi, F., and Roberts, J. (1991). Tactile/kinesthetic stimulation effects on sympathetic and adrenocortical function in preterm infants. *Journal of Pediatrics,* in press.

Laing, D. G., and Panhuber, H. (1978). Neural and behavioral changes in rats following continuous exposure to an odor. *Journal of Comparative Physiology, 124,* 259–65.

Laing, D. G., and Panhuber, H. (1980). Olfactory sensitivity of rats reared in an odorous or deodorized environment. *Physiology and Behavior, 25,* 555–58.

Landauer, T. K., and Whiting, J.W.M. (1964). Infantile stimulation and adult stature of human males. *American Anthropologist, 66,* 1007–28.

Landauer, T. K., and Whiting, J.W.M. (1981). Correlates and consequences of stress in infancy. In R. H. Monroe, R. L. Monroe, and B. B. Whiting (Eds.), *Handbook of cross-cultural human development* (pp. 355–75). New York: Garland STPM Press.

LaTorre, J. C. (1968). Effect of differential environmental enrichment on brain weight and on acetylcholinesterase and cholinesterase activities in mice. *Experimental Neurology, 22,* 493–503.

Levanthal, A. G., and Hirsch, H.V.B. (1975). Cortical effect of early selective exposure to diagonal lines. *Science, 190,* 903–4.

Levine, S. (1962). Plasma-free corticoid response to electric shock in rats stimulated in infancy. *Science, 135,* 795–96.

Levine, S. (1968). Influence of infantile stimulation on the response to stress during preweaning development. *Developmental Psychobiology, 1,* 67–70.

Levine, S., and Alpert, M. (1959). Differential maturation of the central nervous system as a function of early experience. *AMA Archives of General Psychiatry, 1,* 403–5.

Levine, S., Alpert, M., and Lewis, G. W. (1958). Differential maturation of adrenal response to cold stress in rats manipulated in infancy. *Journal of Comparative and Physiological Psychology, 51,* 774–77.

Levine, S., Chevalier, J. A., and Korchin, S. J. (1956). The effects of early shock and handling on later avoidance learning. *Journal of Personality, 24,* 475–93.

Levine, S., and Cohen, C. (1959). Differential survival to leukemia as a function of infantile stimulation in DBA-2 mice. *Proceedings of the Society for Experimental Biology and Medicine, 102,* 53–54.

Levine, S., Haltmeyer, G. C., Karas, G., and Denenberg, V. H. (1967). Physiological and behavioral effects of infantile stimulation. *Physiology and Behavior, 2,* 55–59.

Levine, S., and Mullins, R. F. (1966). Hormonal influences on brain organization in infant rats. *Science, 152,* 1585–592.

Levine, S., and Otis, L. S. (1958). The effects of handling before and after weaning on the resistance of albino rats to later deprivation. *Canadian Journal of Psychology, 12,* 103–8.

Lieb, S. A., Renfield, G., and Guidubaldi, J. (1980). Effects of early intervention and stimulation on the preterm. *Pediatrics, 66,* 83–90.

Meaney, M. J., Aitken, D. H., Bodnoff, S. R., Iny, L. J., Tatarecvicz, J. E., and Sapolsky, R. M. (1985). Early postnatal handling alters glucocorticoid receptor concentrations in selected brain regions. *Behavioral Neuroscience, 99,* 765–70.

Meaney, M. J., Aitken, D. H., van Berkel, C., Bhatnagar, S., and Sapolsky, R. M. (1988). Effect of neonatal handling on age-related impairments associated with the hippocampus. *Science, 239,* 766–68.

Meyer, M. E., and McCormick, C. E. (1978). Unconditioned responding in mice as a function of early handling and shock intensity. *Psychological Record, 28,* 571–74.

Mistretta, C. M., and Bradley, R. M. (1978). Effects of early sensory experience on brain and behavioral development. In G. Gottlieb (ed.), *Studies on the development of behavior and the nervous system* (pp. 215–47). Orlando, FL: Academic Press.

Mogensen, J. (1991). Influence of the rearing conditions on functional properties of the rat's prefrontal system. *Behavioural Brain Research, 42,* 135–42.

Morton, J.R.C., Denenberg, V. H., and Zarrow, M. X. (1963). Modification of sexual development through stimulation in infancy. *Endocrinology, 72,* 439–42.

Muir, D. W., and Mitchell, D. E. (1973). Visual resolution and experience: Acuity deficits in cats following early selective visual deprivation. *Science, 180,* 420–22.

Mushynski, W. E., Levitan, I. B., and Ramirez, G. (1973). Competition hybridization studies on brain ribonucleic acid from rats reared in enriched and deprived environments. *Journal of Neurochemistry, 20,* 309–17.

Pettigrew, J. D., and Freeman, R. D. (1973). Visual experience without lines: Effect on developing cortical neurons. *Science, 182,* 599–601.

Pfeifer, W. D., Rotundo, R., Myers, M., and Denenberg, V. H. (1976). Stimulation in infancy: Unique effects of handling. *Physiology and Behavior, 17,* 781–84.

Rabinovitch, M. S., and Rosvald, H. E. (1951). A closed-field intelligence test for rats. *Canadian Journal of Psychology, 5,* 122–28.

Rausch, P. B. (1981). Effects of tactile and kinesthetic stimulation on premature infants. *Journal of Obstetric, Gynecologic and Neonatal Nursing, 10,* 34–37.

Rauschecker, J. P., and Singer, W. (1981). The effects of early visual experience on the cat's visual cortex and their possible explanation by Hebb synapses. *Journal of Physiology, 310,* 215–39.

Reasner, D. S. (1987). Spatially selective alteration of the mitral cell layer: A critical review of the literature. *Chemical Senses, 12,* 365–79.

Renner, M. J., and Rosenzweig, M. R. (1987). *Enriched and impoverished environments. Effects on brain and behavior,* New York: Springer-Verlag.

Rice, R. D. (1977). Neurophysiological development in premature infants following stimulation. *Developmental Psychology, 13,* 69–76.

Rosenzweig, M. R., and Bennett, E. L. (1969). Effects of differential environments on brain weights and enzyme activities in gerbils, rats and mice. *Developmental Psychobiology, 2,* 87–95.

Rosenzweig, M. R., and Bennett, E. L. (1978). Experiential influences on brain anatomy and brain chemistry in rodents. In G. Gottlieb (Ed.), *Studies on the development of behavior and the nervous system* (pp. 289–327). Orlando, FL: Academic Press.

Rosenzweig, M. R., Bennett, E. L., Alberti, M., Morimato, H., and Renner, M. J. (1982). Effects of differential environments and hibernation on ground squirrel brain measures. *Society for Neuroscience Abstracts, 8,* 669.

Rosenzweig, M. R., Bennett, E. L., and Diamond, M. C. (1972a). Chemical and anatomical plasticity of brain: Replications and extensions. In J. Gaito (Ed.), *Macromolecules and behavior,* 2nd ed. (pp. 205–77). New York: Appleton-Century-Crofts

Rosenzweig, M. R., Bennett, E. L., and Diamond, M. C. (1972b). Brain changes in response to experience. *Scientific American, 226,* 22–29.

Rosenzweig, M. R., Krech, D., Bennett, E. L., and Diamond, M. C. (1962). Effects of environmental complexity and training on brain chemistry and anatomy: A replication and extension. *Journal of Comparative and Physiological Psychology, 55,* 429–37.

Rosenzweig, M. R., Bennett, E. L., Diamond, M. C., Wu, S.-Y, Slagle, R. W., and Saffran, E. (1969). Influences of environmental complexity and visual stimulation on development of occipital cortex in rat. *Brain Research, 14,* 427–45.

Rosselli-Austin, L., and Williams, J. (1990). Enriched neonatal odor exposure leads to increased numbers of olfactory bulb mitral and granule cells. *Developmental Brain Research, 51,* 135–37.

Russell, P. A. (1971). "Infantile stimulation" in rodents: A consideration of possible mechanisms. *Psychological Bulletin, 75,* 192–202

Saari, M. J., Fong, S., Shivji, A., and Armstrong, J. N. (1990). Enriched housing masks deficits in place navigation induced by neonatal monosodium glutamate. *Neurotoxicology and Teratology, 12,* 29–32.

Scafidi, F. A., Field, T. M., Schanberg, S. M., Bauer, C. R., Tucci, K., Roberts, J., Morrow, C., and Kuhn, C. M. (1990). Massage stimulates growth in preterm infants: A replication. *Infant Behavior and Development, 13,* 167–88.

Scafidi, F. A., Field, T. M., Schanberg, S. M., Bauer, C., Vega-Lahr, N., Garcia, R., Poirier, J., Nystrom, G., and Kuhn, C. M. (1986). Effects of tactile/kinesthetic stimulation on the clinical course and sleep/wake behavior of preterm infants. *Infant Behavior and Development, 9,* 91–105.

Scarr-Salapatek, S., and Williams, M. L. (1973). The effects of early stimulation on low-birth-weight infants. *Child Development, 44,* 94–101.

Schaefer, T. (1978). Infantile handling and body temperature change in the rat. I. Initial investigations of the temperature hypothesis. *Transactions of the New York Academy of Sciences, 30,* 977–84.

Schiffman, H. R. (1990). *Sensation and Perception.* New York: John Wiley & Sons.

Scott, S., Cole, T., Lucas, P., and Richards, M. (1983). Weight gain and movement patterns of very low birthweight babies nursed on lambswool. *Lancet, 264,* 1014–16.

Siqueland, E. R. (1970). Biological and experimental determinants of exploration in infancy. Paper presented at First National Biological Congress, Detroit.

Sjoden, P.-O. (1976). Effect of neonatal thyroid hormone stimulation and differential preweaning rearing on spatial discrimination learning in rats. *Physiological Psychology, 4,* 515–20.

Solkoff, N., Yaffe, S., Weintraub, D., and Blase, B. (1969). Effects of handling on the subsequent development of premature infants. *Developmental Psychology, 1,* 765–68.

Stell, M., and Riesen, A. (1987). Effects of early environments on monkey cortex. Neuroanatomical changes following somatomotor experience: Effects of layer III pyramidal cells in monkey cortex. *Behavioral Neuroscience, 101,* 341–46.

Sullivan, R. M., and Leon, M. (1986). Early olfactory learning induced an enhanced olfactory bulb response in young rats. *Developmental Brain Research, 27,* 278–82.

Sullivan, R. M., and Leon, M. (1987). One-trial olfactory learning enhances olfactory bulb responses to an appetitive conditioned odor in 7-day-old rats. *Developmental Brain Research, 35,* 307–11.

Tretter, F., Cynoder, M., and Singer, W. (1975). Modification of direction selectivity of neurons in the visual cortex of kittens. *Brain Research, 84,* 143–49.

Turner, A. M., and Greenough, W. T. (1985). Differential rearing effects on rat visual cortex synapses. I. Synaptic and neuronal density and synapses per neuron. *Brain Research, 329,* 195–203.

Uphouse, L. L., and Bonner, J. (1975). Preliminary evidence for the effects of environmental complexity on hybridization of rat brain RNA to rat unique DNA. *Developmental Psychobiology, 8,* 171–78.

Volkmar, F. R., and Greenough, W. T. (1972). Rearing complexity affects branching of dendrites in the visual cortex of the rat. *Science, 176,* 1445–447.

Walsh, R. N., Budtz-Olsen, O. E., Torok, A., and Cummins, R. A. (1970). Environmentally induced changes in the dimensions of the rat cerebrum. *Developmental Psychobiology, 4,* 115–22.

Walsh, R. N., Cummins, R. A., and Budtz-Olsen, O. E. (1973). Environmentally induced changes in the dimensions of the rat cerebrum: A replication and extension. *Developmental Psychobiology, 6,* 3–7.

Warren, J. M., Zerweck, C., and Anthony, A. (1982). Effects of environmental enrichment on old mice. *Developmental Psychobiology, 15,* 13–18.

Werboff, J., and Havlena, J. (1963). Febrile convulsions in infant rats and later behavior. *Science, 142,* 684–85.

Weiner, I., Schnabel, I., Lubow, R. E., and Feldon, J. (1985). The effects of early handling on latent inhibition in male and female rats. *Developmental Psychobiology, 18,* 291–97.

Weinberg, J., Krahn, E. A., and Levine, S. (1978). Differential effects of handling on exploration in male and female rats. *Developmental Psychobiology, 11,* 251–59.

Weininger, O. (1956). The effects of early experience on behavior and growth characteristics. *Journal of Comparative and Physiological Psychology, 49,* 1–6.

Whiting, J.W.M. (1965). Menarcheal age and infant stress in humans. In F. A. Beach (Ed.), *Sex and behavior* (pp. 221–33). New York: John Wiley & Sons.

Wiesel, T. N., and Hubel, D. H. (1963). Single-cell responses in striate cortex of kittens deprived of vision in one eye. *Journal of Neurophysiology, 26,* 1003–17.

Will, B. E., Rosenzweig, M. R., Bennett, E. L., Hebert, M., and Morimoto, H. (1977). Relatively brief environmental enrichment aids recovery of learning capacity and alters brain measures after postweaning brain lesions. *Journal of Comparative and Physiological Psychology, 91,* 35–38.

Wilson, D. A., Willner, J., Kurz, E. M., and Nadel, L. (1986). Early handling increases hippocampal long-term potentiation in young rats. *Behavioral and Brain Research, 21,* 223–27.

Wilson, M., Warren, J. M., and Abbott, L. (1965). Infantile stimulation, activity, and learning by cats. *Child Development, 36,* 843–53.

Wong, R. (1972). Infantile handling and associative processes in rats. *British Journal of Psychology, 63,* 101–8.

Wong, R., and Judd, L. (1973). Infantile handling and successive spatial reversal learning in rats. *Behavioral Biology, 8,* 391–97.

Wong, R., and Wong, B. (1978). Infantile handling and learning: A critical review. *American Journal of Psychology, 91,* 23–33.

Woo, C. C., Coopersmith, R., and Leon, M. (1987). Localized changes in olfactory bulb morphology associated with early olfactory learning. *Journal of Comparative Neurology, 263,* 113–25.

Wyly, M. V., Denenberg, V. H., DeSantis, D., Burns, J. K., and Zarrow, M. X. (1975). Handling rabbits in infancy: In search of a critical period. *Developmental Psychobiology, 8,* 179–86.

Zarrow, M. X., Denenberg, V. H., Haltmeyer, G. C., and Brumaghin, J. T. (1967). Plasma and adrenal corticosterone levels following exposure of the two-day-old rat to various stressors. *Proceedings of the Society for Experimental Biology and Medicine, 125,* 113–16.

Zarrow, M. X., Philpott, J. E., Denenberg, V. H., and O'Connor, W. B. (1968). Location of ^{14}C-4-corticosterone in the 2-day-old rat and a consideration of the mechanism involved in early handling. *Nature, 218,* 1264–265.

7
Play

Bafflement, delight, and lively intellectual fascination are three
human responses to animal play. Although play may be difficult
and even unrewarding to study, it is never dull. On the contrary.
Play enriches: through the artistry of its movements and contexts, through the intellectual richness of the controversy it
engenders, and through still debated benefits to the player.

R. Fagen, 1984

Children engage in activities we assume to be nonserious, purposeless, and
enjoyable. We call these activities *play*. The young of nonhuman species also
play. Have not most of us observed behaviors of puppies, kittens, and even baby
hamsters that we are subjectively certain to be frolicsome. We rarely question
those subjective impressions. But what if we did? If our impressions are replaced
by objective analyses, is the establishment of a separate category of behavior jus-
tified?

Play *must* be unique, it has been argued, because it differs in form from adult
behavior. Loizos (1966), for one, contended that, unlike "serious" behavior,
playful activities are exaggerated, repetitive, and incomplete. Others, however,
are of a different mind. Schlosberg (1947) stated that the reason certain behaviors of young organisms are incomplete or otherwise inadequate has to do with
stimulus-response associations rather than with a concept as vague and unin-
formative as play. He wrote that "enough has been said to indicate that the category 'playful activity' is so loose that it is almost useless for modern psychology." In a similar vein, Lazar and Beckhorn (1974) contended that play as a
category is redundant—that it is nothing more than an immature form of adult
behavior.

Despite such criticism, play is generally viewed, as least implicitly, as a separate category of behavior consisting of activities that consume much of the
youngs' waking hours. As such, parsimony dictates that play must serve a function—that it must in some manner contribute to behavioral development.

Although play has been the focus of a good deal of research throughout the
past two decades or so, its systematic study presents more conceptual and methodological difficulties than does the analysis of any other factor assumed to influence development. The reason is twofold. First, a generally acceptable definition
of play does not exist. This fact should not be surprising given the exceedingly

wide range of activities commonly subsumed under the rubric *play,* activities such as tumbling and wrestling by young rodents, "stalking" of a ball of yarn by kittens, rough-housing of young nonhuman primates, mutual chasing and fleeing by puppies, and "pretend" games of children, to name but a few. Second, the function or functions of play, although having been the subject of a great deal of speculation commencing formally during the nineteenth century, remain within the realm of conjecture.

Given these serious difficulties, why, then, do investigators devote time and resources to such an elusive topic? As alluded to above, play is believed to be exhibited by members of all mammalian species. This presumed universality— that it is engaged in most often by immature organisms—and in keeping with the belief that nature is purposeful, leads inevitably to the conclusion that play *must* be important, perhaps even essential, for normal development; if it were not needed, it would not exist. Therefore regardless of the difficulties, it is believed that the study of play can add significantly to our understanding of the forces that shape development.

Prior to discussing the research, let us first consider in some detail the difficulties involved in defining play activity and in delineating its function. Such discussion promotes a better appreciation of both the methodologies that have been developed to assess play and the data themselves.

DIFFICULTIES WITH THE PLAY CONCEPT

Definitional Problem

What is play? To begin with, play is a subset of behaviors that are believed to occur "only when the animal's essential needs have been satisfied and not in stressful situations" (Poole & Fish, 1975). Therefore although play may have long-term consequences, unlike serious behavior it serves no *immediate* function, appearing to be purposeless (Bekoff & Byers, 1981). It is assumed that play is most characteristic of the immature animal, exhibited at relatively low levels by adults.[1]

Despite the fact that many juvenile behaviors presumably have no immediate function and are considered to be playful, they often are similar to behaviors exhibited by adults within a serious context. It is seen, for example, with "play fighting," an often used dependent measure in laboratory studies of play. As described by Panksepp, Siviy, and Normansell (1984):

> [when] rat pups are placed together in a nonthreatening environment, they rapidly begin to exhibit vigorous fighting: animals chase and pounce on each other, sometimes unilaterally, sometimes mutually with rapid role reversals. They repeatedly poke and nip each other, often at the nape of the neck but also on the ventral surface when one animal is pinned. . . .[p. 466]

---

[1]Adults, of course, do play. However, most of their play involves organized activities. Here we are concerned with the rather spontaneous activities mainly exhibited by youngsters.

The behaviors associated with play fighting in juvenile rats—offensive acts including chasing, wrestling, and biting as well as defensive maneuvers that serve to avoid such contact (Pellis & Pellis, 1987)—are similar to acts observed when adults fight (Takahashi & Lore, 1983). This comparability between play and serious behavior is illustrated in Figure 7.1. Various components of play fighting in the Stellar sea lion, such as the offensive neck bite and the submissive open mouth, are virtually identical to those observed between aggressing adults (see Figure 7.1). The similarity between juvenile and adult behavior certainly blurs the distinction between play fighting and serious behavior.

Putting aside the issue of similarity, one could argue that the fighting-like behavior of the young animals must be playful because it rarely leads to serious injury (Reinhardt & Reinhardt, 1982). Even if we overlook the fact that serious injury is not an inevitable outcome of an aggressive encounter among adults (the ritualized rutting contests of male deer are a good example), might it not be that juveniles are simply physically incapable of inflicting damage? One also could contend that juvenile aggression-like activities must be playful because they are positive; young animals acquire an instrumental response when rewarded with the opportunity to engage in them (Humphreys & Einon, 1981). However, adults also acquire responses when reinforced by the opportunity to fight (Myer & White, 1965; Tellegen, Horn, & Legrand, 1969; Van Hemel, 1972).

It must not be overlooked that the similarity between what have been termed playful acts and serious behavior is also found in nonsocial situations. Dangle a ball of yarn in front of a kitten, and in all likelihood it will assume the characteristic feline stalking posture and then pounce. Although almost universally regarded as play, the acts of stalking and pouncing are similar to those of the adult after encountering an object of prey.

Given the similarities between particular activities of the immature animal and adult behaviors, it becomes problematical as to whether to classify the former as play. Simply stated, an act cannot be designated play merely because the actor is young. According to some researchers, a way out of this dilemma is to demonstrate that, although juvenile and adult behaviors are similar, they do differ in a number of significant aspects. As Hole and Einon (1984) stated, "The most powerful criterion for considering a behaviour as 'play' is the extent to which it employs unique behaviour patterns." This point has been demonstrated within the context of fighting by showing that juveniles direct bites to body areas differing from those selected by adults. More will be said about this later.

Unfortunately, even the demonstration of differences between certain juvenile and adult behaviors does not completely alleviate the problem of defining play. Again it must be asked on what empirical basis can the behavior of the juvenile be designated *play?* Is the behavior truly nonserious and enjoyable? Are the individuals really having fun?

It seems unlikely that an adequate behavioral definition of play can ever be formulated. This deficiency leaves the researcher with three options. One is to conclude that play is not within the purview of scientific inquiry. A second is to conduct research despite the inability to adequately define the subject matter under investigation. A third is to define play differently, perhaps in nonbehav-

Figure 7.1 Fighting component "bite neck" in a serious adult fight (above) and in a mock-fight between 6-week-old pups (below). (From Gentry, "The development of social behavior through play in the Stellar sea lion." *American Zoologist, 14*, 391–403. © 1974 by The American Society of Zoologists. Reprinted by permission.)

ioral terminology. Panksepp (1986), opting for the latter, maintained that play is best defined neurobiologically:

> Because play has to be generated by distinct brain activities, a lasting definition would specify the locations and properties of the circuits instigating the behavior universally recognized as play. Accordingly, play would come to be scientifically defined with respect to concrete brain processes that generate the myriad behaviors traditionally subsumed by the concept. [p. 33]

However, even this novel approach is problematical because it requires *a priori* that certain behaviors be designated play.

Functional Problem

The lack of an adequate behavioral definition is not the only difficulty surrounding the topic of play. Another, and one equally troubling, is that the function or functions of play have not been adequately delineated.[2] This problem is not due to a lack of interest, as formal theories of play have been available since the latter portion of the nineteenth century. Rather, the problem lies with the fact that play is difficult if not impossible to manipulate *independently.* If you recall, the function of early olfactory experience was ascertained by controlling the odors to which the youngster is exposed. Play, however, cannot be as easily manipulated. To control the play experience of young animals one is forced to impose other conditions on the youngster, such as periods of social isolation[3] or cohabitation with an older animal, conditions that themselves could influence the dependent measure.

Because play is not easily amenable to manipulation, the ascription of function often has been inferred from dataless theoretical analyses, from impressions gleaned from careful observation of play behavior, and from the existence of a relation within individual subjects between amount of play and the rate at which another behavior develops. Although the latter technique can be useful, like any correlational analysis it relies on variability. That is, the amount of play must differ sufficiently among individuals for it to be related statistically to the ontogeny of a later-appearing behavior. However, the naturally occurring variability in amount of play is frequently too small to permit a meaningful correlation to be established.

Now that you have been made aware of the difficulties involved in the functional anaysis of play, let us briefly consider some of the ideas concerning function that have emerged over the years, beginning with some of the earliest notions.

---

[2] Is it possible that play serves no adaptive significance? Owing to the costs associated with the behavior, such as the risk of accidental injury, energy expenditure, and death by predation, it is difficult to imagine that no benefits accrue. Regarding the latter, Hole (1991) reported that rats exhibit a preference for playing away from exposed areas, thereby reducing the risk of predation.

[3] Numerous studies have purportedly shown that play deprivation leads to adverse effects during later life (Einon & Morgan, 1977; Einon & Potegal, 1991; Sahakian, Robbins, Morgan, & Iverson, 1975). Unfortunately these studies are compromised by the imposition of periods of social isolation during early periods of development.

The first formal theory of play is found in Spencer's 1878 textbook, *The Principles of Psychology*. He asserted that whereas animals relatively low on the phylogenetic scale are continually occupied by activities requisite for survival (seeking food and shelter, escaping from predators, and so forth), higher order animals, because of their more complex nervous systems, "are not wholly absorbed in providing for immediate needs" (p. 628). Furthermore, that they engage in more complex patterns of behavior enables them to be better nourished. This enhanced nutritional status coupled with the fact these higher order animals essentially have time to spare from engaging in survival-related activities lead at times "to an energy somewhat in excess of immediate needs" (p. 629). Play, which results when an energy surplus occurs at a time during which survival-related activities are not being performed, functions to discharge this surplus energy by permitting certain mental/behavioral processes to be exercised. The exact form play behavior assumes depends on the length of time particular "nerve centers" have been inactive; those inactive for long periods become unusually susceptible to discharge. Wrote Spencer:

> Every one of the mental powers, then, being subject to this law, that its organ when dormant for an interval longer than ordinary becomes unusually ready to act . . . it happens that a simulation of those activities is easily fallen into, when circumstances offer it in place of the real activities. Hence play of all kinds—hence this tendency to superfluous and useless excercise of faculties that have been quiescent. [pp. 629–630]

In contrast, Groos (1898) argued that play is not simply a mechanism for dealing with surplus energy but, rather, serves as practice for instinctive behaviors exhibited later in life. Accordingly, if there was no such thing as play, instinctive activities such as predation would have to be exhibited perfectly on the initial attempts; if not the animal would starve. Hence:

> all youthful play is founded on instinct. These instincts are not so perfectly developed, not so stamped in all their details on the brain, as they would have to be if their first expressions were to be in serious acts. Therefore they appear in youth, and must be perfected during that period by constant practice. [Groos, 1898, p. 79]

For Groos, then, "Animals cannot be said to play because they are young and frolicsome, *but rather they have a period of youth in order to play" (p. 75).*

Just how well does Groos's notion of play apply to humans? Not well at all, according to Hall (1908), who asserted that play cannot be practice for behaviors the child will eventually exhibit because those future behaviors are unpredictable. Instead, play serves the function of recapitulating the serious behavior of our ancestors:

> True play never practices what is phyletically new, and this, industrial life often calls for. It exercises many atavistic and rudimentary functions, a number of which will abort before maturity, but which live themselves out in play like the tadpoles tail, that must be both developed and used as a stimulus to the growth of legs which will otherwise never mature. [p. 202]

Hall went on to predict that "if the form of every human occupation were to change today, play would be unaffected save in some of its superficial imitative forms" (p. 202). Hall was obviously influenced by the industrial revolution, which required adults to acquire skills that could not be presaged by the play of the child. Of course, the behaviors of interest to Hall were far removed from the instinctual activities that formed the basis of Groos's theory.

It is apparent that major differences in interpreting the function of play were present from the outset of formal theorizing, and such differences remain. Beyond the functions attributed to play by Spencer, Groos, and Hall, play also has been viewed as promoting muscle growth and general physical capacity (Fagen, 1976), social relationships (Baldwin & Baldwin, 1974; Bekoff, 1974), tool use (Beck, 1980; Huffman & Quiatt, 1986), motor skills (Chalmers & Locke-Haydon, 1984), and problem-solving (Smith & Simon, 1984). Play may also help the child to bridge the gap between fantasy and reality (Partington & Grant, 1984) and to assimilate psychologically painful experiences (Wälder, 1933).

Due primarily to the inability to manipulate early playful experience, the myriad functions ascribed to play are predominatly theoretically rather than empirically based. That and the lack of an acceptable definition of play make play behavior a difficult and controversial topic for developmental researchers. Although this chapter is not the appropriate forum for lengthly speculative discussion about the nature and function of play, it would be remiss to omit discussion of research devoted to illuminating the factors that influence that behavior. To facilitate the discussion, let us make the following four assumptions: (1) play comprises a separate category of behavior; (2) play is predominantly displayed by immature organisms; (3) play differs from "serious behavior" in that it serves no immediate function of consequence other than providing the organism with stimulation (which, given the information considered in Chapter 6, may itself be important); and (4) the adaptive significance of play becomes manifest later in development.

"Play fighting" has been and continues to be the behavior of choice for those who study play under controlled laboratory conditions. The reasons for this are fourfold. First, the behavior is relatively easy to quantify. Second, it is readily engaged in by standard laboratory animals such as rats and hamsters. Third, the behavior possesses face validity, as it has a conspicuously playful appearance. As Panksepp et al (1984) remakred, "Clearly, the mock fighting is rarely 'taken seriously' by either animal." Finally, it is believed that play fighting is important developmentally, permitting the organism "to excercise, practice and refine the skills [needed] in future social encounters" (Panksepp et al., 1984). Their assertion is bolstered by data showing that juvenile rats that more often than not get the better of their playmates during play fighting tend to be dominant in adult life (Normansell, 1984, as cited by Panksepp et al., 1984). Taylor (1980) also reported that the amount of play fighting correlates positively with the amount of ostensibly serious fighting behavior exhibited by adults. For these reasons the preponderance of data pertaining to play are derived from analyzing play fighting. Consequently, play fighting is the focus of our discussion.

PLAY FIGHTING

Play fighting, also referred to as rough-and-tumble play, is exhibited by members of many species including our own. Although an encounter is generally devoid of most adult communicative behaviors that serve to signal threat or submission (Aldis, 1975; Bekoff, 1972), the "playmates" do engage in species-typical patterns of activities of both the offensive and defensive variety. Play fighting, which rarely results in serious physical injury, often includes many role reversals; animals rapidly alternate between attacking and defending. An example of discrete behaviors that comprise play fighting is given in Table 7.1 for the Columbian ground squirrel.

Certain behaviors that occur just prior to play fighting may also be included under the play fighting category. It is important that one member of the pair "inform" the other that what is to follow is play rather than a serious aggressive act. This form of preplay communication has been studied by Bekoff (1974), who identified in dogs what he called a "bow." As seen in Figure 7..2, the bow serves as a prelude to a bout of play fighting in beagle puppies. Because it is especially important that the mature dog also communicate the impending occurrence of a playful advance so the other does not "mistake" it for a serious attack, it should not be surprising that the bow also is exhibited by adults (see Figure 7.3). Bekoff also described preplay signals of the wolf, which include exaggerated head and body movements (head-tossing and side-to-side swaying of the shoulders) and high leaping in the fox (see Figure 7.4). To my knowledge information is unavailable concerning the possibility of preplay fighting communicative behavior in rodents.

The frequency with which bouts of play fighting are exhibited is age-dependent. Rats, for example, begin to display the behavior at about day 15 or 16, just after their eyes open. It reaches its peak at 30 to 40 days and then slowly declines (Baenninger, 1967; Taylor, 1980). Similar relations between age and play fighting have been reported for many species including the squirrel monkey (Rosenblum, 1968), polecat (Poole, 1966), ferret (Lazar & Beckhorn, 1974), cat (Martin, 1982, as cited in Martin & Bateson, 1985), and hamster (Pellis & Pellis, 1988a).

The inclination to label interaction between juveniles as a form of *fighting* attests to its similarity to aggressive behaviors observed among adults. However, it does differ from adult aggressive behavior with regard to the target of attack and defensive posturing. This point was demonstrated for the hamster by Pellis and Pellis (1988b), who isolated pairs of male littermates for 24 hours, reintroduced them into their home cage, and filmed the ensuing encounter. Data from the same pairs were collected at 6-day intervals beginning on day 25 and continuing through the early adult stage. Adult fighting was observed beginning on day 80 by placing an intruder into the home cage of another animal. When young (25 to 50 days), most bites are directed anterior to the shoulders, especially to the cheeks. Pellis and Pellis (1988a) referred to the cheeks as an *amicable* target because they are normally contacted during sexual encounters rather than dur-

Table 7.1 Operational definitions of the behavioral components of play in the Columbian ground squirrel

Behavioral Component	Definition
Approach	Walking toward another animal.
Arch back	Upward convex bending of the spine, hindlegs vertically extended.
Belly-up	Lying on back with all four legs spread and raised upward; mouth held open.
Bite	Bringing teeth into contact with another animal and closing them.
Box	Two animals facing each other, rearing up on hindlegs with forepaws extended, striking one another with forepaws.
Break off	Stopping or diverting attention from the play bout (for > 5 seconds) without either animal leaving the vicinity.
Chase	Running after a moving animal.
Fight	Similar to wrestling but with escalated biting, kicking (with hindlimbs), and usually vocalization by one or both animals.
Follow	Walking pursuit of another animal.
"Greeting"	Head extended toward another animal, often with a slight lowering of forebody; mouth open; head rotated and mutual contact of naso-oral areas.
Into burrow	Moving either slowly or quickly into a burrow entrance.
Mount	Jumping onto other animal's lower back and grasping it with forelimbs.
No reaction	Although in contact with or near other animal, no response to behavior of other animal perceivable.
Pause	Brief stop (< 5 seconds) in play; animals still directing attention to each other.
Pounce	Jumping or leaping onto another animal.
Push away	Kicking using each hindleg (simultaneously or successively).
Run away	Hurriedly running from another animal without pursuit.
Rush	Running toward another, with the other animal not moving away.
Side jump	Animal sitting with four paws on the ground, leaps laterally, usually in a direction away from the other animal.
Tail bush	Piloerection of the tail.
Wrestle	Grasping or clinging to each other, two animals perform whole-body rolling, with no vocalization.

Source: From Waterman. Social play in free-ranging Columbian ground squirrels, *Spermophilus Columbianus. Ethology* 77:225–236. © 1988 by Paul Parey. Reprinted by permission.

ing mutual investigation by strange mature males. In contrast, however, adults tend to direct bites posterior to the shoulders, mainly to the rump.

Encounters between pairs of younger and older hamsters also differ with regard to defensive behavior. For 80-day-old and older subjects the most common mode of defense is to flee, followed by the attainment of an upright posture. The least likely defensive reaction is to lay on the back. Younger hamsters, however, do not flee and rarely adopt an upright posture. Instead, in almost all cases they lie supine.

Figure 7.2 Play of two 30-day-old beagles. The dog on the right performs a "bow," and his littermate approaches. (From Bekoff, "Social play and play-soliciting by infant canids." *American Zoologist, 14,* 323–40. © 1974 by The American Society of Zoologists. Reprinted by permission.)

These age-related differences in offensive and defensive behavior led Pellis and Pellis (1988b) to conclude that

> play-fighting remains distinct from serious fighting throughout development, from weaning, through to sexual maturity and early adulthood. These data refute the hypothesis that, in the hamster, play-fighting is a form of not very aggressive adult fighting, and support the hypothesis that play-fighting is a distinct form of behavior in this species. [p. 335]

The data also can be used to refute the notion that play fighting is practice for serious fighting; what is practiced during play is not what is used during a genuine aggressive encounter.

Figure 7.3 A "bow" performed by the dog on the right. (From Bekoff, "Social play and play-soliciting by infant canids." *American Zoologist, 14,* 323–40. © 1974 by The American Society of Zoologists. Reprinted by permission.)

Figure 7.4 High leaping during play-soliciting by a red fox. (From Bekoff, "Social play and play-soliciting by infant canids." *American Zoologist, 14,* 323–40. © 1974 by The American Society of Zoologists. Reprinted by permission.)

Similar findings have been obtained from the rat. Serious fighting is characterized by bites directed at the opponent's rump, lower back, and flanks, whereas play fighting involves contact with the nape of the neck (Pellis & Pellis, 1987). Furthermore, the contact with the nape, made orally or with the snout, rarely involves biting. Another behavior commonly observed when young rats are paired and one that has come to be used as a measure of play fighting is called "pinning," when one animal has its back on the ground with the other on top of or poised above it (Bolles & Woods, 1964; Hole, 1988).

The differences in form between the encounters of juvenile animals relative to those of adults are not universal, however. In many species, such as the American black bear (Henry & Herrero, 1974), cattle (Reinhardt & Reinhardt, 1982), European polecat (Poole, 1972), and Stellar sea lion (Gentry, 1974), the "combative" behaviors of juveniles and adults are virtually identical. Fortunately, the species that do exhibit clear differences, rats and hamsters, are of the standard laboratory variety.

Now that play fighting has been described in some detail, we are ready to examine the factors that affect its display. Let us begin with the influence of experience and then move on to physiological factors.

Experience

Does the lack of play experience affect future play behavior? If play is regulated by an underlying motivational system, play *deprivation* should lead to a subsequent *increase* in the frequency or intensity of play activity in much the same way as food deprivation enhances eating activity. Müller-Schwarze (1968) reported a minimal effect of play deprivation in deer and concluded that, at least for that species, there is no specific source of play motivation. On the other hand, Panksepp and Beatty (1980) described a marked influence of deprivation in the rat. They compared rats weaned and isolated on day 18 of life to others weaned but not isolated from littermates. On day 21 the behavior of pairs of same-sex, similarly aged youngsters was observed for 5 minutes in a separate test cage. Three days of isolation exerted a profound effect; whereas nonisolated animals play fought for less than a third of the observation period, isolated subjects usually play fought throughout the entire period. It also was reported that as little as 8 hours of isolation was sufficient to increase play fighting, whereas reductions of play fighting occurred after isolated animals were permitted as little as 1 hour of social stimulation. Panksepp and Beatty concluded that "play has the hallmarks of a regulated process" and suggested that it may be controlled by some facet of brain neurochemistry. More is said about this subject later.

The procedure used by Panskepp and Beatty to produce play deprivation consisted of depriving the subjects of social stimulation, and it is possible that social rather than play deprivation was responsible for the enhancement of play fighting. If so, it would explain the discrepancy between the findings of Panksepp and Beatty and those of Müller-Schwarze (1968), who reported little effect of play deprivation on subsequent play activity of deer. Instead of preventing play by isolating them, Müller-Schwarze offered the fawn a milk bottle whenever play activity was about to begin. Because the bottle always elicited drinking, playing was prevented.

Panksepp et al. (1984) considered the possibility that the enhancement of play is caused by social rather than play deprivation. They did so by reducing play experience but in the absence of social deprivation. It was accomplished in two ways. First, a young rat was housed with an older animal known to normally play less. Second, a pair of young rats was kept in a cage "which contained a 'jungle gym' insert which retards vigorous rough-and-tumble play while still allowing for bodily contact." Should these manipulations enhance play fighting over the level shown by similarly aged young animals kept in standard cages, one could conclude that play *reduction* (it cannot be called deprivation because low levels of play do occur) rather than social deprivation is responsible. The results are shown in Figure 7.5. It is apparent that the two manipulations, although not as influential as social deprivation, do enhance subsequent play fighting. Thus the enhancement of play fighting following periods of social isolation in the rat is at least in part due to play deprivation.

Relatively brief periods of maternal separation also have been shown to influence subsequent levels of play behavior. Capitanio and Reite (1984) compared the play fighting of four pigtail macaque monkeys having undergone a 10-day

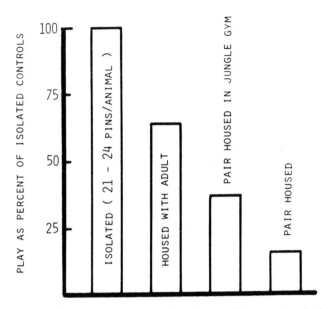

Figure 7.5 Effects of various housing conditions on level of play, as a percentage of that obtained by animals isolated for 24 hours prior to a 5-minute play session. (From Panksepp et al., "The psychobiology of play: Theoretical and methodological perspectives." *Neuroscience and Biobehavioral Review, 8,* 465–92. © 1984 by Pergamon Press. Reprinted by permission.)

period of maternal separation to that of five nonseparated animals. Maternal separation, which took place when the subjects were between 5 and 7 months old, consisted in removing the mother while allowing the offspring to remain in their social group made up of adult males, adult females, and other young. Behavioral observations were made between 1.5 and 3.0 years after the separation experience. The results were clear; maternally separated animals played about half as much as did controls.

The influence of housing space on play fighting has been examined as well (Klinger & Kemble, 1985). Small litters (four pups) of 35- to 39-day-old rats played more frequently than large litters (eight pups) when the size of the living enclosure remained relatively small. Increasing the size of the enclosure led to increased play fighting in eight-pup litters. Therefore, play fighting in rats is affected significantly by housing space.

Physiology

Brain

Numerous attempts have been made to delineate the neural involvement in play fighting by observing juveniles after destruction of discrete regions of their brains. It should be emphasized, however, that data obtained in this manner may be difficult to interpret, especially when the outcome involves a behavioral decline. Diminution or elimination of play fighting may be a by-product of general debilitation resulting from the inflicted brain damage rather than indicative of the destruction of a specific play behavior-controlling neural mechanism. The data become more persuasive, however, if complementary information is presented that attests to the subject's general behavioral competence or when the result consists of an augmentation of play fighting. Furthermore, even if the behavior remains *unchanged* following destruction of a certain portion of the brain, one cannot completely dismiss its involvement in play fighting. It is possible that play fighting is governed by a neural circuit with redundant features. While having the capacity to maintain play fighting in the face of damage to one or more of its redundant aspects, under *normal* conditions the *entire* circuit may function. With these cautionary notes in mind, we can now review the research.

The involvement of the neocortex in the ontogeny of various species-typical behaviors was the focus of a study by Murphy, MacLean, and Hamilton (1981). Neocortices of 1- and 2-day-old hamsters were eliminated by either the application of heat or aspiration, and their behavioral development was compared to that of intact controls. The time of emergence of many behaviors including digging, seed cracking, hoarding, nest building, and play fighting was *unaffected* by decortication. However, because Murphy et al. subjected play fighting behavior to neither a precise topographical nor temporal analysis, it is conceivable that although the behavior did emerge at the normal time it differed qualitatively or quantitatively from that of intact animals. This possibility is supported by Normansell and Panksepp's (1984) findings with decorticate rats. Whereas the major components of play fighting are present, the amount of time spent engaged in the activity is half that of normals.

Murphy et al. (1981) did make an important observation regarding the influence of subcortical tissue. Four hamsters that sustained destruction of some subcortical limbic tissue in addition to the elimination of the neocortex were normal in practically all respects except that they displayed no play fighting. Neural control of play fighting therefore may reside in subcortical tissue, a possibility considered in the studies described below.

The involvement of the amygdala in the fighting behavior of adult rats prompted Meaney, Dodge, and Beatty (1981) to ask if that structure also plays a role in play fighting. Bilateral electrolytic lesions of the amygdala were performed in 21- and 22-day-old rats that were subsequently tested for play fighting between days 26 and 40. As seen in Figure 7.6, lesions attenuated the play fighting of males but not females, a finding perhaps related to the observation that males normally exhibit more play fighting than females. (Sex differences in play fighting are considered in the following section.) To conclude from these data that the amygdala is part of a neural circuit related *specifically* to the initiation of play fighting is premature, as amydalectomized rats also are deficient in nonplay fighting activities (Panksepp et al., 1984).

A decrease in play fighting also has been observed following damage to other subcortical areas of the rat brain. Beatty and Costello (1983) reported that lesions of the anterior hypothalamus and ventromedical nucleus of the hypothalamus

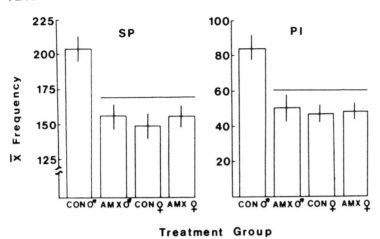

Figure 7.6 Frequency (mean ± SEM) of social play (SP, left panel) and play initiation (PI, right panel) responses of control (CON) and amygdalectomized (AMX)
rats. Horizontal lines denote groups that were not statistically different. (From
Meaney et al., "Sex-dependent effects of amygdaloid lesions on the social play of
pubertal rats." *Physiology and Behavior, 26,* 467–72. © 1981 by Pergamon Press.
Reprinted by permission.)

are effective, as are lesions of the thalamus (dorsomedial thalamus and parafas-
cicular region) (Siviy & Panksepp, 1985 [as cited by Siviy & Panksepp, 1987]).
It is important to note that whereas thalamic damage reduces play fighting, it
does not affect general activity levels (Panksepp et al., 1984). Lastly, extensive
damage to the medial preoptic-anterior hypothalamus decreases play fighting
(Dodge, 1981, as cited by Meaney, Stewart, & Beatty, 1985) whereas damage
restricted to the medial preoptic nucleus is without effect (Leedy, Vela, Popolow,
& Gerall, 1980).

The only case in which play fighting is increased after brain damage involves
the septal area. Rats given septal lesions on day 23 exhibit elevated levels of play
fighting between days 27 and 41 (Beatty, Dodge, Thaylor, Donegan, & Godding,
1982).

Does the amygdala together with regions of the hypothalamus and thalamus
form a circuit that normally *activates* play fighting? Does the septum normally
inhibit the behavior? A good deal of additional experimentation is required to
delineate play-related brain circuitry providing, of course, that the brain is
indeed "wired" in such a behaviorally discrete manner.

Hormones

Data derived from both *descriptive* and *manipulative* research have implicated
the endocrine system in play fighting. Descriptive studies have found a sex difference in the amount and intensity of play fighting, and studies involving hor-

monal manipulations report consequent and predictable alterations in the behavior.

Descriptive Research

Data from various studies reveal that males play fight more than females. Devore (1963) and Owens (1975), describing the behavior of free-ranging baboons, reported that by the age of 2 years juvenile males play more roughly and for longer periods of time than females. Females, on the other hand, spend more time with adult females and newborn infants of the troop. A sex difference in play fighting is also reflected in the makeup of play groups, which invariably include more juvenile males than females; in hamadryas baboons the ratio may be as high as 8:1 (Kummer, 1971). More intense play fighting by the male also has been observed in rhesus monkeys (Goldfoot & Wallen, 1978; Goy, 1978). In contrast, a difference in play fighting was not observed between female and male gorillas (Brown, 1988).

Regarding humans, the findings of Goldberg and Lewis (1969) may indirectly bear on the issue of sex differences. Sixty-four children were observed separately at 6 months of age and again at 13 months in a situation that allowed them to play with specially selected toys in the presence of their mothers. Girls were observed to be more reluctant than boys to leave the mother, and their play behavior was charaterized as being of a quiet style. In contrast, "Boys were independent, showed more exploratory behavior, played with toys requiring gross motor activity, were more vigorous, and tended to run and bang in their play" (p. 30). That young boys are more vigorous in their play than girls may portend a greater proclivity for boys to play fight later in development.

Blurton-Jones (1976) directly observed play fighting among 3- to 5-year-old nursery school children. Play fighting, which is remarkably similar to that exhibited by nonhuman primates (see Figure 7.7), consists of the following seven movement patterns: running, chasing and fleeing, wrestling, jumping up and down, beating at one another with an open hand without actually hitting, beating at one another with an object without actually hitting, and laughing. As exhibited by nonhumans, roles assumed during the play fight rapidly alternate; the aggressor becomes the victim and vice versa. According to Blurton-Jones, play fighting is readily distinguishable from truly hostile behavior, which in children is often precipitated by theft of property. Of importance here is the observation that males engage in more play fighting than females. Unfortunately, we are made privy neither to the number of children studied nor to any quantifiable aspect of the data.

A female–male difference in play fighting also has been reported in nonprimate species. Gentry (1974) observed that male Stellar sea lions exhibit many more components of play activities than do females, and Goldman and Swanson (1975) reported a similar finding for hamsters.

Most of the data pertaining to the role of the endocrine system in play fighting have been obtained from the rat. Olioff and Stewart (1978) computed the amount of time same-sex pairs of rats engaged in play fighting during 10-minute observation sessions held in a test chamber. This assessment technique is known

Figure 7.7 Rough-and-tumble play is as common in human young as it is in the young of other species, such as 6- to 8-year-old chimpanzees. (From Blurton-Jones, *Play—Its Role in Development and Evolution.* © 1976 by Basic Books. Reprinted by permission.)

as the *paired encounter* procedure. Data were obtained when the animals were 22, 26, and 30 days of age. When the data were summed across the three ages it was found that males spent almost twice as much time playing as did females. Owing to a slight increase in play fighting among females and a decrease among males, no sex difference was seen when the animals were retested on day 40. Subsequent investigations employing variants of the paired encounter procedure also yielded a sex difference in favor of the male (Birke & Sadler, 1983; Holloway & Thor, 1983; Thor and Holloway, 1985).

Unanimity is not to be had, however, for reports also appeared in which reliable sex differences in the play fighting of paired male and female rats were *not* observed (Panksepp & Beatty, 1980; Panksepp et al., 1984; Takahashi & Lore, 1983). These disparate findings may be related, at least in part, to certain aspects of the paired encounter procedure. According to Thor and Holloway (1984a), a sex difference is more likely to emerge if tests are conducted in the home cage of one member of the pair following several days of social isolation. Pellis and Pellis (1990) proposed that the probability of observing a sex difference is increased if familiar rather than strange juveniles are paired.

Beyond nuances such as those mentioned above, the paired encounter procedure may suffer overall from its artificiality. Young rats do not normally find themselves in dyads, let alone same-sex dyads, and they do not often encounter novel environments such as those provided by the test chamber. Sex differences in play fighting have been reported consistently using the more natural *focal animal* procedure, which consists in housing the juveniles in groups that are left undisturbed throughout the testing period. Observations are made for brief periods throughout the day, with data usually gathered across a number of days.

Unlike the disparate findings from experiments using the paired encounter procedure, most investigations using the focal observation technique do report reliable sex differences. Meaney and Stewart (1981), for example, kept animals in groups of six and made 20-second observations 70 times a day. Between the ages of 26 and 40 days males play fought about 40% more frequently than did females. Similar findings have been presented by Beatty et al. (1982), Meaney and McEwen (1986), and Meaney, Stewart, Paulin, & McEwen (1983).

Whether a sex difference in the play fighting of juvenile rats is found depends in large measure on methodology. A male–female difference is much more likely to be observed under conditions of ongoing social interaction than under circumstances in which animals are removed from the group and paired in a strange environment. In any event, such descriptive research does not by itself warrant ascribing to the endocrine system a role in the development of play fighting. To do that one must examine the behavior following direct hormonal manipulations.

Manipulative Research

The effect of hormonal manipulation on play fighting of the rat was first demonstrated by Olioff and Stewart (1978), who injected some 1-day-old males and females with testosterone while the remaining animals received only the sesame oil vehicle within which the hormone was dissolved. The results, depicted in Figure 7.8, are as follows: (1) oil-treated males play fought more than oil-treated females; (2) testosterone-treated females engaged in more play than did oil-treated females but did not differ from oil-treated males; (3) testosterone-treated males did not differ from oil-treated males or from testosterone-treated females.

A confirmatory and more detailed account was subsequently provided by Meaney and Stewart (1981). They reasoned that since early androgen exposure augments play fighting in the female, gonadectomy of young males should *reduce* it. Because the notion of preferential female differentiation (see Chapter

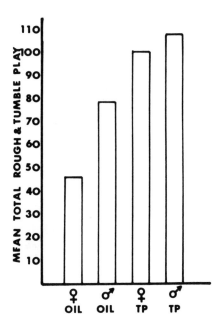

Figure 7.8 Rough-and-tumble play scores (means) for oil-treated (OIL) and testosterone-treated (TP) male and female rats on tests run at 22, 26, and 30 days of age. (From Olioff and Stewart, "Sex differences in the play behavior of prepubescent rats." *Physiology and Behavior, 20,* 113–15. © 1978 by Pergamon Press. Reprinted by permission.)

3) assumes that ovarian secretions play little if any role in sexual differentiation, it also was predicted that neither gonadectomy nor estrogen treatment would alter levels of play fighting of the female. Both predictions were confirmed. Males gonadectomized on day 1 (but not on day 23) exhibited a subsequent decline of play fighting when assessed between days 26 and 40, *and* the play behavior of females was unaffected by gonadectomy performed on day 1 and by estradiol treatment on the first and second day of life.

Meaney and Stewart's results reveal that the expression of play fighting is influenced by the presence of androgen during early development. By day 23, however, the hormone is unnecessary, as gonadectomy on that day does not affect the behavior. Beatty, Dodge, Traylor, and Meaney (1981) further demarcated the period during which androgen stimulation is necessary by showing that gonadectomy of the male as early as day 10 did not affect the subsequent display of the behavior. Therefore although androgen prior to day 10 of life is required to produce a male-typical level of play fighting, its presence is not necessary during the period within which play fighting is exhibited.

Despite the fact that the administration of testosterone alters the propensity to play fight, it is possible that the effect actually is caused by another hormone. After testosterone enters a neuron, a small fraction of it may be converted to the estrogen estradiol or to another androgen, 5α-dihydrotestosterone. We already have seen that estradiol does not influence play fighting when given to a female. Meaney and Stewart (1981) further showed that 5α-dihydrotestosterone also is ineffective. Therefore testosterone rather than one of its by-products is responsible for the development of male-typical levels of play fighting.

An issue often considered by those concerned with hormones and behavior is brain localization. Precisely where in the brain does a hormone exert its influence? This was addressed vis-a-vis play fighting by Meaney and McEwen (1986), who placed various amounts of testosterone in the amygdala of 1-day-old female rats. The amygdala was chosen because it contains androgen receptors and because amygdaloid lesions made on day 21 or 22 reduce play fighting of males to female levels while producing no effect on females (Meaney et al., 1981). Females given the largest amount of testosterone play fought at rates indistinguishable from those of males, a finding that implicates the amygdala in the testosterone-produced enhancement of play fighting. Whether other brain regions also yield facilitatory effects following direct testosterone application awaits the results of further experimentation.

Testosterone is not the only hormone that influences play fighting. Glucocorticoids also are effective. Male rats administered corticosterone on days 1 and 2 or on days 3 and 4 displayed a reduction in play fighting, whereas those treated on days 9 and 10 or daily from days 26 to 40 were unaffected (Meaney & Stewart, 1983; Meaney, Stewart, & Beatty, 1982). Females, on the hand, are unaffected by corticosterone treatment regardless of when it is given. This result implies that an attenuation of play fighting also should be evident in males that have been exposed to glucocorticoid-releasing stressful stimuli during early life. To my knowledge, this possibility has not been examined.

Because glucocorticoids neither adversely affect circulating levels of testosterone nor influence the intracellular receptor binding of that hormone and because portions of the brain contain glucocorticoid receptors, Meaney et al. (1985) believed that glucocorticoids act *independently* to attenuate play fighting. Exactly how it might be accomplished is unknown.

Data culled from nonhuman primates also implicate the endocrine system in the development of play fighting. As mentioned in Chapter 3 (see Figure 3.6), Goy and Phoenix (1971) discovered that female rhesus monkeys exposed prenatally to an abnormally high amount of testosterone exhibit levels of rough-and-tumble play typical of those shown by males. The period of testosterone sensitivity in the rhesus monkey encompassess a segment of prenatal development but, unlike in the rat, apparently not postnatal development. Neither testosterone treatment of 3- to 4-month-old females (Joslyn, 1973) nor castrating males at birth (Goy, 1970) affect play fighting.

It also is worth reiterating (see Chapter 3) that human females exposed prenatally to higher-than-normal levels of androgen were reported to show an enhanced preference for "boys'" toys and for a male-like expenditure of physical energy during play (Ehrhardt & Baker, 1977; Ehrhardt & Money, 1967). We do not know, however, if these girls engaged in elevated levels of play fighting.

Neurochemistry

Identification of the neurochemical substrate of play fighting consists in administering pharmacological agents that affect specific central nervous system neurotransmitter function. In so doing, neuronal transmission and thus play behavior itself should be affected. Ideally, one wishes to uncover a drug with *behavioral specificity,* one that affects only play fighting. Such specificity would mitigate against the argument that an effect on play fighting is secondary to an overall behavioral alteration. Moreover, it also is desirous to achieve *pharmacological specificity* by demonstrating that complementary strategies, the administration of an agonist or antagonist, either yield opposite behavioral effects or neutralize one another.

Play fighting has been assessed following the administration of numerous drugs. The results have been summarized by Thor and Holloway (1984b) and are shown in Table 7.2. It is apparent that most centrally active drugs tend to influence play fighting and that with few exceptions the effect consists in a decrease in the behavior.

Detailed descriptions of the experiments that assess the effect of the myriad drugs listed in Table 7.2 on play behavior would be tedious and, more importantly, probably not a fruitful exercise given the episodic nature of much of the work. Instead, we focus on the most programmatic of the research, that of Panksepp and his colleagues. Their research is derived from an overall program designed to explore the involvement of the endogenous brain opioid system (endorphins) in social behavior and in what has been referred to as social emotions (Panksepp, Herman, Vilberg, Bishop, & De Eskinazi, 1978). If you recall (see Chapter 5), Panksepp contends that brain opioids mediate social affect—specifically, that opioids reduce the distress associated with social separation.

Panksepp et al. (1978) discovered that the administration of the opioid morphine increases the pinning behavior associated with play fighting, whereas the opioid anatgonist naloxone decreases pinning. Furthermore, because morphine at the dosage used by Panksepp somewhat *reduces* motor activity, it seems highly unlikely that it increases play fighting through a nonspecific attenuating effect on general activity. Similarly, naloxone, although reducing play, produces no significant effect on activity (Siegel, Jensen, & Panksepp, 1985). Because morphine was especially effective in juveniles having been isolated just prior to the play fighting session (Panksepp employed the paired encounter procedure), it was suggested that "morphine, by reducing the isolation distress produced a central state which was more compatible with vigorous play." Similar findings were later reported by Beatty and Costello (1982) and Panksepp, Jalowiec, DeEskinazi, and Bishop (1985).

If a morphine-stimulated nervous system is indeed more suitable for vigorous play, morphine-treated juvenile rats should tend to be dominant (exhibit more pinning) during play encounters, whereas animals administered the antagonist naloxone should tend to be less dominant (pinned more often). These predictions were tested by Panksepp et al. (1985), who in one experiment found that naloxone markedly decreased and morphine modestly increased pinning. Morphine also tended to increase the dominance of submissive animals, and naloxone tended to decrease the dominance of dominant animals. Normansell and Panksepp (1990) further reported that the central opioid system, while affecting the expression of play, presumably does not influence the motivation to play. Whereas morphine-treated rats engaged in more play fighting and naloxone-treated animals less play fighting than controls, neither treatment affected the

Table 7.2 Drug effects on social play in juvenile rats

Investigator (s)	Drug(s)	Dose (mg/kg)	Effect
Einon et al. 1978	D-Amphetamine	2	Decrease
	Chlorpromazine	2	Decrease
Panksepp et al. 1980	Naloxone	0.5–5.0	Decrease
	Morphine	0.5–2.0	Increase (isolates)
Panksepp 1980	Chlorpromazine	1	Decrease
	D-Amphetamine	1	Decrease
	Fenfluramine	2.5–10.0	Decrease
	Naloxone	1–5	Decrease
	Quipazine	5–10	Decrease (marked)
	Methysergide	5	Increase
	Morphine	0.5–1.0	Increase (isolates)
			Decrease (nonisolates)
Humphreys et al.	D-Amphetamine	2	Decrease
1981	Chlorpromazine	2–8	Decrease
Beatty et al. 1982	D-Amphetamine	0.125–1.000	Decrease
	Methylphenidate	0.5–4.0	Decrease
Beatty et al. 1982	Naloxone	1–10	Decrease
Normansell et al. 1982	Naloxone	1	Decrease (slower entry to play chamber)
Siviy et al. 1982	Naloxone	1	Decrease (food-deprived)
Beatty, 1983	Methylscopolamine	0.125–1.000	None
	Scopolamine	0.125–1.000	Decrease
Beatty et al. 1983	D-Amphetamine	0.25–1.00	Decrease
	4-OH-amphetamine	0.25–4.00	Decrease
Holloway et al. 1983	Caffeine	10–40	Decrease
Siviy et al. 1983	Morphine	1	Increase
Thor et al. 1982	Scopolamine	0.3–4.0	Decrease
	Methylscopolamine	3	None

acquisition of a spatial discrimination task (T maze) reinforced by the opportunity to play fight.

The findings of Panksepp and his colleagues place play fighting within the wider context of social-emotional behavior and may be indicative of a modulatory role for endogenous opioids. However two important issues relating to the generality of the findings must be addressed. First, do manipulations of the opioid system affect play fighting in species other than the rat? Second, are opioids effective in situations other than those for which periods of social isolation precede the pairing of animals? The fact that opioids have been implicated in emotional expression instigated by social isolation and that the opioid enhancement of play fighting is principally seen in juveniles following periods of isolation suggest that the data may not generalize to play fighting displayed during the more naturally occurring long-term social interactions such as those assessed with the focal animal technique.

Table 7.2 (*Continued*)   Drug effects on social play in juvenile rats

Investigator(s)	Drug(s)	Dose (mg/kg)	Effect
Thor et al. 1983	Caffeine		Decrease
	D-Amphetamine		Decrease
	Methylphenidate		Decrease
Beatty et al. 1984	Amphetamine	0.5–1.0	Decrease
	Haloperidol	0.05–0.80	Decrease
	Chlorpromazine	0.5–5.0	Decrease
	Phenoxybenzamine	0.5–20.0	Decrease
	Propranolol	10–20	Decrease
	Clonidine	0.05–0.20	Decrease
	a-Methyltyrosine	100	None
	Ephedrine	10–80	Decrease
	Apomorphine	0.125–1.000	Increase
Holloway et al. 1984	Caffeine	5–40	Decrease (acute)
		9–150	Increase (chronic)
Thor et al. 1984	Scopolamine	20 (daily)	Increase (following withdrawal)
Thor et al. 1984	D-Amphetamine	6–12 (daily)	Decrease (no effect after 1st day of exposure)
Holloway et al.	Caffeine	0–10	Decrease
	Haloperidol	0–10	Decrease
	2-Chloroadenosine	0–10	Decrease (caffeine and 2-chloroadenosine given together reverse the effects of the other)

Source: From Thor and Holloway. Social play in juvenile rats: a decade of methodological and experimental research. *Neuroscience and Biobehavioral Reviews* 8:455–464. © 1984 by Pergamon Press. Reprinted by permission.

CONCLUDING COMMENTS

Experimental analysis of play or, more accurately, of play fighting, consists primarily in determining how the central nervous system governs its display. It is done by observing the behavior of brain-damaged animals, animals with altered brain chemistry, and hormonally aberrant subjects. It appears to me that the most persuasive data concerning the control of play fighting have been derived from studies involving the endocrine system, in particular the influence of androgen. Observations of ongoing social behavior reveal that males play fight more frequently and more intensely than females. Moreover, straightforward experimental maneuvers yield predictable results; young females exposed to androgen subsequently play at levels characteristic of the male, whereas males with much reduced levels of androgen come to resemble females. Androgen therefore permanently modifies a component of the brain that governs play fighting behavior.

The link between androgen and play fighting should come as no great surprise in view of the similar relation between androgen and serious fighting behavior. One might instead be struck by the efficiency of a system in which two behaviors—nonserious fighting and serious fighting—share the same biological substrate. On the other hand, the system might not be efficient at all. Rather, the fact that the proclivities to engage in two putatively distinct but similar forms of behavior are both regulated by androgen may mean that the behaviors are actually one and the same, that the adult version differs somewhat owing to physical maturation and to experience obtained during the juvenile period. So we have come full circle, returning to the question posed at the beginning of the chapter. Is play a separate class of behavior? Regardless of whether it is distinct behavior, however, the primary issue is ascertaining the functional significance of that early-exhibited activity. Accordingly, the focus of research with nonhuman animals perhaps should be shifted away from the question of how play is controlled to the much more difficult task of assessing the function, if any, it serves in behavioral development.

REFERENCES

Aldis, O. (1975). *Play fighting.* Orlando, FL: Academic Press.

Baenninger, L. P. (1967). Comparison of behavioural development in socially isolated and grouped rats. *Animal Behaviour, 15,* 312–23.

Baldwin, J. D., and Baldwin, J. I. (1974). Exploration and social play in squirrel monkeys *(Saimiri). American Zoologist, 14,* 303–15.

Beatty, W. W., and Costello, K. B. (1982). Naloxone and play fighting in juvenile rate. *Pharmacology, Biochemistry and Behavior, 17,* 905–7.

Beatty, W. W., and Costello, K. B. (1983). Medial hypothalamic lesions and play fighting in juvenile rats. *Physiology and Behavior, 31,* 141–5.

Beatty, W. W., Dodge, A., Traylor, K., Donegan, J., and Godding, P. (1982). Septal lesions increase play fighting in juvenile rats. *Physiology and Behavior, 28,* 649–52.

Beatty, W. W., Dodge, A. M., Traylor, K. L., and Meaney, M. J. (1981). Temporal boundary of the sensitive period for hormonal organization of social play in juvenile rats. *Physiology and Behavior, 26,* 241–43.

Beck, B. B. (1980). *Animal tool behavior: The use of stone.* New York: Garland.

Bekoff, M. (1972). The development of social interaction, play and metacommunication in mammals: An ethological perspective. *Quarterly Review of Biology, 47,* 412–34.

Bekoff, M. (1974). Social play and play-soliciting by infant Canids. *American Zoologist, 14,* 323–40.

Bekoff, M., and Byers, J. A. (1981). A critical reanalysis of the ontogeny and phylogeny of mammalian social and locomotor play: An ethological hornet's nest. In K. Immelmann, G. W. Barlow, L. Petrinovich, and M. Mains (Eds.), *Behavioral development: The Beielefeld Interdisciplinary Project* (pp. 296–337). Cambridge: Cambridge University Press.

Birke, L. I. A., and Sadler, D. (1983). Progestin-induced changes in play behaviour of the prepubertal rat. *Physiology and Behavior, 30,* 341–47.

Blurton-Jones, N. (1976). Rough-and-tumble play among nursery school children. In J. S. Bruner, A. Jolly, and K. Sylva (Eds.), *Play—Its role in development and evolution* (pp. 352–63). New York: Basic Books.

Bolles, R. C., and Woods, P. J. (1964). The ontogeny of behaviour in the albino rat. *Animal Behaviour, 12,* 427–41.

Brown, S. G. (1988). Play behaviour in lowland gorillas: Age differences, sex differences, and possible functions. *Primates, 29,* 219–28.

Capitanio, J. P., and Reite, M. (1984). The roles of early separation experience and prior familiarity in the social relations of pigtail macaques: A descriptive multivariate study. *Primates, 25,* 475–84.

Chalmers, N. R., and Locke-Haydon, J. (1984). Correlations among measures of playfulness and skillfulness in captive common marmosets *(Callithrix jacchus jacchus). Developmental Psychobiology, 17,* 191–208.

DeVore, I. (1963). Mother-infant relations in free-ranging baboons. In H. L. Rheingold (Ed.), *Maternal behavior in mammals* (pp. 305–35). New York: John Wiley & Sons.

Ehrhardt, A. A., and Baker, S. W. (1977). Males and females with congenital adrenal hyperplasia: A family study of intelligence and gender-related behavior. In P. A. Lee, L. P. Plotnick, A. A. Kowarski, and C. J. Migeon (Eds.), *Congenital adrenal hyperplasia* (pp. 447–61.) Baltimore: University Park Press.

Ehrhardt, A. A., and Money, J. (1967). Progestin-induced hermaphroditism: IQ and psychosexual identity in a study of ten girls. *Journal of Sex Research, 3,* 83–100.

Einon, D. F., and Morgan, M. J. (1977). A critical period for social isolation in the rat. *Developmental Psychobiology, 10,* 123–32.

Einon, D., and Potegal, M. (1991). Enhanced defense in adult rats deprived of playfighting experience as juveniles. *Aggressive Behavior, 17,* 27–40.

Fagen, R. M. (1976). Exercise, play and physical training in animals. In P. P. G. Bateson and P. H. Klopher (Eds.), *Perspectives in ethology,* vol. 2 (pp. 227–53). New York: Plenum Press.

Gentry, R. L. (1974). The development of social behavior through play in the Steller sea lion. *American Zoologist, 14,* 391–403.

Goldberg, S., and Lewis, M. (1969). Play behavior in the year-old infant: Early sex differences. *Child Development, 40,* 21–32.

Goldfoot, D. A., and Wallen, K. (1978). Development of gender role behaviors in heterosexual and isosexual groups of infant rhesus monkeys. *Recent Advances in Primatology, 1,* 155–60.

Goldman, L., and Swanson, H. H. (1975). Developmental changes in pre-adult behavior in confined colonies of golden hamsters. *Developmental Psychobiology, 8,* 137–50.

Goy, R. W. (1970). Early hormonal influences on the development of sexual and sex-related behavior. In F. O. Schmitt (Ed.), *The neurosciences: Second study program* (pp. 196–206). New York: Rockefeller University Press.

Goy, R. W. (1978). Development of play and mounting behavior in female rhesus virilized prenatally with esters of testosterone or dihydrotestosterone. *Recent Advances in Primatology, 1,* 449–62.

Goy, R. W., and Phoenix, C. H. (1971). The effects of testosterone propionate administered before birth on the development of behavior in genetic female rhesus monkeys. In C. Sawyer and R. Gorski (Eds.), *Steroid hormones and brain function* (pp. 193–202). Berkely: University of California Press.

Groos, K. (1898). *The play of animals.* New York: Appleton and Company.

Hall, G. S. (1908). *Adolescence: Its psychology and its relation to physiology, anthropology, sex, crime and education,* vol. I. New York: Appleton and Company.

Henry, J. D., and Herrero, S. M. (1974). Social play in the American black bear: Its similarity to Canid social play and an examination of its identifying characteristics. *American Zoologist, 14,* 371–89.

Hole, G. (1988). Temporal features of social play in the laboratory rat. *Ethology, 78,* 1–20.

Hole, G. (1991). Proximity measures of social play in the laboratory rat. *Developmental Psychobiology, 24,* 117–33.

Hole, G. J., and Einon, D. F. (1984). Play in rodents. In P. K. Smith (Ed.), *Play in animals and humans* (pp. 95–117). Oxford: Basic Blackwell Publisher.

Holloway, W. R., and Thor, D. H. (1983). Caffeine: Effects on the behaviors of juvenile rats. *Neurobehavioral Toxicology and Teratology, 5,* 127–37.

Huffman, M. A., and Quiatt, D. (1986). Stone handling by Japanese macaques *(Macaca fuscata):* Implications for tool use of stone. *Primates, 27,* 413–23.

Humphreys, A. P., and Einon, D. F. (1981). Play as a reinforcer for maze-learning in juvenile rats. *Animal Behaviour, 29,* 259–70.

Joslyn, W. D. (1973). Androgen-induced social dominance in infant female rhesus monkeys. *Journal of Psychology and Psychiatry, 14,* 137–45.

Klinger, H. J., and Kemble, E. D. (1985). Effects of housing space and litter size on play behavior in rats. *Bulletin of the Psychonomic Society, 23,* 75–77.

Kummer, H. (1971). *Primate societies: Group techniques of ecological adaptation.* Chicago: Aldine Atherton.

Lazar, J. W., and Beckhorn, G. D. (1974). The concept of play or the development of social behavior in ferrets *(Mustela putorious). American Zoologist, 14,* 405–14.

Leedy, M. G., Vela, E. A., Popolow, H. B., and Gerall, A. A. (1980). Effects of prepubertal medial preoptic area lesions on male sexual behavior. *Physiology and Behavior, 24,* 341–46.

Loizos, C. (1966). Play in mammals. In P. A. Jewell and C. Loizos (Eds.), *Play, exploration and territory in mammals* (pp. 6–8). London: Zoological Society of London.

Martin, P., and Bateson, P. (1985). The influence of experimentally manipulating a component of weaning on the development of play in domestic cats. *Animal Behaviour, 33,* 511–18.

Meaney, M. J., and McEwen, B. S. (1986). Testosterone implants into the amygdala during the neonatal period masculinize the social play of juvenile rats. *Brain Research, 398,* 324–28.

Meaney, M. J., and Stewart, J. (1981). Neonatal androgens influence the social play of prepubescent rats. *Hormones and Behavior, 15,* 197–213.

Meaney, M. J., and Stewart, J. (1983). The influence of exogenous testosterone and corticosterone on the social behavior of prepubertal male rats. *Bulletin of the Psychonomic Society, 21,* 232–34.

Meaney, M. J., Dodge, A. M., and Beatty, W. W. (1981). Sex-dependent effects of amygdaloid lesions on the social play of pubertal rats. *Physiology and Behavior, 26,* 467–72.

Meaney, M. J., Stewart, J., and Beatty, W. W. (1982). The effects of neonatal glucocorticoids on the social play of juvenile rats. *Hormones and Behavior, 16,* 475–91.

Meaney, M. J., Stewart, J., Paulin, P., and McEwen, B. (1983). Sexual differentiation of social play in rat pups is mediated by the neonatal androgen-receptor system. *Neuroendocrinology, 37,* 85–90.

Meaney, M. J., Stewart, J., and Beatty, W. W. (1985). Sex differences in social play: The socialization of sex roles. *Advances in the Study of Behavior, 15,* 1–58.

Muller-Schwarze, D. (1968). Play deprivation in deer. *Behaviour, 31,* 144–62.

Murphy, M. R., MacLean, P. D., and Hamilton, S. C. (1981). Species-typical behaviors of hamsters deprived from birth of the neocortex. *Science, 213,* 459–61.

Myer, J. S., and White, R. T. (1965). Aggressive motivation in the rat. *Animal Behaviour, 13,* 430–33.

Normansell, L. A., and Panksepp, J. (1984). Play in decorticate rats. *Society for Neuroscience Abstracts, 10,* 612.

Normansell, L., and Panksepp, J. (1990). Effects of morphine and naloxone on play-rewarded spatial discrimination in juvenile rats. *Developmental Psychobiology, 23,* 75–83.

Olioff, M., and Stewart, J. (1978). Sex differences in the play behavior of prepubescent rats. *Physiology and Behavior, 20,* 113–15.

Owens, N. W. (1975). Social play behaviour in free-living baboons, *Papio anubis. Animal Behaviour, 23,* 387–408.

Panksepp, J. (1981). The ontogeny of play in rats. *Developmental Psychobiology, 14,* 327–32.

Panksepp, J. (1986). The psychobiology of prosocial behaviors: Separation distress, play, and altruism. In C. Zahn-Waxler, E. M. Cummings, and R. Iannotti (Eds.), *Altruism and aggression: Biological and social origin* (pp. 465–92). Cambridge: Cambridge University Press.

Panksepp, J., and Beatty, W. W. (1980). Social deprivation and play in rats. *Behavioral and Neural Biology, 30,* 197–206.

Panksepp, J., Herman, B. H., Vilberg, T., Bishop, P., and DeEskinazi, F. G. (1978). Endogenous opioids and social behavior. *Neuroscience and Biobehavioral Reviews, 4,* 473–87.

Panksepp, J., Siviy, S., and Normansell, L. (1984). The psychobiology of play: theoretical and methodological perspectives. *Neuroscience and Biobehavioral Reviews, 8,* 465–92.

Panksepp, J., Jalowiec, J., DeEskinazi, F. G., and Bishop, P. (1985). Opiates and play dominance in juvenile rats. *Behavioral Neuroscience, 99,* 441–53.

Partington, J. T., and Grant, C. (1984). Imaginary playmates and other useful fantasies. In P. K. Smith (Ed.), *Play in animals and humans* (pp. 217–140). Oxford: Basil Blackwell Publisher.

Pellis, S. M., and Pellis, V. C. (1987). Play-fighting differs from serious fighting in both target of attack and tactics of fighting in the laboratory rat *Rattus norvegicus. Aggressive Behavior, 13,* 227–42.

Pellis, S. M., and Pellis, V. C. (1988a). Identification of the possible origin of the body target that differentiates play fighting from serious fighting in Syrian golden hamsters *(Mesocricetus auratus). Aggressive Behavior, 14,* 437–49.

Pellis, S. M., and Pellis, V. C. (1988b). Play-fighting in the Syrian golden hamster *Mesocricetus auratus Waterhouse,* and its relationship to serious fighting during post-weaning development. *Developmental Psychobiology, 21,* 323–37.

Pellis, S. M., and Pellis, V. C. (1990). Differential rates of attack, defense, and counterattack during the developmental decrease in play fighting by male and female rats. *Developmental Psychobiology, 23,* 215–31.

Poole, T. B. (1966). Aggressive play in polecats. In P. A. Jewell and C. Loizos (Eds.), *Play, exploration and territory in mammals* (pp. 23–37). London: Zoological Society of London.

Poole, T. B. (1972). Diadic interactions between pairs of male polecats *Mustela furo* and *Mustela Furo × M. putorius)* under standrdized environmental conditions during the breeding season. *Zeitschrift fur Tierpsychologie, 30,* 45–58.

Poole, T. B., and Fish, J. (1975). An investigation of playful behaviour in *Rattus norvegicus* and *Mus musculus* (Mammalia). *Journal of the Zoological Society, London, 175,* 61–71.

Potegal, M., and Einon, D. (1989). Aggressive behaviors in adult rats deprived of play
    fighting experience as juveniles. *Developmental Psychobiology, 22,* 159–66.
Reinhardt, V., and Reinhardt, A. (1982). Mock fighting in cattle. *Behaviour, 81,* 1–13.
Rosenblum, L. A. (1968). Mother-infant relations and early behavioral development in
    the squirrel monkey. In L. A. Rosenblum and R. W. Cooper (Eds.), *The squirrel
    monkey* (pp. 164–79). Orlando, FL: Academic Press.
Sahakian, B., Robbins, T., Morgan, M. J., and Iverson, S. (1975). The effects of psycho-
    motor stimulants on stereotypy and locomotor activity in socially deprived and
    control rats. *Brain Research, 84,* 195–205.
Schlosberg, H. (1947). The concept of play. *Psychological Review, 54,* 229–31.
Siegel, M. A., Jensen, R. A., and Panksepp, J. (1985). The prolonged effects of naloxone
    on play behavior and feeding in the rat. *Behavioral and Neural Biology, 44,* 509–
    14.
Siviy, S. M., and Panksepp, J. (1987). Dorsomedial diencephalic involvement in juvenile
    play in rats. *Behavioral Neuroscience, 99,* 1103–13.
Smith, P. K., and Simon, T. (1984). Object play, problem-solving and creativity in chil-
    dren. In P. K. Smith (Ed.), *Play in animals and humans* (pp. 199–216). Oxford:
    Basil Blackwell Publisher.
Spencer, H. (1878). *The principles of psychology,* vol. II. New York: Appleton & Com-
    pany.
Takahashi, L. K., and Lore, R. K. (1983). Play fighting and the development of agonistic
    behavior in male and female rats. *Aggressive Behavior, 9,* 217–27.
Taylor, G. T. (1980). Fighting in juvenile rats and the ontogeny of agonistic behavior.
    Journal of Comparative and Physiological Psychology, 94, 953–61.
Tellegen, A., Horn, J. M., and Legrand, R. G. (1969). Opportunity for aggression as a
    reinforcer in mice. *Psychonomic Science, 14,* 104–5.
Thor, D. H., and Holloway, W. R. (1984a). Sex and social play in juvenile rats *(Rattus
    norvegicus). Journal of Comparative Psychology, 98,* 276–84.
Thor, D. H., and Holloway, W. R. (1984b). Social play in juvenile rats: A decade of meth-
    odological and experimental research. *Neuroscience and Biobehavioral Reviews,
    8,* 455–64.
Thor, D. H., and Holloway, W. R. (1985). Play soliciting behavior in prepubertal and
    postpubertal male rats. *Animal Learning and Behavior, 13,* 327–30.
Van Hemel, P. E. (1972). Aggression as a reinforcer: Operant behavior in the mouse-kill-
    ing rat. *Journal of the Experimental Analysis of Behavior, 17,* 237–45.
Walder, R. (1933). The psychoanalytic theory of play. *Psychoanalytic Quarterly, 2,* 208–
    24.
Waterman, J. M. (1988). Social play in free-ranging Columbian ground squirrels, *Sper-
    mophilus columbianus. Ethology, 77,* 225–36.

8

Learning and Memory

The mechanism of the conditioned reflex is ready in all its parts
from the day of birth.   I. Pavlov, 1928

We are so much accustomed to this lack of the impressions of
childhood that we are apt to overlook the problem underlying it
and are inclined to explain it as a self-evident consequence of
the rudimentary character of the mental activities of children.
Actually, however, a normally developed child of three or four
already exhibits an enormous amount of highly organized mental functioning in the comparisons and inferences which he
makes and in the expression of his feelings; and there is no obvious reason why amnesia should overtake psychical acts, which
carry no less weight than those of a later age.   S. Freud, 1899

Survival depends in large measure on the organism's ability to acquire behaviors
that allow it to meet challenges posed by an often-changing environment. Those
environmental challenges, although at times ephemeral, often persist for days,
weeks, or even throughout a lifetime. A particular behavior, then, must be sustained for as long as the eliciting circumstance exists. Furthermore, a particular
environmental condition, once gone, may reappear. Thus information regarding the relation between that condition and a behavior must be accessible to the
organism so it can react efficiently should a similar situation arise. That is to say,
the organism must be able to acquire a behavior that allows it to meet an environmental demand, to exhibit the behavior for as long as necessary, and to retain
information about it for future use.

The ability to acquire behavior is present prior to birth or hatching. If you
recall from Chapter 2, the behavior of embryos can be modified using both classical and instrumental conditioning procedures. However, because of both the
immaturity of their central nervous systems and their restricted environmental
niche, embryonic conditioning is of a rudimentary sort. The ability to learn relations between stimuli and between stimuli and responses truly blossoms, however, once the organism emerges from the confines of the relatively safe, maternally buffered amniotic environment into a comparatively bewildering world in
which the burden to survive is soon placed squarely on its shoulders. The intent
of this chapter is to chronicle the postembryonic development of learning and
remembering.

Before proceeding to a discussion of the research, an issue relating directly to both methodological considerations and the interpretation of data must be considered. The issue, familiar to those involved in the study of conditioning and learning and one that takes on added significance when dealing with the developing organism, is the distinction between learning and performance. Learning is a theoretical concept that cannot be measured directly. Rather, it is inferred from a subject's performance. The problem, then, is to determine whether a given factor affects learning *or* performance, whether it influences the organism's capacity to modify its behavior or its ability to perform the appropriate response. A prime example concerns age. Suppose that 12-day-old rats deprived of milk for 4 hours can be trained to perform a certain voluntary response, with milk serving as reinforcement, whereas identically treated 6-day-olds do not acquire the response. Is it evidence that the 6-day-old lacks the capacity for instrumental learning? Certainly not. It might be that the 6-day-old is incapable of performing the response, that 4 hours of food deprivation is an insufficient motivator for them or that milk is an inappropriate reinforcer for the younger subjects. Regarding the latter, rats are unable to differentiate some types of positive reinforcement from negative reinforcement until the second week of life (Camp & Rudy, 1988).

Distinguishing factors that affect learning from those that influence performance presents a practical problem with regard to the design of experiments concerned with the ontogeny of learning and memory because it is often the case that the physical requirement of a task effectively differs for animals of different ages. It is much more difficult for a 3-day-old rat to traverse a straight alley than it is for a 10-day-old. In other words, it is more difficult for the younger animals to *perform.* In this example one can attempt to equate the physical demands by testing the 3-day-olds in a shortened version of the alley.

Although the learning–performance dichotomy must of necessity be of major concern, it is not the only issue that has to be considered. Others include the discernment of actual age-related differences in the ability to remember a previously acquired behavior from a secondary effect produced by an amount of original learning and, as alluded to above, equating levels of motivation and reinforcement among subjects of varying age, to recite but a few. A valuable discussion of the difficulties that confront those who conduct research into the ontogeny of learning and memory is provided by Spear (1978).

Now that some of the important general concerns pertaining to the study of learning and memory have been explored, we are ready to consider substantive issues. Let us begin with acquisition of the classically conditioned response and then consider acquisition of the instrumental response.

ACQUISITION

Classical Conditioning

Classical conditioning was viewed originally as a procedure whereby a formerly neutral stimulus (the *conditioned stimulus,* or CS) acquires the capacity to elicit a response (the *conditioned response,* or CR). Now, however, it is considered to be more than a procedure for imbuing stimuli with response-eliciting properties. It is thought to be a means by which organisms obtain predictive knowledge about their environment. That is, the CS permits the organism to anticipate and thus prepare for the arrival of a stimulus (unconditioned stimulus, or UCS) that will reflexively evoke a particular response (unconditioned response, or UCR).

Data from Nonhumans

The earliest demonstration of classical conditioning in young animals was reported by Caldwell and Werboff (1962). A CS consisting of a vibrating rod applied to the chest was paired with electrical shock delivered to the foreleg (UCS) of newborn rats (their exact ages were not stated) that were suspended in a harness. Shock elicited flexion of the leg, the UCR. The *interstimulus interval* (ISI), the time between the onset of the CS and onset of the UCS was either 300, 600, 1200, or 2400 msec. The results are depicted in Figure 8.1. With repeated

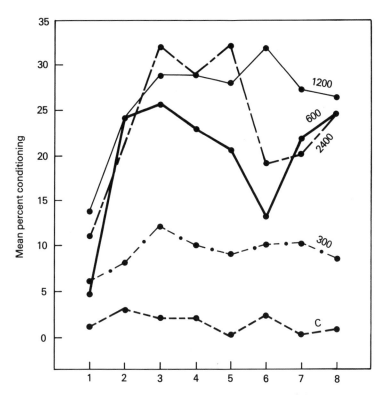

Figure 8.1 Mean percentages of conditioned responses for newborn rats trained according to a classic conditioning procedure with intervals between conditioned (CS) and unconditioned stimuli (UCS) of 300, 600, 1200, and 2400 ms. Control animals (C) were presented only with the CS. (From Caldwell and Werboff, "Classical conditioning in newborn rats." *Science, 136,* 1118–119. © 1962 by The American Association for the Advancement of Science. Reprinted by permission.)

pairing the CS acquired the ability to elicit the leg flexion response with the most effective ISIs being between 600 and 2400 msec. According to the authors, the level of conditioning exhibited by the neonates, especially those given the ISI of 2400 msec., is similar to that exhibited by adults.

Caldwell and Werboff's findings suggest that the rat's capability to display classical conditioning does not evolve during the course of early postnatal development but, rather, is present at birth at a level comparable to that of the adult. According to Rudy and his associates, however, classical conditioning may not necessarily appear in younger animals because it is dependent on maturation of the sensory system, which conveys information about the CS. Hyson and Rudy (1984) exposed 10-, 12-, 14- and 16-day-old rat pups to paired presentations of a either a 90-dB, 2000-Hz continuous tone (CS) and a 10% sucrose solution infused directly into the mouth via a cannula implanted in the cheek (UCS) *or* a 90-dB, 22-Hz train of clicks and the UCS. The UCS elicited a mouthing response that was eventually evoked by the CS. Ten training sessions were given daily.

The data revealed that age is a decisive factor in determining the effectiveness of CS–UCS pairings; regardless of the type of auditory CS, a continuous tone or clicks, pairings of the CS and UCS given prior to day 14 were ineffective in establishing conditioning. Because the external ear is closed on day 10 and is fully open by day 14, the inability to establish conditioning prior to day 14 may have been caused by the fact that the auditory CS was attenuated. However, it appears not to have been the case because pups less than 14 days of age, although they do not acquire the CR, do respond reflexively to auditory stimulation. Also, increasing the intensity of the CS does not facilitate conditioning. Stated Hyson and Rudy:

> From this pattern of results it appears that the processes through which acoustic stimulation exerts its control over reflexive behaviors are *dissociated* during ontogenesis. The processes that mediate reflexive reactions appear functional prior to those that support the learning reflected in the establishment of the conditioned responding. [p. 278]

They speculated that the capacity to form an association between an auditory CS and a UCS is dependent on the stage of development of the ascending auditory system, which matures in the following caudal-rostral direction: cochlea→ brainstem→midbrain→thalamus→auditory cortex. Therefore reflexive reactions to sound require that auditory signals reach only caudal structures of the ascending auditory system, whereas learning to respond in a particular manner to an auditory stimulus requires that auditory input reach rostral structures.

Moye and Rudy (1985) and Vogt and Rudy (1984) presented similar findings regarding the visual and gustatory system, respectively. Although 15-day-old rats can detect a flashing 6-W lamp, unlike 17-day-olds they are unable to acquire an association between that visual stimulus and a UCS of electrical shock. Similarly, whereas 6-day-old pups can discern the presence of sucrose, the ability to associate its taste (CS) with illness produced by injections of lithium chloride

(UCS) and thus eventually avoid the sucrose, a phenomenon referred to as *taste aversion learning,* does not emerge until day 12. In both cases it is conjectured that learning depends on relevant sensory system development, a process that proceeds in a caudal to rostral direction. Again, complex behavior such as learning requires that information pertaining to the CS reach higher levels of the nervous system than does relatively simple reflexive behavior. However, such information need not reach cortical sensory areas, as classical conditioning *can* be acquired by decerebrate animals including rabbits (McCormick & Thompson, 1984), cats (Norman, Buchwald, & Villablanca, 1977), and man (Bernston, Tuber, Ronca, & Bachman, 1983).

How, then, can the findings of Rudy and co-workers be reconciled with those of Caldwell and Werboff (1962), who reported successful classical conditioning of 1-day-olds with a tactile CS produced by a vibrating rod placed on the chest? It is possible that the disparity involves differential maturation rates of the various sensory systems—that the sensory system responsive to tactile stimulation matures earlier than the others. According to Gottlieb (1971) and Scherrer (1968), sensory systems subserving touch and kinesthesis do mature earlier than systems that subserve other modalities.

Rudy and Cheatle (1977) also reported that 2-day-old rats exposed to the novel odor of lemon (CS) and then *immediately* injected with illness-producing lithium chloride (UCS) avoided that odor when tested on day 8. This event is referred to as *odor aversion learning.* They later found (Rudy & Cheatle, 1979), however, that 2- and 4-day-olds were unable to acquire the aversion if a short delay were imposed between exposure to the odor and lithium injection. In contrast, 8-day-old rats exhibit conditioning following up to a 90-minute delay between CS offset and UCS onset.

Odor aversion learning is not the only instance in which younger animals cannot tolerate delays between CS and UCS. It is generally the case that the ability to bridge a delay interval increases with advancing age (Kucharski, Richter, & Spear, 1985; Miller, Jagielo, & Spear, 1989; Steinert, Infurna, Jardular, & Spear, 1979). Moye and Rudy (1987) reported that 21-day-old but *not* 17-day-old rats exhibit suppression of activity in response to the presentation of an auditory CS that had been paired 30 seconds after its offset with electrical shock. The data are depicted in Figure 8.2. Similar findings were reported when the CS was the onset of a light.

Does this mean, then, that subjects younger than a certain age are unable to acquire any information when a delay is imposed between CS and UCS? Apparently not. Miller, Molina, and Spear (1990) made the important observation that whereas 4-day-old rats do not avoid an odor when a 15-minute delay is imposed between its cessation and the imposition of an illness-producing UCS, they do, at a later time, avoid another stimulus that has been paired with that odor. Therefore, although the 4-day-olds did not avoid the odor, the odor must nevertheless have acquired negative properties. In other words, learning *did* take place, but it was not displayed as one would expect. "The results suggest that outcomes appearing to represent age-related differences in associative learning may in some instances be more appropriately viewed as representing ontoge-

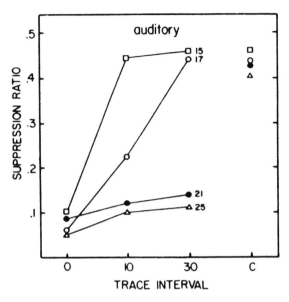

Figure 8.2 Mean suppression ratios obtained during the test from subjects trained when 15, 17, 21, and 25 days old. Intervals between the CS and UCS were 0, 10, or 30 seconds. Subjects in the control condition (C) received unpaired presentations of the CS and UCS. (From Moye and Rudy, "Ontogenesis of trace conditioning in young rats: Dissociation of associative and memory processes." *Developmental Psychobiology, 20,* 405–14. © 1987 by John Wiley & Sons. Reprinted by permission.)

netic differences in the way in which acquired associations are manifested in behavior" (Miller et al., 1990).

The acquisition of a classically conditioned response depends not only on the sensory modality of the CS and the temporal relation between the CS and UCS but also on other factors. One has to do with the nature of the UCS. Haroutunian and Campbell (1979) reported that odor aversion learning can be produced in rats 8 days of age and older by pairing an odor with one of the following: (1) an injection of illness-producing lithium; (2) electrical shock to the paws; (3) shock directed to internal, visceral tissue. Prior to day 8, however, only the illness-producing stimulus and shock to internal tissue promote odor aversion; shock to the paws is ineffective. Prior to day 8, then, only internal (interoceptive) aversive stimuli can serve as an effective UCS. Therefore the level of nervous system maturation as it relates to the UCS also is a factor in determining the outcome of a classical conditioning procedure.

In addition to the nature of the UCS, other factors, probably related in some manner to the uniqueness of the youngster's ecological niche, also can determine if conditioning will transpire. This point is perhaps best exemplified by an experiment on the development of taste aversion learning. Young rats learn to avoid a novel taste (CS) when it is paired with the administration of an illness-producing substance (UCS) (Campbell & Alberts, 1979). They even learn to avoid a novel taste when it is present in mother's milk (Galef & Sherry, 1973). (The taste of mother's milk is manipulated by feeding her a diet adulterated with a flavoring agent.) This result was shown by removing the flavored milk from the mammary gland, infusing it with a syringe into the pup's mouth, and then making the pup sick. Later the pup avoids solid foods adultered with that flavor. Nonetheless, Martin and Alberts (1979) discovered that aversion to the flavor present in mother's milk is *not* acquired if the milk is obtained *through nursing.* In other words, if a hungry pup is allowed to nurse from a dam whose milk has been flavored and then made ill, it subsequently fails to avoid similarly flavored foods. "It is as if there is a sanctity to maternal cues, making them immune to aversive conditioning" (Martin & Alberts, 1979).

Data from Humans

Unlike research on classical conditioning of nonhuman young that commenced only about three decades ago, research with human infants began almost nine decades ago with the publication of two papers the same year, 1907. One was by Bogen (translated by Brackbill & Thompson, 1967) who studied a 3.5-year-old child whose esophagus was constricted as a result of ingesting lye. Although the child was able to swallow food and drink liquids, the narrow esophagus caused vomiting, thereby prohibiting those substances from reaching the stomach. As a result, food and drink had to be placed directly into the stomach through a fistula. Bogen used that fistula to collect gastric secretions. Chewing and swallowing meat, as expected, produced gastric secretion. However, secretion also was found after the child was permitted only to observe meat or was merely talked to about meat. Later, the sound of a trumpet was paired either with the sight of meat or with food-related conversation. In both cases the trumpet alone came to evoke gastric secretion.

The other publication was by Krasnogorskii (translated by Brackbill & Thompson, 1967) who observed sucking, swallowing, and mouth opening on the part of a 14-month-old in response to the sight of a glass of milk. These behaviors also appeared in reaction to a bell that had been paired with the milk. "There is no doubt whatsoever that the ringing of the bell after its combination with the unconditioned stimulus became a conditional stimulus."

These early investigations heralded the study of classical conditioning in human infants, an enterprise that has continued, albeit sporadically, for almost 90 years (Fitzgerald & Brackbill, 1976; Fitzgerald and Porges, 1971; Rovee-Collier, 1986). The early studies, as well as many performed later, were greatly influenced by Pavlov's work on conditioned salivation. As a consequence, they dealt almost exclusively with UCSs that were food-related, thereby limiting the UCRs and CRs to responses that were ingestion-related. It since has been shown that conditioning also can be established in infants with UCSs of an aversive sort.

Aversive UCSs. The most famous (or infamous) example of the use of an aversive UCS is the study of Watson and Raynor (1920) in which an 11-month-old boy named Albert served as the subject. Albert was a robust, lively child who initially exhibited no hesitation in playing with various animate and inanimate objects such as white rats, dogs, monkeys, cotton wool, and blocks. The conditioning procedure consisted in striking a steel bar with a hammer just as the child touched the white rat. The loud noise apparently frightened Albert for he fell forward and buried his face in the mattress. The procedure was repeated for a second time when Albert again touched the rat. A week later when the rat was presented he vacillated in reaching for it, and when the animal nuzzled his hand he quickly withdrew it. After three additional pairings of the sight of the rat with the noise, Albert reacted to the presentation of the rat by whimpering and turning away. After two more pairings he was a distraught child.

> The instant the rat was shown the baby began to cry. Almost instantly he turned sharply to the left, fell over, raised himself on all fours and began to crawl away ever so rapidly that he was caught with difficulty before he reached the edge of the mattress. [p. 5]

It was later demonstrated that responsiveness to the rat had generalized to a rabbit, a Santa Claus mask, cotton wool, a fur coat, and even to Watson's white hair.

Watson and Raynor believed that they had produced a conditioned fear response to white fluffy objects by pairing a CS (rat) with an aversive UCS (loud noise). Here, then, the genesis of a phobic reaction can be accounted for by classical conditioning rather than by psychoanalytically inspired explanations, which Watson abhorred. Watson and Raynor conjured up the following scenario:

> The Freudians twenty years from now, unless their hypotheses change, when they come to analyze Albert's fear of a seal skin coat—assuming that he comes to analysis at that age—will probably tease from him the recital of a dream which upon their analysis will show that Albert at three years of age attempted to play with the pubic hair of the mother and was scolded violently for it. [p. 14]

Despite Watson and Raynor's presumption that Albert's fear of the rat and consequently of other furry white objects was established through classical conditioning, another possibility has been suggested. According to Church (cited by Rovee-Collier, 1987), the true operation may have in fact been *instrumental* conditioning. This idea is proposed because initially the child was exposed to the aversive stimulus after he actually touched the rat, hence an instrumental punishment procedure that served to suppress touching. Although a correct argument, later pairings of the noise with just the sight of the rat certainly exacerbated Albert's reactions, leading to crying and escape behavior. The genesis of Albert's fear, then, appears to involve a combination of classical and instrumental conditioning procedures.

A lesser known early demonstration of infant conditioning with an aversive UCS was that of Jones (1930), which had to do with changes in electrical resistance of the skin or galvanic skin response (GSR) in a 7-month-old. (The GSR is produced by administering relatively mild electrical shock, which causes perspiration, thus reducing skin resistance.) The sound of an armature striking an induction coil was presented for 20 seconds and was paired during the final 10 seconds with the mild electrical shock that elicited the GSR. After only six training trials the GSR was elicited by presentation of the sound. Moreover, conditioning was maintained upward of 2 weeks after the CS–UCS pairings.

Another means of studying the efficacy of an aversive UCS with young subjects, and one that has received some attention of late (Fitzgerald & Brackbill, 1976; Hoffman, Cohen, & DeVido, 1985; Lintz, Fitzgerald, & Brackbill, 1967), involves the eye-blink response, a protective reaction readily produced by a puff of air directed at the eye or by a tap on the glabella, the flat region of skin between the eyebrows. Little, Lipsitt, and Rovee-Collier (1984) paired a 70-dB, 1000-Hz tone with a 400-msec puff of air delivered to the corner of the infant's eye. Both the ISI (500 msec and 1500 msec) and age of the subjects (10, 20, and 30 days) were varied. Infants as young as 10 days exhibit eye-blink conditioning if the ISI is 1500 msec, substantially longer than optimal ISIs found for adults of most mammalian species.

As we have seen, infants can be classically conditioned using positive and aversive UCSs. Furthermore, neutral stimuli of various kinds can serve as CSs. A type of CS that has not been considered and one that may play a significant role in development consists of the passage of fixed intervals of time. Conditioned stimuli of this sort provide the basis for what is referred to as *temporal conditioning.*

Temporal Conditioning. Marquis (1941) provided the first evidence of temporal conditioning in infants by showing that infants who had been on a 3-hour feeding schedule for 9 days and then were shifted to a 4-hour schedule displayed an increase in general motor activity, fussiness, and crying about 30 minutes *prior* to the 4 hour feeding. She concluded that the passage of 3 hours served as a CS that elicited a CR best described as "expectancy" of milk. When the expectancy was not met, crying and fussiness ensued.

Krachkovskaia (1959) observed that elevations of leukocytes, which are related to the maturation of the infant's digestive processes and which occur by the first week of life, also are subject to temporal conditioning. Whereas the elevated leukocyte count that appears after a feeding ("digestive leukocytosis") is explicable in purely physiological terms, the elevated leukocyte count seen *before* a feeding must lend itself to a different interpretation, namely, that it is a CR formed in response to the passage of time between one meal and the next. This supposition was tested by obtaining the leukocyte count in infants shifted to a 4-hour from a 3-hour feeding schedule. On the first day of the change, elevated levels of white blood cells appeared prior to what would have been the 3-hour feeding. By the second day, before the eighth feeding, the leukocyte count did not increase in response to the old feeding schedule but, instead, increased prior to feeding on the new regimen.

Later studies of temporal conditioning have employed a more refined methodology including CSs of much shorter durations. Fitzgerald, Lintz, Brackbill, and Adams (1967), for example, examined conditioned pupillary constriction and dilation by exposing some 26- to 86-day-old infants every 20 seconds to the onset of a 100-W blue light bulb. The light remained lit for 4 seconds. Others were exposed every 20 seconds to the offset of the bulb; it remained off for 4 seconds. Eventually, infants in the first group began to exhibit pupillary constriction prior to the onset of the light, whereas subjects in the second group showed pupillary dilation prior to the offset of the light.

Infants do not invariably acquire a temporally conditioned response, however. Whether they do so depends on the nature of the CR. Attempts to temporally condition an eye-blink response and sucking have been unsuccessful (Brackbill, Lintz, & Fitzgerald, 1968; Abrahamson, Brackbill, Carpenter, & Fitzgerald, 1970, respectively).

Rovee-Collier (1987) has addressed the potential import of temporal conditioning to the developing organism. She stated:

> Temporal information may be one of the earliest aspects of the environment to be incorporated into the infant's representation of the structure of its niche. For the young of many mammalian and avian species, the ability to learn the particular timing of critical events and to anticipate them has immediate and direct survival implications. [p. 114]

Effect of age. Before concluding the discussion of the acquisition of classically conditioned responding in human infants, we must consider whether the capacity to exhibit a CR is age-related. If you recall, nonhuman subjects have the capacity to acquire a CR soon after birth. However, whether they do so depends on the level of maturation of the sensory system corresponding to the modality of the CS. Do similar findings apply to human infants?

First, newborn humans, like nonhumans, can be classically conditioned. Blass, Ganchrow, and Steiner (1984) have demonstrated that infants 2 to 48 hours old can acquire a conditioned response. The CS consisted of stroking the middle of the infant's forehead with the index finger once per second for 10 seconds, and the UCS was delivery of a sucrose solution directly into the mouth. The UCS elicited UCRs termed "head-orient" and "pucker-suck." Both the experimental group and one control group underwent 18 training trials. However, the experimental group received the UCS immediately after receipt of the tactile CS, whereas the control group received it following variable periods (10, 20, and 30 seconds) after cessation of the CS. A second control group received only the UCS. The findings were clear. Whereas all groups of infants exhibited comparable levels of head-orienting responses throughout the training trials, head-orienting of the experimental subjects occurred predominantly during the CS portion of each trial. In contrast, head-orienting of the control infants were distributed equally throughout the entire trial. Similar findings were obtained for the other CR, pucker-suck. Therefore, head-orienting and pucker-suck reactions of the experimental group generally anticipated the UCS and thus were considered CRs.

After the acquisition phase the subjects were placed on an extinction schedule, exposed only to the CS. The experimental subjects not only exhibited the expected decline in conditioned responding, they also evidenced a marked behavioral change, described by Blass et al. thusly:

> After 1 or 2 extinction trials, the infant's expression appeared to be that of surprise, which gave way to a frowning or angry face, to be followed by crying or whimpering. Crying was short-lived; and at its termination, the infants generally slept. [p. 230]

That the bout of emotional behavior exhibited by seven of eight of the infants was not simply caused by the withholding of the UCS is shown by the fact that only 1 of the 16 control subjects cried during the extinction phase. Therefore the experimental infants apparently became upset because the expectancy elicited by the CS that milk would be forthcoming was not met.

Sullivan et al. (1991) also report what they believe to be successful classical conditioning of 1-day-olds. These investigators paired a CS consisting of the odor of citrus with a UCS of stroking accessible areas of the infant's body. The UCS elicited an increase in general activity. After repeated pairings the CS came to elicit head-turning toward the source of the odor. Here, then, what was designated as the CR (head-turning) differed markedly from the UCR.

Humans, like nonhumans, appear to be capable of acquiring a CR soon after birth. Does the nature of the CS determine if conditioning will occur, a situation that exists in animals? Kasatkin (Kasatkin & Levikova, 1935a,b; see also reviews of his work by Brackbill and Koltsova, 1967, and Razran, 1933) believed that the functional development of the sensory system dictates when a given stimulus can successfully serve as a CS. (This position should be familiar, as it is a precursor to Rudy's [Hyson and Rudy, 1984; Moye and Rudy, 1985] proposal concerning the development of conditioning in nonhuman subjects.) Kasatkin (1972) later amended his position to include the effectiveness of the UCS. However, according to their own data and those of others, Fitzgerald and Brackbill(1976) concluded that, in addition to the nature of the CS and UCS, conditionability depends on the infant's state (whether it is quiet, crying, hungry, sleepy, and so forth), individual differences in its initial response to the CS, and on the complexity of the task. A combination of these factors probably contributes to many of the reported failures to establish classical conditioning in immature humans (Fitzgerald & Brackbill, 1976; Kasatkin, 1972).

Instrumental Conditioning

Unlike a classically conditioned response, which is reflexively elicited by a formerly neutral stimulus, an instrumental response is voluntary and exists within the organism's behavioral repertoire prior to conditioning. Instrumental conditioning consists in strengthening a response by making reinforcement contingent on its performance. Thus by making food available following a right turn in a T maze, the probability of turning right in the maze increases; and by making reinforcement contingent on a lever press response, the rate of lever pressing markedly increases. Instrumental conditioning therefore is the "comprehension" of a relation between a response and reinforcement.

Data from Nonhumans

Tasks of two sorts typically have been used to assess the young organism's ability to acquire an instrumental response. One, called an appetitive task, procures positive reinforcement; and the other, an avoidance task, averts negative reinforcement. Regarding the latter, both *active* avoidance, a problem requiring the emission of a response, and *passive* avoidance, one requiring that responding be withheld, have been used.

Appetitive Conditioning. The initial experiments on the ontogeny of appetitive conditioning made use of animals old enough to ingest solid food, thereby permitting the food to be used as reinforcement. Amsel and associates (Amsel and Chen, 1976; Burdette, Brake, Chen, & Amsel, 1976; Chen & Amsel, 1975) demonstrated that rats as young as 17 days can be trained to traverse a straight alley. Moreover, preweaning animals respond in an adult manner to the schedule of reinforcement; those reinforced intermittently are more persistent in responding during extinction than those maintained on a continuous reinforcement schedule. It was also found that responding in the face of nonreward, especially for subjects intermittently reinforced, is *inversely* related to age.

The use of a more natural source of reinforcement, nipple attachment, permitted Amsel, Burdette and Letz (1976) to study the instrumental learning capacity of animals much younger than those that attained the ability to ingest solid food. Ten-day-old pups were separated from their mothers and placed in a temperature-controlled holding cage. Training trials in a straight alley began 8 hours later. Reinforcement consisted in allowing the infant to attach to its anesthetized mother's nipple for 15 seconds. Sucking did not produce nourishment, however, because the anesthetic blocks milk release from the mammary gland. As mentioned previously, this response is known as *nonnutritive sucking.* On nonreward trials the mother was not present, and the pup was removed when it reached the end of the alley. The data are shown in Figure 8.3. It is apparent that the time taken to reach the end of the runway decreased on the first five reinforced trials. The times remained low following a 15-minute interval during which the animals were returned to a holding cage. Response times then increased during five subsequent nonreinforced trials, declined during the next five reinforced trials, and so on.

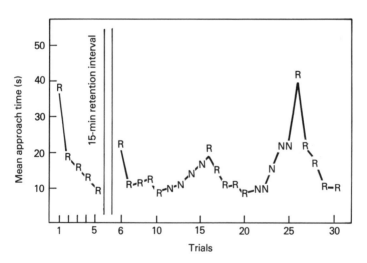

Figure 8.3 Mean approach time during rewarded (R) and nonrewarded (N) trials. (From Amsel et al., "Appetitive learning, patterned alteration, and extinction in 10-day-old rats with non-lactating suckling as reward." *Nature, 262,* 816–818. © 1976 by Macmillan Magazines. Reprinted by permission.)

Also using nonnutritive sucking as reinforcement, Kenney and Blass (1977) trained rats in a Y maze. A correct response was reinforced with access to the nipples for 30 seconds. An incorrect response also brought the youngsters into contact with the adult female. However, the nipples facing that arm of the maze were made inaccessible by covering them with gauze. Animals as young as *7 days* learned to discriminate between the right and left arms of the maze. There was no reliable differences between 7-, 12-, 17-, and 21-day-olds in terms of trials required to reach the learning criterion.

Even *1-day-old* rats are capable of acquiring an instrumental response when reinforcement is of the appetitive type. Johanson and Hall (1979), using the ingenious device depicted in Figure 8.4, rewarded food-deprived infants with an infusion of 3 to 4 ul of milk directly into their mouths whenever they probed upward into a cloth-covered paddle. They results are depicted in Figure 8.5. It is clear that 1-day-olds acquired the paddle-probing instrumental response. Furthermore, they also learned to discriminate a paddle that produced reinforcement from one that did not. Each paddle was labeled with a distinctive odor (odorants were placed in the cloth triangle suspended underneath the paddle— see Figure 8.4). The neonates came to reliably probe the paddle that led to reinforcement and to ignore the one associated with no reinforcement. Using a similar paddle-pressing procedure, Moran, Lew, and Blass (1981) found that 3-day-olds acquire the response when reinforced by 500-msec bursts of electrical stimulation directed at the lateral hypothalamus.

That rats as young as 1 day of age can acquire a positively reinforced instrumental response is a fairly amazing feat given the immaturity of the infant central nervous system (Goldman, 1976). However, experiments using positive

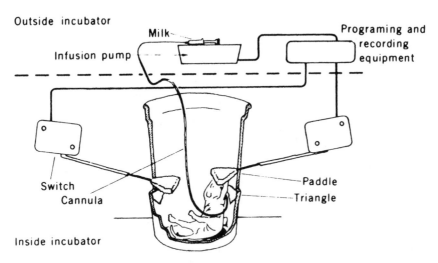

Figure 8.4 Apparatus used to administer milk directly into a rat pup's mouth contingent on a paddle press response. (From Johanson and Hall, "Appetitive learning in 1-day-old rat pups." *Science, 205,* 419–21. © 1979 by The American Association for the Advancement of Science. Reprinted by permission.)

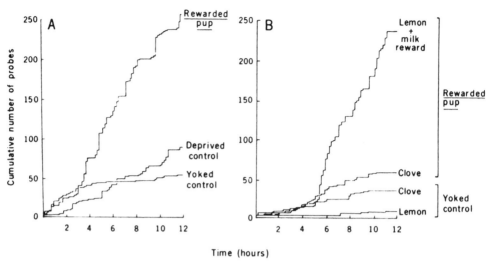

Figure 8.5 (A) Cumulative number of probes (for 10-minute intervals) into the paddle made by a representative 1-day-old pup that was rewarded with an oral infusion of milk. A littermate (yoked control) that received milk only when the experimental pup probed its paddle and a "deprived control" that received no milk made considerably fewer probes over the 12 hours of testing. (B) Pups appeared to have learned to discriminate the paddle that produced reinforcement from one that did not. The pup's yoked control littermate did little probing and did not show discrimination. (From Johanson and Hall, "Appetitive learning in 1-day-old rats." *Science, 205,* 419–21. © 1979 by The American Association for the Advancement of Science. Reprinted by permission.)

reinforcement rarely directly compare the performance of animals of varying ages. (An exception is the Kenney and Blass study [1977] cited above in which they reported no differences in trials to criterion among groups of variously aged rat pups.) Without age comparisons it is difficult to draw conclusions about the ontogeny of appetitive learning. We do not know, for example, if 1-day-old rats learn the paddle-probing response of Johanson and Hall (1979) as readily as do 5-day-olds. Such is not the case, however, for studies in which subjects learn to avoid aversive stimulation.

Avoidance Conditioning. Riccio and Schulenburg (1969) used a passive avoidance procedure in which 10-, 15-, 20-, 30-, and 100-day-old rats were shocked whenever they stepped from one side of the apparatus (the "safe" side) to the other. The subjects were trained until they remained on the safe side for 180 seconds or until they underwent seven trials. As seen in Figure 8.6, most of the 100-day-olds met the learning criterion after having received only a single shock, whereas most of the 20- and 30-day-olds required two shocks. The 10- and 15-day-olds, in contrast, were inferior; the former required six punishments, and many of the 15-day-olds never met the criterion. The findings led Riccio and

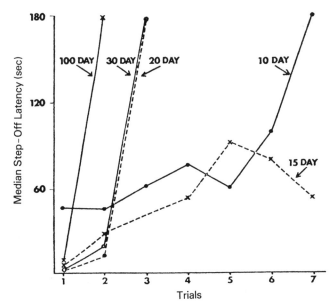

Figure 8.6 Median step-off latencies as a function of training trials in different age groups. (From Riccio and Schulenburg, "Age-related deficits in acquisition of a passive avoidance response." *Canadian Journal of Psychology, 23,* 429–37. © 1969 by The Canadian Psychological Association. Reprinted by permission.)

Schulenburg to conclude "that the ability to acquire a passive avoidance response improves with age in the rat, but that even very young rats are capable of learning to avoid." A similar pattern of results was obtained by Schulenburg, Riccio, and Stikes (1973) and Stehouwer and Campbell (1980).

Blozovski and Cudennec (1980) examined passive avoidance learning with a somewhat different procedure. Animals were placed in a chamber cooled to a discomforting 23°C from which they could cross into another chamber that was warmed to 27°C. Entering the warm chamber, however, led to the delivery of electrical shock. Animals were tested for a maximum of 10 trials or until they remained in the cool chamber for 300 seconds. Other animals were treated similarly except that shock was not delivered. As depicted in Figure 8.7, conditioning, albeit at a low level, begins to appear by day 11 and from that time performance increases steadily.

Myslivecek and Hassmannova (1980, 1990) used a similar technique. Animals were goaded to enter a shock chamber by passing a stream of air over them; but as was the case with cold, animals preferred to avoid the shock by staying still. Whereas this experiment too found that passive avoidance learning improves with age, rats only hours old did meet the learning criterion. However, the criterion—the amount of time the subject must remain in the safe area of the experimental chamber—was only 60 seconds, much less than that used by

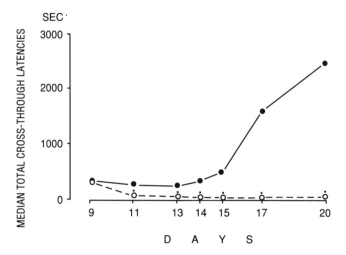

Figure 8.7 Ontogenetic development of a step-through locomotor passive-avoidance learning task in the rat measured by the median total cross-through latencies as a function of age (● = conditioning; ○ = control; * = statistically significant difference). (From Blozovsky and Cudennec, "Passive-avoidance learning in the young rat." *Developmental Psychobiology, 13,* 513–18. © 1980 by John Wiley & Sons. Reprinted by permission.)

Blozovski and Cudennec (1980) and others. Myslivecek and Hassmannova argued that the previously reported inferior passive avoidance learning in very young rats is due mainly to too stringent a criterion, that is, too strict a definition of learning.

Although age is directly related to rate of passive avoidance learning and to asymptotic performance level, age appears to contribute little to the learning of an active avoidance response. According to Campbell and Campbell (1962), acquisition by 18-day-old rats of a task that required them to move from one side of an apparatus in which they had previously received electrical shock to the safe side did not differ in any respect from that of 100-day-olds. Similarly, 21- to 25-day-old rats learned to cross to the safe side of a chamber in response to a flashing light that signaled impending shock at a rate similar to that of 60- to 70-day-olds (Feigley & Spear, 1970). Other data (Goldman & Tobach, 1967; Kirby, 1963; Riccio, Rohrbaugh, & Hodges, 1968) also have attested to the fact that young rats learn about as well as adults when confronted with an avoidance problem requiring an active response. Additional studies should be performed to assess the performance of younger animals.

Why do young animals appear to be on a par with adults in acquiring an active avoidance response but are inferior to them when challenged with an avoidance task necessitating the withholding of behavior? The answer may lie with the *cholinergic* neurotransmitter system. The cholinergic system has been hypothesized to facilitate transmission among neurons involved in volitional inhibition or suppression of behavior (Carlton, 1969; Carlton & Markiewicz, 1971). It is possible, then, that because young animals possess an immature cholinergic system, they are deficient in response inhibition and therefore are deficient in the acquisition of a passive avoidance response.

Support for this position comes from various sources. The cholinergic system has been found to mature gradually; significant increases in the concentration of acetylcholine are found in the rat brain from birth to the third week of life (Crevier, 1958; Ladensky, Consolo, Peri, & Garattini, 1972; Matthews, Nadler, Lynch, & Cotman, 1974). Functional analyses also reveal that the cholinergic system matures by the third week of life (Campbell, Lytle, & Fibiger, 1969), although others believe it may mature somewhat earlier (Smith, Spear, & Spear, 1979). Furthermore, Wilson and Riccio (1976) reported that administration of scopolamine, a drug that blocks central cholinergic transmission, increases the number of trials required by 18-, 21-, and 30-day-old rats to acquire a passive avoidance response. Fifteen-day-old subjects were unaffected, suggesting that the cholinergic system matures significantly by day 18. Similar findings have been reported for mice; behavioral suppression as assessed by passive avoidance comes under cholinergic control about day 15, the time at which scopolamine first produces performance deficits (Ray & Nagy, 1978). Later investigations consisted in placing anticholinergic compounds directly into discrete nuclei of the developing rat brain in an attempt to localize sites involved in response inhibition. According to Blozovski and Hennocq (1982) and Blozovski and Dumery (1987), both the hippocampus and the amygdala play a major role.

We have seen that the young animal has the capacity to acquire both appetitively and aversively motivated instrumental responses. Whereas there does not appear to be significant age-dependent effects with regard to the former (although few studies have directly compared animals of different ages), younger subjects exhibit deficits in aversively reinforced tasks requiring response inhibition. It would be informative to determine whether those deficits are related to response inhibition in general or to inhibition associated specifically with aversive stimuli. This question could be addressed by making *positive reinforcement* contingent on the inhibition of behavior.

Facilitation of Instrumental Conditioning. Before leaving the topic of the ontogeny of learning in nonhuman animals, let us briefly consider two factors that can facilitate the acquisition of instrumental responding. One involves stimulation from the home environment. Sixteen-day-old rats show enhanced acquisition of a passive avoidance response if they are trained in the presence of soiled bedding from their home cage (Smith & Spear, 1978). A similar effect has been observed with an active avoidance task (Misanin, Lariveri, Turns, & Turns, 1986). Even the presence during acquisition of a nontypical nest odor such as banana to which the animal has been previously exposed can be facilitative (Wigal, Kucharski, & Spear, 1984).

How stimuli from an animal's home cage facilitate avoidance learning is not understood. According to Smith and Spear (1981), when animals are removed from the safe nest environment their level of emotional arousal increases, thereby interfering in some manner with their ability to make appropriate use of cues in the learning situation. Put simply, they may have difficulty paying attention. Thus the introduction of familiar home cage stimuli such as odor may facilitate learning by reducing levels of arousal.

A second factor that can affect instrumental learning is the nursing experience itself. Cramer, Pfister, and Haig (1988), in a clever and important series of experiments, proposed that if the demands of a conditioning task are similar to those of the nursing situation, acquisition of the instrumental response should be facilitated. They draw the following analogy between suckling, which for the rat involves repeatedly shifting from one nipple to another, and behavior in a radial arm maze (see Figure 8.8):

> The suckling rat, then, can maximize its intake by withdrawing the milk from the nipple to which it is attached during the (milk) letdown and then quickly moving to another, unsuckled nipple and withdrawing its contents. In many ways, the task demands placed on adult rats solving a radial maze are somewhat similar. First, both the maternal ventrum and the maze present a spatial array of food sites. Second, in the pattern of discrete milk letdowns characteristic of rat lactation, each nipple is filled with a limited amount of milk once every few minutes. By comparison, each arm of the maze is baited at the beginning of the test session. Third, the milk in the nipple can be depleted by suckling, just as the arm of the maze is depleted once the rat has run down it and eaten the pellet. Returning immediately to the nipple or arm is not rewarded by additional milk or food, respectively. Both the infant rat suckling nipples and the adult rat solving the spatial maze can maximize intake by visiting each site—nipple or maze arm—once and only once. [p. 3]

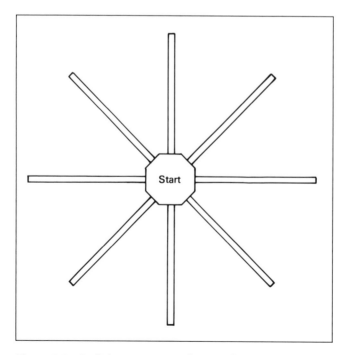

Figure 8.8   Radial arm maze. Each arm is baited only once.

The similarities between the demands of suckling and those of the radial maze led Cramer et al. to predict that animals that had had restricted nipple-shifting experience should exhibit relatively poor radial maze learning.

Groups of five 5-day-olds were given to foster mothers having the full complement of 12 nipples or to mothers having only four nipples (eight had been surgically removed). Other animals from litters containing 10 pups were allowed to remain with their natural, intact mother. Beginning on day 22 the pups were given preliminary training in the maze. They were weaned on day 24, and testing commenced the following day. The results are shown in Figure 8.9. Regardless of litter size and thus the ratio of pups to nipples, pups exposed to many nipples during the suckling period learned the maze much more quickly than did those exposed to few nipples. A second experiment verified the effectiveness of the independent variable; rats exposed to many nipples do indeed perform more nipple-shifting responses than those exposed to relatively few nipples.

Cramer et al. then addressed the issue of what nipple-shifting experience contributes to conditionability. Does it only facilitate spatial learning tasks, or might it affect all forms of learning? The influence of nipple-shifting may be specific to spatial learning because exposure to differential numbers of nipples affected neither the acquisition of a food reinforced lever-pressing response nor a visual discrimination task in which the onset or offset of a light signaled the availability of reinforcement contingent on a lever press. It seems, then, that the experience gained by moving from nipple to nipple in an attempt to maximize the availability of milk can facilitate the learning of a task that also requires movement from place to place to maximize the availability of food. As the authors

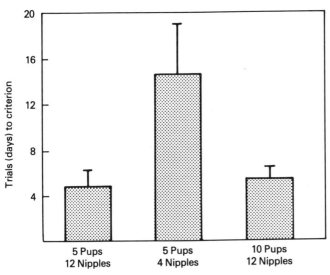

Figure 8.9 Trials (days) to criterion on an eight-arm radial maze for rats from different rearing conditions (mean ± SEM). (From Cramer et al., "Experience during suckling alters later spatial learning." *Developmental Psychobiology, 21,* 1–24. © 1988 by John Wiley & Sons. Reprinted by permission.)

remarked, though, the fact that exposure to many nipples affects acquisition of the difficult eight-arm radial maze but not the relatively simple lever-press response does not exclude the possibility that the facilitative effect of nipple shifting is not specific to spatial learning but facilitates the learning of difficult problems in general. Regardless of its specificity, however, the extent to which the influence of nipple-shifting experience or the lack thereof persist into adult life should next be ascertained. Furthermore, the findings of Cramer et al. raise the possibility that additional forms of early behavioral experience also may affect the organism's later learning ability.

Data from Humans

Free Operant Procedure. Reports of instrumental conditioning of human infants did not appear in the literature until 1960. Since then reports have surfaced regularly and in large number. Most of the research has used the *free operant* procedure in which the infant is permitted to control its response rate and thus modulate the amount of reinforcement obtainable within a fixed time period. The results of those investigations reveal that stimuli of many types can serve as reinforcement for a variety of responses such as head turning, panel pressing, and vocalizing. Effective rewards have included sugar water (Kobre & Lipsitt, 1972), milk (Papousek, 1961), music (Butterfield & Siperstein, 1972), nonnutritive sucking (Siqueland, 1968), and the sight of an adult (Koch, 1968), to name but a few. Furthermore, there appears to be no relation between type of reinforcer and the type of response capable of being strengthened.

The data also reveal that infants can be instrumentally conditioned beginning soon after birth. As you may recall from Chapter 2, for example, newborn infants modulate the rate at which they engage in nonnutritive sucking when the sound of their mother's voice is made contingent upon particular rates of sucking (DeCasper & Fifer, 1980).

Conjugate Reinforcement Procedure. Whereas most infant conditioning studies have used the conventional method of reinforcement—providing rewards of an invariant magnitude for each reinforced response—some studies have employed a different procedure in which the rate or vigor of the operant response determines the intensity of reinforcing stimulation. This relation between response and reward is called a *conjugate* schedule of reinforcement. It is believed by some that a conjugate schedule more accurately mirrors the normal pattern of interaction between the infant and its environment than do standard reinforcement schedules.

> There are numerous examples of this (conjugate) schedule in "real" life. When an infant sucks, each minimally adequate suck produces milk, and the faster and/or more vigorous the sucks, the more continuous and voluminous is the flow. Similarly, when an infant cries, the mother approaches; but the haste of her approach as well as the number and intensity of her concurrent vocalizations are controlled by the rate and intensity of the infant's cries. . . . Thus conjugate reinforcement schedules offer the organism an opportunity to reap benefits commensurate with the energy invested in obtaining them. [Rovee-Collier, 1983, pp. 67–68]

The conjugate reinforcement schedule was first used with infants by Lipsitt, Pederson, and DeLucia (1966), who placed 12-month-olds in front of a darkened viewing box. They were permitted to observe a rotating and colorful clown by pressing a panel that turned on a light. Increases in response rate up to two or three presses per second produced a gradual increase in the frequency and intensity of the illumination. Infants exhibited reliable increases in response rate when reinforcement was available and reliable decreases in rate during extinction.

The conjugate reinforcement technique has since been used to study the learning capacity of infants younger than 12 months. It has been accomplished, in part, by replacing the panel press with responses more suitable for younger infants. One such response is nonnutritive sucking. Sucks exceeding a particular threshold of intensity, as measured by a pressure transducer placed within the nipple, are reinforced with visual stimulation proportional in intensity to the rate of all suprathreshold responses.

Kalnins and Brune (1973) made the clarity of a silent colored motion picture contingent on the sucking rate of 5-week-old infants. Twelve infants exposed initially to a blurred image could gradually bring it into focus by sucking, and 12 others initially exposed to a clear picture could blur it as a function of their sucking. After training, half of the infants in each group were placed in the opposite treatment condition. Infants initially given a blurred image exhibited rapid increases in suck rates; and when the condition was reversed they displayed a rapid decrease in sucking. Subjects given the clear image, however, did not increase their rates of sucking even after reversal of the treatment condition. This finding indicates that something more than stimulus change is required to reinforce nonnutritive sucking.

Siqueland (1969a,b) has demonstrated conditioning in infants as young as 1 month. These infants exhibited increases in the rate of high intensity sucking when reinforced with brief access to a colored triangle on a dark background. Furthermore, when the color of the triangle was changed, the response rate increased, demonstrating that the infants had habituated to the original color of the triangle.

Conjugate reinforcement also has been used in conjunction with kicking-produced changes in visual stimulation. A ribbon is attached from the infant's leg to a mobile suspended overhead, enabling the infant to move the mobile by kicking (see Figure 8.10). Consequently, the amount of visual stimulation (viz., movement of the mobile) is directly proportional to the frequency and intensity of the kicks.

Data derived from 10-week-olds (Rovee & Rovee, 1969) are shown in Figure 8.11. Reinforcement contingency obviously exerted a profound effect on the rate of kicking; the response rate increased markedly when reinforcement was available and declined to the preconditioning level during extinction.

The efficacy of "mobile" conjugate reinforcement has been confirmed many times with infants of various ages (Ohr, Fagen, Rovee-Collier, Hayne, & Vander Linde, 1989; Rovee-Collier & Dufault, 1991). Davis and Rovee-Collier (1983) did report, however, that 8 weeks is about the earliest at which infants can be conditioned.

Infants not only exhibit "simple" conditioning, they also display discrimination learning (Rovee-Collier & Capatides, 1979). Two mobiles differing in both color and pattern were presented for alternating 2-minute periods to 3-month-olds. During the initial phase of the experiment both mobiles were associated with reinforcement; the infant could move each by kicking. During the second, or discrimination, phase, the infant was permitted to move one of the mobiles but not the other. During the final phase, the infant again was permitted to move both mobiles.

The infants learned to respond differentially to the two mobiles; during the second phase the kicking rate gradually increased when the mobile associated with reinforcement was presented and declined to the mobile associated with nonreinforcement. This differential responding disappeared during the third phase, when kicking increased to the mobile previously associated with nonreinforcement. Rovee-Colier and Capatides pointed out that the ability of the infants

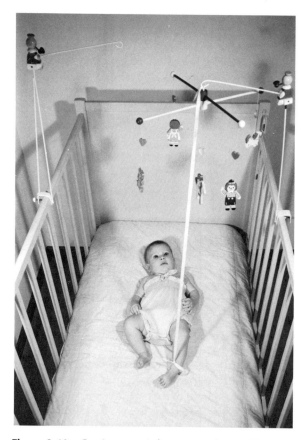

Figure 8.10 Conjugate reinforcement derived from kicking-produced changes in visual stimulation. (Courtesy of Dr. C. Rovee-Collier, Rutgers University.)

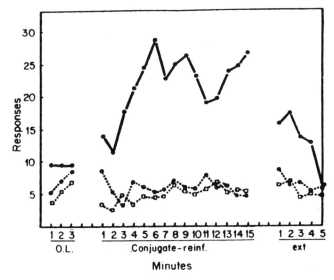

Figure 8.11 Mean footkicks of 10-week old infants during successive minutes of baseline (O.L. = operant level), acquisition (conjugate reinforcement), and extinction (ext.). Only the experimental group (solid line) received conjugate reinforcement; visual-somesthetic (● . . . ●) and visual-only (□ . . . □) control groups received noncontingent mobile stimulation during the 15-minute acquisition phase. (From Rovee and Rovee, "Conjugate reinforcement of infant exploratory behavior." *Journal of Experimental Child Psychology, 8,* 33–39. © 1969 by Academic Press. Reprinted by permission.)

to inhibit responding when confronted with a stimulus associated with nonreinforcement calls into question the claim that prior to 7 to 8 months infants lack the ability to volitionally inhibit goal-directed behavior (Kagen, Kearsley, and Zelaza, 1978).

RETENTION   *essay & nonhuman data*

Not only must the organism learn associations between aspects of its environment and behavior, it must also retain what has been learned for use at a later time. Put simply, the associations must be remembered. If it were not the case, experiences of many types would soon be lost; and so much effort would be spent relearning past associations that the developing organism would have time for little else. Let us turn our attention to memory and forgetting and address the following questions: To what extent do young organisms retain associations? What is the relation between age and retention? To what extent do older organisms retain associations acquired during early life? How can the forgetting of associations acquired during early life be alleviated?

Data from Nonhumans

"Conspicuous in the literature on memory in rodents is the relative lack of research on the emergence of memory, or on memory during that developmental stage of the organism when neurological change is occurring at a most rapid rate." With that opening statement, Misanin, Nagy, Keiser, and Bowen (1971) presented the seminal report on the ontogeny of memory in infant animals. Rats at 5, 7, 9, and 11 days of age were placed in a straight alley in which electrical shock was delivered through the metal grid floor. Escape from the shock required that the subject touch the end wall of the goal compartment. The principal dependent measure was the number of competing responses as defined by a 180-degree turn in a direction away from the goal. A decrease in the number of competing responses was assumed to be indicative of improvement in performance. Animals were given 25 trials a day for 3 consecutive days.

Although rats of all ages showed improved performance within a daily training session, only the 9- and 11-day-olds made fewer competing responses on days 2 and 3 relative to the first day of training. The 5- and 7-day-olds behaved on days 2 and 3 as if they had never before been in the maze. After eliminating the possibilities that the decrease in competing responses by the 9- and 11-day-olds was caused by fatigue or habituation to shock, it was deduced that their enhanced performance on days 2 and 3 is attributable to retention across a 24-hour period—that they remembered something about the task from one day to the next. Hence the capacity to retain information across a 24 hour period emerges on about day 9 of life.

Misanin et al. (1971) also reported that younger animals can retain information, but that they have a much shorter retention span than older animals. For example, 7-day-olds can retain only over a 1-hour period. Nagy, Newman, Olsen and Hinderliter (1972) provided similar findings for mice; 9-day-olds can retain information for at least 96 hours, whereas the retention capacity of younger animals is much shorter, less than 6 hours for 5- and 7-day-olds.

Nagy and Mueller (1973) considered the possibility that what appears to be the emergence of a 24-hour retention capacity at 9 days may actually be a manifestation of a higher level of learning by 9-day-old animals relative to younger animals. They addressed that possibility by giving 7- and 9-day-old mice 0, 10, 25, or 40 trials in the straight alley escape task and then testing them 24 hours later. Whereas none of the four groups of 7-day-olds exhibited retention, retention was displayed by the 9-day-olds, even those given only 10 acquisition trials. That the 9-day-olds exhibited retention when the degree of original learning was varied suggests that the superior performance of 9-day-olds is due to the emergence of the capacity to remember information over a 24-hour time span rather than to an enhanced level of original learning. This conclusion is strengthened by the fact that even though the acquisition performance of 7-day-olds given 40 training trials is similar to that of 9-day-olds allowed 25 training trials, the 7-day-olds still showed no retention when tested 24 hours later.

The studies of Misanin and Nagy (see also Missanin, Haigh, Hinderliter, & Nagy, 1973; Nagy, Pagano, & Gable, 1976) make two important points. One is that the capacity to learn and the capacity to retain develop at different rates; learning antedates retention. Second, retention improves with advancing age.[1] Similar conclusions were later reached by others. Campbell and Alberts (1979), for example, studied the retention of taste aversion learning in 10-, 12-, 15-, and 20-day-old rats after intervals of 1, 5, and 10 days. They found that although taste aversion is acquired by pups of all three ages, less retention is displayed by the 10- and 12-day-olds relative to the 15- and 20-day-olds (see Figure 8.12). Stehouwer and Campbell (1980) assessed retention following the acquisition of a passive avoidance task in which shock was administered when the rats made contact with the cage walls. Retention increased from about 6 hours in 10-day-olds to 5 days in 15-day-olds.

Although the capacity to retain information generally increases with advancing age, a major determinant of memory span seems to be task-specific. Misanin et al. (1971) reported that by 9 days of age rats retain a passive avoidance response for 24 hours. However, the passive avoidance task of Stenhouwer and Campbell (1980) yields only 6 hours of retention in 10-day-olds. Furthermore, 10-day-olds recall a learned taste aversion over a 5-day period (Campbell &

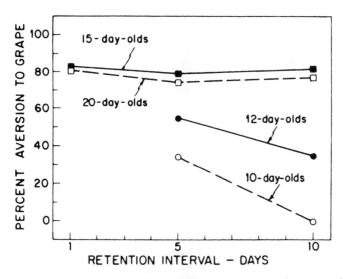

Figure 8.12 Retention of conditioned aversion to the taste of grape juice in rat pups of various ages as a function of the retention interval. (From Campbell and Alberts, "Ontogeny of long-term memory for learned taste aversions." *Behavioral and Neural Biology, 25,* 139–56. © 1979 by Academic Press. Reprinted by permission.)

[1]The relation between retention and age applies only to altricial animals. The precocial guinea pig trained at 3 days of age to run to a particular side of a T maze in order to escape shock exhibits a level of retention at 75 days of age virtually identical to that of an animal trained initially as an adult and retested 72 days later (Campbell, 1984). Therefore the level of neurological maturity at the time of original learning plays an important role in the capacity to retain information.

Alberts, 1979). This relation between retention and task received further support from Bachevalier and Blozovski (1980), who classically conditioned a leg flexion response using a vibrotactile CS and shock UCS in 0-, 2-, 3-, and 4-day-old rats. Testing revealed that *all* animals, even those less than a day old at the time of original learning, retained the CS–CR association for 24 hours.

Although the ability to retain information of any sort for even a brief period of time obviously depends on the attainment of a minimal level of neurological maturation, there is no precise point in postnatal development demarcating organisms that can from those that cannot remember over relatively long periods of time. Rather, characteristics of the task determine the length of time over which information is retained. The fact that classically but not instrumentally conditioned responses can be retained over a 24-hour period by rats less than 1 day of age suggests that task complexity might be a relevant dimension if one assumes that classical conditioning, because of its involuntary nature, is indeed a simpler form of learning than instrumental conditioning.

Infantile Amnesia

Whereas data unequivocally show that infants can acquire information and retain it over varying periods of time, much of what is acquired during early life is eventually lost; both adult humans and nonhumans alike recall little about their infancy and childhood. Dudycha and Dudycha (1941) described five studies with human subjects in which the average ages of the earliest reported memories are 3.0, 3.0, 3.5, 3.7, and 3.8 years. Mare (cited by Spear, 1978), reviewing 270 autobiographies, found that only three authors described events that occurred prior to the age of 2 and that only 13 authors discussed events taking place prior to the age of 3. The exaggerated loss of memories of events that occurred during early life is referred to as *infantile amnesia*.

Alleviation of Infantile Amnesia

The cause of infantile amnesia, although subject to a great deal of speculation (Spear, 1978), is not known. What is known is how infantile amnesia can be alleviated. Campbell and Jaynes (1966), in their now classical paper, suggest one mechanism by which early learning experiences can be preserved.

> Although obvious and disarmingly simple, it yet seems to the authors of such neglected importance as to warrant this note and the coining of a term for it. By *reinstatement* we denote a small amount of an experience over the developmental period which is enough to maintain an early learned response at a high level, but is not enough to produce any effect in animals which have not had the early experience. [p. 478]

Their reinstatement concept was derived from an experiment in which 25-day-old rats acquired an association between a stimulus and electrical shock. It was accomplished by placing rats in the apparatus illustrated in Figure 8.13. The black compartment had a grid floor through which shock could be delivered. Shock was not delivered when the animals were in the white compartment. Two groups of animals were placed in the black compartment, the door was closed,

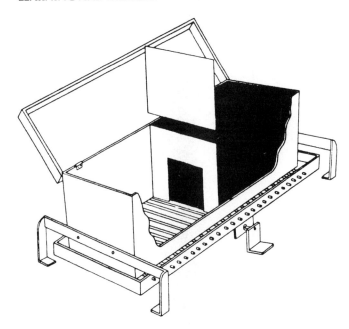

Figure 8.13 Apparatus used for studying retention of conditioned fear in animals of different ages. (From Campbell, *Comparative Perspectives on the Development of Memory*. © 1984 by Lawrence Erlbaum Associates. Reprinted by permission.

and shock was administered in 2-second bursts about every 20 seconds for 5 minutes. A control group of rats was treated identically except that shock was not given. During the next month one shock, the reinstatement, was given 7, 14, and 21 days after the original training session. Reinstatements, which were administered in the black compartment, were given to one of the early shock groups and to the control group. Animals spent time in the white compartment either before or after receiving reinstatements. The second early shock group was also placed in the black compartment, but reinstatements were not given.

At 53 days of age the animals were tested by placing them in the black compartment with the door removed, enabling them to run into the white compartment. The data from this experiment are depicted in Figure 8.14. Only the animals that had had early experience with shock *and* the reinstatements behaved as if they remembered that black was associated with punishment, as they spent most of the session in the safe white compartment. Animals given reinstatement but not the early fear training showed no evidence of having acquired a fear of the black compartment. Therefore, the reinstatement stimulus by itself is incapable of establishing the learned fear response. Its efficacy depends on a previously established memory.

According to Campbell and Jaynes (1966), infantile amnesia can be alleviated by exposing animals to a truncated form of the original conditioning experience, by "reminding" them about the event. Their reinstatement consisted in expo-

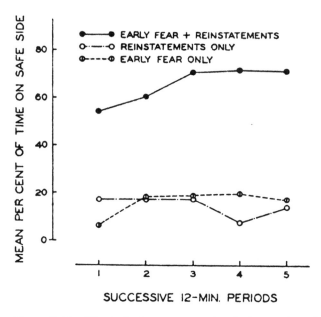

Figure 8.14   Effect of reinstatement of early fear on later behavior (From Campbell and Jaynes, "Reinstatement." *Psychological Review, 73,* 478–80. © 1966 by The American Psychological Association. Reprinted by permission.)

sure to the CS and UCS. However, exposure to only the CS or the UCS also has been shown to facilitate retention (Richardson, Ebner, & Riccio, 1981; Silvestri, Rohrbaugh, & Riccio, 1970; Spear & Parsons, 1976).

Infantile amnesia also can be alleviated by ensuring that stimuli present within the context of the original learning situation are also present during later testing. This form of alleviation has been called *contextual matching.* Solheim, Hensler, and Spear (1980) demonstrated that young animals trained to perform an active avoidance response in the presence of an odor and tested in the presence of a different odor exhibit a retention deficit relative to animals that were trained and tested in the presence of the same odor. Contextual matching of internal stimuli also is effective. Twenty-one-day-old rats injected with pentobarbital just prior to passive avoidance training exhibited better retention when tested after pentobarbital treatment than animals that received the drug during acquisition and saline during testing (Richardson, Riccio, & Jonke, 1983). Illness induced by lithium injections also facilitates retention if the animals are ill during both acquisition and the retention test (Richardson, Riccio, & Axiotis, 1986).

The lack of contextual matching may account, at least in part, for the inability to remember events that occur during infancy and childhood. As Rovee-Collier and Hayne (1987) stated:

the probability of reencountering portions of the identical context of our early experiences, real or perceived, diminishes substantially as time passes, as our environment changes, and as we grow and change. Because physical and perceptual changes are more rapid during infancy than during any later period of development, this factor may play a particularly major role in infantile amnesia. [pp. 231–232]

That contextual matching facilitates later performance is not surprising if the phenomenon is viewed within the well-known framework of stimulus control. As initially described by Skinner (1938), context associated with reinforced responding acts as a "setting event," or *discriminative stimulus,* that signals the availability of reinforcement. During the course of conditioning, behavior comes to be controlled by the discriminative stimulus; that is, responding occurs only when the discriminative stimulus is present. If contextual stimuli are actually discriminative stimuli, it is no wonder that their absence during a later testing episode can lead to poor performance. Viewed in this way, the concept of contextual matching is redundant and can be dispensed with.

Data from Humans

Visual Attention Studies

Human infants from 2 to 12 months of age are traditionally believed to be able to retain information for only a matter of minutes (see reviews by Olson, 1976; Werner & Perlmutter, 1979). This conclusion is based on data from studies of visual attention. An example of such a study is one in which infants are briefly exposed to a stimulus and after a delay are presented with that same stimulus and a novel stimulus. The idea is that infants will have habituated to the familiar stimulus during its initial presentation, therefore preferring to gaze at the novel stimulus. Should the infant prefer the novel stimulus, by definition it must remember the original stimulus. By delaying the presentation of the original stimulus plus the novel stimulus for various periods of time, one can determine the upper limit of the infant's retention capacity. With this procedure novelty preferences have been reported with delays of up to 15 minutes (Strauss, 1981, as cited by Rovee-Collier and Hayne, 1987).

Another type of visual attention procedure is the delayed response task, which involves varying the time between the presentation of a visual stimulus and reinforcement. Diamond and Doar (1989) attracted an infant's attention by holding up a toy. As the infant watched, the toy was placed into one of two "hiding wells." The wells were then concealed with identical covers. After a delay of 0 to 12 seconds, during which time the infant was distracted so as to break its fixation on the positive hiding well, the infant was allowed to reach for and, if successful, play with the toy. How long a delay can infants tolerate between exposure to the toy and the opportunity to obtain it by reaching into the correct hiding well? How long can they remember the location of the toy? Again, it is shown that infants have a remarkably short retention capacity; only 50% of 12-month-olds were able to reach the learning criterion (14 correct responses to 16 trials) with a delay of 8 seconds; none tolerated a delay of 12 seconds. Similar findings have been presented by Brody (1981), among others.

The data from these visual attention experiments warrant only a single conclusion, namely, that human infants lack the capacity to retain information for periods longer than a few minutes. Or do they? According to the research of Rovee-Collier and associates, infant retention must be measured in days and even weeks, surely not in minutes. This disparity of major proportion has to do with how retention is assessed. Instead of the customary visual attention task, Rovee-Collier performed a conditioning analysis of infant memory similar to that used with nonhuman infants. This novel approach has elicited criticism from various quarters because it assumes that human memory and nonhuman memory are basically the same, a supposition at variance with the established view that human memory involves

> the conscious recollection of having experienced an event before. This very narrow definition restricts the concept of memory solely to verbally competent humans. From this perspective, the development of memory is synonymous with the development of language, and no evidence of memory can, by definition, be obtained either for humans prior to the age that they can verbally articulate their sense of "past" or for any nonhuman species including nonhuman primates. [Rovee-Collier and Hayne, 1987, p. 232]

Conditioning Studies

Using the kicking-produced "mobile" conjugate reinforcement technique described earlier, Greco et al. (1986) and Sullivan, Rovee-Collier, and Tynes (1976) subjected 2- and 3-month-old infants, respectively, to 2- 15-minute acquisition sessions on consecutive days followed sometime later by a 15-minute long-term retention session. The data are presented in Figure 8.15. To account for individual differences in response rate, the data are converted to retention ratios by dividing response rate during the long-term retention test by the response rate during the preceding session. As seen in Figure 8.15, 3-month-olds exhibited significant retention after as long as an 8-day delay between acquisition and the retention test. The 2-month-olds could withstand a delay of 24 hours.

The results of Rovee-Collier's conditioning analysis (see also review by Rovee-Collier & Hayne, 1987) clearly showed that infants are able to retain information for a much longer period of time than has previously been reported from visual attention research. Furthermore, retention can be enhanced by the method of reinstatement. As shown in Figure 8.15, by 14 days the 3-month-olds no longer remembered the conditioning task. However, retention *is* displayed at 14 days if 24 hours prior to the retention test the infants are exposed to a moving mobile (the mobile is moved by the experimenter, not the infant) for 3 minutes (Rovee-Collier, Patterson, & Hayne, 1985). To be an effective reinstating stimulus the mobile must be virtually identical to the mobile used during acquisition; even a slight change renders it ineffectual.

Rovee-Collier and associates showed clearly that within the context of a conditioning analysis human infants possess the capacity to retain information about an event for periods of time well beyond the few seconds or minutes reported by investigators who assess memory with visual attention tasks. One must ask why the two methods of assessing retention capacity produce such disparate findings. Rovee-Collier (1983) believed it has to do with the fact that,

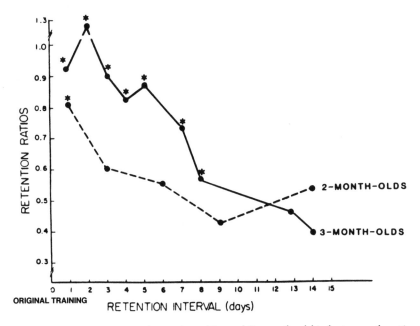

Figure 8.15 Mean retention ratios of 2- and 3-month-old infants as a function of the retention interval (* = retention). (From Greco et al., "Ontogeny of early event memory: I. Forgetting and retrieval by 2- and 3-month olds." *Infant Behavior and Development, 9,* 441–60. © 1986 by Ablex Publishing Corporation. Reprinted by permission.)

unlike visual attention procedures, the instrumental conditioning technique allows the infant to control its environment and "that the greater the degree of control infants are allowed to exert over their sources of environmental stimulation, the more robust are the demonstrations of their learning and memorial prowess."

As convincing as the data of Rovee-Collier and her associates are to some, they have not persuaded others who consider human memory to be distinct from the relatively simple ability of nonhumans and human infants participating in Rovee-Collier's conditioning studies to merely recognize stimuli. As Strauss and Carter (1984) contended:

> In general this research has demonstrated that, beginning at an early age, infants possess some relatively sophisticated recognitory abilities. For the most part, these abilities appear to be developmentally invariant and quite similar to the recognitory abilities of other infrahuman species. Yet, does this research truly reflect the developing memorial abilities of the infant? We suggest that research conducted thus far is still extremely limited . . . that future infant research will benefit more by focusing on issues common to the adult and developmental memory literature than on current models of animal learning and memory. [pp. 318–319]

Until such time as the fundamental differences in the conception of human memory are resolved, if ever, consensus will not be reached concerning the human infant's ability to remember, as well as the infant's development of memorial capacity.

CONCLUDING COMMENTS

Beginning at a very early age humans and nonhumans alike possess the ability to form associations between stimuli and between responses and their outcomes. Moreover, organisms retain those associations for periods of time as determined by age and characteristics of the task. Although retention or memory can be augmented by exposing the organism to stimuli connected with the original learning experience, most associations formed during early life are eventually forgotten, a phenomenon referred to as infantile amnesia.

Is it possible that the exaggerated forgetting of events that transpires during early life has some functional significance? Are most events that occur during our infancy and early childhood of so little import that they do not warrant the expenditure of what may be a finite amount of memory storage capacity? Or might many of those early events interfere with potentially important associations to be formed later? Curiously, virtually no attention has been paid to the possible utility of infantile amnesia. A functional analysis of infantile amnesia, although a difficult undertaking, may add to our understanding of the ontogeny of learning and memory.

REFERENCES

Abrahamson, D., Brackbill, Y., Carpenter Y., and Fitzgerald, H. E. (1970). Interaction of stimulus and response in infant conditioning. *Psychosomatic Medicine, 32,* 319–25.

Amsel, A., Burdette, D. R., and Letz, R. (1976). Appetitive learning, patterned alternation, and extinction in 10-day-old rats with non-lactating suckling as reward. *Nature, 262,* 816–18.

Amsel, A., and Chen, J. S. (1976). Ontogeny of persistence: Immediate and long-term persistence in rats varying in training age between 17 and 65 days. *Journal of Comparative and Physiological Psychology, 90,* 808–20.

Bachevalier, J., and Blozovski, D. (1980). Acquisition and retention of classical conditioning in the newborn rat. *Developmental Psychobiology, 13,* 519–26.

Bernston, C. G., Tuber, C. G., Ronca, A. E., and Bachman, D. S. (1983). The decerebrate human: Associative learning. *Experimental Neurology, 81,* 77–88.

Blass, E. M., Ganchrow, J. R., and Steiner, J. E. (1984). Classical conditioning in newborn humans 2–48 hours of age. *Infant Behavior and Development, 7,* 223–35.

Blozovski, D., and Cudennec, A. (1980). Passive avoidance learning in the young rat. *Developmental Psychobiology, 13,* 513–18.

Blozovski, D., and Dumery, V. (1987). Development of amygdaloid cholineergic mediation of passive avoidance learning in the rat. *Experimental Brain Research, 67,* 70–76.

Blozovski, D., and Hennocq, N. (1982). Effects of antimuscarinic cholinergic drugs injected systemically or into the hippocampal-entorhinal area upon passive avoidance learning in young rats. *Psychopharmacology, 76,* 351–8.

Bogen, H. (1967). Conditioning gastric secretions. Trans. in Y. Brackbill and G. G. Thompson (Eds.), *Behavior in infancy and early childhood* (pp. 231–36). New York: Free Press.

Brackbill, Y., and Kottsova, M. M. (1967). Conditioning and learning. In Y. Brackbill and G. G. Thompson (Eds.), *Behavior in infancy and early childhood* (pp. 138–51). New York: Free Press.

Brackbill, Y., Lintz, L. M., and Fitzgerald, H. E. (1968). Differences in the autonomic and somatic conditioning of infants. *Psychosomatic Medicine, 30,* 193–201.

Brody, L. R. (1981). Visual short-term cued recall in infancy. *Society for Research in Child Development, 52,* 242–50.

Burdette, D. R., Brake, S., Chen, J.-S., and Amsel, A. (1976). Ontogeny of persistence: Immediate extinction effects in preweaning and weaning rats. *Animal Learning and Behavior, 4,* 131–38.

Butterfield, E. C., and Siperstein, G. N. (1972). Influence of contingent auditory stimulation upon non-nutritional suckle. In J. Bosma (Ed.), *Oral sensation and perception: The mouth of the infant* (pp. 231–54). Springfield, IL: Charles C Thomas.

Caldwell, D. F., and Werboff, J. (1962). Classical conditioning in newborn rats. *Science, 136,* 1118–19.

Camp, L. L., and Rudy, J. W. (1988). Changes in the categorization of appetitive and aversive events during postnatal development of the rat. *Developmental Psychobiology, 21,* 25–42.

Campbell, B. A. (1984). Reflections on the ontogeny of learning and memory. In R. Kail and N. E. Spear (Eds.), *Comparative perspectives on the development of memory,* (pp. 23–35). Hillsdale, NJ: Lawrence Erlbaum Associates.

Campbell, B. A., and Alberts, J. R. (1979). Ontogeny of long-term memory for learned taste aversions. *Behavioral and Neural Biology, 25,* 139–56.

Campbell, B. A., and Campbell, E. H. (1962). Retention and extinction of learned fear in infant and adult rats. *Journal of Comparative and Physiological Psychology, 55,* 1–8.

Campbell, B. A., and Jaynes, J. (1966). Reinstatement. *Psychological Review, 73,* 478–80.

Campbell, B. A., Lytle, L. D., and Fibiger, H. C. (1969). Ontogeny of adrenergic arousal and cholinergic inhibitory mechanisms in the rat. *Science, 166,* 635–6.

Carlton, P. L. (1969). Brain-acetylcholine and inhibition. In J. Tapp (Ed.), *Reinforcement and behavior* (pp. 111–35). Orlando, FL: Academic Press.

Carlton, P. L., and Markiewicz, L. (1971). Behavioral effects of atropine and scopolamine. In E. Furchgott (Ed.), *Pharmacological and biophysical agents and behavior* (pp. 345–73). Orlando, FL: Academic Press.

Chen, J.-S., and Amsel, A. (1975). Retention and durability of persistence acquired by young and infant rats. *Journal of Comparative and Physiological Psychology, 89,* 238–45.

Cramer, C. P., Pfister, J. P., and Haig, K. A. (1988). Experience during suckling alters later spatial learning. *Developmental Psychobiology, 21,* 1–24.

Crevier, M. A. (1958). A histochemical and biochemical study of the polysaccharidic substances of the developing nervous system of the rat in relation with the appearance of cholinesterase activity. *Canadian Journal of Biochemistry, 36,* 275–88.

Davis, J., and Rovee-Collier, C. K. (1983). Alleviated forgetting of a learned contingency in 8-week-old infants. *Developmental Psychology, 19,* 353–65.

DeCasper, A. J., and Fifer, W. P. (1980). Of human bonding: Newborns prefer their mothers' voices. *Science, 208,* 1174–76.

Diamond, A., and Doar, B. (1989). The performance of human infants on a measure of frontal cortex function, the delayed response task. *Developmental Psychobiology, 22,* 271–94.

Dudycha, G. J., and Dudycha, M. M. (1941). Childhood memories: A review of the literature. *Psychological Bulletin, 38,* 668–82.

Feigley, D. A., and Spear, N. E. (1970). Effect of age and punishment condition on long-term retention by the rat of active- and passive-avoidance. *Journal of Comparative and Physiological Psychology, 73,* 515–26.

Fitzgerald, H. E., and Brackbill, Y. (1976). Classical conditioning in infancy: Development and constraints. *Psychological Bulletin, 83,* 353–76.

Fitzgerald, H. E., Lintz, L. M., Brackbill, Y., and Adams, G. (1967). Time perception and conditioning an autonomic response in human infants. *Perception and Motor Skills, 24,* 479–86.

Fitzgerald, H. E., and Porges, S. W. (1971). A decade of infant conditioning and learning research. *Merrill Palmer Quarterly, 17,* 79–117.

Galef, B. G., and Sherry, D. F. (1973). Mother's milk: A medium for transmission of cues reflecting the flavor of mother's diet. *Journal of Comparative and Physiological Psychology, 83,* 374–78.

Goldman, P. S. (1976). Maturation of the mammalian nervous system and the ontogeny of behavior. *Advances in the Study of Behavior, 7,* 1–89.

Goldman, P. S., and Tobach, E. (1967). Behavior modification in infant rats. *Animal Behaviour, 15,* 559–62.

Gottlieb, G. (1971). Ontogenesis of sensory function in birds and mammals. In E. Tobach, L. A. Aronson, and E. Shaw (Eds.), *The biopsychology of behavioral development* (pp. 211–47). Orlando, FL: Academic Press.

Greco, C., Rovee-Collier, C., Hayne, H., Griesler, P., and Earley, L. (1986). Ontogeny of early event memory: I. Forgetting and retrieval by 2- and 3-month olds. *Infant Behavior and Development, 9,* 441–60.

Haroutunian, V., and Campbell, B. A. (1979). Emergence of interoceptive and exteroceptive control of behavior in rats. *Science, 205,* 927–29.

Hoffman, H. S., Cohen, M. E., and DeVido, C. J. (1985). A comparison of eyelid conditioning in adults and infants. *Infant Development and Behavior, 8,* 247–54.

Hyson, R. L., and Rudy, J. W. (1984). Ontogenesis of learning: II. Variation in the rat's reflexive and learned responses to acoustic stimulation. *Developmental Psychobiology, 17,* 263–83.

Johanson, I. B., and Hall, W. G. (1979). Appetitive learning in 1-day-old rat pups. *Science, 205,* 419–21.

Jones, H. E. (1930). The retention of conditioned emotional reactions in infancy. *Journal of Genetic Psychology, 37,* 485–98.

Kagen, J., Kearsley, R. B., and Zelaza, P. R. (1978). *Infancy: Its place in development.* Cambridge, MA: Harvard University Press.

Kalnins, I. V., and Bruner, J. S. (1973). The coordination of visual observations and instrumental behavior in early infancy. *Perception, 2,* 307–14.

Kasatkin, N. I. (1972). First conditioned reflexes and the beginning of the learning process in the human infant. In G. Newton and A. H. Reisen (Eds.), *Advances in psychobiology* (pp. 289–313). New York: John Wiley & Sons.

Kasatkin, N. I., and Levikova, A. M. (1935a). On the development of early conditioned reflexes and differentiations of auditory stimuli in infants. *Journal of Experimental Psychology, 18,* 1–19.

Kasatkin, N. I., and Levikova, A. M. (1935b). The formation of visual conditioned reflexes in infants during the first year of life. *Journal of General Psychology, 12,* 416–35.

Kenney, J. T., and Blass, E. M. (1977). Suckling as incentive to instrumental learning in preweanling rats. *Science, 196,* 898–89.

Kirby, R. H. (1963). Acquisition, extinction, and retention of an avoidance response in rats as a function of age. *Journal of Comparative and Physiological Psychology, 56,* 158–62.

Kobre, K. R., and Lipsitt, L. P. (1972). A negative contrast effect in newborns. *Journal of Experimental Child Psychology, 14,* 81–91.

Koch, J. (1968). Conditioned orienting reactions to persons and things in 2-5 month old infants. *Human Development, 11,* 81–91.

Krachkovskaia, M. V. (1959). Reflex changes in the leukocyte count of newborn infants in relation to food intake. *Pavlov Journal of Higher Nervous Activity, 9,* 193–99.

Krasnogorskii, N. I. (1967). The formation of conditioned reflexes in the young child. Trans. in Y. Brackbill and G. G. Thompson (Eds.), *Behavior in infancy and early childhood* (pp. 257–79). New York: Free Press.

Kucharski, D., Richter, N. G., and Spear, N. E. (1985). Conditioned aversion is promoted by memory of CS. *Animal Learning and Behavior, 13,* 143–51.

Ladensky, H., Consolo, S., Peri, G., and Garattini, S. (1972). Changes in acetylcholine and choline concentrations and choline acetyltransferase activity in the developing rat brain: Effects of polythiouracil. *Archives Internationales de Pharmacodynamie et de Therapie, 196* (suppl), 133–35.

Lintz, L. M., Fitzgerald, H. E., and Brackbill, Y. (1967). Conditioning the eye blink to sound in infants. *Psychonomic Science, 7,* 405–6.

Lipsitt, L. P., Pederson, L. J., and DeLucia, C. A. (1966). Conjugate reinforcement of operant conditioning in infants. *Psychonomic Science, 4,* 66–68.

Little, A. H., Lipsitt, L. P., and Rovee-Collier, C. (1984). Classical conditioning and retention of the infant's eyelid response: Effects of age and interstimulus interval. *Journal of Experimental Child Psychology, 37,* 512–24.

Marquis, D. P. (1941). Can conditioned responses be established in the newborn infant? *Journal of Genetic Psychology, 39,* 479–92.

Martin, L. T., and Alberts, J. R. (1979). Taste aversions to mother's milk: The age-related role of nursing in acquisition and expression of a learned association. *Journal of Comparative and Physiological Psychology, 93,* 430–45.

Matthews, D. A., Nadler, J. V., Lynch, G. S., and Cotman, C. W. (1974). Development of cholinergic innervation in the hippocampal formation of the rat: I. Histochemical demonstration of acetylcholinesterase activity. *Developmental Biology, 36,* 130–41.

McCormick, D. A., and Thompson, R. F. (1984). Cerebellum: Essential involvement in the classically conditioned eyelid response. *Science, 223,* 296–99.

Miller, J. S., Jagielo, J. A., and Spear, N. E. (1989). Age-related differences in short-term retention of the separable elements of a conditioned odor aversion. *Journal of Experimental Psychology: Animal Behavior Processes, 15,* 194–201.

Miller, J. S., Molina, J. C., and Spear, N. E. (1990). Ontogenetic differences in the expression of odor-aversion learning in 4- and 8-day-old rats. *Developmental Psychobiology, 23,* 319–30.

Misanin, J. R., Haigh, J. M., Hinderliter, C. F., and Nagy, Z. M. (1973). Analysis of response competition and nondiscriminated escape training of neonatal rats. *Journal of Comparative and Physiological Psychology, 85,* 570–80.

Misanin, J. R., Lariviere, N. A., Turns, A. E., and Turns, C. F. (1986). The effect of home cage stimuli on acquisition and retention of an active avoidance response in previsual rats. *Developmental Psychobiology, 19,* 37–47.

Misanin, J. R., Nagy, Z. M., Keiser, E. F., and Bowen, W. (1971). Emergence of long-term memory in the neonatal rat. *Journal of Comparative and Physiological Psychology, 77,* 188–99.

Moran, T. H., Lew, M. F., and Blass, E. M. (1981). Intracranial self-stimulation in 3-day-old rat pups. *Science, 214,* 1366–68.

Moye, T. B., and Rudy, J. W. (1985). Ontogenesis of learning: VI. Learned and unlearned responses to visual stimulation in the infant hooded rat. *Developmental Psychobiology, 18,* 395–409.

Moye, T. B., and Rudy, J. W. (1987). Ontogenesis of trace conditioning in young rats: Dissociation of associative and memory processes. *Developmental Psychobiology, 20,* 405–14.

Myslivecek, J., and Hassmannova, J. (1980). Passive avoidance learning in newborn rats. *Proceedings of the International Union of Physiological Science, 14,* 602.

Myslivecek, J., and Hassmannova, J. (1990). Early inhibitory learning in the rat: I. Learning and memory development. *Developmental Psychobiology, 23,* 119–28.

Nagy, Z. M., and Mueller, P. M. (1973). Effects of amount of original training upon onset of a 24-hour memory capacity in neonatal mice. *Journal of Comparative and Physiological Psychology, 85,* 151–59.

Nagy, Z. M., Newman, J. A., Olsen, P. L., and Hinderliter, C. F. (1972). Ontogeny of memory in the neonatal mouse. *Journal of Comparative and Physiological Psychology, 81,* 380–93.

Nagy, Z. M., Pagano, M. R., and Gable, T. (1976). Differential development of 24-hour capacities of two components of *t* maze escape learning by infant mice. *Animal Learning and Behavior, 4,* 25–29.

Norman, R. J., Buchwald, J. S., and Villablanca, J. R. (1977). Classical conditioning with auditory discrimination of the eye blink in decerebrate cats. *Science, 195,* 551–3.

Ohr, P. S., Fagen, J. W., Rovee-Collier, C., Hayne, H., and Vander Linde, E. (1989). Amount of training and retention by infants. *Developmental Psychobiology, 22,* 68–80.

Olson, G. M. (1976). An information processing analysis of visual memory and habituation in infants. In T. J. Tighe and R. N. Leaton (Eds.), *Habituation: Perspectives from child development, animal behavior, and neurophysiology* (pp.239–77). Hillsdale, NJ: Lawrence Erlbaum Associates.

Papousek, H. (1961). Conditioned head rotation in infants in the first months of life. *Acta Paediatrica, 50,* 565–76.

Ray, D., and Nagy, Z. M. (1978). Emerging cholinergic mechanisms and ontogeny of response inhibition in the mouse. *Journal of Comparative and Physiological Psychology, 92,* 335–49.

Razran, G. H. S. (1933). Conditioned responses in children: A behavioral and quantitative review of experimental studies. *Archives of Psychology, 23,*123–31.

Riccio, D. C., and Schulenburg, C. J. (1969). Age-related deficits in acquisition of a passive avoidance response. *Canadian Journal of Psychology, 23,* 429–37.

Riccio, D. C., Rohrbaugh, M., and Hodges, I. A. (1968). Developmental aspects of passive and active avoidance learning in rats. *Developmental Psychobiology, 1,* 108–11.

Richardson, R., Ebner, D. L., and Riccio, D. C. (1981). Effects of delayed testing on passive avoidance of conditioned fear stimuli in young rats. *Bulletin of the Psychonomic Society, 18,* 211–14.

Richardson, R., Riccio, D. C., and Axiotis, R. (1986). Alleviation of infantile amnesia in rats by internal and external contextual cues. *Developmental Psychobiology, 19,* 453–62.

Richardson, R., Riccio, D. C., and Jonke, T. (1983). Alleviation of infantile amnesia in rats by means of a pharmacological contextual state. *Developmental Psychobiology, 16,* 511–18.

Rovee, C. K., and Rovee, D. T. (1969). Conjugate reinforcement of infant exploratory behavior. *Journal of Experimental Child Psychology, 8,* 33–39.

Rovee-Collier, C. K. (1983). Infants as problem solvers: A psychobiological perspective. In M. D. Zeiler and P. Harzem (Eds.), *Advances in analysis of behavior,* vol. 3 (pp. 63–101). New York: John Wiley & Sons.

Rovee-Collier, C. (1986). The rise and fall of infant classical conditioning research: Its promise for the study of early development. In L. P. Lipsitt and C. Rovee-Collier (Eds.), *Advances in infancy research* (pp. 139–58). Norwood, NY: Ablex Publishing Corp.

Rovee-Collier, C. (1987). Learning and memory in infancy. In J. D. Osofsky (Ed.), *Handbook of infant development* (pp. 98–148). New York: John Wiley & Sons.

Rovee-Collier, C. K., and Capatides, J. B. (1979). Positive behavioral contrast in 3-month-old infants on multiple conjugate reinforcement schedules. *Journal of the Experimental Analysis of Behavior, 32,* 15–27.

Rovee-Collier, C., and Dufault, D. (1991). Multiple contexts and memory retrieval at three months. *Developmental Psychobiology, 24,* 39–49.

Rovee-Collier, C., and Hayne, H. (1987). Reactivation of infant memory: Implications for cognitive development. *Advances in Child Development and Behavior, 20,* 185–238.

Rovee-Collier, C., Patterson, J., and Hayne, H. (1985). Specificity in the reactivation of infant memory. *Developmental Psychobiology, 18,* 559–74.

Rudy, J. W., and Cheatle, M. D. (1977). Odor aversion learning in neonatal rats. *Science, 198,* 845–46.

Rudy, J. W., and Cheatle, M. D. (1979). Ontogeny of associative learning: Acquisition of odor aversion by neonatal rats. In N. E. Spear and B. A. Campbell (Eds.), *Ontogeny of learning and memory* (pp. 157–88). Hillsdale, NJ: Lawrence Erlbaum Associates.

Scherrer, J. (1968). Electrophysiological aspects of cortical development. *Progress in Brain Research, 22,* 480–89.

Schulenburg, C. J., Riccio, D. C., and Stikes, E. R. (1973). Acquisition and retention of a passive-avoidance response as a function of age in rats. *Journal of Comparative and Physiological Psychology, 74,* 75–83.

Silvestri, R., Rohrbaugh, M., and Riccio, D. C. (1970). Conditions influencing the retention of learned fear in young rats. *Developmental Psychology, 2,* 389–95.

Siqueland, E. R. (1968). Reinforcement patterns and extinction in human newborns. *Journal of Experimental Child Psychology, 6,* 431–32.

Siqueland, E. R. (1969a). The development of instrumental exploratory behavior during the first year of human life. Paper presented at the meeting of the Society for Research in Child Development, Santa Monica, CA.

Siqueland, E. R. (1969b). Further development in infant learning. Paper presented at the meeting of the 19th International Congress of Psychology, London.

Skinner, B. F. (1938). *The behavior of organisms.* East Norwalk, CT: Appleton & Lange.

Smith, G. J., and Spear, N. E. (1978). Effects of the home environment on withholding behaviors and conditioning in infant and neonatal rats. *Science, 202,* 327–29.

Smith, G. J., and Spear, N. E. (1981). Home environmental stimuli facilitate learning of shock-escape spatial discrimination in rats 7–11 days of age. *Behavioral and Neural Biology, 30,* 327–29.

Smith, G. J., Spear, L. P., and Spear, N. E. (1979). Ontogeny of cholinergic mediation of behaviors in the rat. *Journal of Comparative and Physiological Psychology, 93,* 636–47.

Solheim, G. S., Hensler, J. G., and Spear, N. E. (1980). Age-dependent contextual effects on short-term active avoidance retention in rats. *Behavioral and Neural Biology, 30,* 250–99.

Spear, N. E. (1978). *The processing of memories: Forgetting and retention.* Hillsdale, NJ: Lawrence Erlbaum Associates.

Spear, N. E., and Parsons, P. (1976). Analysis of a reactivation treatment: Ontogeny and alleviated forgetting. In D. Medin, R. Davis, and W. Roberts (Eds.), *Processes of animal memory* (pp. 135–65). Hillsdale, NJ: Lawrence Erlbaum Associates.

Stehouwer, D. J., and Campbell, B. A. (1980). Ontogeny of passive avoidance: Role of task demands and development of species-typical behaviors. *Developmental Psychobiology, 13,* 385–98.

Steinert, P. A., Infurna, R. N., Jardular, M. F., and Spear, N. E. (1979). Effects of CS concentration on long-delay taste aversion learning in preweanling and adult rats. *Behavioral and Neural Biology, 27,* 487–502.

Strauss, M. S., and Carter, P. (1984). Infant memory: Limitations and future directions. In R. Kail and N. E. Spear (Eds.), *Comparative perspectives on the development of memory* (pp. 317–24). Hillsdale, NJ: Lawrence Erlbaum Associates.

Sullivan, M. W., Rovee-Collier, C. K., and Tynes, D. M. (1979). A conditioning analysis of infant long-term memory. *Child Development, 50,* 152–62.

Sullivan, R. M., Taborsky-Barba, L., Mendoza, R., Itano, A., Leon, M., Cotman, C. W., Payne, T. F., and Lott, I. (1991). Olfactory classical conditioning in neonates. *Pediatrics, 87,* 511–17.

Vogt, M. B., and Rudy, J. W. (1984). Ontogenesis of learning: I. Variation in the rat's reflexive and learned response to gustatory stimulation. *Developmental Psychobiology, 17,* 11–33.

Watson, J. B., and Raynor, R. (1920). Conditioned emotional reactions. *Journal of Experimental Psychology, 3,* 1–14.

Werner, J. S., and Perlmutter, M. (1979). Development of visual memory in infants. *Advances in Child Development and Behavior, 14,* 2–56.

Wigal, T., Kucharski, D., and Spear, N. E. (1984). Familiar contextual odors promote discrimination learning in preweanling but not in older rats. *Developmental Psychobiology, 17,* 555–70.

Wilson, L. M., and Riccio, D. C. (1976). Scopolamine's effect on passive avoidance behavior in immature rats. *Developmental Psychobiology, 9,* 245–54.

9

Transitions: Weaning
and Puberty

At a time when the first beginnings of sexual satisfaction are still linked with the taking of nourishment, the sexual instinct has a sexual object outside the infant's own body in the shape of his mother's breast. It is only later that the instinct loses that object. . . .

As we all know, it is not until puberty that the sharp distinction is established between the masculine and feminine characters. From that time on, this contrast has a more decisive influence than any other upon the shaping of human life.

S. Freud, 1905

Development consists of a multitudinous number of transitions the totality of which transform the immature organism into the adult. Of those transitions, two of the most important from a psychological standpoint have been selected for discussion here. One is weaning, the passage from nursing to independent feeding. This event not only is important for nutritional reasons, but for some species it marks emancipation from the mother, eliminating her role in the developmental process. A second is puberty, the transition from a nonreproductive to a reproductive state or, from a behavioral perspective, the transition from a state of assexuality to one of sexuality.

WEANING

Except for a small number of precocial species such as the guinea pig, which can survive from birth in the absence of the mother, obtaining mothers' milk is indispensable to the survival of the infant mammal. Beyond providing the sole source of nourishment, milk and nursing also contribute to development in other ways. For example, the infant's vulnerability to infection is reduced because the colostrum, the milk formed immediately after parturition, contains antibodies that reduce such vulnerability (Barlow et al., 1974). Not only does the contact between mother and newborn necessitated by nursing assist in keeping the infant warm, but the long periods of time mothers spend with their young (5-day-old rat pups spend 70% to 80% of the day suckling [Plaut, 1974]) ensure the availability of an adult to defend against predators.[1] The odors associated with nursing have even been implicated in psychosexual development as expressed in a male's later selection of a mate (Fillion & Blass, 1986). Of course the degree to which the infant's need to suckle is satisfied has been viewed by some as a major determinant of personality development.

At some point, however, the youngster must become emancipated, at least physically, from its mother. This discussion focuses on the factors involved in the process of emancipation, the transition from nursing to the independent ingestion of foods typical of those consumed by adults of that species.

Suckling and Independent Feeding

A comparison of suckling to independent feeding reveals a number of similarities and differences that may provide insight into the processes that promote the transition between the two states.

Similarities

Beyond the fact that both suckling and independent feeding enable nutrients to be brought from without to within, the behaviors also correspond in two other ways. First, suckling as well as feeding is regulated by changes in internal state. This point was first demonstrated by Houpt and Epstein (1973), who deprived neonatal rats of milk but not maternal care by removing them from their mothers and placing them with a nonlactating maternally behaving foster mother. They remained with the foster mother for 4 hours. The young were weighed 4 hours after being returned to a lactating female. Deprivation influenced the subsequent intake of neonates as young as 1 day of age; they gained an average of 100% more than nondeprived controls (0.4 g versus 0.2 g, respectively). Similar results were obtained from 3- to 7-day-old young (see Figure 9.1).

Houpt and Epstein also asked if stomach loading depresses subsequent food intake of neonatal rats as it is known to do to adults. The procedure was the same as that used to assess the influence of deprivation except that at the termination of the 4-hour fasting period half of the animals (3- to 7-day-olds) were given a stomach load of either 0.4 g synthetic dogs' milk, 0.4 g nonnutritive kaolin (clay) mixed with distilled water, or 0.4 to 0.7 g of distilled water. The remaining animals were given no stomach load. As seen in Figure 9.2, both nutritive and nonnutritive loads depressed subsequent intake. Water was the least effective presumably because it empties much more quickly from the stomach than do milk and kaolin (see also Drewett, 1978, and Houpt & Houpt, 1975). Reduction of intake by stomach loading also has been reported with kittens (Keopke & Pribram, 1971) piglets (Stephens, 1975), and puppies (Stanley, 1970).

Neonates, like adults, have the ability to regulate their intake in response to

---

[1]When the mother herself is a source of prey, it may be advantageous for her to spend as little time as possible with the young. This situation is the case for the rabbit. It leaves the offspring almost immediately after their birth and returns to feed them approximately once every 24 hours (Zarrow, Denenberg, & Anderson, 1965).

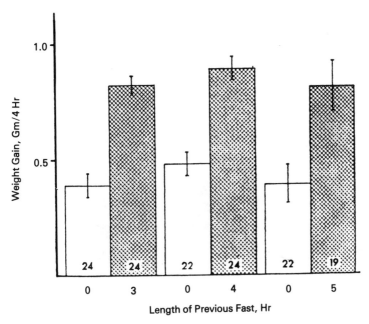

Figure 9.1 Effect of deprivation on subsequent weight gain in suckling rats. Cross-hatched columns represent mean weight gain of previous fasted rats; clear columns represent mean weight gain of nonfasted rats. Vertical lines represent the SE. Numbers within columns are the number of rats tested. (From Houpt and Epstein, "Ontogeny of controls of food intake in the rat: GI gill and glucoprivation." *American Journal of Physiology, 225*, 58–66. © 1973 by The American Physiological Society. Reprinted by permission.)

internal changes associated with prior ingestion. How do they it? By simply observing neonates of various species it becomes apparent that regulation is *not* accomplished by varying the amount of time at the nipple, as most of the time spent by the neonate with their mother is consumed by nipple attachment. Attachment occurs even when it does not procure milk. Milk is available only when secreted into the mammary ducts in response to the release of the pituitary hormone oxytocin. For the rat, it occurs at 5- to 20-minute intervals (Lincoln, Hill & Wakerley, 1973), yet attachment is virtually continuous.

That regulation of milk intake is not achieved by relinquishing the nipple has been verified experimentally by Blass, Hall, and Teicher (1979b); stomach-loaded rat pups governed their intake appropriately but did not leave the nipple. Similarly, Lorenz, Ellis, and Epstein (1982) reported that latency to attach to the nipple and frequency of attachment are unaffected by small stomach loads, which decrease milk intake. By day 20, however, those same loads reduced the frequency of attachment. Regulation by the neonate, then, must be related to the sucking response itself. Brake and colleagues (Brake, Sager, Sullivan, & Hofer, 1982; Brake, Wolfson, & Hofer, 1979) measured sucking by recording the electrical activity of jaw muscles. They reported that 3- to 20-day-old rats do

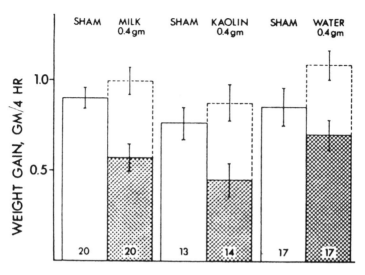

Figure 9.2 Effect of gastrointestinal fill on weight gain following deprivation in suckling rats 3 to 7 days old. Clear columns bounded by solid lines represent mean weight gain of rats that had been gastrically intubated only; cross-hatched columns represent mean weight gain of rats given a stomach load. Clear columns bounded by dashed lines represent stomach load. Height of right-hand column of each pair of columns represents total calculated weight gain including stomach load. (From Houpt and Epstein, "Ontogeny of controls of food intake in the rat: GI fill and glucoprivation." *American Journal of Physiology, 225,* 58–66. © 1973 by The American Physiological Society. Reprinted by permission.)

indeed modify their sucking response as a function of changes in nutritional status, sucking more frequently and with greater intensity after periods of milk deprivation. Furthermore, sucking is reduced by stomach loads of milk.

The adjustment of the sucking response itself probably in part explains the failure of nursing animals to regulate in a situation in which sucking behavior is functionally divorced from milk intake, that is, when a fixed amount of milk is provided to the pup regardless of the frequency and intensity of its sucks. Such a situation was created by Hall and Rosenblatt (1977) by infusing milk directly into the rat pup's mouth while it was attached to the nipple of a nonlactating female. Milk was infused at 1-minute intervals through a polyethylene cannula affixed to the back of the tongue. In this situation the 5- and 10-day-old pups, deprived of nourishment for 8 hours, consumed abnormally large quantities of milk, eventually becoming bloated, having difficulty breathing, and turning blue. Only then did they leave the nipple. Despite this seemingly painful condition, if the snout was cleaned and breathing restored the pup would reattach. This failure to regulate, in addition to being caused by the inability of the infant to adjust milk intake by modifying its sucking response, is also likely due to the fact that milk was made available at 1-minute intervals rather than at the 5- to 20-minute intervals characteristic of normal nursing.

The ability to respond to nutritional status by adjusting intake is present from an early age. It does not mean, however, that the neonate is in possession of a fully mature food regulatory mechanism, as a number of manipulations that affect the food intake of the adult are ineffective when applied to the neonate. These manipulations are considered in the following section.

A second similarity between nursing and independent feeding is that, like the latter, nursing can serve as reinforcement for the acquisition of an instrumental response. Kenny and Blass (1977) removed 6-, 11-, 16-, and 20-day-old pups from their mothers and, 24 hours later, placed them in a Y maze. An anesthetized *nonlactating* female was placed on its side in such a way as to permit the pups access to her nipple area regardless of whether they approached the female from the right or the left arm of the maze. For some of the young subjects traversing the left arm resulted in access to the nipples, whereas traversing the right arm led to nipples wrapped in gauze. The opposite was true for the other subjects. Choosing the correct arm (that which allowed contact with the nipples) was reinforced by allowing the animals 30 seconds of nonnutritive suckling (remember that the adult was not lactating). The results were clear. All subjects, regardless of age, came to reliably choose the arm that led to the uncovered nipples. Moreover, all subjects exhibited retention of the correct response when retested 48 later, requiring fewer trials than originally needed to attain the learning criterion.

These data are noteworthy in two respects. First, they further demonstrate that the capacity to acquire an instrumental response and to retain it are present from an early age. Second, sucking *itself* must be positive because it can reinforce an operant response without yielding milk. Whether nonnutritive sucking is innately reinforcing or it has acquired reinforcing properties through its association with milk is not known.

Although nonnutritive sucking has reinforcing properties, sucking that yields milk is even more rewarding, especially for older pups. Fourteen-day-old rat pups ran down a straight alley faster when the response was reinforced by access to a lactating female than by access to a nonlactating female (Letz, Burdette, Gregg, Kittrell, & Amsel, 1978). According to Kenney, Stoloff, Bruno & Blass (1979), when given a choice, 17- and 21-day-olds, but not 10- and 12-day-olds, prefer nutritive to nonnutritive sucking.

Differences

Although both nursing and independent feeding are regulated in part by internal states and they both are reinforcing, nursing and independent feeding differ in a number of respects beyond the fact that they require markedly different motor behaviors. One striking difference involves the role of olfactory stimuli. Whereas odor is not necessary with regard to independent feeding, it plays a crucial role in suckling. Teicher and Blass (1976) discovered this fact when they observed that 4- to 5-day-old rats do not attach to nipples that have been washed. If, however, cleansed nipples are coated with a distillate of the nipple wash or with pups' saliva, nipple attachment is reinstated. These findings were replicated by Blass, Teicher, Cramer, and Bruno (1977) and extended to pups aged 2 through 11 days. Suckling, then, appears to be elicited by a substance found in the pups' saliva, one the pups themselves deposit on the nipples. Because Blass et al. never observed pups to lick nipples prior to attaching to them, they concluded that the substance must be volatile and an olfactory cue. Their conclusion has been supported by other data showing that anosmia induced by irrigating the nasal passage with zinc sulfate or by removing the olfactory bulbs also disrupts suckling (Singh, Tucker, & Hofer, 1976; Teicher, Flaum, & Williams, 1978). Anosmia induced close to the time of weaning, although disrupting suckling, does not affect the transition to solid food (Alberts, 1976).

The participation of the pups' own saliva in the elicitation of nipple attachment does not, however, account for the *initial* sucking response, which of course is performed in the absence of their saliva on the nipples. The control of this first response in the newborn was addressed by Teicher and Blass (1977). Their findings are shown in Figure 9.3. As can be seen, both mothers' saliva and amniotic fluid reinstate nipple attachment when applied to a washed nipple. Other substances, such as saliva from a virgin female and mother's urine, are without effect. The mother, then, apparently applies a substance to her nipples that evokes the initial suckling response. Whether that substance is found separately in both saliva and amniotic fluid or solely in the latter is not known because amniotic fluid is ingested by the mother during delivery and the cleaning of the young.

Another difference between nursing and independent feeding pertains to internal controls. As discussed above, the infant rat, like the adult, can regulate its food intake, and it does so from birth. However, unlike the adult, for which regulation is controlled by various mechanisms, the infant depends primarily, if not exclusively, on stimuli arising from distension of the stomach. In other words, a number of factors that modify independent feeding are without effect in the nursing animal. One such factor involves blood glucose. Whereas decreases in blood glucose cause sated adult animals to consume relatively large quantities of food, similar declines in the young animal are without influence. This point was initially made by Teitelbaum, Cheng, and Rozin (1969) and later confirmed by Lytle, Moorcraft, and Campbell (1971), who reduced blood glucose in rats of various ages by administering insulin. Using body weight as the index of food intake, Lytle et al. (1971) found that insulin increased food intake of 25-day-old and older rats but not of 15- and 20-day-olds regardless of whether the latter had access to the mother or to solid food. This finding also was obtained by Houpt and Epstein (1973), who lowered blood glucose by administering 2-deoxy-D-glucose. Lytle et al. (1971) further reported that amphetamine, which produces anorexia in the adult, was ineffective prior to day 15 of age. Similarly, the stomach hormone cholecystokinin, which inhibits feeding in adult rats also has been reported to be ineffective in 5- and 10-day-olds (Blass, Beardsley, & Hall, 1979a). In the Blass et al. experiment, however, milk was delivered directly into the pup's mouth by tongue cannulation while it was sucking on the nipple of a nonlactating animal. Consequently, the finding that cholecystokinin did not cause a cessation of milk intake may have more to do with the procedure than with the hormone itself: Remember that 5- and 10-day-olds given oral infusions

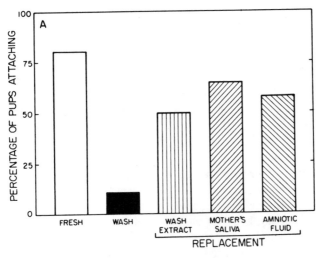

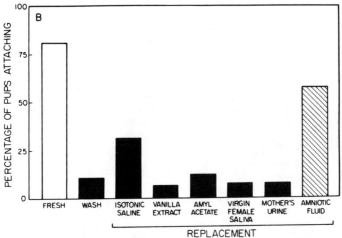

Figure 9.3 Percentage of pups attaching for their first suckling experience. (A) Conditions: on the fresh mother; after nipple wash; after a distillate of the wash; parturient mother's saliva, or amniotic fluid was painted on the nipples. (B) Conditions: on the fresh mother; after nipple wash; and after replacement with isotonic saline, vanilla extract, amyl acetate, virgin female saliva, parturient mother's urine. The effect of amniotic fluid replacement is included for comparison. (From Teicher and Blass, "First suckling response of the newborn albino rat: The roles of olfaction and amniotic fluid." *Science, 198,* 635–36. © 1977 by The American Association for the Advancement of Science. Reprinted by permission.)

must be nearly drowned in milk before they leave the nipple. Cholecystokinin may be involved in the cessation of *normal* milk intake.

Transition

Study of the weaning process raises the fundamental question of whether nursing is the youthful form of independent feeding. As a youthful or less mature form of a later behavior, and assuming that adult-like behaviors are an elaboration of infantile behaviors, one would predict that if nursing is prevented, deficits in independent feeding behavior would occur. It also would be expected that independent feeding would not emerge until a sufficient amount of nursing has transpired. That is, independent feeding should become evident only relatively late into the preweaning period. Let us begin with the first supposition, namely, that the elimination of nursing behavior should deleteriously affect independent feeding.

Hall (1975) elegantly demonstrated that nursing is *not* an essential prelude to independent feeding, that rats deprived of nursing experience wean and grow normally. A cannula was placed in the stomach of 12- to 48-hour-old rats through which an artificial diet could be administered (see Figure 9.4). The

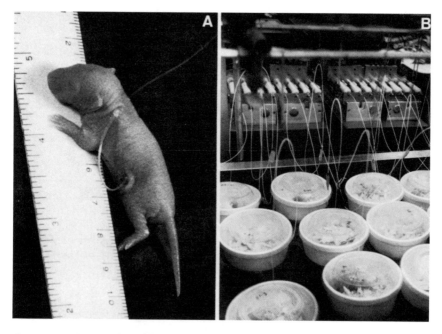

Figure 9.4   (A) A 2-day-old rat pup with its intragastric cannula in place. (B) Pups are housed in cups that float in a temperature-controlled waterbath. The cannula can be seen emerging from the lids of the cups and passing overhead to syringes mounted on infusion pumps. Diet was infused continuously. (From Hall, "Weaning and growth of artificially reared rats." *Science, 190,* 1313–315. © 1975 by The American Association for the Advancement of Science. Reprinted by permission.)

infants were kept isolated in Styrofoam cups floating in a bath of warm water. Although the artificially reared rat pups weighed less at weaning on day 18 than did those normally reared, their median time to ingest 0.5 g of solid food was identical to that of normals. Furthermore, the "artificially reared rats appeared to walk to the food supply and eat in the same fashion as pups reared normally and seemed to experience no difficulty in identifying or ingesting their first oral food." Moreover, the growth rates of artifically reared and normal animals were similar. Nursing, then, appears to be nonessential for the emergence of autonomous feeding in rats.

It is not known if nursing is necessary for the ingestion of solid food in primates. Subjects, such as Harlow's monkeys, that are isolated from their mothers from birth do eventually accept solid food. However, unlike the infant rats described above that were totally deprived of oral milk ingestion, isolated monkeys were bottle-fed. Therefore they did have nursing experience albeit in the absence of the mother. Nevertheless, it has been reported that their later ingestive behavior is not completely normal. Miller, Caul, and Mirsky (1971) examined three 9-year-old monkeys that had been totally isolated for the first year of life. Relative to three 9-year-old normally reared controls, isolates consumed about 30% more food per meal over the course of a 6-month free feeding period. Despite this elevated food intake, however, they did not gain more weight than the controls. No explanation for the finding was offered.

Let us now consider the second prediction that follows from the assumption that suckling is indispensable for the appearance of independent feeding, namely, that the latter should not arise until the later stage of the nursing period. In other words, because independent feeding develops serially from nursing, it cannot appear until a significant amount of nursing has transpired. As demonstrated by Hall, however, infant rats have the capacity to exhibit adult-like feeding patterns if they are tested away from the mother. Hall (1979) initially observed that when isolated incubator-reared infant rats are given direct oral infusions of a liquid diet they respond not like they are nursing but rather like they are eating independently, licking and "mouthing" the food so as to move it to the back of the mouth for swallowing. That these mature feeding-like behaviors are not simply peculiar to the oral infusion procedure was shown by Hall and Bryan (1980), who reported that newborn rats consume moistened powdered laboratory food, sucrose, or milk when the substances are placed on the floor of a warm test chamber. Furthermore, with the exception of 12-day-olds, the amount of intake is positively related to hours of food deprivation (see Figure 9.5).

Other factors in addition to food deprivation modulate the independent feeding of infants as they do in adults. The anorexic amphetamine, which has no influence on nursing prior to day 15 of age (Lytle et al., 1971), suppresses independent feeding of pups as young as 3 days (Hall & Williams, 1983). Norepinephrine, which induces feeding in adult rats when infused into particular areas of the brain, elicits milk intake in sated 10-day-olds feeding away from the dam (Epstein, 1984).

Hall's observations cast doubt on the view that nursing is a juvenile form of autonomous feeding by revealing that both forms of ingestive behavior occur at

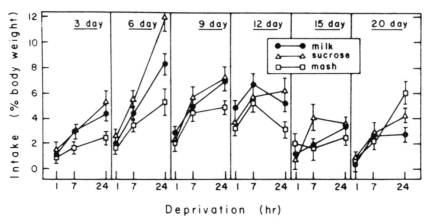

Figure 9.5   Intakes (mean ± SE) of various solutions at different ages and deprivations. (From Hall and Bryan, "The ontogeny of feeding in rats: II. Independent ingestive behavior." *Journal of Comparative Physiological Psychology, 94,* 746–56. © 1980 by The American Psychological Association. Reprinted by permission.)

an early age. Nursing and feeding, then, appear to be distinct behaviors, with the latter observable *only* when the infant is placed in the extraordinary position of being separated from the mother and forced to seek out and ingest food. Ordinarily, autonomous feeding, although within the infant's capability, is not exhibited. The issue, then, is one of identifying the mechanism or mechanisms that suppress nursing, thereby permitting independent feeding to come to the fore. For the rat the transition is completed at about the end of the fourth postpartum week when the young prefer autonomous feeding to nursing (Stoloff & Blass, 1983).

Mechanisms

Mother–Infant Interaction. Not surprisingly, both nursing and the transition to independent ingestion are in large part the result of a synchronous relationship between the mother and its infants. This synchrony is seen even with regard to the secretion of milk. During the early portion of the lactation period the availability of milk is dependent on the mother's receipt of stimuli associated with suckling, such as tactile stimulation of the nipple by the infants. Such stimuli reflexively cause the pituitary hormone prolactin to be released, which in turn promotes milk secretion (Grosvenor & Whitworth, 1974). The elimination of suckling-related stimulation, then, has the immediate effect of attenuating prolactin release. In addition, however, the removal of those stimuli also diminishes the ability of *subsequent* suckling-related stimuli to release the hormone (Grosvenor, Mena, & Schaefgen, 1967). Therefore suckling stimulation serves two functions: the immediate release of prolactin and maintenance of the responsiveness of the prolactin-releasing mechanism.

As the young mature and begin to spend time away from the mother (for the rat this period commences with eye-opening on day 14) the availability of suckling-related stimuli markedly declines. Why, then, is milk secretion not affected? As demonstrated with rats by Grosvenor, Maiweg, and Mena (1970), on about day 14 prolactin, in addition to being released by suckling-related stimuli, is also secreted in response to pup-emitted stimuli such as odor and sound, which can be perceived by the adult from afar. Here then is a clear example of mother–infant synchrony: the release of prolactin by nonsuckling pup-related stimuli coincident with the development of pups' exploratory behavior.[2]

Maternal behavior also is synchronized with the changing physical characteristics of the young. Normally rats begin to consume solid food on about day 16, and by day 30 they no longer suckle (Babicky, Ostadalova, Parizek, Kolar, & Bibr, 1970). Part of the reason why suckling ceases is that the mother treats older pups differently from younger ones, spending considerably less time nursing the former (Addison & Alberts, as cited by Hall & Williams, 1983; Cramer, Thiels, & Alberts, 1990; Rosenblatt, 1965). However, if the mother is made to treat the older pup as if it were younger, the pup nurses for a period well beyond 30 days. This phenomenon was shown by Pfister, Cramer, and Blass (1986) who placed a single 21-day-old pup with a foster litter of 16-day-olds and its mother. This procedure was repeated every 5 days until the subjects either reached sexual maturity or stopped nursing. Nursing was assessed every fifth day by food-depriving the animal for 24 hours and placing it with an anesthetized dam for 45 minutes.

The percentage of experimental and normal rats attaching to a nipple expressed as a function of their age is shown in Figure 9.6. It is obvious that nursing continued well beyond the time of normal weaning; one third of the animals continued to suckle at 60 days of age and some even at day 65 (see Figure 9.7). Nursing also was observed up to day 45 in the nest setting, in which solid food and water were freely available. These data suggest that the nursing female normally contributes to the weaning process by altering her responsiveness to older pups. In our own species the maternal factor not only contributes to individual differences in weaning age but collectively leads to cultural differences. As Popkin, Bilsborrow, and Akin (1982) reported, it is not uncommon for mothers in certain cultures to continue to nurse up to the third year of life.

Serotonergic System. The coincidence in young rats between a major change in the control of suckling and the maturation of a neurotransmitter system prompted investigators to determine if that neurotransmitter system is involved in the weaning process. The change in suckling is as follows: Prior to about 13 days of age both food-deprived and nondeprived rat pups attach to a nipple, whereas subsequent to day 13 only deprived young reliably attach (Hall, Cramer, & Blass, 1975, 1977). Therefore at about day 13 the nursing animal becomes somewhat adult-like in that the presence of food in the absence of a state of depletion is often not sufficient to elicit ingestive behavior. Because the seroto-

---

[2]The acquisition by nonsuckling stimuli of the ability to cause release of prolactin may be a useful system within which to examine the influence of conditioning on hormonal regulation. Perhaps the nonsuckling stimuli (CS/s) acquire the capacity to elicit prolactin release only after being paired with the suckling stimuli (UCS/s).

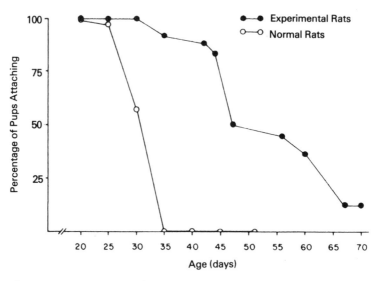

Figure 9.6 Percentage of experimental and normal rat pups attaching to the nipples of an anesthetized dam during a 45-minute test. All subjects were deprived for 24 hours. Tests were repeated at approximately 5-day intervals. (From Pfister et al., "Suckling in rats extended by continuous living with dams and the preweanling litters." *Animal Behavior, 34,* 415–20. © 1986 by Academic Press. Reprinted by permission.)

Figure 9.7 A 65-day-old rat attaching to a nipple of an anesthetized dam. (From Pfister et al., "Suckling in rats extended by continuous living with dams and the preweanling litters." *Animal Behavior, 34,* 415–20. © 1986 by Academic Press. Reprinted by permission.)

nergic neurotransmitter system matures at that time and has been implicated in adult ingestive behavior (Blundell, 1984; Loizou & Salt, 1970), it was logical to ask if serotonin is involved in the transition from nursing to independent feeding; in other words, does serotonin inhibit suckling?

The initial experiments, performed by Nock, Williams, and Hall (1978), involved the administration of two drugs, *methysergide* and *quipazine.* Methysergide antagonizes the action of serotonin by blocking serotonin receptors in the brain, whereas quipazine increases brain serotonergic activity by directly stimulating serotonergic receptors. If serotonin normally inhibits suckling in older offspring, methysergide, by antagonizing the action of serotonin, should reinstate suckling behavior. The prediction was supported; whereas only 25% of 20-day-old rats injected with saline attached to the nipples of an anesthetized dam, 100% of methysergide-injected subjects did so. A second prediction involved quipizine. Because it enhances brain serotonergic activity, one would expect the drug to inhibit suckling. Although Nock et al. found that quipizine did not inhibit suckling, it did reduce it significantly; the treated animals spent significantly less time attached to nipples than did controls. Lastly, because methysergide blocks serotonin receptors and quipizine directly stimulates those receptors, methysergide also should antagonize the effect of quipizine. It does. Twenty-day-olds administrated *both* methysergide and quipizine spent as much time attached to nipples as did saline-injected controls.

The findings of Nock et al. (1978) were confirmed by Williams, Rosenblatt, and Hall (1979), who also reported that the ability of methysergide to induce suckling behavior is age-dependent; it is effective in rat pups as old as 39 days, an age at which food deprivation normally does *not* induce such behavior, but is ineffective in 10-day-olds and in animals over 40 days. Williams et al. also made the important point that the effects reported by Nock et al. are not caused by other extraneous actions of methysergide and quipizine but, rather, that they are specific to alterations of the serotonergic system. Metergoline, another serotonin antagonist, and fenfluramine, a serotonin releaser, also yield the expected effects on suckling.

The influence of serotonergic receptor blockade on nursing behavior is seen not only when the young are allowed access to a nipple but also when they are permitted to choose between a nipple and solid food. Stoloff and Supinski (1984) placed 20-, 25-, and 30-day-old food-deprived rats in a Y maze that contained an anesthetized dam with six accessible nipples in one goal and a dam with six inaccessible nipples but solid food and water in the other goal. Each subject was given 45 trials. Regardless of age, young rats administered methysergide chose the goal containing the accessible nipples more often than controls. The greatest effect was observed in 30-day-olds, which normally select the suckling stimulus on one third of the trials. Animals administered methysergide chose the suckling stimulus 50% of the time. Furthermore, on those trials in which the food goal was chosen, fewer methysergide-treated subjects than controls ate the solid food.

Modification of the serotonergic system by pharmacological manipulations supports the idea that the serotonergic system plays a role in the weaning process. As Williams et al. (1979) stated:

> We speculate that the natural emergence of a functional serotonin system in rat pups may be, in part, the physiological basis of the initiation of the weaning process. As the (serotonergic) system develops, suckling is inhibited. This mechanism would free pups, which before this time suckled continuously, to investigate other food sources. The decline in maternal behavior and the dam's rejection of her pups' attempts to suckle may also contribute to the weaning process. [p. 424]

The data, however, have been criticised by Leshem and Kreider (1987) on two counts. First, they stated that drugs that have been used to block serotonergic receptors such as methysergide have relatively poor serotonergic specificity. That is, the drugs produce a number of *non*serotonergic-related effects. Second, they suggested that because the drugs are administered by injection rather than directly placed into the brain, their principal influence may be on peripherally produced serotonin, which is mainly associated with the gastrointestinal tract. Therefore a change in ingestive behavior observed as a consequence of drug administration could be caused by altering gastrointestinal function rather than by directly influencing suckling.

Lesham and Kreider addressed their criticisms by placing the serotonin-specific neurotoxin 5,7-dihydroxytryptamine (5,7-DHT) directly into the third ventricle of the 3-day-old rat brain. This manipulation produces a permanent depletion of brain serotonin by destroying serotonin-producing neurons. Therefore if serotonin is involved in the transition from suckling to independent ingestion, weaning should be delayed or even eliminated in rats administered 5,7-DHT. The data supported the findings obtained with the peripherally injected drugs; 5,7-DHT-treated food-deprived animals exhibited significantly more nipple attachment than controls up until day 37 of age. Nevertheless, because suckling did cease after day 37 despite serotonin depletion, Lesham and Kreider concluded that serotonin, although involved in the weaning process, does not play an essential role. This conclusion is unwarranted, however, because 5,7-DHT treatment of 3-day-olds does not deplete serotonin but, rather, causes an average reduction relative to control levels of only 50% as assessed at 7 weeks of age. Although reduced, the levels of serotonin may have been sufficient to eventually cause a cessation of suckling.

Food Selection

We have seen that the infant rat possesses two distinct modes of ingestive behavior. It not only suckles but also has the capability to ingest food independent of the mother. Weaning, then, consists of the suppression of suckling, thereby allowing independent feeding to eventually become the sole means by which food is ingested. The changing interaction between mother and young, as well as maturation of the serotonergic system, contribute significantly to the transition from nursing to independent feeding. From that point in time, the youngster is nutritionally on its own, required to devote a major portion of its time to foraging for food. How does the weanling know what to ingest? Its chances of survival are enhanced, of course, if it ingests items that are normally ingested by adult members of the species rather than novel items that could be toxic.

Information pertaining to food selection is provided in two ways. One is that weanlings often approach adults and begin to feed in their vicinity (Galef, 1971; Galef & Clark, 1971). This maneuver, then, increases the probability that the weanling ingests foods currently ingested by the adults. A second involves information provided by the mother during the lactation period. Galef and Henderson (1972) fed two nursing rats solely with standard laboratory fare and two others with food normally preferred over the standard diet. The lactating rats were never fed in the maternity cage. Rather, they were only fed outside of the home cage for three 1-hour periods each day. Thus the young animals were never exposed to solid foods in the maternity cage, nor did they experience the mother ingesting solid foods at any time during the preweaning period. On days 17 to 23 the young were placed in a choice apparatus that contained both the standard and preferred foods, and the amount of intake of each was recorded over a 3-hour period. The results were that pups whose mothers were fed the standard, nonpreferred diet ate more of that food than pups whose mothers were given the preferred diet. We see, then, that the diet consumed by the nursing female is highly influential in determining the food preference of her young, even overriding the presence of a highly palatable food. Similar findings were reported by Galef and Sherry (1973).

The influence of maternal diet also has been examined by Sullivan et al. (1990), who recorded both behavioral preference and olfactory bulb neural activity (as assessed by the uptake of 2-DG) in rat pups in relation to maternal diet. In their first experiment, newborn rats were reared either by mothers fed a standard laboratory diet or by others fed a diet high in sucrose, which has been shown to alter the normal maternal odor (Leon, 1975). On postnatal day 19 some of the pups were placed in a Y maze and allowed to choose between normal maternal odor in the form of soiled bedding from a cage that had housed a normally fed lactating female and abnormal maternal odor emitted by bedding taken from a cage that had housed a nursing female given the sucrose-based diet. Other pups were injected with 2-DG and presented with bedding from a cage containing a normally fed female. Afterward they were killed and the olfactory bulbs assessed for the uptake of 2-DG.

Early olfactory exposure influenced both behavior and neuronal activity. Regarding the former, animals that had been raised by mothers fed the normal diet (i.e., young that had experienced normal maternal odor) reliably selected the arm of the maze leading to bedding from cages that had housed normally fed females; the opposite was true for pups raised by females fed the high sucrose diet. Furthermore, a small but statistically reliable effect was found for 2-DG uptake. Pups raised with normal maternal odor exhibited enhanced 2-DG uptake in response to the presentation of bedding from a normal-odor cage. Pups raised with altered maternal odor did not exhibit enhanced 2-DG uptake to normal maternal odor. The results are shown in Figure 9.8.

A second experiment consisted in raising *all* neonates with mothers fed the sucrose-based diet. Half of the mothers, however, were given a sucrose-based diet

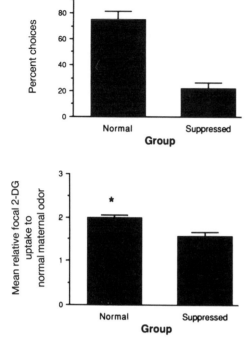

Figure 9.8 Behavioral (top) and focal olfactory bulb 2-DG uptake (bottom) responses to normal maternal odor in 19-day-old pups raised with mothers fed either a normal diet (Normal) or a sucrose-based diet that suppressed the dominant maternal odor (Suppressed). (* = statistical significance between groups.) (From Sullivan et al., "Modified behavioral and olfactory bulb responses to maternal odors in preweanling rats." *Developmental Brain Research*, 53, 243–47. © 1990 by Elsevier Science Publishers. Reprinted by permission.)

adulterated with peppermint. As shown in Figure 9.9, the findings replicated the results of the first experiment; pups exhibited a behavioral preference and augmented olfactory bulb neuronal activity to the familiar odors.

Diet-produced changes in the taste or odor of their mother's milk, or perhaps in the odor of the mother herself, may be the mechanism by which the young gain familiarity with the foods the adult has ingested. Yet why should animals favor familiar stimuli, and how are such predilections established? As stated previously, such preferences are advantageous to the developing organism if we assume that familiar stimuli tend to be safer than novel stimuli. How such preferences are established is another matter. According to Zajonc (1971), the preferences are innate. Sullivan et al. (1990) offered a different explanation:

> A variety of stimuli have been shown to function as a reward to pups, ranging from tactile stimulation to intra-oral milk infusions. Within the nest, these stimuli are provided by the dam. Thus, the pup's association of maternal odors with stimulation provided during maternal care can result in a learned preference for those odors, and a concomitant change in pup brain function. [p. 246]

This explanation of course does not account for food preferences ostensibly established *prior* to birth (Hepper, 1988).

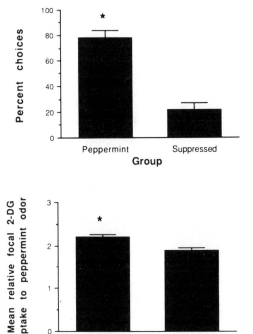

Figure 9.9 Behavioral (top) and focal olfactory bulb 2-DG uptake (bottom) responses to peppermint odor of 19-day-old pups raised with mothers fed either a sucrose-based diet adulterated with peppermint (Peppermint) or a sucrose-based diet that suppressed the dominant maternal odor (Suppressed). (* = statistical significance between groups.) (From Sullivan et al., "Modified behavioral and olfactory bulb responses to maternal odors in preweanling rats." *Developmental Brain Research, 53,* 243–47. © 1990 by Elsevier Science Publishers. Reprinted by permission.)

Concluding Comments

The research on suckling and weaning is noteworthy in two respects. On the one hand it has uncovered factors both internal and external to the young animal that control both processes. On the other hand, the research has demonstrated conclusively that although the infant normally engages in suckling behavior it is capable of independent feeding should it be required to do so if the lactating adult is removed. Therefore suckling and independent feeding are separate behaviors, present concurrently and related only insofar as both are concerned with the intake of nourishment. The research makes the important point that not all behaviors that appear early in development are primitive or juvenile forms of adult behavior.

PUBERTY

Puberty consists in myriad changes that mark the transition from nonreproductive to reproductive status. It is a passage that not only entails maturation of the physical attributes requisite for successful mating but requires the emergence of the motivation to engage in reproductive behavior. Of course other behaviors indirectly related to reproduction, such as territorial marking and fighting, also make their appearance.

Here we are concerned with those factors that determine when puberty occurs and, in the extreme case, whether it transpires at all. The timing of puberty is a significant consideration, having a number of implications with regard to reproductive potential or fitness. For example, as Clark, Spencer, and Galef (1986) reported, female gerbils that reach puberty relatively early have more litters containing more young per litter than late-maturing females. Consequently the early-maturing animals have more than twice as many offspring as do the later maturing animals. Also, early-maturing gerbils give birth to and wean a greater proportion of females than do their late-maturing counterparts. The adaptive value of the latter is unclear.

Before discussing the forces that contribute to the timing of puberty, let us first briefly consider the mechanisms that control its onset.

Neuroendocrine Control of Puberty

The mechanisms that regulate puberty have been the subject of intense scrutiny for many years. It is generally agreed (Ojeda & Urbanski, 1988; Plant, 1988) that at a particular point in development the arcuate nucleus of the hypothalamus secretes *gonadotropin-releasing hormone* (GnRH), which is transported by a system of ducts to the anterior portion of the pituitary gland. The pituitary, in response to GnRH, increases its secretion of the two gonadotropins, *luteinizing hormone* and *follicle-stimulating hormone.* As the name implies, gonadotropins act on the gonads, causing them to augment their secretion of estrogen, androgen, and progesterone. This increase in levels of gonadal hormones effects sexual maturation in both females and males.

Although a great deal is now understood about the neuroendocrine control of puberty, a *precise* description of the developmental changes the hypothalamus must undergo to enable it to secrete GnRh is lacking (Foster, Karsch, Olster, Ryan, & Yellon, 1986; Reiter & Grumbach, 1982). Moreover, although various factors such as adrenal secretions (Gorski & Lawton, 1973), prolactin (Gelato, Meites, & Wuttke, 1978), endogenous brain opioids (Wilkinson & Landymore, 1989), and nerve growth factor (Lara, McDonald, & Ojeda, 1990) have been implicated, specification of the mechanism or mechanisms that trigger the process culminating in puberty remains elusive. Reiter and Grumbach (1982) even suggested that the changes leading to puberty commence early in development, that the "hypothalamic-pituitary-gonadal system in the human differentiates and functions during fetal life and early infancy, is suppressed to a low level of activity for almost a decade during childhood, and is reactivated during puberty. In this light, puberty represents not the initiation of pulsatile secretion of GnRH and, thus, of pituitary gonadotropins, but the reactivation after a protracted period of quiescent or absent activity, of the GnRH neurosecretory neurons."

Regardless of the questions that remain to be answered, it is agreed that a decisive endocrinological stage is the rising levels of gonadal hormones. Elevated levels of gonadal hormones modify internal organs related to reproduction, cause the appearance of secondary sexual characteristics, and in females lead to the first ovulation. Behaviorally, gonadal hormones activate particular portions of the brain, thereby providing the impetus or motivation to engage in reproduction-related activities. Thus males gonadectomized prior to puberty exhibit virtually no male sexual behaviors, and gonadectomized females fail to become sexually receptive. An exception is the human female, for whom it is generally agreed that sexual motivation is nonhormonally regulated.[3]

Like other aspects of development, puberty is not determined *solely* by physiological maturation. Instead, it results from an interplay between such maturation and the environment. The outcome of this interaction determines if and when puberty will occur. The balance of this discussion focuses on the influence of the early environment, specifically day length, uterine position, odor, population density, nutrition, and stress.

Day Length

Female rats exposed to constant illumination commencing from either the day of birth or from day 21 display an acceleration of puberty as assessed by the age at which the vaginal membrane ruptures. (Rupturing of the vaginal membrane, referred to as *vaginal opening,* is a commonly used index of puberty in the female rat; the first mating generally occurs within the ensuing 3 hours. Vaginal opening normally takes place between day 35 and 36 [Hashizume & Ohashi, 1984].) Animals kept under constant illumination exhibit vaginal opening about 5 days earlier than do controls maintained on a light–dark illumination schedule (Fiske, 1941; Turscott, 1944). Furthermore, continuously light-exposed animals also display the initial ovulation earlier than controls (Relkin, 1968). Both the advancement of vaginal opening and ovulation are apparently caused by an increased level of follicle-stimulating hormone, as the pituitaries from light-exposed subjects have a greater ability than those from controls to induce ovarian growth following transplant into recipient females (Fiske, 1941).

Although there is general agreement concerning the puberty-accelerating influence of constant illumination in the rat, the effect of total darkness is unclear. Early studies did find that exposure to constant darkness produced a retardation of sexual maturation. Luce-Clausen and Brown (1939) reported that female rats kept in darkness beginning from the day of birth exhibited on average an 8-day delay in vaginal opening. Retardation also was found for animals blinded either at birth (Browman, 1938) or on day 15 (Turscott, 1944). Later work, however, yielded contradictory findings. Orbach and Kling (1966), for example, reported no effect of blinding performed between days 6 and 10, whereas Relkin (1967) showed that darkness can *accelerate* development by about 4 days if darkness is imposed from the day of birth. Should 21 days of exposure to light precede total darkness, puberty is retarded.

Because prepubertal animals are rarely if ever exposed to interminable illumination or darkness, you might ask what the relevance of these data are to

---

[3]Adams, Gold, and Burt (1978) have presented evidence of a rise in female-initiated sexual activity at the time of ovulation. Further exploration into the role of the endocrine system in female libido is in order.

understanding development. The answer to that reasonable query resides in related research, which demonstrates that the onset of sexual maturation varies as a function of the *duration* of light to which the youngster is exposed. In other words, living in a continuously illuminated environment is not required to affect the onset of puberty. Rather, the timing of puberty is related to light exposure in a quantitative manner. Because the amount of daylight varies as a function of season, the time of birth may normally contribute to the timing of puberty. Let us examine the results of studies that varied the duration of light exposure.

Duration of Light Exposure

Lecyk (1962) performed one of the earliest studies in which separate groups of prepubertal males and females were exposed to various durations of light. The experiment, begun on September 22, consisted in placing voles under gradually increasing light approximating the natural change in duration occurring between March 21 and June 24. Another group was kept under a constant 16/8 hour light/dark cycle, and a third group was exposed to 8 hours of light until November 5 when the duration was increased gradually to 13 hours by December 6. A control group was exposed only to natural light.

The results were clear. By early December all but the control animals reached puberty. The latter exhibited no signs of sexual maturation. Lecyk (1963) also demonstrated the converse, namely, that sexual maturation can be completely inhibited by exposing 10-day-old voles of either sex to gradually decreasing illumination or by exposing them to 7 hours of light a day.

Thibault et al. (1966) exposed male volves to either 5, 10, 15, or 20 hours of illumination a day. As shown in Figure 9.10, animals given 15 and 20 hours of exposure had heavier testes than those exposed for 5 or 10 hours. Unfortunately, these investigators did not include a control group exposed to natural lighting conditions.

Similar findings were obtained from the white-footed mouse (Johnston & Zucker, 1980). Differences were seen between animals exposed from birth to either 10 or 14 hours of light. Males exposed to the short day length had significantly smaller testes than those exposed to 14 hours of light. Furthermore, complete spermatogenesis was found in 75% of long-day-length animals by day 60, whereas *no* animal exposed to the short day length showed complete spermatogenesis even by day 100. Comparable findings were obtained from females. Short-day-length subjects had smaller uteri than long-day-length mice. The ovaries of short-day-length animals, also smaller, did not begin to reach maturity until day 90, whereas those of all the long-day-length animals became mature by day 50.

Johnston and Zucker (1979) reported that prepubertal cotton rats also are influenced by duration of light exposure. Relative to males exposed to a day-length of 14 hours, those exposed to 10 hours of light had smaller testes and lighter seminal vessicles. Whereas *all* of the females exposed to the long day length exhibited vaginal opening by day 50, it was found for only 50% of the short-day-length subjects.

The lamb presents a different and somewhat more complicated picture. Females kept from birth on a long-day-length regimen exhibit a *delay* in puberty

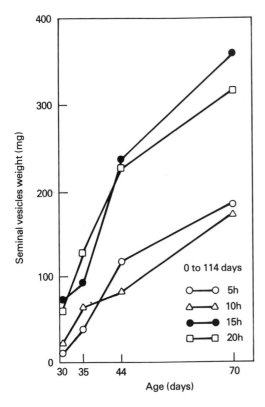

Figure 9.10 Influence of various day/light ratios on seminal vesicle weights in the field vole. (Adapted from Thibault et al., "Regulation of breeding season and oestrous cycles by light and external stimuli in some mammals." *Journal of Animal Science, 25,* 119–42. © 1966 by The American Society of Animal Science. Reprinted by permission.

(Yellon & Foster, 1985). This finding suggests, then, that short day lengths should promote puberty, but they do not. Lambs exposed to 9 hours of light a day are similar to animals maintained on long day lengths; the initiation of ovulation is delayed. Because lambs are typically born in the spring, the young experience a particular sequence of day lengths; the increasing day lengths of spring and summer are followed by the shortened day lengths of fall. In fact, *both* long and short day lengths are essential; 1 week of long day lengths commencing at 21 weeks of age followed by continuous exposure to short day lengths leads to the onset of reproductive cycles. According to Foster, Yellon, and Olsert (1985), "the lamb maintains a 'photoperiod history' [using] the long days of spring and summer as a reference to time puberty to the short days of autumn."

The influence of light on the nonhuman primate also has been investigated. Wilson et al. (1988) raised some spring-born female rhesus monkeys beginning at 12 months of age in outdoor enclosures under natural conditions and others indoors in a light-controlled (12 hours of light daily) environment. Overall, then, the latter were exposed to more light stimulation than the animals housed outdoors. The distribution of first ovulation dates is shown in Figure 9.11. The difference between the groups is obvious; most indoor-raised subjects reached puberty sooner than animals kept outdoors. Light therefore accelerates development in this nonhuman primate.

What of the human primate? I know of only a single study that bears on the issue of light and human sexual maturation. Zacharias and Wurtman (1964)

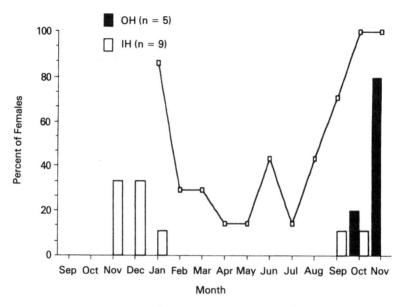

Figure 9.11 Distribution of first ovulation for rhesus monkeys housed in outdoor (OH) or indoor (IH) enclosures is indicated by bar graph. Line graph indicates the percentage of IH females that had ovulated by 32 months of age (*n* = 7) and continued to ovulate during ensuing months. (From Wilson et al., "Effects of natural versus artificial environment on the tempo of maturation in female rhesus monkeys." *Endocrinology, 123,* 2653–661. © 1988 by The Endocrine Society. Reprinted by permission.)

compared age at menarche in blind and normally sighted girls. Blindness was associated with earlier menarche, especially if blindness was accompanied by a loss of light perception. Comparing normally sighted subjects to those deprived of both form and light perception, it is found that whereas 50% of the former reached the first menstrual cycle by the 149th month, 50% of the visually deprived subjects attained it at 140 months. Unless blindness is associated with some other physiological change that could affect the onset of sexual maturity, the *absence* of light appears to *foster* sexual maturity in the human female.

Mechanism of Action

How does lighting condition exert its influence? It is believed that it affects the timing of puberty by altering the rate at which the pineal gland synthesizes and releases the hormone *melatonin.* Because melatonin is released by the pineal during periods of darkness, the duration of the release directly reflects duration of the dark period. Therefore animals exposed to long day length should exhibit a shorter period of melatonin release than animals kept on short day length— and they do. Foster, Olster, and Yellon (1985), for example, reported that lambs exposed to 9 hours of light a day display a significantly greater duration of melatonin release than do subjects exposed to 15 hours of light. "'This ability of the pattern of melatonin release to conform to the prevailing photoperiod endows it with the potential to serve as a timekeeping hormone in the sexually immature lamb" (Foster, 1988).

Other and more direct data also implicate melatonin as the agent responsible for the effect of light on the timing of puberty. Denervation of the pineal, a procedure that eliminates melatonin release, prevents a puberty-inducing photoperiod from bringing on ovulation in the lamb (Yellon & Foster, 1986). This adverse effect of denervation can be overcome by a melatonin replacement regimen.

Much remains to be learned about the role of melatonin in the timing of puberty. Although a relatively clear picture is emerging for its function in the sheep and rhesus monkey, much less is understood about its relation to puberty in other species. Furthermore, its site of action is unclear. Whereas evidence speaks for a direct effect on particular areas of the brain (Cordinali, Vacas, & Boyer, 1979; Kao & Weisz, 1977), other data suggest that melatonin may act directly on the pituitary (Martin, McKeel, & Sattler, 1982; Yamashita, Mieno, Shimizu, & Yamashito, 1978) in addition to the possibility that it acts directly on the gonad (Brzezinski, Seibel, Lynch, Deng, & Wurtman, 1987; Ellis, 1969).

Uterine Position

As you recall from Chapter 3, the fetal female's location in utero relative to that of male fetuses influences its development in various ways. Generally, females that have spent their prenatal period adjacent to male fetuses look and act more like males than females that have been contiguous to no males. Apropos to this discussion is that uterine position appears to modulate the timing of puberty. Female mice having been situated between two males (2M females) in utero were found to have an average age at vaginal opening of 37.3 days in contrast to 34.2 days for females situated between no males (0M). Females located adjacent to a single male (1M) had an average score of 35.7 days (McDermott, Gandelman, & Reinisch, 1978).

Uterine position similarly affects female rats (Meisel & Ward, 1981) and gerbils (Clark & Galef, 1988). Regarding the latter, age at vaginal opening of the gerbil is normally distributed bimodally. Some females mature early, exhibiting an average of 15.9 days at vaginal opening in contrast to an average of 35.2 days for the others (Clark et al., 1986). Clark and Galef (1988) found that uterine position accounts, in part, for that bimodality. Females located adjacent to one or two male fetuses were less likely to reach sexual maturity early than females contiguous no males. Nearly all (95.5%) of the 0M subjects were early maturers, in contrast to 57.5% and 41.1% for the 1M and 2M females, respectively. This finding is of special significance for the gerbil, as the maturation rate is related to reproductive ability (early maturing gerbils have more offspring).

Odors

Animals emit airborne chemicals (odors) that produce various physiological and behavioral changes on the part of other animals *of the same species*. These odors, called *pheromones,* influence various aspects of reproduction. For example, they can signal the state of sexual readiness, provide the basis for recognizing previous mating partners, and regulate ovarian cyclicity. Of relevance here is that pheromones can both advance and delay puberty.

Advancement of Puberty

The earliest evidence that olfactory stimuli can advance the onset of sexual maturation was presented by Vandenbergh (1969), who exposed groups of six 21-day-old sexually immature female mice to either adult males or to odors from adult males. Females exposed to intact (but not castrated) males placed directly in their cages reached vaginal opening and first estrus earlier than did females kept in a room containing no males (see Table 9.1).

Vaginal opening and first estrus also were reached sooner by females kept in cages containing an adult male that was separated from them by a wire mesh partition. The latter finding showed that physical contact was not an element in male-produced puberty advancement. In fact, the male need not be present at all. Merely placing soiled bedding from a cage containing an adult male into the females' cages advanced puberty, a finding that prompted Vandenberg to conclude that it is the male's odor that accelerates puberty in immature females, specifically an odor contained in the urine. Since Vandenberg's discovery, male-emitted puberty-accelerating pheromone has been found for species as diverse as the hamster (Levin & Johnston, 1986), cow (Izard & Vandenbergh, 1982), tamarin (Epple & Katz, 1980), and pig (Brooks & Cole, 1970).

The failure of a castrated male to accelerate puberty when placed in the cage of an immature female suggested that androgen is involved in the formation of the pheromone. This finding was confirmed by Lombardi, Vandenberg and Whitsett (1976), who reported that phermonal activity of male urine, which declines within 2 days of castration of the donor, can be reinstated within 24

Table 9.1 Mean age in female mice at two measures of sexual maturation after varying forms of exposure to male influence

Treatments	No.	Vaginal opening ± se		First estrus ± se	
Physical exposure					
Intact male present	24	30.9*	0.80	39.6*	0.61
Castrate male present	24	39.3	2.09	54.6	1.50
Restricted exposure					
Male behind mesh	23	31.2*	0.65	40.6*	1.07
Activated male odor	24	29.5*	0.94	42.3*	0.98
Solitary male odor	24	32.7	0.53	45.4†	1.48
No male odor	24	34.9	0.92	54.6	2.91

*Significantly earlier than no male odor treatment at .01 level.

†Significantly earlier than all older ages in same column at .05 level.

Source: Adapted from Vandenberg. Male odor accelerates female sexual maturation in mice. *Endocrinology* 84:658–660. © 1969 by The Endocrine Society. By permission.

hours by a single injection of testosterone. In that experiment the dependent variable was uterine weight. The uterus is particularly sensitive to the puberty-accelerating pheromone, increasing in weight within 48 hours after exposure of the female to it (Wilson, Beamer, & Whitten, 1980). The influence of various dosages of testosterone propionate on pheromonal production of castrate males is shown in Figure 9.12.

Because the puberty-accelerating pheromone is androgen-dependent and androgen levels are influenced by social status, Lombardi and Vandenbergh (1977) asked if the pheromone itself is affected by social status. The answer is yes, at least in mice. Only urine from dominant males advanced puberty; urine from subordinate animals had absolutely no effect.

Although for most of the research the influence of the puberty-accelerating pheromone is assessed by determining the time of vaginal opening or the first ovulation, some experiments have used a more direct index of sexual maturation: hormone levels. Bronson and Desjardins (1974) and Bronson and Maruniak (1976) determined levels of various hormones as immature females were exposed directly to an adult male or to urine from a male. Within 1 to 3 hours of exposure the females exhibited a marked increase in luteinizing hormone (LH) secretion followed by a 15- to 20-fold increase in circulating levels of estrogen (estradiol). It is concluded that the puberty-accelerating pheromone exerts

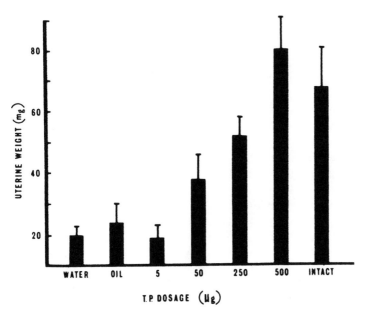

Figure 9.12 Uterine weight response of juvenile female mice after exposure to urine from castrated male mice receiving various doses of testosterone propionate (T.P.) and from intact mice. (From Lombardi et al., "Androgen control of the sexual maturation pheromone in house mouse urine." *Biology of Reproduction, 15,* 179–86. © 1976 by The Society for the Study of Reproduction. Reprinted by permission.)

its effect on the immature female mice by way of LH release, which in turn triggers the ovarian release of estradiol. The fall in estradiol levels on the morning of day 3 leads to the occurrence of ovulation later that day.

Once a pheromone has been identified through its action, a complete picture of it can emerge only after it has been isolated and identified chemically. Regarding the puberty-accelerating pheromone produced by the male, Vandenbergh, Whitsett, and Lombardi (1975) reported that it is associated with the protein component of the urine. Vandenbergh, Finlayson, Dobrogosz, Dills, & Kost (1976), using column chromatography, found a fraction that exhibited pheromonal activity. Because the active fraction does *not* contain androgenic material, and because the puberty-accelerating pheromone *is* androgen-dependent (see above), the involvement of androgen in the genesis of the pheromone must be that of producing a critical nonandrogenic substance. More recently Nishimura, Utsumi, and Yuhara (1983), using gas chromatography, presented evidence suggesting that the pheromone is either isoamylamine or isobutylamine. A definitive statement concerning the identification of the pheromone in male mouse urine must await further research.

Urine from males is not the only source of a puberty-accelerating pheromone for the immature female. According to Drickamer and Hoover (1979), urine from pregnant and lactating mice also advances the onset of puberty as determined by the timing of the first estrous cycle. Urine from both sources requires a minimum of about 3 days of exposure to be effective (Drickamer, 1984). Drickamer (1982a) also reported that the urine from a singly caged sexually receptive female has puberty-accelerating properties.

The data show clearly that chemicals contained in the urine accelerate the onset of sexual maturity in the female. What purpose do these pheromones ultimately serve? According to Drickamer (1982b), they act to communicate the fact that the environment is favorable for reproduction. The environment must be favorable if it contains adult males, pregnant and lactating females, and other females that are sexually receptive. It is therefore to the young female's advantage to reach sexual maturity quickly.

Unlike female puberty, relatively little is known about the possible pheromonal acceleration of sexual maturity in the male. This lack of information is likely do as much to the difficulty of gauging the onset of puberty in males relative to females as it is to assuming that the female reproductive system is more modifiable than that of the male. In any event, an experiment by Maruniak, Coquelin, and Bronson (1978) bears mentioning in this regard. They reported that prepubertal male mice secrete LH in response to the urine of adult females. However, the hormonal response disappears after repeated exposure to the urine. Moreover, whereas the weight of their reproductive organs increases after cohabitation with adult females from days 20 to 36, no such effect is seen in other males after cohabitation on days 30 to 42. The data, in general agreement with those of Fox (1968), Svare, Bartke, and Macrides (1978), and Vandenbergh (1971), leave a great deal unanswered concerning the influence of the adult female on the attainment of sexual maturation in the male.

Delay of Puberty

Various investigators had observed that puberty occurs later in group-housed female mice than it does when they are housed singly (Champlin, 1971; Vandenbergh, Drickamer, & Colby, 1972). Drickamer (1974) went on to study this puberty-suppressing phenomenon in detail by housing 21-day-old female mice singly or in differentially sized groups. The results are summarized in Table 9.2. It is apparent that the onset of vaginal opening and first estrus were delayed in grouped animals and that the magnitude of the delay was related to the size of the group. It also can be seen that group-housed mice weigh more than those kept alone.

In a second experiment, singly housed prepubertal females exposed to only the urine from group-housed females (kept four per cage), unlike those exposed to urine from singly housed donors, were found to be virtually identical to animals that had been kept in groups. They, too, showed a delay in vaginal opening and first estrus, as well as elevated body weight. Somewhat surprisingly, in view of the role of the male gonad in the production of the puberty-accelerating pheromone, puberty-delaying properties were contained in the urine of both adult *and* prepubertal grouped females. In the final study of the series Drickamer determined that the puberty-delaying pheromone appears in the urine only when the group-housed females are permitted to interact physically; when kept in the same cage but separated by wire mesh barriers, their urine fails to delay puberty. Drickamer (1977) subsequently reported that 3 to 7 days of pheromone exposure during the first postweaning week is required to produce the delay.

Table 9.2 Mean age and body weight for vaginal introitus and first vaginal estrus for female mice housed at different densities (18 mice per treatment)

Density	Vaginal Introitus		First Estrus	
	Age	Weight	Age	Weight
1/cage	26.1(.6)	17.5(.7)	30.4(.6)	21.1(.6)
2/cage	27.6(.5)	18.5(.5)	33.6(.7)	22.9(.6)
3/cage	28.1(.6)	18.6(.7)	34.1(1.1)	22.6(.7)
5/cage	28.7(.6)	18.9(.7)	34.1(.9)	22.6(.4)
7/cage	29.7(.7)	19.9(.8)	37.1(1.1)	24.1(.4)
9/cage	29.9(.7)	19.7(.7)	37.6(.8)	24.2(.3)
$F(df = 5/102)$	5.34	1.90	9.12	5.11
p	$<.05$	$.05 < p < .10$	$<.05$	$<.05$

Note: The F-ratios from one-way analyses of variance and associated probabilities are given at the bottom of each column. Within a vertical column those means not connected by the same vertical line are significantly different at the .01 level.

Source: From Drickamer. Sexual maturation of female house mice: Social inhibition. *Developmental Psychobiology* 7:257–265. © 1974 by John Wiley & Sons. Reprinted by permission.

306

Interestingly, whereas externally voided urine from only group-housed females contains the pheromone, urine taken directly from the bladder contains the pheromone regardless of whether the donor was housed singly or in a group (McIntosh & Drickamer, 1977). This finding means, then, that the absence of the pheromone in externally voided urine of nongrouped females is determined by a mechanism located between the bladder and urethra. McIntosh and Drickamer believe the mechanism resides in the urethra itself because the urine from grouped females loses its puberty-delaying property when it is incubated in homogenized urethras obtained from isolated females. Group-housing therefore somehow prevents the urethra from deactivating the pheromone.

Because the urine of group-housed prepubertal as well as adult females contains the puberty-delaying pheromone, the absence of any ovarian involvement in its production should come as no surprise (Drickamer, McIntosh, & Rose, 1978). The adrenal gland, however, does play an essential role (Drickamer & McIntosh, 1980). Voided urine and urine taken directly from the bladder of group-housed adrenalectomized subjects do not contain the puberty-delaying pheromone. Therefore production of the pheromone is dependent on one or more adrenal hormones.

Whereas most of the data concerning the puberty-delaying pheromone has been derived from the mouse, the inhibition of female sexual maturation by other females has been found for some other species. They include the California vole (Batzli, Getz, & Hurley, 1977), gerbil (Payman & Swanson, 1980), pig (Clark, Faillance, Tribble, Orr, & Bell, 1985), and marmoset (Abbott & Hearn, 1978).

As was true for research on puberty-accelerating pheromones, few data exist concerning puberty delay in the male. Lawton and Whitsett (1979) exposed weanling male deer mice to soiled bedding removed from a cage containing an adult male or to urine collected from an adult male. After a 5-week exposure period, both groups had lighter seminal vesicles than did the controls.

The rate of sexual maturation of the male California vole also is affected by olfactory stimuli. Rissman, Sheffield, Kratzmann, Firtune, and Johnston (1984) found that puberty, as assessed at 45 days of age by androgen level and seminal vesicle weight, can be delayed when the weanlings are exposed to bedding from their mother's cage in contrast to bedding from a cage containing an unrelated male. Exposure to father's bedding produces an intermediate effect on androgen levels and no effect on the weight of the seminal vesicles. As to the function of the pheromone, Rissman et al. speculated as follows:

> Exposure to family chemical cues may even be prolonged if young males remain in their natal territories, as young montane voles do when population density is high. . . . In dense populations, dispersal opportunities and food may be limited, and may severely reduce the chances of success with a new litter, especially for nulliparous parents. By delaying sexual maturation, the young male (or female) may be able to build up body mass and fat supplies, thus increasing his chances of successful dispersal and/or reproduction when the opportunities are better. [p. 330]

Population Density

It has long been known that when a population reaches a certain magnitude it ceases to grow and eventually declines. Although this cessation and decline of population growth have in a number of instances been related to a scarcity of food, they also ensue even in the face of unlimited resources (Brown, 1953), occurrences that gave impetus to numerous investigations devised to ascertain how such "'nonstarvation"-induced population reduction is achieved. The results of those inquiries have shown that population size is reduced by inhibition of reproduction due to diminished fertility, increased prenatal and postnatal mortality, disruption of maternal behaviors, and *inhibition of sexual maturation.* We focus here on the latter. Two techniques have been used to examine endogenous population controlling mechanisms. One involves the observation of naturally occurring populations of various densities (density = the number of individuals per unit area) and the other consists in examining artificially created populations of differing densities. Let us begin with natural populations.

Natural Populations

Southwick (1958) captured virtually entire populations of mice inhabiting 40 separate corn stacks varying in population density. Density was estimated by dividing the number of postweaning mice (those weighing a minimum of 7.6 g) by the cubic meter capacity of the stack. The stacks were grouped into the following four density classes: low (<0.5 weaned mice per cubic meter); medium (0.5 to 2.0); high (2.0 to 6.0); very high (>6.0). When the ovaries were examined, it was found that the proportion of females judged by body weight as being of postpubertal age that were capable of reproducing varied inversely as a function of density; 98.5%, 93.6%, 87.9%, and 83.7% of the females from the low, medium, high, and very high density populations, respectively, were fecund. A reliable difference in fecundity was not found for males. Similar data were obtained from voles (Chitty; 1952), lemmings (Krebs, 1963), and rabbits (Lloyd, 1964, as cited by Sodleir, 1969).

Although the data garnered from these and other studies point to an association between density and sexual maturation, a methodological problem inherent in the comparison of natural populations makes interpretation of the findings difficult. The problem is that the various populations comprising a given study most likely have been in existence for varying periods of time, and those populations with the greatest densities are probably older than less dense populations. Because differences in the maturity of a population may be related to differences in population structure and social behaviors, which might themselves influence puberty, it is problematical whether a change in the timing of puberty is causally related to density, age of the population, or a combination of the two. This difficulty can be alleviated by constructing artificial populations.

Artificial Populations

A number of studies have shown that as artificially created freely growing populations reach a certain magnitude, more and more females fail to reach sexual maturity. Crowcroft and Rowe (1957), for example, founded four colonies of wild house mice, each with one adult male and two adult females. Each triad was placed in a pen of 6 square feet containing nesting boxes and an unlimited supply of food and water. Every 2 weeks throughout the course of the study the animals were examined and counted. The growth and subsequent leveling off of the populations are shown in Figure 9.13. Commencing at the second 5-month period, most of the females did not attain vaginal opening. Terman (1965) reported similar findings; when density reached a certain magnitude, which varied from population to population, most of the females produced no litters, suggesting that many failed to reach sexual maturity. Density-dependent inhibition of puberty also has been reported by Christian (1956), Clarke (1955), and Lidicker (1966), among others.

Data pertaining to males are unclear. Although Crowcroft and Rowe (1957) and Jean-Faucher, Berger, De Turickhaim, Veyissere, and Jean (1981) found virtually no effect of density on male sexual maturation, Christian (1956) did report a delay of puberty.

Mechanisms

Data derived from both natural and artificial populations reveal that a dense population is often associated with inhibition of female sexual maturation. An obvious question, then, is how density exerts its influence. It has been suggested by Christian (Christian, 1963; Christian, Lloyd, & Davis, 1965) that behavioral factors associated with grouping, especially heightened levels of aggression, are the source of stress. Stress in turn activates the pituitary-adrenal axis. As demonstrated by Christian et al. (1965), ACTH administration can readily inhibit sexual maturation in female mice. The ovaries of mice treated with the hormone daily for 12 weeks beginning on day 21 showed absolutely no sign of ovulating, as neither follicles nor corpora lutea were present. Because ACTH is effective in both intact and adrenalectomized animals, one can conclude that ACTH produces the effect directly rather than through the release of corticosterone. Moreover, whereas ACTH has little effect on male reproductive function in house mice, it does inhibit testicular maturation in voles.

All of the endocrinological research of which I am aware has focused on the relation between population density and the pituitary-adrenal system. It would likely be fruitful, however, to include other endocrine measures. In this regard it is worth noting that Armario, Garcia-Marquez, and Jolin (1987) have reported that crowded *adult* rats exhibit lower serum levels of growth hormone.

Another mechanism that can serve to delay puberty in dense populations involves pheromones. Massey and Vandenbergh (1980) established freely growing populations of wild mice on two "'highway islands" (cloverleaf sections of a major highway). One of these populations eventually became dense, and the

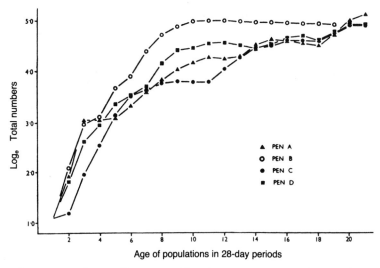

Figure 9.13 Rates of increase of four house-mouse populations. (From Crowcroft and Rowe, "The growth of confined colonies of the wild house-mouse (*Mus musculus L.*)." *Proceedings of the Zoological Society, London, 129,* 359–70. © 1957 by Academic Press. Reprinted by permission.)

other remained sparse. These investigators discovered that only urine collected from females from the dense population when that population was at its maximum density had puberty-delaying properties in immature females. Urine of females from the sparsely populated island and urine from animals of the dense population collected when density had not reached its peak were without effect.

Nutrition

Although it had been known for some time that for many species, including humans pubertal onset is preceded by a growth spurt (Frisch, 1974; Tanner, 1962), it was sometime later that puberty was found to be related *causally* to growth. Kennedy and Mitra (1963), in their seminal study, reared infant rats in either small (3 pups) or large (18-20 pups) litters. This procedure furnished the following three groups of weanlings differentiated by body weight: "'optimally grown" (>40 g), "'retarded" (between 20 and 25 g) and "'very retarded" (<15 g). At weaning on day 21 all of these animals had unlimited access to food. Other animals were underfed after weaning; after being reared in normal-sized litters of 7 to 9 pups until weaning, they were placed on a restricted feeding schedule that virtually stopped their growth for 10 days. The amount of food intake was then adjusted so that they gained 10 g, after which they were maintained at that weight for 10 days. This procedure was repeated until they reached 75 g, which occurred on about day 65. (Animals raised in large litters and then given unlimited access to food reach a weight of 75 g by day 45.)

Ages at vaginal opening, the first estrus, and first mating are summarized in

Table 9.3. It is apparent that puberty was delayed in animals restricted in their preweaning or postweaning growth rates relative to optimally grown animals. Furthermore, postweaning growth restriction delayed the onset of the first estrus and first mating more than did preweaning restriction. Restricted growth also interfered with the interrelation of the three indices of puberty. "In most optimally grown rats the vagina opened, oestrus occurred and successful mating took place on the same day, whereas most retarded rats did not show oestrus until a day or two after vaginal opening and even then did not mate until the second, third or even fourth cycle" (Kennedy and Mitra, 1963).

How does restricted rate of growth inhibit the onset of puberty? Lambs fed a diet that retards growth exhibit not only a significant delay in the onset of puberty but also a reduction in plasma levels of LH, surges of which are a critical factor in the initiation of puberty (Fitzgerald, 1984; Fitzgerald, Michel, & Butler, 1982; Foster & Olster, 1985). Data also are indicative of a similar situation in the rhesus monkey (Dubey, Cameron, Steiner, & Plant, 1986). The next question, then, is *how* restricted growth affects the secretion of LH. The answer is not known, although data from adult rats suggest that restricted feeding activates an opioid-sensitive neural pathway that directly inhibits LH secretion (Dyer, Mansfield, Corbet, & Dean, 1985).

Sexual maturation also is influenced by the content of the diet. Kirtley and Maher (1979) fed one group of weanling rats a high fat diet composed of 20% corn oil and another a low fat diet containing 5% oil. Both diets were of equal caloric value. The average day on which the high fat group displayed vaginal opening was 32.8 compared to a mean of 39.7 days for the low fat subjects. The high fat group also reached first estrus (mean 33.2 days) earlier than did the other group (mean 40.8 days). It should be noted that at the time of vaginal opening and first estrus both groups exhibited similar indexes of obesity (body weight/nasoanal length $\times$ 100). Comparable results are reported by Frisch, Hegsted, and Yoshinago (1975), who also found no differences in caloric intake between

Table 9.3 Effect of growth rate and feeding on the weight and age of puberty in rats

Parameter	Optimal Growth	Retarded Growth	Very Retarded Growth	Underfed
Age (days: mean ± SD)				
Vaginal opening	38.1 ± 5	43.4 ± 4	49.0 ± 6	46.7 ± 14
Estrus	38.4 ± 5	46.6 ± 6	50.6 ± 6	68.8 ± 14
Mating	41.1 ± 6	51.0 ± 10	56.7 ± 9	76.3 ± 15
Weight (g: mean ± SD)				
Vaginal opening	91.3 ± 12	78.0 ± 9	83.2 ± 12	62.7 ± 18
Estrus	92.7 ± 11	89.2 ± 14	90.4 ± 14	105.2 ± 9
Mating	102.4 ± 15	99.1 ± 21	102.0 ± 18	124.2 ± 25

Note: The groups are arranged in order of age at first estrus.

Source: Adapted from Kennedy and Mitra. Body weight and food intake as initiating factors for puberty in the rat. *Journal of Physiology* 166:408–418. © 1963 by The Physiology Society. By permission.

the high and low fat groups at the time of vaginal opening and first estrus. They speculated that the attainment of a particular body composition of fat to lean body mass or to total body weight may be a necessary condition for the onset of puberty. Lastly, prepubertal male and female rats exhibit a delay in sexual maturation when fed a diet low in protein (Glass, Mellitt, Vigersky, & Swerdloff, 1979; Ramaley, 1981).

Stress

A novel theory, proposed by Belsky, Steinberg, and Draper (1991), links life experience with reproductive behavior. These investigators believe that humans "'vary their mating and childrearing behavior in accordance with the contextual conditions in which they develop, so as to maximize their reproductive success." For example, individuals who grow up in dangerous and stressful environments have a greater chance of reproductive success if they reproduce at an early age, prior to experiencing potentially life-threatening conditions. This idea could explain the greater prevalence of the early teen pregnancies of individuals living in inner cities.

One prediction from this theory is that girls growing up in a stressful environment will exhibit an advancement of puberty. In other words, since they reproduce at an earlier age relative to those reared in nonstressful environments, perhaps they also reach puberty sooner. The prediction was supported. Of 81 girls for whom puberty commenced at 12 or earlier, 49% had grown up in homes where the father was absent. This situation was true for only 24% of girls who did not exhibit puberty until 14 years or older. Similar findings have been presented by Moffit, Caspi, and Belski (1990) and by Surbey (1990). Steinberg (1988) also reported that girls who had experienced relatively high levels of familial conflict displayed a greater degree of sexual maturation over the course of a year than did controls. With regard to the mechanism, Belsky et al. (1991) suggest that stress causes the individual to be more biologically reactive to environmental factors that have the potential to accelerate puberty. Such factors could include pheromones.

The findings of Belsky et al. (1991) and the others are certainly intriguing. However, the relation between stress and early sexual behavior may be indirect and not causal. For example, perhaps families experiencing conflict offer the children less parental supervision and guidance than families in which conflicts are at a minimum. Thus more children of the former might be expected to experiment with sex, among other things. Additional data are clearly needed before one can conclude that early stress does indeed foster earlier reproduction and, for that matter, earlier puberty.

Concluding Comments

Research with nonhuman subjects has revealed that environmental factors help regulate the onset of puberty. Relative to animals, little is known about how the environment affects human puberty. Although it is unlikely that early-maturing humans necessarily produce more offspring than those maturing later, the timing of puberty undoubtedly influences social development. Uncovering the relation between human sexual maturation and such variables as climate, nutrition, population density, stress, and family composition might well be a fruitful undertaking.'

REFERENCES

Abbott, D. H., and Hearn, J. P. (1978). Physical, hormonal and behavioral aspects of sexual development in the marmoset monkey, *Callithrix jacchus. Journal of Reproduction and Fertility, 53,* 155–66.

Adams, D. B., Gold, A. R., and Burt, A. D. (1978). Rise in female-initiated sexual activity at ovulation and its suppression by oral contraceptives. *New England Journal of Medicine, 299,* 1145–150.

Alberts, J. R. (1976). Olfactory contributions to behavioral development in rodents. In R. L. Doty (Ed.), *Mammalian olfaction* (pp. 67–94). Orlando, FL: Academic Press.

Armario, A., Garcia-Marquez, C., and Jolin, T. (1987). Crowding-induced changes in basal and stress levels of thyrotropin and somatotropin in male rats. *Behavioral and Neural Biology, 48,* 334–43.

Babicky, A., Ostadalova, I., Parizek, J., Kolar, J., and Bibr, B. (1970). Use of radioisotope techniques for determining the weaning period in experimental animals. *Physiologia Bohemaslovaca, 19,* 457–67.

Barlow, B., Santulli, T. V., Heird, W. C., Pitt, J., Blanc, W. A., and Schullinger, J. N. (1974). An experimental study of acute neonatal enterocolitis—the importance of breast milk. *Journal of Pediatric Surgery, 9,* 587–94.

Batzli, G. O., Getz, L. L., and Hurley, S. S. (1977). Suppression of growth and reproduction in microtine rodents by social factors. *Journal of Mammalogy, 58,* 583–91.

Belsky, J., Steinberg, L., and Draper, P. (1991). Childhood experience, interpersonal development, and reproductive stategy: An evolutionary theory of socialization. *Child Development,* in press.

Blass, E. M., Beardsley, W., and Hall, W. G. (1979a). Age-dependent inhibition of suckling by cholecystokinin. *American Journal of Physiology, 236,* E567–70.

Blass, E. M., Hall, W. G., and Teicher, M. H. (1979b). The ontogeny of suckling and ingestive behaviors. *Progress in Psychobiology and Physiological Psychology, 8,* 243–99.

Blass, E. M., Teicher, M. H., Cramer, C. P., and Bruno, J. P. (1977). Olfactory, thermal, and tactile controls of suckling in preauditory and previsual rats. *Journal of Comparative and Physiological Psychology, 91,* 1248–260.

Blundell, J. E. (1984). Serotonin and appetite. *Neuropharmacology, 23,* 1537–51.

Brake, S. C., Sager, D. J., Sullivan, R., and Hofer, M. A. (1982). The role of intraoral and gastrointestinal cues in the control of sucking and milk consumption in rat pups. *Developmental Psychobiology, 15,* 529–41.

Brake, S. C., Wolfson, V., and Hofer, M. A. (1979). Electromyographic patterns associated with non-nutritive sucking in 11–13-day-old rat pups. *Journal of Comparative and Physiological Psychology, 93,* 760–70.

Bronson, F. H., and Desjardins, C. (1974). Circulating concentrations of FSH, LH, estradiol, and progesterone associated with acute male-induced puberty in female mice. *Endocrinology, 94,* 1658–88.

Bronson, F. H., and Maruniak, J. A. (1976). Differential effects of male stimuli on follicle-stimulating hormone, luteinizing hormone, and prolactin secretion in prepubertal female mice. *Endocrinology, 98,* 1101–108.

Brooks, P. H., and Cole, D.J.A. (1970). The effect of the presence of a boar on the attainment of puberty in gilts. *Journal of Reproduction and Fertility, 23,* 435–40.

Browman, L. G. (1938). Effect of bilateral optic enucleation on certain reproductive phenomena in rats under various light conditions. *Anatomical Record, 72* (suppl.), 122–38.

Brown, R. Z. (1953). Social behavior, reproduction, and population changes in the house-mouse *(Mus musculus). Eccological Monographs, 23,* 217–40.

Brzezinski, A., Seibel, M. M., Lynch, H. J., Deng, M. H., and Wurtman, R. J. (1987). Melatonin in human preovulatory follicular fluid. *Journal of Clinical Endocrinology and Metabolism, 64,* 865–67.

Champlin, A. K. (1971). Suppression of oestrous in grouped mice: The effects of various densities and the possible nature of the stimulus. *Journal of Reproduction and Fertility, 27,* 233–41.

Chitty, D. (1952). Mortality among voles *(Microtus agrestis)* at Lake Vyrnwy, Montgomeryshire in 1936–9. *Philosophical Transactions of the Royal Society of London* (B), *236,* 505–52.

Christian, J. J. (1956). Adrenal and reproductive responses to population size in mice from fully growing populations. *Ecological Monographs, 37,* 258–73.

Christian, J. J. (1963). The pathology of overpopulation. *Military Medicine, 128,* 571–603.

Christian, J. J., Lloyd, J. A., and Davis, D. E. (1965). The role of endocrines in the self-regulation of mammalian populations. *Recent Progress in Hormone Research, 21,* 501–71.

Clark, J. R., Faillace, L. S., Tribble, L. F., Orr, D. E., and Bell, R. W. (1985). Effects of composition and density of the group and "'pheromone" treatment on puberty in gilts reared in confinement. Presented at the 2nd International Conference on Pig Reproduction, Columbia, MO.

Clark, M. M., and Galef, B. G. (1988). Effects of uterine position on rate of sexual development in female Mongolian gerbils. *Physiology and Behavior, 42,* 15–18.

Clark, M. M., Spencer, C. A., and Galef, B. G. (1986). Reproductive life history correlates of early and late sexual maturation in female Mongolian gerbils *(Meriones unquiculatus). Animal Behaviour, 34,* 551–60.

Clarke, J. R. (1955). Influence of numbers on reproduction and survival in two experimental vole populations. *Proceedings of the Royal Society of London* (B), *144,* 68–85.

Cordinali, D. P., Vacas, M. I., and Boyer, E. E. (1979). Specific binding of melatonin in bovine brain. *Endocrinology, 105,* 437–41.

Cramer, C. P., Thiels, E., and Alberts, J. R. (1990). Weaning in rats: I. Maternal behavior. *Developmental Psychobiology, 23,* 479–93.

Crowcroft, P., and Rowe, F. P. (1957). The growth of confined colonies of the wild house-mouse *(Mus musculus L.). Proceedings of the Zoological Society of London, 129,* 359–70.

Drewett, R. F. (1978). Gastric and plasma volume in the control of milk intake in suckling rats. *Quarterly Journal of Experimental Psychology, 30,* 755–64.

Drickamer, L. C. (1974). Sexual maturation of female house mice: Social inhibition. *Developmental Psychobiology, 7,* 257–65.

Drickamer, L. C. (1977). Delay of sexual maturation in female house mice by exposure to grouped females or urine from grouped females. *Journal of Reproduction and Fertility, 51,* 77–81.

Drickamer, L. C. (1982a). Acceleration and delay of puberty in female mice by urinary chemosignals from other females. *Developmental Psychobiology, 15,* 433–45.

Drickamer, L. C. (1982b). Acceleration and delay of first vaginal oestrus in female mice by exposure to grouped females or urine from grouped females. *Journal of Reproduction and Fertility, 51,* 77–81.

Drickamer, L. C. (1984). Acceleration of puberty in female mice by a urinary chemosignal from pregnant or lactating females: Timing and duration of stimulation. *Developmental Psychobiology, 17,* 451–55.

Drickamer, L. C., and Hoover, J. E. (1979). Effects of urine from pregnant and lactating female house mice on sexual maturation of juvenile females. *Developmental Psychobiology, 12,* 545–51.

Drickamer, L. C., and McIntosh, T. K. (1980). Effects of adrenalectomy on the presence of a maturation-delaying pheromone in the urine of female mice. *Hormones and Behavior, 14,* 146–52.

Drickamer, L. C., McIntosh, T. K., and Rose, E. A. (1978). Effects of ovariectomy on the presence of a maturation-delaying pheromone in the urine of female mice. *Hormones and Behavior, 11,* 131–37.

Dubey, A. K., Cameron, J. L., Steiner, R. A., and Plant, T. M. (1986). Inhibition of gonadotropin secretion in castrated male rhesus monkeys *(Macaea mulatta)* induced by dietary restriction: Analogy with the prepubertal hiatus of gonadotropin release. *Endocrinology, 118,* 518–25.

Dyer, R. G., Mansfield, S., Corbet, H., and Dean, A.D.P. (1985). Fasting impairs LH secretion in female rats by activating an inhibitory opioid pathway. *Journal of Endocrinology, 105,* 91–97.

Ellis, L. C. (1969). The direct action of melatonin and serotonin on testicular androgen production in vitro. *Journal of Reproduction and Fertility, 18,* 159.

Epple, G., and Katz, Y. (1980). Social influences on first reproductive success and related behaviors in the saddle-back tamarin *Saguinus fuscicollis Callitrichidae. International Journal of Primatology, 1,* 171–84.

Epstein, A. N. (1984). The ontogeny of neurochemical systems for control of feeding and drinking. *Proceedings of the Society for Experimental Biology and Medicine, 175,* 127–34.

Fillion, T. J., and Blass, E. M. (1986). Infantile experience with suckling odors determines adult sexual behavior in male rats. *Science, 231,* 729–31.

Fiske, V. M. (1941). Effect of light on sexual maturation, estrous cycles and anterior pituitary of the rat. *Endocrinology, 29,* 189–96.

Fitzgerald, J. A. (1984). The effect of castration, estradiol and LHRH on LH secretion of lambs fed different levels of dietary energy. *Journal of Animal Science, 59,* 460–69.

Fitzgerald, J., Michel, F., and Butler, W. R. (1982). Growth and sexual maturation in ewes: Dietary and seasonal effects modulating luteinizing hormone secretion and first ovulation. *Biology of Reproduction, 27,* 864–70.

Foster, D. L. (1988). Puberty in female sheep. In E. Knobil, J. D. Neill, L. L. Ewing, G. S. Greenwald, C. L. Markert, and D. W. Pfaff (Eds.), *The physiology of reproduction,* vol. 2 (pp. 1739–62). New York: Raven Press.

Foster, D. L., Karsch, F. J., Olster, D. H., Ryan, K. D., and Yellon, S. M. (1986). Determinants of puberty in a seasonal breeder. *Recent Progress in Hormone Research, 42,* 331–84.

Foster, D. L., and Olster, D. H. (1985). Effect of restricted nutrition in the lamb: Patterns of tonic luteinizing hormone (LH) secretion and competency of the LH surge. *Endocrinology, 116,* 375–81.

Foster, D. L., Olster, D. H., and Yellon, S. M. (1985). Neuroendocrine regulation of puberty by nutrition and photoperiod. In C. Flamigni, S. Venturali, and J. Givens (Eds.), *Adolescence in females: Endocrinological development and implications on reproductive function (pp. 1–21). Chicago: Year Book Medical Publications.*

Foster, D. L., Yellon, S. M., and Olsert, D. H. (1985). Internal and external determinants of the timing of puberty in the female. *Journal of Reproduction and Fertility, 75,* 327–44.

Fox, K. A. (1968). Effects of prepubertal habitation conditions on the reproductive physiology of the male house mouse. *Journal of Reproduction and Fertility, 17,* 75–85.

Frisch, R. E. (1974). Critical weight at menarche, initiation of the adolescent spurt, and control of puberty. In M. M. Grumbach, G. D. Grove, and F. E. Mayer (Eds.), *Control of onset of puberty* (pp. 406–23). New York: John Wiley & Sons.

Frisch, R. E., Hegsted, D. M., and Yoshinago, K. (1975). Body weight and food intake at early estrus of rats on a high-fat diet. *Proceedings of the National Academy of Sciences, 72,* 4172–176.

Galef, B. G. (1971). Social effects in the weaning of domestic rat pups. *Journal of Comparative and Physiological Psychology, 75,* 341–57.

Galef, B. G., and Clark, M. M. (1971). Social factors in the poison avoidance and feeding behavior of wild and domestic rat pups. *Journal of Comparative and Physiological Psychology, 75,* 358–62.

Galef, B. G., and Sherry, D. F. (1973). Mother's milk: A medium for transmissions of cues reflecting the flavor of mother's diet. *Journal of Comparative and Physiological Psychology, 83,* 374–78.

Gelato, M. C., Meites, J., and Wuttke, W. (1978). Adrenal involvement in the timing of puberty in female rats: Interaction with serum prolactin levels. *Acta Endocrinologica, 89,* 590–98.

Glass, A. R., Mellitt, R., Vigersky, R. A., and Swerdloff, R. S. (1979). Hypoandrogenism and abnormal regulation of gonadotropin secretion in rats fed a low-protein diet. *Endocrinology, 104,* 438–42.

Gorski, M. E., and Lawton, I. E. (1973). Adrenal involvement in determining the time of onset of puberty in the rat. *Endocrinology, 93,* 1232–34.

Grosvenor, C. E., Maiweg, H., and Mena, F. (1970). A study of factors involved in the development of the exteroceptive release of prolactin in the lactating rat. *Hormones and Behavior, 1,* 111–20.

Grosvenor, C. E., Mena, F., and Schaefgen, D. A. (1967). Effect of non-suckling interval and duration of suckling on the suckling-induced fall in pituitary prolactin concentration in the rat. *Endocrinology, 81,* 449–53.

Grosvenor, C. E., and Whitworth, N. (1974). Evidence for a steady rate of secretion of prolactin following suckling in the rat. *Journal of Dairy Science, 57,* 900–12.

Hall, W. G. (1975). Weaning and growth of artificially reared rats. *Science, 190,* 1313–15.

Hall, W. G. (1979). The ontogeny of feeding in rats: I. Ingestive and behavioral responses to oral infusions. *Journal of Comparative and Physiological Psychology, 93,* 977–1000.

Hall, W. G., and Bryan, T. E. (1980). The ontogeny of feeding in rats: II. Independent ingestive behavior. *Journal of Comparative and Physiological Psychology, 94,* 746–56.

Hall, W. G., Cramer, C. P., and Blass, E. M. (1975). Developmental changes in suckling of rat pups. *Nature, 258,* 318–20.

Hall, W. G., Cramer, C. P., and Blass, E. M. (1977). The ontogeny of suckling in rats:

Transition towards adult ingestion. *Journal of Comparative and Physiological Psychology, 91,* 1141–155.

Hall, W. G., and Rosenblatt, J. S. (1977). Sucking behavior and intake control in the developing rat. *Journal of Comparative and Physiological Psychology, 91,* 1232–247.

Hall, W. G., and Williams, C. L. (1983). Suckling isn't feeding, or is it? A search for developmental continuities. *Advances in the study of behavior, 13,* 219–54.

Hashizume, K., and Ohashi, K. (1984). Timing of sexual receptivity and the release of gonadotrophins during puberty in female rats. *Journal of Reproduction and Fertility, 72,* 87–91.

Hepper, P. G. (1988). Adaptive fetal learning: Prenatal exposure to garlic affects postnatal preferences. *Animal Behaviour, 36,* 935–36.

Houpt, K. A., and Epstein, A. N. (1973). Ontogeny of controls of food intake in the rat: GI fill and glucoprivation. *American Journal of Physiology, 225,* 58–66.

Houpt, K. A., and Houpt, T. R. (1975). Effect of gastric loads and food deprivation on subsequent food intake in suckling rats. *Journal of Comparative and Physiological Psychology, 88,* 764–72.

Izard, M. K., and Vandenbergh, J. G. (1982). Priming pheromones from oestrus cows increase synchronization of oestrus in dairy heifers after PGF-2 injection. *Journal of Reproduction and Fertility, 66,* 189–96.

Jean-Faucher, C., Berger, M., De Turickheim, M., Veyissere, G., and Jean, C. (1981). Effects of dense housing on the growth of reproductive organs, plasma testosterone levels and fertility of male mice. *Journal of Endocrinology, 90,* 397–402.

Johnston, P. G., and Zucker, I. (1979). Photoperiodic influences on gonadal development and maintenance in the cotton rat, *Sigmodon hispidus. Biology of Reproduction, 21,* 1–8.

Johnston, P. G., and Zucker, I. (1980). Photoperiodic regulation of reproductive development in white-footed mice *(Peromyscuc leucopus). Biology of Reproduction, 22,* 983–89.

Kao, L.W.L., and Weisz, J. (1977). Release of gonadotrophin-releasing hormone (Gn-RH) from isolated, perfused medial-basal hypothalamus by melatonin. *Endocrinology, 100,* 1723–26.

Kennedy, GX. C., and Mitra, J. (1963). Body weight and food intake as initiating factors for puberty in the rat. *Journal of Physiology, 166,* 408–18.

Kenny, J. T., and Blass, E. M. (1977). Suckling as incentive to instrumental learning in preweanling rats. *Science, 196,* 898–99.

Kenny, J. T., Stoloff, M. L., Bruno, J. P., and Blass, E. M. (1979). Ontogeny of preference for nutritive over non-nutritive suckling in albino rats. *Journal of Comparative and Physiological Psychology, 93,* 752–59.

Keopke, J. E., and Pribram, K. H. (1971). Effect of milk on the maintenance of sucking behavior in kittens from birth to six months. *Journal of Comparative and Physiological Psychology, 75,* 363–77.

Kirtley, D., and Maher, R. (1979). Effect of an isocaloric high-fat diet on initiation of puberty in Osborne-Mendel rats. *Biology of Reproduction, 21,* 331–38.

Krebs, C. J. (1963). Lemmign cycle at Baker Lake, Canada, during 1959–62. *Science, 140,* 674–76.

Lara, H. E., McDonald, J. K., and Ojeda, S. R. (1990). Involvement of nerve growth factor in female sexual development. *Endocrinology, 126,* 364–75.

Lawton, A. D., and Whitsett, J. M. (1979). Inhibition of sexual maturation by a urinary pheromone in male prairie deer mice. *Hormones and Behavior, 13,* 128–38.

Lecyk, M. (1962). The effect of the length of daylight on reproduction in the field vole *Microtus arvalis. Zoologica Polonica, 12,* 189–97.

Lecyk, M. (1963). The effect of short day length on sexual maturation in young individuals of the vole *Microtus arvalis. Zoologica Polonica, 13,* 77–86.

Leon, M. (1975). Dietary control of maternal pheromone. *Physiology and Behavior, 14,* 311–19.

Leshem, M., and Kreider, M. (1987). Brain serotonin depletion and nipple attachment in rat pups. *Pharmacology, Biochemistry and Behavior, 27,* 7–14.

Letz, R., Burdette, D. R., Gregg, B., Kittrell, E. M., and Amsel, A. (1978). Evidence for a transitional period for development of persistence in infant rats. *Journal of Comparative and Physiological Psychology, 92,* 856–66.

Levin, R. N., and Johnston, R. E. (1986). Social mediation of puberty: An adaptive female strategy? *Behavioral Biology, 46,* 308–24.

Lidicker, W. (1966). Ecological observations on a feral house mouse population declining to extinction. *Ecological Monographs, 36,* 27–50.

Lincoln, D. W., Hill, A., and Wakerley, J. B. (1973). The milk ejection reflex of the rat: An intermittent function not abolished by surgical levels of anesthesia. *Journal of Endocrinology, 57,* 459–76.

Loizou, L. A., and Salt, P. (1970). Regional changes in monoamines of the rat brain during postnatal development. *Brain Research, 20,* 467–70.

Lombardi, J. R., and Vandenberg, J. G. (1977). Pheromonally induced sexual maturation in females: Regulation by the social environment of the male. *Science, 196,* 545–46.

Lombardi, J. R., Vandenbergh, J. G., and Whitsett, J. M. (1976). Androgen control of the sexual maturation pheromone in house mouse urine. *Biology of Reproduction, 15,* 179–86.

Lorenz, D. N., Ellis, S. B., and Epstein, A. N. (1982). Differential effects of upper gastrointestinal fill on milk ingestion and nipple attachment in the suckling rat. *Developmental Psychobiology, 15,* 309–30.

Luce-Clausen, E. M., and Brown, E. F. (1939). The use of isolated radiation in experiments with the rat: III. Effects of darkness, visable and infrared radiation on three succeeding generations of rats. *Journal of Nutrition, 18,* 551–55.

Lytle, L. D., Moorcraft, W. H., and Campbell, B. A. (1971). Ontogeny of amphetamine anorexia and insulin hyperphagia in the rat. *Journal of Comparative and Physiological Psychology, 77,* 388–93.

Martin, J. E., McKeel, D. W., and Sattler, C. (1982). Melatonin directly inhibits rat gonadotroph cells. *Endocrinology, 110,* 1079–84.

Maruniak, J. A., Coquelin, A., and Bronson, F. H. (1978). The release of LH in male mice in response to female urinary odors: Characteristics of the response in young males. *Biology of Reproduction, 18,* 251–55.

Massey, A., and Vandenbergh, J. G. (1980). Puberty delay by a urinary cue from female mice in feral populations. *Science, 209,* 821–22.

McDermott, N. J., Gandelman, R., and Reinisch, J. M. (1978). Contiguity to male fetuses influences ano-genital distance and time of vaginal opening in mice. *Physiology and Behavior, 20,* 661–63.

McIntosh, T. K., and Drickamer, L. C. (1977). Excreted urine, bladder urine, and the delay of sexual maturation in female house mice. *Animal Behavior, 25,* 999–1004.

Meisel, R. L., and Ward, I. L. (1981). Fetal female rats are masculinized by male littermates located caudally in the uterus. *Science, 213,* 239–42.

Miller, R. E., Caul, W. F., and Mirsky, I. A. (1971). Patterns of eating and drinking in socially isolated rhesus monkeys. *Physiology and Behavior, 7,* 127–34.

Moffitt, T., Caspi, A., and Belsky, J. (1990). Family context, girl's behavior, and the onset of puberty: A test of a sociobiological model. Paper presented at the Biennial Meeting of the Society for Research in Adolescence, Atlanta, GA.

Nishimura, K., Utsumi, K., and Yuhara, M. (1983). Isolation of puberty accelerating pheromone from male mouse urine. *Japanese Journal of Animal Reproduction, 29,* 24–31.

Nock, B., Williams, C. L., and Hall, W. G. (1978). Suckling behavior of the infant rat: Modulation by a developing neurotransmitter system. *Pharmacology, Biochemistry and Behavior, 8,* 277–80.

Ojeda, S. R., and Urbanski, H. F. (1988). Puberty in the rat. In E. Knobil et al. (Eds.), *The physiology of reproduction* (pp. 1699–37). New York: Raven Press.

Orbach, J., and Kling, A. (1966). Effect of sensory deprivation on onset of puberty, mating, fertility and gonadal weight in rats. *Brain Research, 3,* 141–54.

Payman, B. C., and Swanson, H. H. (1980). Social influence on sexual maturation and breeding in the female Mongolian gerbil *Meriones unguiculatus. Animal Behaviour, 28,* 528–35.

Pfister, J. F., Cramer, C. P., and Blass, E. M. (1986). Suckling in rats extended by continuous living with dams and the preweanling litters. *Animal Behaviour, 34,* 415–20.

Plaut, S. M. (1974). Adult-litter relations in rats reared in single and dual-chambered cages. *Developmental Psychobiology, 7,* 111–20.

Plant, T. M. (1988). Puberty in primates. In E. Knobil et al. (Eds.), *The Physiology of Reproduction,* vol. II (pp. 1763–88). New York: Raven Press.

Popkin, B. M., Bilsborrow, R. E., and Akin, J. S. (1982). Breast-feeding patterns in low-income countries. *Science, 218,* 1088–90.

Ramaley, J. A. (1981). Puberty onset in males and females fed a high-fat diet. *Proceedings of the Society for Experimental Biology and Medicine, 166,* 294–96.

Reiter, E. O., and Grumbach, L. (1982). Neuroendocrine control mechanisms and the onset of puberty. *Annual Review of Physiology, 44,* 595–613.

Relkin, R. (1967). Pineal function in relation to absolute darkness and sexual maturation. *American Journal of Physiology, 213,* 999–1011.

Relkin, R. (1968). Combined effects of hypothalamic lesioning and light in the advancement of puberty. *Endocrinology, 82,* 865–69.

Rissman, E. F., Sheffield, S. D., Kratzmann, M. B., Firtune, J. E., and Johnston, R. E. (1984). Chemical cues from families delay puberty in male California voles. *Biology of Reproduction, 31,* 324–31.

Rosenblatt, J. S. (1965). The basis of synchrony in the behavioral interaction between mother and her offspring in the laboratory rat. In B. M. Faas (Ed.), *Determinants of infant behavior,* vol. 3 (pp. 3–43). London: Methuen.

Singh, P. J., Tucker, A. M., and Hofer, M. A. (1976). Effects of nasal $ZnSO_4$ irrigation and olfactory bulbectomy on rat pups. *Physiology and Behavior, 17,* 373–82.

Sodleir, M.F.S. (1969). *The ecology of reproduction in wild and domestic mammals.* London: Methuen.

Southwick, C. H. (1958). Population characteristics of house mice living in English corn ricks: Density relationships. *Proceedings of the Zoological Society of London, 131,* 163–75.

Stanley, W. C. (1970). Feeding behavior and learning in neonatal dogs. In *Oral sensation and perception,* 2nd symp. (pp. 242–90). Springfield, IL: Charles C Thomas.

Steinberg, L. (1988). Reciprocal relation between parent-child distance and pubertal maturation. *Developmental Psychology, 24,* 122–28.

Stephens, D. B. (1975). Effects of gastric loading on the sucking response and voluntary milk intake of neonatal piglets. *Journal of Comparative and Physiological Psychology, 88,* 796–805.

Stoloff, M. L., and Blass, E. M. (1983). Changes in appetitive behavior in weaning-age rats: Transitions from sucking to feeding behavior. *Developmental Psychobiology, 16,* 439–54.

Stoloff, M. L., and Supinski, D. M. (1984). Control of suckling and feeding by methysergide in weaning albino rats: A determination of Y-maze preference. *Developmental Psychobiology, 18,* 273–85.

Sullivan, R. M., Wilson, D. A., Wong, R., Correa, A., and Leon, M. (1990). Modified behavioral and olfactory bulb responses to maternal odors in preweanling rats. *Developmental Brain Research, 53,* 243–47.

Surbey, M. (1990). Family composition, stress, and human menarche. In F. Bercovitch and T. Ziegler (Eds.), *The socioendocrinology of primate reproduction* (pp. 134–45). New York: Alan R. Liss.

Svare, B., Bartke, A., and Macrides, F. (1978). Juvenile male mice: An attempt to accelerate testis function by exposure to adult female stimuli. *Physiology and Behavior, 21,* 1009–13.

Tanner, J. M. (1962). *Growth and adolescence.* Oxford: Blackwell Scientific Publications.

Teicher, M. H., and Blass, E. M. (1976). Suckling in newborn rats: Eliminated by nipple lavage, reinstated by pup saliva. *Science, 193,* 422–25.

Teicher, M. H., and Blass, E. M. (1977). First suckling response of the newborn albino rat: The roles of olfaction and amniotic fluid. *Science, 198,* 635–36.

Teicher, M. H., Flaum, L. E., and Williams, M. (1978). Survival, growth and suckling behavior of neonatally bulbectomized rats. *Physiology and Behavior, 21,* 553–61.

Teitelbaum, P., Cheng, M., and Rozin, P. (1969). Development of feeding parallels its recovery after hypothalamic damage. *Journal of Comparative and Physiological Psychology, 67,* 430–44.

Terman, C. R. (1965). A study of population growth and control exhibited in the laboratory by prairie deer mice. *Ecology, 46,* 890–95.

Thibault, C., Courit, M., Martinet, L., Mauleon, P., Du Mesnil Du Busson, F., Ortavant, P., Pelletier, J., and Signoret, J. P. (1966). Regulation of breeding season and oestrous cycles by light and external stimuli in some mammals. *Journal of Animal Science, 25* (suppl.), 119–42.

Turscott, B. L. (1944). Physiological factors in hypophyseal and gonadal interaction: I. Light and the follicular mechanism of the rat. *Journal of Experimental Zoology, 95,* 291–99.

Vandenbergh, J. G. (1969). Male odor accelerates female sexual maturation in mice. *Endocrinology, 84,* 658–60.

Vandenbergh, J. G. (1971). The influence of the social environment on sexual maturation in male mice. *Journal of Reproduction and Fertility, 24,* 383–90.

Vandenbergh, J. G., Drickamer, L. C., and Colby, D. R. (1972). Social and dietary factors in the sexual maturation of female mice. *Journal of Reproduction and Fertility, 28,* 397–405.

Vandenbergh, J. G., Finlayson, J. S., Dobrogosz, W. J., Dills, S. S., and Kost, T. A. (1976). Chromatographic separation of puberty accelerating pheromone from male mouse urine. *Biology of Reproduction, 15,* 260–65.

Vandenbergh, J. G., Whitsett, J. M., and Lombardi, J. R. (1975). Partial isolation of a pheromone accelerating puberty in female mice. *Journal of Reproduction and Fertility, 43,* 515–23.

Watson, R. H., and Gamble, L. C. (1961). Puberty in the Merino ewe with special reference to the influence of season of birth upon its occurrence. *Australian Journal of Agricultural Research, 12,* 124–38.

Wilkinson, M., and Landymore, K. M. (1989). Do brain opioid peptides regulate the onset of puberty? In R. G. Dyer and R. J. Bicknell (Eds.), *Brain opioid systems in reproduction* (pp. 70–91). New York: Oxford University Press.

Williams, C. L., Rosenblatt, J. S., and Hall, W. G. (1979). Inhibition of suckling in weaning-age rats: A possible serotonergic mechanism. *Journal of Comparative and Physiological Psychology, 93,* 414–29.

Wilson, M. C., Beamer, W. G., and Whitten, W. K. (1980). Puberty acceleration in mice: I. Dose-response effects and lack of critical time following exposure to male mouse urine. *Biology of Reproduction, 22,* 864–72.

Wilson, M. E., Gordon, T. P., Rudman, C. G., and Tanner, J. M. (1988). Effects of a natural versus artificial environment on the tempo of maturation in female rhesus monkeys. *Endocrinology, 123,* 2653–661.

Yamashita, K., Mieno, M., Shimizu, T., and Yamashito, E. (1978). Inhibition by melatonin of the pituitary response to luteinizing hormone releasing hormone in vivo. *Journal of Endocrinology, 76,* 487–91.

Yellon, S. M., and Foster, D. L. (1985). Alternate photoperiods time puberty in the female lamb. *Endocrinology, 116,* 2090–97.

Yellon, S. M., and Foster, D. L. (1986). Melatonin rhythms time photoperiod-induced puberty in the female lamb. *Endocrinology, 119,* 44–49.

Zacharias, L., and Wurtman, R. J. (1964). Blindness: Its relation to age of menarche. *Science, 144,* 1154–55.

Zajonc, R. B. (1971). Attraction, affiliation and attachment. In J. F. Eisenberg, W. S. Dillon, and J. F. Ripley (Eds.), *Man and beast* (pp. 141–79). Washington D.C.: Smithsonian Institutions Press.

Zarrow, M. X., Denenberg, V. H., and Anderson, C. O. (1965). Rabbit: Frequency of suckling in the pup. *Science, 150,* 1835–36.

Author Index

Veridiano, N. P., 107
Vermeulen, E., 35
Vernon, J. A., 114
Vessey, M. P., 106
Veyissere, G., 308
Vigersky, R. A., 311
Vilberg, T., 156, 233
Villablanca, J. R., 245
Vince, M. A., 18, 36–38
Visitini, F., 5
Visser, G. H. A., 15
Vogel, E., 101
Vogt, M. B., 244
Vogt, R. C., 75
Volkmar, F. R., 188
vom Saal, F. S., 62, 76–77, 79
Vorderman, A., 114

Waddell, W. J., 92
Wade, G. N., 65–66
Wakerley, J. B., 280
Walder, R., 219
Walker, D., 36
Walker, S., 112
Wallace, C. S., 188, 191–92
Wallace, R. B., 187
Wallen, K., 228
Walser, E. S., 38
Walsh, R. N., 187, 191
Ward, I. L., 78–79, 100, 301
Ward, O. B., 79
Warren, J. M., 184, 191
Waterman, J. M., 221
Watson, J. B., 12, 247–48
Weaver, D. R., 18, 43
Webb, M. A., 95, 97
Weckin, S., 111
Weinberg, J., 153, 170
Weiner, H., 147, 153
Weiner, I., 174
Weiner, L., 93, 97, 99
Weininger, O., 168
Weintraub, D., 178, 180
Weiss, K., 106
Weisz, J., 78–79, 100, 301
Wellman, G., 36
Wenger, E., 5–7
Werboff, J., 91, 111, 175, 243–45
Werner, J. S., 269
West, J. R., 100
Whalen, R. E., 60, 63
Whimbey, A. E., 170
White, B. L., 133
White, N. R., 18
White, R. T., 215
Whiting, J. M. W., 176–77
Whitsett, J. M., 302–304, 306
Whitten, W. K., 303
Whitworth, N., 288
Wiener, S. G., 152, 153–55

Wiens, J. A., 43–44
Wiesel, T. N., 194, 197
Wigal, T., 257
Wilkinson, M., 296
Williams, C. L., 287, 289, 291–92
Williams, J., 199
Williams, M., 284
Williams, M. L., 178–79
Williamson, H. O., 106
Willner, J., 170
Wilson, D. A., 170, 293–95
Wilson, G. S., 114
Wilson, J. D., 54
Wilson, L. M., 257
Wilson, M., 184
Wilson, M. C., 303
Wilson, M. E., 299–300
Wilson, W., 17
Windle, W. F., 5, 10
Winick, M., 168
Winslow, J. T., 156
Wise, W. E., 102
Wolf, K. A., 140, 143
Wolfson, V., 281
Wong, B., 174
Wong, R., 174, 293–95
Woo, C. C., 200
Wood, C., 36
Wood, J. W., 110
Wood, S., 36
Woodcock, J. M., 184
Woodruff, K. S., 101
Woods, J. R., 102, 104
Woods, P. J., 223
Wooton, B., 140
Wurtman, R. J., 299–301
Wuttke, W., 296
Wyly, M. V., 171

Yaffe, S., 178
Yaffe, S. J., 109–10
Yalom, I. D., 70
Yam, J., 106
Yamashita, K., 301
Yamashito, E., 301
Yanai, J., 109–10
Yedwab, J., 110
Yellon, S. M., 296, 299–301
Yoottanasumpun, V., 104–105
Yoshinago, K., 310
Young, J. F., 106
Young, L. D., 143
Young, W. C., 58–59
Yuhara, M., 304
Yutzey, D. A., 67, 169–70
Yuwiler, A., 184

Zacharias, L., 299–300
Zajonc, R. B., 294
Zappia, J. V., 18

Subject Index